ALBERT BLOCH
1882 – 1961

ALBERT BLOCH
THE AMERICAN BLUE RIDER

EDITED BY
HENRY ADAMS
MARGARET C. CONRADS
ANNEGRET HOBERG

PRESTEL

This book has been published in conjunction with the exhibition *Albert Bloch: The American Blue Rider* held at The Nelson-Atkins Museum of Art, Kansas City, Missouri, 26 January – 16 March 1997; Städtische Galerie im Lenbachhaus, Munich, Germany, 16 April – 29 June 1997; and the Delaware Art Museum, Wilmington, 3 October – 7 December 1997.

This catalogue and the accompanying exhibition have received generous support from the Marguerite Munger Peet Museum Trust, Marguerite Peet Foster and UMB Bank, n.a., Co-Trustees. Additional financial assistance has been provided by Arvin Gottlieb, Crawford L. Taylor, Jr., The National Endowment for the Arts, a federal agency, and The Missouri Arts Council, a state agency.

Front cover: *The Green Domino* (detail), see cat. 19

Frontispiece: Albert Bloch, 1917

Die Deutsche Bibliothek – CIP-Einheitsaufnahme
Albert Bloch: the American Blue Rider; The Nelson-Atkins Museum of Art, Kansas City, 26 January - 16 March 1997, Delaware Art Museum, Wilmington, 3 October - 7 December / [in conjunction with the Exhibition Albert Bloch: The American Blue Rider]. Ed. by Henry Adams … [Ms. ed. by Simon Haviland. Contributions by Annegret Hoberg transl. from the German by Michael Robertson]. – Munich; New York: Prestel, 1997
Dt. Ausg. u.d.T.: Albert Bloch
ISBN 3-7913-1778-4
NE: Bloch, Albert [Ill.]; Adams, Henry [Hrsg.]; Exhibition Albert Bloch – The American Blue Rider ‹1997, Kansas City, Mo. u.a.›; Nelson-Atkins Museum of Art ‹Kansas City, Mo.›

Prestel-Verlag
Mandlstrasse 26 · D-80802 Munich, Germany
Tel. (89) 381709-0; Fax (89) 381709-35
and 16 West 22nd Street, New York, NY 10010, USA
Tel. (212) 627-8199; Fax (212) 627-9866

Prestel books are available worldwide.
Please contact your nearest bookseller or write to either of the above addresses for information concerning your local distributor.

Manuscript edited by Simon Haviland
Contributions by Annegret Hoberg translated from the German by Michael Robertson, Augsburg
Research assistance provided by Julie Aronson

Typeset and designed by Wigelprint, Munich
Lithography by Fischer-Repro, Frankfurt
Printed by Pera Druck Matthias GmbH, Munich
Bound by Almesberger, Salzburg

Printed in Germany

ISBN 3-7913-1778-4

Printed on acid-free paper

FOREWORD

The story of Albert Bloch — both his art and life — has until now been largely unknown in the world of American art. In each of the various phases of his career, Bloch created works that stir the intellect and feed the soul. As a young illustrator for the St. Louis *Mirror*, he distilled the important political and cultural issues into elegant yet biting satire that set the tone for two decades of caricature. As the only American member of the Blue Rider, he made remarkable contributions to the rich fabric of early modernism. Finally, removing himself to Lawrence, Kansas, away from major art centers, Bloch continued his pilgrim's journey searching for ancient truths, while educating two generations of Midwestern painters. *Albert Bloch: The American Blue Rider* illuminates in detail for the first time the full range of this extraordinary artist's work.

Bringing *Albert Bloch: The American Blue Rider* to fruition has truly been an international effort, with much hard work on both sides of the Atlantic. The Städtische Galerie im Lenbachhaus has been our very able partner in this endeavor, and we thank Dr. Helmut Freidl, Director, and Dr. Annegret Hoberg, Curator, for their good efforts in co-organizing this project and hosting the exhibition at their museum. Dr. Hoberg has exercised her considerable talents in the most collegial fashion as co-curator and author, co-editor, and coordinator of this volume. We also extend our thanks to Dr. Henry Adams, who, while curator of American art at the Nelson-Atkins, initiated this project, and then continued to serve as co-curator and essayist. Dr. David Cateforis of the University of Kansas not only has provided a study of Bloch's Lawrence years in an essay here, but has willingly assisted us throughout the project. It is thanks to the good people at our publisher, Prestel-Verlag, that the design and production of this book are so very handsome. To all the lenders, listed elsewhere, we thank you for sharing your treasures with us. We are delighted that the exhibition will have a second American showing at the Delaware Art Museum, and we are grateful to Stephen Bruni, Director, Nancy Miller Batty, Chief Curator, and Mary Holohan, Registrar, for their endeavors.

In Kansas City, Margaret C. Conrads, Samuel Sosland Curator of American Art, has served with Drs. Hoberg and Adams as co-editor of this book. She has also organized the many facets of the exhibition, and has been especially aided in this task by Julie Aronson, Assistant Curator of American Art, and Cindy Cart, Associate Registrar, as well as the many staff members at the Nelson-Atkins upon whom we rely for all exhibitions. To Scott A. Heffley, Conservator of Paintings, we are very grateful for the instrumental role he played in the origins of this project and for conserving many of the paintings seen in the exhibition and on the pages of this book.

Arvin Gottlieb and Crawford L. Taylor, Jr., gave early financial assistance to this project, and we are grateful for their recognition of the importance of Albert Bloch and their generosity. The major sponsor for the project, the Marguerite Munger Peet Museum Trust, Marguerite Peet Foster and UMB Bank, n.a., Co-Trustees, carries on the wonderful tradition of supporting American art begun by Mrs. Peet in her lifetime, and we thank the officers of the Trust, Mrs. Adam Foster, R. Crosby Kemper, and Steve Campbell for their cooperation.

Without Anna Bloch, the artist's widow, *Albert Bloch: The American Blue Rider* — both the exhibition and this volume — could not have been realized. We are truly indebted to Mrs. Bloch for the generosity she has extended to us through loans, sharing of her unequaled knowledge and extensive archives, and her never-ending good will.

Marc F. Wilson
Director
The Nelson-Atkins Museum of Art

ALBERT BLOCH – CHRONOLOGY

Annegret Hoberg

1882

Albert Bloch is born in St. Louis, Missouri, on 2 August, the second of five children. His father, Theodore Bloch (d. 1934), a wholesale merchant, was of Bohemian Jewish ancestry and had emigrated to the United States from Protivin, near Prague; his mother, Emilie Scheider (d. 1920), came from a middle-class German Jewish family.

1898–1900

While still in high school, Albert Bloch takes extra drawing classes at a private school and he leaves Central High School in St. Louis before graduation, at age 16, in order to devote himself exclusively to art. From 1898 to 1900 he attends the St. Louis School of Fine Arts (later incorporated into the city's Washington University).

1905–07

In 1905 William Marion Reedy, editor of the St. Louis satirical weekly the *Mirror*, hires Bloch as a full-time contributor. By 1913 Bloch has contributed to the *Mirror* more than 250 caricatures, including 191 "Kindly Caricatures" of public figures, over 100 cartoons, and 31 covers, as well as numerous articles.

Around 1905–06 Bloch starts to paint and takes part-time courses again at the St. Louis School of

Fine Arts under Dawson Dawson-Watson, an Englishman. In December 1905 Bloch marries Hortense Altheimer, daughter of a Jewish plantation owner in Pine Bluff, Arkansas, living with relatives in St. Louis.

Early in 1906 Albert and Hortense Bloch move to New York, where their first son, Bernard, is born the following year.

1908–10

At the end of 1908 on the advice of Reedy, who had recognized and wished to encourage his artistic talent, Bloch travels to Europe to continue his studies. In December he embarks in New York for Southampton, England, with his family, traveling across France to Munich. In early 1909 they move into an apartment at Kurfürstenstrasse 59 in Schwabing, then Munich's thriving artists' district. During his early years in Munich, up to 1913, Bloch receives a monthly allowance from Reedy.

Bloch soon abandons his original plan to continue his art studies at the Academy in Munich. He attends evening classes at private schools in the city and pursues his studies mostly on a self-taught basis, visiting museums and occupying himself a great deal with German literature, including contemporary works. Up to 1913 he continues to supply drawings and reviews, as well as articles, to the *Mirror* in St. Louis.

In the winter of 1910 Bloch visits Paris to study art.

1911

Apparently not long after his return from Paris, in early 1911, Bloch discovers the illustrated catalogue of an exhibition of the "Neue Künstlervereinigung München" (NKVM; New Artists' Union, Munich) at the Thannhauser Gallery in Munich; the exhibition had closed in September 1910. This was the association from which the Blue Rider group would secede two years later. Bloch sees immediately that the works illustrated in the catalogue embody an approach similar to his own and he makes efforts to contact the NKVM.

Bloch's mother, Emilie, in New York

Bloch's father, Theodor Bloch, in St. Louis

(Left) Bloch, in Strauss's studio in St. Louis, 1905

Bloch in Strauss's studio in
St. Louis, 1905

Hortense Bloch, Bloch's first wife, and
their son Bernard, c. 1908

Bloch in his Munich studio, 1911

In May Bloch sees an exhibition by two members of the NKVM, Pierre Girieud and Franz Marc, at the Thannhauser Gallery.

In the summer he works in Dachau, to the north of Munich, made popular as a place for *plein-air* studies by the "New Dachau" school of painting and its successors.

Probably in the fall of 1911 Wassily Kandinsky visits Bloch's studio, introduced by an artist friend. Not long after, Kandinsky returns with other members of the NKVM to view Bloch's paintings. Subsequently, Kandinsky and Marc make efforts to have Bloch included as a guest exhibitor at the NKVM exhibition being planned for December 1911. However, the jury rejects the proposal since Bloch is not a member. Kandinsky and Marc then encourage Bloch to participate in the Blue Rider exhibition, which is currently being organized on short notice and will mark their final break with the NKVM. The "First Exhibition by the Editorial Board of The Blue Rider," held from 18 December 1911 to 1 January 1912 at the Thannhauser Gallery, includes six paintings by Bloch — a remarkably large number.

1912

Eight drawings by Bloch are included in the second Blue Rider exhibition, "The Blue Rider: Black and White," consisting solely of works on paper and held from February to April at the Hans Goltz Gallery in Munich.

Together with other members of the Blue Rider, Bloch is invited to exhibit at the important "Sonderbund" exhibition in Cologne from May to September, on which the "Armory Show," held in New York the following year, is modeled. One painting by Bloch is included in the German exhibition.

During preparations for the "Sonderbund" project, a dispute arises between the organizing commission in Cologne and the members of the Blue Rider, who feel that the exhibition is not adequately representing them as a group. Along with August Macke, who grew up in the Rhineland cities of Cologne and Bonn, Bloch tries to mediate in the dispute, making a stop in Cologne and Barmen in May on his way to America.

Bloch has already agreed to take part in the exhibition "Works Rejected by the Sonderbund," for which the Blue Rider group has found a suitable space at Herwarth Walden's Der Sturm Gallery in Berlin. In this first exhibition at Der Sturm Gallery — "The Blue Rider, Franz Flaum, Oscar Kokoschka, Expressionists," held from March to May — Bloch shows the same paintings as at the first Blue Rider exhibition in Munich, with the addition of *Impression Sollnhofen*. The latter is reproduced in the *Blaue Reiter Almanac*, edited by Kandinsky and Marc and published in May 1912.

In June Bloch leaves for America for four months, partly in order to ask for financial support from his wife's relatives in St. Louis.

1913

Together with other Blue Rider artists, Bloch is included in the "Public National Post-Impressionist Exhibition" (Nemzetközi Postimpresszionista Kiállitás) in Budapest, at which a large number of important works by the German Expressionists are shown.

May sees Bloch's first large one-man exhibition, of 38 paintings, at the Kunstsalon Max Dietzel in Munich.

Further financial support from Reedy not being forthcoming, Bloch asks Marc to help him look for a new benefactor.

In the summer of 1913 Bloch visits Marc in Sindelsdorf (Upper Bavaria) and views several important paintings that have just been completed in his studio.

Again due to the urgings of Marc and Kandinsky, Bloch is invited to take part in the "First German Autumn Salon" at Walden's Der Sturm Gallery in Berlin in September — the most important exhibition of international modern art to be held at a private gallery in Germany. All of the Blue Rider artists are represented, along with Paul Klee and Lyonel Feininger.

In October Kandinsky recommends Bloch to the well-known American collector Arthur Jerome Eddy in Chicago, who had purchased a painting of Kandinsky's at the "Armory Show" in New York earlier in the year and also had been collecting works by other Blue Rider artists. Eddy purchases

twenty-five of Bloch's paintings, giving the artist's work a prominent place in his collection.

Immediately after the "First German Autumn Salon," which Bloch only just manages to see before it closes in Berlin, he presents his first one-man exhibition at Walden's Der Sturm Gallery — a retrospective of his work to date, consisting of 42 paintings.

1914

In January two paintings from Bloch's one-man show at Walden's Der Sturm Gallery are included in the exhibition "New Painting" at the Ernst Arnold Gallery, featuring work by members of the NKVM and Blue Rider, as well as by Feininger, Oskar Kokoschka, and Egon Schiele.

In the spring Bloch encounters for the first time the journal *Die Fackel*, edited by Karl Kraus in Vienna, and becomes an enthusiastic reader of Kraus's writings.

The outbreak of World War I in August 1914 prevents two exhibitions of Bloch's work, in Essen and Barmen, from taking place. Marc is drafted into military service, Kandinsky returns to Russia, and two other Blue Rider artists, Alexei Jawlensky and Marianne von Werefkin, emigrate to Switzerland.

Bloch's financial position once again becomes difficult; Eddy is almost the only purchaser of his works.

1915

In May Bloch spends a few days with his family in Kochel, and strengthens his ties with Marc's wife, Maria.

In July, during his first period of leave from the front, Franz Marc visits Bloch, with whom he has been corresponding frequently. Bloch decides to translate Marc's essay "The European Idea," written in the trenches, into English.

In July and August the Art Institute of Chicago presents a one-man show of Bloch's work, containing 25 paintings, most of them from the Eddy collection. The exhibition then travels to the City Art Museum in St. Louis.

1916

Up to the end of the war Bloch receives numerous opportunities to exhibit his work, thanks mainly to the efforts of Herwarth Walden. At the beginning of 1916 his work is represented by a selection of important recent drawings and watercolors in the exhibition "Graphic Works" at Der Sturm Gallery in Berlin.

In March he exhibits with Klee at Der Sturm Gallery, showing 16 recent paintings.

In May two of Bloch's paintings from this last exhibition are shown in the Sturm exhibition "Expressionists, Cubists" at the Herzogliches Museum in Braunschweig, together with works by Klee, Marc, Heinrich Campendonk, Max Ernst, Gabriele Münter, and others.

Paintings by Bloch are also included in group exhibitions at Der Sturm Gallery in Berlin in the summer and at Gummesons Konsthandel in Stockholm. His work on paper is also featured at the Sturm exhibition in the fall in Berlin and again in Stockholm.

Bloch's second son, Walter, is born and the family moves to a larger apartment, at Konradstrasse 5 in Schwabing.

For financial reasons, Bloch takes on a number of private pupils, including, from 1916 on, the young painter Emmy Klinker from Barmen.

In December, at the instigation of Klee, Bloch is invited to exhibit at the Kunstverein in Jena, together with Campendonk.

1917

In February–March Bloch participates in the Sturm exhibition in the Corray Gallery in Basel, Switzerland, along with other Blue Rider artists and Swedish modernists.

In April Bloch and Campendonk attend at the cemetery at Kochel the reburial of the remains of Franz Marc, who had been killed in action in March 1916 on the French front.

In May Bloch's work, including a large number of new paintings, appears in a large-scale joint exhibition at Walden's Der Sturm Gallery in Berlin, this time with Harald Kauffmann.

The same collection of paintings, plus a few others, travels in July to the Kunstsalon Ludwig Schames in Frankfurt am Main, where it is shown along with works by Stanislaus Stückgold.

In the general exhibition at Der Sturm Gallery in June Bloch's work is exhibited alongside that of Campendonk, Feininger, Kandinsky, Klee, Umberto Boccioni, Gino Severini, and Marc Chagall.

In the summer Bloch spends some time in Berlin.

In December he is given another one-man exhibition, of 21 paintings, at the Kunstverein in Jena and shows a smaller number at the Kunstsalon Schames in Frankfurt.

1918

In April Bloch holds a one-man exhibition at the Munich gallery "Das Reich," at the instigation of Campendonk and Walter Dexel.

Bernard Bloch in a traditional Bavarian outfit, c. 1911

Bloch in Bauer's studio, c. 1916

Emmy Klinker, c. 1916

In June Der Sturm Gallery's sixty-fourth exhibition presents "Albert Bloch, Emmy Klinker, Elisabeth Niemann, Kurt Schwitters." Germany's surrender at the end of the war and conditions in Munich after the proclamation of a Republic, prompt Bloch to leave Germany and return to the USA.

He contributes a few political caricatures to the newly founded journal *Der Ararat*, published by the Munich art dealer Hans Goltz.

1919

From March to May Bloch and his family stay with his artist friend Gordon McCouch in Porto di Ronco, near Ascona, Switzerland.

In May he travels to America via Paris and Le Havre and stays for almost a year with his relatives in St. Louis.

During this period, the Hans Goltz Gallery in Munich presents the most extensive retrospective of Bloch's work to date, with 104 works and an illustrated catalogue.

Bloch's work is also shown in the fall at the "Fifth General Exhibition" at Goltz's gallery.

1920

In May Bloch's last one-man exhibition in Germany takes place at the Kunstverein in Jena, under the direction of Dexel.

In August Bloch returns, on his own, for what will be his last visit to Europe. Initially, he stays for several months near Ascona, where McCouch arranges accommodations for him.

In November Bloch receives a residence permit for Munich and travels to the Bavarian capital.

He spends the winter clearing out his apartment and stays mainly with his friend Emmy Klinker on Schwabing's Schellingstrasse.

Bloch in Ascona, Tessin, c. 1920-21

Bloch on the terrace of his house in Lawrence, c. 1925

Bloch's father, Theodor, in St. Louis, August 1925

1921–22

At the beginning of January Bloch spends a few days with Klinker in her home town of Barmen in the Ruhr region, visiting her father, legal counselor Richard Klinker, who has established an impressive collection of Bloch's work.

In February–March Bloch and Emmy Klinker stay for two weeks in Vienna, where he attends three lectures by Karl Kraus. He then spends a few more weeks in Ascona, saying his farewell to McCouch.

In April Bloch embarks again for the United States, this time with the firm intention of settling there permanently. He arrives in New York in May.

He obtains a job at the Chicago Academy of Fine Arts, where Carl Werntz is the director, teaching the Saturday afternoon color class.

In November a large-scale one-man exhibition of Bloch's work is held at the Daniel Gallery in New York, which acts as his agent for a time. Although the exhibition period is extended and in spite of a good reception in the press, this is to be the last retrospective of his work until 1955. Bloch now deliberately withdraws from the exhibition world.

His financial position difficult, he lives in Chicago in meager circumstances, sending the little he earns to Hortense and his children in St. Louis.

In 1922 he manages to sell two articles on art to the magazines the *Smart Set* and the *Milwaukee Arts Monthly*.

Seven of Bloch's paintings are shown at the "Exhibition of Paintings from the Collection of the Late Arthur Jerome Eddy" in Chicago.

1923

From his friends in Chicago, Bloch hears that a professorship is vacant in the Department of Painting and Drawing at the University of Kansas in Lawrence, and he applies for it in June 1923.

In September Bloch is appointed to a full professorship at the University of Kansas and moves with his family to 1015 Alabama Street in Lawrence.

Bloch begins writing letters to *Die Fackel* editor Karl Kraus, initially under the mysterious signature "AB. A Reader from Kansas."

1924–30

During this period, Bloch becomes intensely involved in his teaching activities as head of the Department of Painting and Drawing at the University. In addition to courses of practical artistic training, he introduces a two-year lecture course in art history, leaving a record of his lectures in extensive manuscripts.

He also writes more and more of his scattered notes for *Ishmael's Breviary*, which he had begun in Munich, mainly including ideas on the philosophy of art, but also recording journal notes, aphorisms, and reminiscences.

Between 1924 and 1930 Kraus prints twelve letters from Bloch in various issues of *Die Fackel*.

In February 1926 Bloch organizes the first reading from Kraus's work at the Department of Germanic Languages at the University of Kansas, reading some excerpts himself.

In March Bloch has a large exhibition at the Kansas City Art Institute, together with Archibald Murray and Karl Mattern. He had met Mattern at the Chicago Academy of Fine Arts and had brought him to Lawrence to teach at the Department. Bloch

shows 38 paintings, more than half of which had been produced in Munich.

The peak of his writing career is reached during 1927–28, when Bloch translates many of Kraus's poems. He has himself formally designated as "authorized translator" by Theodor Haecker from the Austrian author's circle.

In summer 1928 he completes the "Translator's Foreword" to a selection of 89 poems by Kraus. Subsequently, he spends a considerable time looking for a publisher, for the Viennese writer was then completely unknown in the United States. In 1930 the volume *Poems by Karl Kraus: Authorized Translation from the German* is finally published by the Four Seasons Press in Boston.

1931–34

Bloch enters into an extensive correspondence with friends and admirers of Kraus in the German-speaking countries, including the writers Mechthilde Lichnowsky (from 1930), Werner Kraft (from 1933), and Hildegard Jone (from 1935).

He meets a young woman named Anna Sylvia Francis from Kansas City, Kansas, who joins the Department of Painting and Drawing in Lawrence first as a student and later as a member of the staff. She lives with the Bloch family, periodically at first and later permanently.

Bloch composes a sequence of love poems dating from around 1934, *The Book of Templeton*, and the drawings in the *Templeton Vignettes*. He copies the poems into the second volume of his extensive unpublished manuscript, *Ventures in Verse*, which in addition to a large number of poems of his own includes translations of the poetry of Goethe, Eduard Mörike, Matthias Claudius, Karl Kraus, Paul Zech and Else Lasker-Schüler. Bloch had begun work on the three volumes of *Ventures in Verse* — its title emulating Kraus's *Worte in Versen* — during the 1920s and continued it until 1941.

In the same year Bloch gives a series of three lectures at the Denver Art Museum. One of the lectures is titled "Kandinksy, Marc, Klee: Criticism and Reminiscences" and contains extensive personal memories of the Blue Rider artists.

1935–36

In August 1935 Bloch receives a letter from Maria Marc, in which she asks him to contribute to a commemorative volume that she is planning for publication on the twentieth anniversary of Marc's death. Bloch immediately sends her an expanded version, translated into German, of the sections on Marc from his Denver lectures. When it emerges that Maria Marc's plans cannot be fully realized in

Greetings to you –
Christmas – New Year '30–31

Bloch's son, Bernard, in St. Louis, August 1925

Bloch's son, Walter, Lawrence, c. 1930

(On the far left) Bloch teaching in the Department of Painting and Drawing, University of Kansas, Lawrence, c. 1930

(Left) Bloch in the studio of his house in Lawrence, c. 1930

Bloch in the studio of his house in Lawrence, c. 1932

Nazi Germany, Bloch himself soon decides to publish his commemorative text, the two other Denver lectures, and several additional essays in a single volume.

This stimulates a renewed correspondence with his old artist friends from the Blue Rider group. In May 1936 Bloch writes to Kandinsky and Klee, requesting permission to reproduce their work. Unfortunately, the book is never published.

In 1936 Bloch shows two of his paintings that he values most highly, *Winter in the Dead Wood* and *Lamentation*, in the "First National Exhibition of American Art" at Rockefeller Center in New York.

He is deeply shaken by the death of Karl Kraus on 12 June.

1937–40

In 1937 the Arthur Jerome Eddy Collection is sold at auction in Chicago, and most of Bloch's works in the collection are scattered far and wide.

Bloch suffers a prolonged period of ill health and produces very few paintings. In 1938 Maria Marc sends him the address of Feininger, who had left

The vacation house The Three Knolls in Falls Village, Connecticut, c. 1939

Bloch and Anna Francis during a summer in Falls Village, c. 1939-40

(Clockwise, from top left)
Bloch and his son Bernard in Falls Village, c. 1940

Nazi Germany and returned to New York, the city of his birth. Bloch immediately gets in touch with Feininger and an extensive, cordial correspondence between the two artists ensues.

In 1939 Feininger invites Bloch to spend the summer near him in Falls Village, Connecticut. Bloch and Anna Francis visit Falls Village for the first time that summer, returning every year until at least 1945.

Around 1940, in New York, Bloch meets Michael Lazarus, an émigré from Vienna and an admirer of Kraus. A lifelong friendship develops between them.

1941–46

Up to 1942 Bloch works intensively on his translation of selected aphorisms by Kraus. In addition, he works on a selection from the extensive manuscript of his *Ventures in Verse* with Lazarus, who searches for a publisher.

In 1943 Lazarus introduces him to the poetry of Georg Trakl and Bloch begins to work on translations of Trakl as well.

Toward the end of the war, the paintings by Bloch in the collections of Bernhard Koehler in Berlin and Richard Klinker in Barmen are destroyed during bombing raids.

Bloch's correspondence with Emmy Klinker in Munich, which had begun during the 1930s, becomes more intensive in the period immediately after the war and continues until his death.

1947–50

Following a heart attack, Bloch retires from the University of Kansas at the beginning of 1947.

In the same year, through the mediation of Lazarus, the selection of his own poems and translations is published in New York under the title *Ventures in Verse: Selected Pieces* by Frederick Ungar, and printed by Martin Jahoda, the son of Kraus's Viennese publisher.

Following an introduction by Oskar Samek, Kraus's lawyer, an intensive flurry of correspondence is exchanged between Bloch and Sidonie Nádherný von Borutin, Kraus's former partner.

In 1949 Hortense Bloch dies in Lawrence.

In the same year Bloch is invited to participate in the large-scale exhibition "Der Blaue Reiter," held at the Haus der Kunst in Munich, which attracts a

Bloch and Anna Francis in Falls Village, c. 1943

Bloch in his studio, in front of the painting *Jordan*, c. 1946

Hortense Bloch in Lawrence, c. 1940

Bloch, his son Walter and Anna Francis in Falls Village, c. 1940 great deal of attention in Germany. At first, Bloch hesitates to participate, but eventually two of his paintings from the collection of Emmy Klinker in Munich are included.

1951–62

Bloch marries Anna Francis on 26 January 1951.

In the winter of 1954–55 the Curt Valentin Gallery in New York presents the first exhibition of work by the Blue Rider artists to be held in America. Bloch is represented by one painting, as are the other members of the group who are still living, Münter and Campendonk.

In September 1955 The University of Kansas Museum of Art in Lawrence presents a retrospective of Bloch's work, including 40 paintings. The exhibition travels in the spring of 1956 to the Renaissance Society at the University of Chicago. For the catalogue, Bloch writes a letter to the Museum's Director, Edward A. Maser, in which he articulates his artistic convictions and his present attitude toward the art of the Blue Rider group.

In 1959 Bloch completes *Impromptu*, which will be his final painting.

After a long illness, Albert Bloch dies on 9 December 1961 in his house in Lawrence.

Bloch in his studio working on a painting he had started in the early 1950s, c. 1958

Bloch in his study during the move of the Department of Painting and Drawing to the Dyche Museum of Natural History, c. 1945

All photographs from the collection of Mrs. Albert Bloch

ALBERT BLOCH:
THE INVISIBLE BLUE RIDER

Henry Adams

In 1984 a woman appeared at the door of the Nelson-Atkins Museum of Art in Kansas City, Missouri, with a stack of battered, discolored canvases. She was Anna Bloch, the widow of the painter Albert Bloch, and she had come to inquire what could be done to conserve these early works by her late husband, who had died in 1961. For over forty years the paintings had lain in a trunk in the corner of an unheated attic studio in Lawrence, Kansas, exposed to great changes of humidity and to extremes of heat and cold.

That the paintings had survived at all was probably a stroke of luck, for in a letter of 1936 to Maria Marc, the widow of the great German painter Franz Marc, Bloch had commented that he would happily destroy all his early work.[1] He had apparently never bothered to unroll these canvases since shipping them back from Germany in 1921.

By 1984 the paintings were cracked and creased, from having been rolled into tubes and subsequently flattened. Nonetheless, Scott Heffley, the young conservator at the museum, remembers feeling a thrill of excitement as the figures of dancing Pierrots and the face of a suffering Christ peered up at him through a brown film of dirt and discolored varnish. Despite their mistreatment, the paintings still communicated amazing vibrancy and life. Moreover, they were clearly pieces of great historic significance, for as Anna confided to him, two of them had been exhibited in the Blue Rider exhibition in Munich, in 1911, the first international show of modern painting and one of the most illustrious events in the history of modern art. Six artists formed the core of the Blue Rider group. Albert Bloch was the only American.

That first encounter between Anna Bloch and Scott Heffley led, through a complex chain of circumstances, to the present exhibition. The encounter itself raises some of the key questions relating to Bloch's curious career. As a young man, Bloch was an intimate of such artistic giants as Wassily Kandinsky and Franz Marc, and from 1911 to 1921 he contributed to a number of shows of modern art in Germany. Why did Bloch refuse to cash in on the celebrity of his early associations and choose to disappear so completely that his work was unknown to the curator of a museum less than an hour's drive from his home? Why, in his later years, did Bloch virtually isolate himself from the art world, from public exhibitions, and from art dealers? Why did he choose to end his career obscurely, conjuring up his private visions in a modest attic studio? Why did he appear to turn his back on modern art? Why, of all the figures in the Blue Rider movement, did Bloch choose to remain the most invisible, the one whose work is almost never shown, and the one whose very name is often omitted from lists of the exhibitors?

Bloch himself made it difficult to provide clear answers to these questions, for when asked to provide information about his life, he was invariably evasive. In a letter of 17 October 1920, to Hans Goltz, the Munich art dealer, publisher, and editor, he noted that he could not imagine anything worth mentioning about his life except that he was born in the United States in 1882, had become a painter, and was still alive.[2] Bloch's most extensive statement about his artistic goals, a letter to Edward Maser of 20 June 1955, is almost equally circumspect. "My career, such as it is," Bloch wrote, "I fear I cannot review for you. There may be those who have followed it — I haven't. I couldn't even tell you where and when it began."[3]

It appears that Bloch wished to become invisible — to let his art speak on its own, without the distraction of a physical being behind it. In a striking passage in his will, dated 1 January 1947, Bloch specified that, "*No photograph of myself* is to be printed in newspapers or periodicals upon this, or, if it can be avoided, any later occasion; nor are they to be given data of any kind for 'obituaries' or any other purpose."[4]

Despite such statements, Bloch scattered his trail with clues for the persistent sleuth. He carefully dated his paintings and sketches, and even compiled scrapbooks to record the names of owners and the exhibition histories of the works created between 1911 and 1919. He was also a voluminous writer and correspondent, who penned letters, poetry, essays, and a fat stack of unpublished lectures. Thus, much material survives from which to piece together Bloch's biography, although notable gaps remain and many of his motives remain a mystery.

Bloch's career spanned different cultures and great physical distances. It began in the German-Jewish neighborhoods of St. Louis; moved to the studios, cafés, and boulevards of Munich; and ended on a university campus, set amidst the vast expanses of the Kansas prairie. Almost by accident, Bloch took part, almost unwillingly, in one of the formative movements of modern art — in a gathering of extraordinary talents at a time when the artistic and spiritual possibilities of the future seemed unlimited. His artistic legacy sheds light on the hopes and aspirations of that moment, while it also betrays, particularly in his late work, his equally profound and haunting disappointments.

Rather than seeking to fix Bloch's position within the history of twentieth-century art, this exhibition has a more modest goal. A final assessment of Bloch's place can be left to future decades. This show simply aspires to bring back into the light a group of his finer creations, both early and late, so that they can again enter the realm of critical and historical awareness. If this project is a success, perhaps some of these works may join the repertory of familiar images of twentieth-century art, and become part of our general visual heritage.

EARLY LIFE

Albert Bloch was born in St. Louis on 2 August 1882, where his father, Theodore Bloch, and two relatives had formed a wholesale grocery business. Nearly half the population of St. Louis was then foreign-born or had foreign-born parents, and within this group a little more than half were German.[5] Bloch's family was Bohemian and Jewish, and dealing with unfriendliness and adversity was very much part of his heritage.

The major events in the lives of Bloch's forbears often seem to have reflected patterns of toleration or persecution. Thus, for example, we know that in 1849 the artist's grandfather, Bernard Bloch, moved from Protivin, ninety miles southwest of Prague, to Strakonice, fifteen miles away, where he married.[6] In that year, following the Revolution of 1848, laws had been liberalized to allow such actions. Before that date, Jews were not allowed to travel; moreover, only the eldest son was permitted to marry, and then only following his father's death.[7]

Bloch's father, Theodore, emigrated to the United States in 1869, at a time when edicts in the Austro-Hungarian Empire were again becoming highly unfavorable to Jews. A few years before, the reactionary Emperor Franz Joseph had canceled the constitution, and he was moving to revoke all the liberties which had recently been granted to minority groups.[8]

Little is known of Albert Bloch's childhood. He was evidently not close to his father, whom he later recalled as "cheerfully taciturn," noting that he allowed no one to break down his "urbane defenses."[9] He seems to have been more deeply attached to his mother, and in his *Ventures in Verse* he wrote of how she would read to him from the fairy tales of Hans Christian Andersen and the brothers Grimm, while his imagination transformed the lamplighted room, with its expressive cast shadows, into a wonderland of dwarfs, giants, deep forests, and haunted fountains. She seems to have supported his artistic aspirations, and he once described her as a "fond listener," whose cheerfulness kept her from ever seeming old.[10] In a letter written in November 1920 to Thekla Bernays, Bloch wrote: "You may have heard from common acquaintances of my mother's recent death … I can't speak of it, or even adequately grasp the ultimate finality of the fact — as yet. She was more to me, meant more in my life than one is led to realize by the word *mother*."[11]

Bloch's early artistic training is briefly sketched in a letter he wrote in 1923 to Harold Butler, the Dean of the School of Fine Arts at the University of Kansas, Lawrence, Kansas. In it Bloch noted that he attended the public schools and the Central High School in St. Louis, "but left the latter before graduation, because by the time I was sixteen the thought of an artistic

career had so taken possession of me that an enforced occupation with anything else amounted to mere drudgery."[12] Bloch's formal training in art was relatively brief, consisting of a course in drawing, which he attended on an extracurricular basis in high school, and two years of study at the St. Louis School of Fine Arts.

Although we have few details, Bloch appears to have been far from a model student. Anna Bloch has charitably written: "He must have given his teachers a bad time; he was gifted beyond them and he knew it."[13] We get hints of Bloch's difficulties from various sources. For example, one of his first satirical drawings for the St. Louis *Mirror* featured Halsey C. Ives, one of his former professors. The text accompanying this sketch, written by Bloch's friend William Reedy, was far from flattering, and seems to specifically allude to Bloch's conflicts with the professor. "Professor Ives," Reedy wrote,

> simply has not been able to adapt himself to the idiosyncracies of his pupils, and this has helped him to smother, to some extent, some promising ingenious individuals. His defect is that of the Washington University in general, a sort of dread of getting away from commonplaces, a fear of brilliancy, a distrust of innovation, a sort of dry, unluminous, unplastic materialism.[14]

Bloch also clearly clashed with Edmund Wuerpel, another of his teachers. In 1925, following Bloch's return to the Midwest from Europe, Wuerpel wrote to him, expressing a desire to renew their acquaintance. Bloch replied with a biting letter, stating that he had no interest or intention of doing so; he had no wish ever to see Wuerpel again. "In the days now more than twenty-five years past," Bloch complained, "you hardly encouraged a desire in me for closer acquaintance with you."[15]

Bloch's hostility to art schools, in fact, became a major tenet of his artistic program. He forcefully expressed this notion, for example, in an essay for the *Mirror*, in June 1910, in which he protested that "the incompetents of our art school faculty at home" could not stimulate "independence of thought and expression."

> What must finally be our artistic salvation in America is a complete secession from the schools, from the academicians: entire freedom of expression, emancipation of man-made rules and theories; nothing less will save us. A genuine artistic impulse is strong enough to conquer all obstacles: the weaklings, in spite of schools and professors, will always go to the wall. Rules forsooth! Who teaches the lark to sing? In Art, in painting, there are fundamental natural laws, which have always existed before art began; they may not be taught in schools. The artist senses them intuitively; he obeys them unconsciously.[16]

WILLIAM REEDY AND THE ST. LOUIS *MIRROR*

Despite his difficulties as an art student, Bloch had no trouble finding work. For three years after leaving art school, from March 1901 until December 1903, he contributed comic strips, political cartoons, and decorative designs to the St. Louis *Star*. Then in 1903, at the age of twenty-one, he moved to New York, where he worked as a free-lance illustrator. In the following years, Bloch seems to have moved back and forth between New York and St. Louis. Bloch's work of this period was technically proficient, but most of his assignments offered little room for personal expression. For the most part he produced conventional Art Nouveau decoration, or illustrated bland topics, such as "How to Rest Gracefully in a Chair," or "Wonderful Fire Fighting Systems at the World's Fair." Throughout this period, however, he also drew continuously from the model and educated himself through extensive reading.

Bloch's big break came in March 1905, at the age of twenty-two, when he was hired by William Marion Reedy, the editor of the weekly St. Louis *Mirror* (whose commentary to some of Bloch's drawings has already been quoted). His encounter with Reedy marked a turning point in Bloch's career. The son of an Irish policeman, Reedy tipped the scales at over three hundred pounds and once boasted that he possessed the "pachydermatous ponderosity of the hippopotamus." He was notorious for his expansive appetites — in food, in literature, in liquor, and in women — having supplemented his formal education under the Jesuits with extensive roamings in the bars and brothels of St. Louis.[17]

Reedy began his career as a journalist and in 1895 assumed the editorial chair of the *Mirror*, which was on the verge of financial collapse. He rapidly transformed it into the city's liveliest magazine of gossip, political commentary, poetry, criticism, and literature. Over a period of thirty years, in part to save money on author's fees, Reedy wrote about half the *Mirror* himself, keeping up a steady stream of commentary on every imaginable topic of current interest. The fame of the magazine, however, rests not so much on Reedy's ponderously expansive prose as in his ability to recognize new talent. Most remarkably, he had an uncanny knack for recognizing gifted young poets, and in the course of his career helped launch the careers of such figures as Vachel Lindsay, Edna St. Vincent Millay, Edwin Arlington Robinson, Carl Sandburg, Robert Frost, Witter Bynner, Louis Untermeyer, Edgar Lee Masters, and even Ezra Pound.

Before Bloch was hired, the *Mirror* had carried no illustrations, and Bloch's drawings immediately changed the whole look of the magazine. Bloch's earliest designs for the *Mirror* were a series of political cartoons which were impressive for their savagery and bite. His first drawing, for example, titled *His Master's Voice*, showed the Mayor of St. Louis, in the guise of a faithful dog, taking orders through a speaking tube from a very fat hog, which represented the special interests.[18] Even today, when we have forgotten the specific people he portrayed, Bloch's drawings of this type still speak forcefully and crudely, even a little viciously, about hypocrisy, political corruption, and false morals. Though nearly a century old, they still carry a powerful shock value. Fairly soon, however, Bloch shifted his major efforts from such political commentaries to a series of satirical portraits titled "Kindly Caricatures," for which Reedy wrote accompanying texts. From 25 May 1905 to 11 February 1909, the series ran with only one or two interruptions for over 160 consecutive issues of the *Mirror*: over the years Bloch represented figures in the fields of politics, academics, art, business, the clergy, the military, medicine, and St. Louis high society.

Despite the friendly-sounding title, Bloch's pen was often dipped in acid, as was Reedy's commentary.

Bloch's political cartoons, reproduced photographically rather than through wood engraving, were executed in a fine-line technique ultimately derived from the work of Thomas Nast. His "Kindly Caricatures," however, were in a different style, reflecting a more up-to-date tendency, that of international Art Nouveau. The drawings were memorable for their remarkable exaggerations — generally speaking a thick concentration of black, treated as an inky, solid mass; or occasionally, the opposite, a design created entirely from a few slender outlines, standing out starkly on the white page, against the repetitive columns of type, like a large window with a beautiful view in an endless expanse of wall.

The execution of these caricatures, particularly after Bloch had gained confidence, was remarkable for its freedom. As we look we can almost feel the artist's sweeping arm movement: we become viscerally involved with the artist's gesture and touch. They create a sculptural reality, with massiveness and grandeur, out of ordinary faces, as if Bloch were drawing not people but the heroically scaled crags and outcroppings of a mountain landscape.

To readers of the time, the style of these caricatures would have carried very definite cultural connotations. For while Bloch's political cartoons for the *Mirror* were rendered in a style associated with lowbrow American newspapers, the caricatures, with their clear reference to Art Nouveau, were associated with the highbrow literary and artistic journals of the continent, such as *The Yellow Book* in London, or *Jugend* or *Simplicissimus* in Munich.[19] Indeed, Bloch's shift of style and subject may well have reflected an editorial decision on the part of Reedy, who doubtless wished to establish his enterprise as different from other St. Louis publications and to ally it with the most fashionable European trends.

In a brief essay on these drawings, Reedy observed that Bloch favored the "bizarre" and "a touch of grossness," and stated that he was particularly drawn to "the German modern school."[20] In fact the principal inspiration for Bloch's caricatures was quite specific: the German satirical magazine *Simplicissimus*. Most of Bloch's drawings reflect the influence of two popular draftsman for this publication, Olaf Gulbransson and Thomas Theodor Heine.[21]

When working in the manner of Gulbransson, Bloch made dramatic use of heavy blacks, in conjunction with slender outlines. Like Gulbransson, he tended to show the head as a kind of pear shape, with heavy jowls, as if it were excessively pulled by gravity, or even made of melting wax. Good examples of this style are Bloch's caricatures of L. D. Kingsland and W. R. Donaldson (figs. 1, 2). When working in the manner of Thomas Theodor Heine, Bloch used contrasts of light and dark somewhat less dramatically, and emphasized instead the rhythmic movement of the line itself, which often abstracts or reduces the form so that it is barely recognizable. Striking examples of this mode are his caricature of F. Louis Soldan (fig. 3) and his striking cover of 10 September 1908, with facing profile portraits of William Howard Taft and William Jennings Bryan.

1. "Kindly Caricatures No. 73: L. D. Kingsland," *Mirror*, 18 October 1906, State Historical Society of Missouri, Columbia

2. "Kindly Caricatures No. 111: W. R. Donaldson," *Mirror*, 6 June 1907, State Historical Society of Missouri, Columbia

3. "Kindly Caricatures No. 15: Louis Soldan," *Mirror*, 31 August 1905, State Historical Society of Missouri, Columbia

If one made a census of the "Kindly Caricatures," it would certainly be Gulbransson's influence which would be the more dominant of the two (fig. 4). Theodor Heine's, however, was to prove the more lasting, since his work anticipated one of the major trends of modern art, a desire to reduce forms to their bare essence — their essential bones (fig. 5). Thus, in some fashion, Bloch's early exposure to Heine made him receptive to the ideas of such modernists as Wassily Kandinsky and Franz Marc, when he encountered them later in Europe. In 1913, when he was living in Germany and had just exhibited in a Blue Rider exhibition, Bloch included a profile of Heine in an article he wrote for the *International*. In the article Bloch declared that he considered Heine to be "the greatest living caricaturist," and went on to praise his work as "an indispensable complement of the literature of modern Germany" and one of its "weightiest by-products."[22]

Bloch's work was at its best when he allowed himself to become most free. Probably the masterpiece of his *Mirror* drawings is his remarkable sketch of the aging actress Sarah Bernhardt, which appeared as a cover of the *Mirror* on 1 March 1906 (fig. 6). This portrait has a freedom that verges on the childlike, and yet zeroes in, almost cruelly, on the haggard features of his subject, to create an impressively vampirelike effect. In a typically overwrought passage, Reedy noted that Bloch had captured Bernhardt's "necrophilistic, satanic power," and had aptly portrayed her as "exotic, morbific, feline, fulgruant, ophidian, and hypnotic."[23]

In histories of American illustration Bloch's drawings for the *Mirror* have never received attention, nor is it surprising that they have been overlooked. The *Mirror* was a little magazine — it was not celebrated for visual design — and it was published in a provincial American city. Aside from Bloch's drawings, the art in the *Mirror* was distinctly mediocre. This oversight is regrettable for Bloch's drawings occupy a notable and important place in the history of American illustration. In this period artists were just making the shift from wood engraving, which required the intervention of the engraver, to photographic reproduction, so-called "process work," which more accurately reproduced the artist's touch. Bloch was one of three American illustrators who recognized the potential of the new methods, the others being the cartoonists Boardman Robinson of the New York *Tribune*, and Robert Minor of the St. Louis *Post-Dispatch*.[24]

Bloch may well have been influenced by Robinson and Minor in certain technical tricks, such as drawing on a very large scale (the photograph could reduce the drawing to any size) and using a variety of media, including pen, brush, and lithographer's crayon, to get a range of textural effects. Robinson and Minor, however, modeled their work on French artists, particularl Honoré Daumier, whereas Bloch was drawn primarily to German sources. Thus, Bloch's work was not only amazingly bold and adventurous for its period, but stylistically distinct from that of other American artists.

The one writer who has recognized Bloch's significance was one who was hardly impartial — William Reedy. Reedy, however, for all his elephantine verbosity, was no mental slouch — his assessement of Bloch's work was singularly apt. He wrote of Bloch's work in 1913: "A large element of the art world has but now come up to the point to which Bloch advanced five years ago…. I cannot help remarking that he pioneered the broad, forceful, realistic method in illustration. He led the breakaway from mere prettiness. He made cartooning a series of social explosions. His drawings were and are dynamite."[25]

In addition to producing drawings, Bloch began writing for the *Mirror* about a year before leaving St. Louis. His first piece, which appeared in December 1907, was a review of New York cultural events of that year. Gossipy in tone, it consisted of eight short blurbs, each accompanied by a caricature.[26] The most interesting of these early writings by Bloch was a short piece he wrote in 1908, "The Work of Henri Matisse." This reviewed the first Matisse exhibition in the United States, which Alfred Stieglitz had organized at his gallery in New York.

The show was Bloch's first true exposure to modern art, and while he later became very critical of Matisse, at this point he was strongly favorable — at least about his drawings — and wrote enthusiastically about his free and abbreviated use of line. Bloch concludes with the description of a lithograph:

> …a female figure indicated in a half dozen flowing lines — mouth, nose and eyes scarcely jotted in — every extraneous detail slurred over and sacrificed to sheer outline. It gives one pause; and few there are who can take it seriously — this thing which a puberous schoolboy might have done in a lewd attempt at a smutty picture. But the artist achieves in these seemingly unconsidered crayon strokes the one thing toward which evidently all his previous efforts have been directed: absolute simplicity, perfect grace; a marvelous purity and poise.[27]

MARRIAGE

Bloch's position on the *Mirror* finally gave him a stable income, and in November 1905, a little more than six months after he joined the magazine, he married Hortense Altheimer, the daughter of a prosperous plantation owner from Pine Bluff, Arkansas. When she met Bloch, Hortense was living in the home of her uncle Benjamin Altheimer, a St. Louis business-man, while attending a local convent school.[28] Bloch apparently fell in love with her four years before their marriage, on New Year's Eve, 1901. Their first child, Bernard, was born two years after their wedding, in 1907.

Bloch's last year as an illustrator in St. Louis was clearly a time when the future seemed to offer unlimited promise. He was newly and apparently happily married, his drawings were widely admired, and he was publishing his first articles and re-views. Indeed, Reedy was clearly delighted with Bloch's work, and eager to see his young protégé develop into an artist of national reputation. However, the *Mirror* constantly teetered on the verge of bankruptcy. "Pay anything!," Reedy once thun-dered, in a letter to Theodore Dreiser. "Money here is the vocative with a vengeance. It is hard work to pay the electric light bill!"[29] Nonetheless, in 1908 Reedy made a remarkable offer: he agreed to pay travel costs and a regular stipend for Bloch to travel to Europe in order to further his artistic training.[30]

Bloch happily accepted, and shortly after Christmas 1908, he, Hortense, and their one-year-old son, Bernard, took the boat from New York to Southampton, spent a little time in London, crossed the channel to Le Havre, and from there took the train to Munich. Although he made brief trips to England, France, Austria, and Switzerland, Munich was to be Bloch's principal home for the next twelve years.

BLOCH'S ARRIVAL IN MUNICH

Reedy had always been interested in what was happening abroad, and looked to Europe for stimulating ideas in literature and art. He once wrote to Bloch: "You'll miss nothing in missing con-temporaneous American books — nothing. All the thinking and imagining is being done in France, Germany, Russia, Italy, and a little in England."[31] Indeed, Bloch's long stay in Munich would utterly transform his artistic thinking, although in ways that Reedy could not have anticipated and was never fully able to accept or understand.

For the next three years Reedy provided Bloch with a regular stipend of about fifty dollars a month, which was just barely enough to live on. No doubt Reedy hoped that Bloch would serve as a foreign correspondent for the *Mirror*, and would send home regular reports of the latest cultural develop-ments. His subsidy continued, however, despite Bloch's failure to provide much satisfaction in this regard.

For Bloch one factor was surely decisive in making him choose Munich over Paris: he was conversant in German, which he had learned from his parents, but did not speak

4. Olaf Gulbransson, *Conrad Dreher as a Hunter*, Draft for *Simplicissimus*, 1910, No. 31, Städtische Galerie im Lenbachhaus, Munich

5. Thomas Theodor Heine, *Neutrality*, Draft for *Simplicissimus*, 1905, No. 45, Städtische Galerie im Lenbachhaus, Munich

6. "Sara" (Sarah Bernhardt), Cover illustration for *Mirror*, 1 March 1906, State Historical Society of Missouri, Columbia

French. In a lecture of 1934, Bloch declared that it was Paris "toward which my soul had yearned," but in fact he had settled in Munich within a few weeks of arriving in Europe, and it must have been his destination from the start.[32]

Throughout the nineteenth century, Munich rivaled Paris as a training center for American artists. As Kandinsky later wrote of this time: "Everyone painted — or wrote poems, or made music, or took up dancing. In every house one found at least two ateliers under the roof."[33] The city housed major museums, as well as cafés, concerts, exhibitions, and publications devoted to artistic topics. Bloch's two favorite satirical magazines, *Simplicissimus* and *Jugend* were both published there. As Bloch wrote to the Chicago collector Arthur Jerome Eddy around 1914, Munich possessed "that indefinable incentive called atmosphere, created by five thousand students and artists, arguing, disputing, theorizing, exhibiting, as only a big colony of students and artists can, in a place so given over to art that arguments and theories command attention and are taken seriously."[34]

ILLUSTRATIONS

For four years, Bloch's illustrations had been one of the mainstays of the *Mirror*, and his departure significantly altered the look of the magazine. "Kindly Caricatures" was the first casualty. Shortly after Bloch's departure, Reedy explained to his readers that the drawings would be temporarily suspended, but he evidently hoped that the series could be revived, and from time to time he sent photographs of potential subjects to Munich.[35] Bloch, however, found this procedure too mechanical, and the closer interaction with Reedy which had stimulated his efforts was lacking. His caricature of Denton Snyder, which appeared in the *Mirror* of February 1909, proved to be his last. His stream of covers also ceased. From 7 January 1909, Reedy made use of an ornamental fleur-de-lis that Bloch had designed earlier, employing it for thirty-nine consecutive issues.

The drawings of Munich that Bloch did send home apparently did not please St. Louis readers. Just after his arrival, he produced four full-page illustrations of Munich, each of which combined a number of different vignettes. The first of these showed copyists and visitors in the Pinakothek; the second, scenes of student life; the third, the readers of different periodicals, each of whom was distinctly characterized; and the fourth, a variety of people seen on the streets.[36]

By the time the last of these drawings had been produced, Bloch had apparently already received negative feedback from home. Rather than change his mode of drawing, however, he titled his last piece "But Surely A. Bloch Can Do Better Than This" (fig. 7). Just what offended his audience is a little unclear, since none of the drawings is radically modern or abstract. They were arranged, however, in a fashion resembling a sketchbook page, and to a St. Louis audience they probably appeared too casual and too spontaneous to be accepted as finished works.

Other than these drawings and a small caricature of the composer Richard Strauss, Reedy published no more drawings by Bloch until December 1912, although Bloch continued to

7. "Munich Sketches: But Surely A. Bloch Can Do Better Than This," *Mirror*, 29 April 1909, State Historical Society of Missouri, Columbia

send him new material. In his letters, Reedy proposed that Bloch try to sell his work to German magazines, which were more in tune with his latest work. In addition, such European success would probably do more for his reputation at home.[37] In accordance with this advice, between 1909 and 1911, Bloch sold twelve of his cartoons to the Berlin weekly *Lustige Blätter*, which was a forum for advanced work of this type by artists such as George Grosz and Lyonel Feininger.[38] These German cartoons by Bloch are in a sketchy, abbreviated style which Reedy dismissed as "hazy confusion," but which was not offputting to the editors of *Lustige Blätter*, since it was similar to the work of the German cartoonist Heinrich Zille, who was a regular contributor to the magazine. Bloch's work as a cartoonist stopped completely, however, around December 1911, the time of the first Blue Rider exhibition. At this time he virtually abandoned caricature to pursue larger artistic ambitions.

WRITINGS FOR THE *MIRROR*

Although his drawings were rejected, after settling in Munich, Bloch continued to write articles for the *Mirror*, and generally speaking, Reedy found them more pleasing and satisfactory than his drawings. In none of these articles did Bloch directly address the issue of modern art, or mention the work of Marc and Kandinsky. Indeed, the lack of primary documentation on these matters, other than Bloch's paintings, is often frustrating. Nonetheless, Bloch's writing for the *Mirror* provides a valuable record of his intellectual development. In fact, his writing evolved in a fashion that exhibits striking parallels with his development as a painter.

Like Bloch's painting, his writings show a general shift in approach from realistic and literal to visionary and subjective. Reedy was dismayed by this development and eventually began to reject the work that Bloch sent home to him. But it took longer for Reedy to turn against Bloch's writings than his drawings. With just two exceptions, he rejected Bloch's drawings after 1909, but he continued to regularly publish his writing until 1912.

Bloch's first two articles from Munich were reviews of cultural events: an oratorio by Richard Strauss and an exhibition of work by American painters. Strauss's piece had been controversial, but in his review of April 1909, Bloch gave it a ringing endorsement. His praise is interesting for the light it sheds on his own knowledge of modern art. Bloch argued that Strauss's music was in keeping with other expressions of the modern spirit, and he approvingly cited its affinities with the work of Auguste Rodin, the French symbolists, Oscar Wilde, Maxim Gorky, Maurice Maeterlinck, Friedrich Nietzsche, George Bernard Shaw, George Moore, Henrik Ibsen, composers such as Richard Wagner, Claude Debussy, Vincent d'Indy, and Gustave Charpentier, and the painters of the Barbizon school, the French Impressionist movement, and the Munich Secession. The roster of writers, composers, sculptors, and painters reveals how avidly Bloch followed modern trends, although the mix of names and tendencies is confusingly diverse. In general he favored work that was rebellious and symbolist in character. His most intense admiration was reserved for Wagner. "Beyond Wagner it is impossible to get," he wrote. "He stands on the highest mountain peak."[39]

Similar in tone was Bloch's review of "American Painting in Germany," which appeared 9 June 1910.[40] Here, however, Bloch more strongly emphasized the theme of rebellion, and, as already noted, lambasted the formal academies of American art. Art had become mechanical, he complained, since "the incompetents of our art school faculty at home" did not stimulate "independence of thought and expression." He pleaded instead for "freedom from the hampering moss-grown theories which have come to be regarded as the rigid basic principles of art, holy and inviolate." Once again, Bloch cited Wagner as an artistic model, comparing the true artist with the figure of Siegfried in Wagner's *Der Ring des Nibelungen*, as he forged his sword.

> The true artist does not disobey the man-made rules, the professorial traditions, he only disregards them; for him they simply do not exist. He sees the task clear before him; forgets everything in the joy of his work. He achieves his purpose; how he arrives at his result is a matter of small moment. Whether a hand or a foot be drawn with academic precision is an indifferent question, depending entirely upon how greatly he is interested in the foot or hand. What does matter to him is that the picture as a whole should express to his satisfaction that which he sets out to express.[41]

Here we have the first full statement of Bloch's artistic credo, and the first expression of a belief that he often restated later — that the artist should not be required to follow other people's rules, but should be allowed to make up his own, to serve his own purposes.

At this point, Bloch shifted from criticism to fiction and poetry. Most of this material was written under the pseudonym of Joseph Strong, and as a consequence, Bloch's authorship was not recognized until quite recently, when it was identified by Werner Mohr.[42] Bloch's pseudonym is a revealing one, given that Reedy sometimes referred to him as "little Albert Bloch" (of course, just about everyone was littler than the gargantuan Reedy). A diffident and shy but inwardly rebellious man, Bloch clearly devised his pseudonym as an emblem of power and strength — of an ability to make others bend to his will.

Four stories of 1910 show Bloch working in a realist vein. The first two provide vignettes of life on the streets. "The Beggar: A Street Corner Story" describes a beggar in the shopping district during the Christmas season.[43] "Derelicts: A Conversational Fragment" recounts the dialogue between a blind man and a prostitute. The prostitute is eager to return to work, to get money for food, but she takes pity on the blind man and decides to lead him home.[44] Thematically, the two stories are related, although the second carries the inverse moral of the first. While "The Beggar" tells of the selfishness of respectable people, "Derelicts" speaks of the Christian generosity of two social outcasts. Reedy was particularly impressed with "Derelicts" and compared it to the work of John Galsworthy, who was then getting a reputation for his novels of London life. As Reedy wrote to Bloch early in July 1910: "Your 'Derelicts' is a very good Galsworthy."[45]

Bloch followed these street stories with two additional fictions, both of which explore the nature of artistic ambition. In "Curtain Speech" an author appears on stage at the end of a performance of his play and denounces the director, the actors, and the producer, all of whom have altered his work out of recognition for commercial reasons. The story, however, ends ironically. At the end of the diatribe we learn that the speech has occurred only in the imagination of the author, actually a timid soul.[46]

In "An Ambition" the author attends a concert and recognizes that the cellist is a former high school classmate — one who had never revealed the slightest hint of ability or talent. After the performance, they join each other for a drink, and the cellist describes his career. He had started out playing in a beer garden, then worked his way up to a theater orchestra. Now he is studying in a conservatory and hopes to join a symphony. Though lacking in unusual ability or talent, his life has been transformed by a noble ambition.[47] It does not take great insight to recognize that both stories dramatize issues that troubled Bloch himself. Like the playwright in the first story, Bloch vacillated between timid retreat and forceful diatribe. Like the cellist in the second, he believed that noble aspiration was more important than technical skill.

On 29 June 1910, shortly after receiving "Curtain Speech," Reedy wrote to Bloch: "Your writings are making a great hit with me. You can exploit your ego and make it caracole as much as you please as long as you send me stuff as comes under your own name or that of Joseph Strong."[48] Despite Reedy's encouragement, however, Bloch let two years go by before he again attempted creative writing for the *Mirror*. In 1912, however, he published four new pieces, all rather short, which were very different from the earlier, realistic stories. "Wehmut" ("Melancholy") describes the complex emotions of a reveler on *Faschingsdienstag* at the peak of the Bavarian lent. The writer smiles and weeps at the same time; he revels yet also feels sad. Both the subject matter of the piece and the tone of bittersweet melancholy are closely analogous to Bloch's paintings of carnival subjects created around this time.[49]

More enigmatic is "Compositions in Monochrome," a series of prose renderings of imaginary pictures, which Bloch composed in his Dachau studio in the summer of 1911. In one the artist is compared to Christ on the cross and is attended by seven naked women, symbolizing the seven virtues, who capture his life's blood in their flasks. In another, an eagle, symbolizing a wise patron, frightens away a flock of cackling jackdaws. Bloch's vignettes are striking both for the violence of their imagery and for the fashion in which they defy literal interpretation and enter the realm of the symbolic and visionary.[50]

The final two pieces deal with the loneliness of the artist, alone on his hilltop, isolated from the rest of mankind. "Prophecy" pictures the artist as a lonely seer, doomed to be scorned and rejected. "Hell shall be his portion upon earth; damned shall he be in the sight of all mankind. His friends shall forsake him, and his next of kin shall sicken at the sound of his name. — Reviled and despised, he shall be cast into the outer Light."[51]

Perhaps Bloch's most moving piece of writing is the poem "Where Is Sanctuary?," which deals with isolation and suffering. Should the artist remain on his hilltop, isolated from mankind? Should he venture into the city, where the money changers rule? Should he seek comfort in organized religion? Should he embrace the lonely sufferings of Christ? Nothing seems to offer comfort to his soul.

> Whither should I flee, seeker after rest and shelter?
> Where is Sanctuary?
> Rocky plain and forest glen refuse me their asylum.
> Nor God, nor Son of God, can still the cry within me.[52]

Reedy seems to have found this new direction in Bloch's writing difficult to grasp and, after publishing a few specimens as an experiment, evidently came to feel that such ventures did not belong in the *Mirror*. Around 1913, for example, Bloch began collecting literary scraps about his life for a collection which he titled "Ishmael's Breviary." In a letter of 8 January 1913, Reedy wrote to Bloch expressing his disapproval:

> Your breviary to hand. I note what you say about it, and I am, of course, pleased to note that you still regard yourself as the center of the universe, and your thoughts as the most important things in the world. The sort of thing you appear to have attempted is one that does not appeal very much to me. The French are the only people who have done it well — Pascal supremely so. In England the most famous collection of these is found in Colton's "Lacon."[53]

As with his drawings, Bloch's writings had progressed to a point where Reedy could no longer follow or understand.

BLOCH'S FIRST GERMAN PAINTINGS

By the time he arrived in Munich, Bloch had produced hundreds of drawings for the *Mirror*, but his experience with oil paint was very limited. About the time of his marriage, he took his first and only lessons in oil technique from an English-born artist named Dawson Dawson-Watson, who had come to the United States in 1893, at the time of the Chicago World's Columbian Exposition, and soon afterwards was hired to teach winter classes at the St. Louis School of Fine Arts. A genial English eccentric, Dawson-Watson had long, unkempt hair and a general air of artistic dishevelment. Nonetheless, he was a master of technical procedures. His lessons, while brief and informal in nature, were evidently sufficient to last a lifetime. Apparently, Bloch never took any further lessons in painting technique.[54]

Reedy had clearly supposed that Bloch would enroll in classes in Munich or otherwise engage in formal training. Instead, Bloch opted to paint on his own and to build up his knowledge through reading and visiting museums. According to Bloch, shortly after his arrival in Munich he visited two former professors at the academy, Leo Samberger, a portraitist, and Hans Volkert, an etcher, and "they definitely discouraged the idea of further academic study." His style had developed too far already, they told him, and "direct academic instruction would rather harm than help me."[55]

Although Bloch's earliest German work often looks quite modern, he had little exposure to "modern painting," as we now understand the term. In Europe the most "modern" influence on his work was the Post-Impressionism of French artists such as Vincent Van Gogh, Paul Cézanne, and Paul Gauguin. Moreover, at this stage Bloch was still so unsure in his taste that, as he later confessed, at an exhibition of the Munich Secession, "I came upon a roomful of Cézannes — and walked right through, unaware that I had been glancing, as I walked away, at anything out of the ordinary."[56]

In Munich, in fact, for the most part, he was surrounded by much less adventurous work and for a time at least was captivated by it. "When I first went abroad," he later wrote, "my chief enthusiasm, side by side with my deep admiration for the great French impressionists — and despite the glaring incompatibility — was that pretentious pseudo-classicist and vulgar mystagogue, Franz von Stuck." Bloch also was briefly captivated by the work of the artists of the Munich Secession, most of whom he eventually looked back upon with horror. "The less you know about it, the less you are missing," he later commented of the Munich painting of this period, "although such figures as Max Liebermann, Corinth, and Slevogt will remain always interesting and important."[57]

Given this unsureness of Bloch's taste, it is striking that his earliest paintings already look impressively radical and bold. Three general factors contributed to this accomplishment: an illustrator's sense of bold pattern and unusual combinations of form, which he carried over from his experience on the *Mirror*; an awareness of French Post-Impressionism; and a German sense of the grotesque.

French influence is often visible in Bloch's earliest efforts. In 1910, he made a brief visit to Paris, to linger at the Café du Dome and to study the work of the Impressionists.[58] Two early still-life paintings provide particularly clear illustrations of French influence and were apparently produced just after this Paris visit. The more striking of the two shows a flowerpot and spiky plant, sitting on a ledge against a yellow background (fig. 8). The bold placement of the motif squarely in the center of the canvas and the roughness of the brushwork give the painting an uncouth directness which recalls Van Gogh and is still a little startling. Dating from about the same time is a still life of an apple and several bananas sitting on a piece of cloth, with tilting planes and carefully angled brushstrokes which recall Cézanne (fig. 9). Both paintings are essentially French in approach, although something about their harshness of effect reveals that they were executed in Munich rather than Paris.

Although these two still-life compositions feel predominantly French, Bloch's portraits of this period strike a more even balance between French and German influences. For example, *Portrait of a Long-Haired Man* (fig. 10) portrays a thin-faced man with a doglike protruding red nose, a bitter mouth, a chin with a

9. *Still Life with Bananas and Apple*, 1911, Mrs. Albert Bloch

8. *Untitled (Plant Still Life)*, 1911, Mrs. Albert Bloch

pronounced underbite, and watery, light blue eyes. He is placed against a bright red background. To some extent one might view this as a Post-Impressionist painting, for the bold flat color brings to mind Van Gogh. The grotesque quality of the drawing, however, has a distinctly German flavor, and recalls the caricatures of *Simplicissimus*, as well as the portraits of early German painters, such as Lucas Cranach and Albrecht Dürer, which Bloch had admired in the Pinakothek, and which also often employ flat red backgrounds. More subdued in color is *Untitled (Portrait of a Man)* (pl. 10) from the same period, showing a gentleman with a curiously mouselike face, with a pointy nose, brown eyes, and enormous mouselike ears. As if to underscore these elements, the pervading color tone in the painting is

mouse-fur brown. Once again, the concept of the painting grows partly out of the French tradition since Edouard Manet, but in this case the effect is even more German and Expressionist in feeling.

These compositions are strikingly bold, but Bloch also produced paintings which, while strong in execution, are more similar in spirit to the general run of Munich work. For example, he spent the summer of 1911 working in a studio in Dachau, just outside Munich, and he was doubtless aware of the work of Adolf Hoelzel, who led a "Dachau School" of landscape painting, which featured rather flat, decoratively arranged shapes and muted colors.[59] Bloch's one surviving Dachau landscape, a modest view of a wall and two houses along a road, reveals a similar decorative treatment and dulled-down palette.

Bloch came particularly close to contemporary German painting in his *Portrait of a Boy* of 1910 (pl. 6), which he exhibited at the Berlin Secession Exhibition of 1911 — the first work he exhibited in Europe. Close study reveals that the painting plays on complementary colors, for the background is a dull orange and the boy's coat a dull green. This contrast, however, is very nearly lost in the general dimness, a kind of muddy brownness similar to the work of Munich portrait painters such as Wilhem Leibl and Franz von Lenbach. What distinguishes Bloch's design from theirs, however, is the broad, flat, abstractly decorative pattern of the brushwork, which ties together different areas, such as the boy's cap and the sleeves of his garment. (This hatching, by the way, is reminiscent of the bold crayon strokes of Bloch's *Mirror* caricatures.) In addition, unlike most German portraits of this period, Bloch completely eschewed any hint of the sentimental. The boy's expression is sour and completely uningratiating.

In general, the early surviving paintings by Bloch are remarkable for their raw, almost primitive quality, and their renunciation of pretty effects. During this period, the most celebrated artist from St. Louis was Richard Miller, who had a studio and art school in Paris and turned out paintings by the dozen of pretty girls in colorful dresses (fig. 11). Bloch's work is so different from Miller's decorative impressionism that it is clear that he avoided such prettiness on purpose. Indeed, on

10. *Portrait of a Long-Haired Man*, 1911, Mrs. Albert Bloch

one occasion, he even wrote a note to himself to avoid creating an effect which was harmonious or agreeable. A drawing of 1913 is inscribed with the words: "Contrasts harsh and discordant. Forbidding — gloomy — cold. Lyrical note strictly to be avoided."[60]

THE BLUE RIDER EXHIBITION

Within two years of his arrival in Munich, Bloch was showing in the first exhibition of the Blue Rider group, a landmark exhibition in the history of modern art. Just how this came about is one of the key questions of Bloch's biography, but unfortunately, there are very few contemporary sources with which to pin down this phase of his career.

Given its prominent place in the history of modern art, it is startling to review how rapidly the Blue Rider movement came and vanished. The two most important figures in the movement, Wassily Kandinsky and Franz Marc, first met in January 1911, and they produced the key achievements of their fellowship — two exhibitions and two books — in a period of just one year, between Spring 1911 and May 1912.

The exhibitions were the first and second Blue Rider exhibitions, which occurred at the Thannhauser Gallery in Munich in December 1911, and at the Goltz Gallery, also in Munich, in February–April 1912. The books were Kandinsky's *Concerning the Spiritual in Art*, which appeared in January 1912, and the *Blaue Reiter Almanac*, edited by Kandinsky and Marc, which appeared in May 1912. The association of Kandinsky and Marc lasted only a little longer, until August 1914, when World War I broke out and placed the two artists on opposite sides of the conflict.

Bloch's most extensive accounts of this period were both written years after the fact: a lecture he delivered in Denver in 1934 and a long letter he wrote to Edward Maser, the director of the Art Museum at the University of Kansas, in 1955 (see pp.

199–207 below). By this time, Bloch's artistic views had shifted somewhat, and both accounts are apparently skewed by this bias. They contain curious omissions and evasions, and although they seem to be generally accurate, a number of their statements are confusing and difficult to interpret.

The most secure form of evidence for this period is that of Bloch's paintings, since he kept a scrapbook with photographs of nearly all his work, dating each piece and recording its ownership and exhibition history. In addition, there is an early photograph of him in his studio, surrounded by a group of his paintings (see p. 10). This must have been taken just before the first Blue Rider exhibition, since one of the pieces in that show, *Harlequinade* (pl. 4), is visible on his easel in the process of being painted. By combining the stylistic evidence of Bloch's paintings with the narrative evidence of his later recollections, and checking both against other forms of evidence, it is possible to work out the general sequence of events with reasonable precision.

In his 1934 lecture, Bloch specified that he learned of Kandinsky's work from an exhibition of the New Artists' Union of Munich, in which several of Kandinsky's paintings were included. He noted that he felt an immediate affinity with Kandinsky's work upon seeing one of his paintings reproduced in the catalogue.[61] Since the first New Artists' Union exhibition of 1909 had no catalogue, Bloch must have been referring to that group's fall 1910 show. Bloch was in Paris at that time — as he later recalled.[62] Thus, he must have encountered Kandinsky's work in the New Artists' Union 1910 catalogue some time after his return to Munich, most likely in the spring of 1911.[63]

After discovering the catalogue, Bloch made contact with Kandinsky, who came to visit his studio with several other members of the New Artists' Union. Bloch mentioned only one of the other visitors by name, Franz Marc, who had only recently

11. Richard Edward Miller, *At the Window*, c. 1912, The Nelson-Atkins Museum of Art, Kansas City, Missouri, Gift of Mrs. Harry G. Woodward, Jr.

12. "Don Quixote," Cover illustration for *Mirror*, 12 November 1908, State Historical Society of Missouri, Columbia

and more calligraphically expressive. It is not surprising to learn that Kandinsky once complained to Bloch, "You draw too well."

It is remarkable that Bloch's first meeting with Kandinsky and Marc should have occurred so shortly before the Blue Rider exhibition, but such a date is supported by the stylistic evidence of Bloch's work. His earliest paintings already show an interest in bold outlines and flat shapes which was compatible with the work of Kandinsky and Marc, and which evidently led them to consider him a kindred spirit. Only very late in 1911, however, did Bloch begin to borrow specific stylistic devices from his two new friends.

13. Wassily Kandinsky, Cover illustration for the *Blaue Reiter Almanac*, 1911, Städtische Galerie im Lenbachhaus, Munich

met Kandinsky himself, after defending his work in print against hostile criticism. In addition, the visitors probably included Adolf Erbslöh, the president of the New Artists' Union, since Bloch mentioned in passing that the mood of the group was friendly, and he had no suspicion of the schism that would soon occur. Bloch stated that this visit occurred "about a year after" the exhibition of the New Artists' Union, and this would suggest that it took place about September 1911, only a few months before the first Blue Rider exhibition, which opened in December.

The radical changes in Bloch's work at this time, and what he derived from Kandinsky, are vividly summed up in one of his drawings, made around 1911, which shows a horse and rider against a mountain landscape (pl. 57). His horse and rider are quickly drawn, but nonetheless reveal great mastery of technique. Naturalistic elements, however, are subsumed — one might even say consumed — by sweeping brushstrokes of black ink, evocative at once of tree and mountain forms, and expressive of the larger, more abstract rhythms of nature. Bloch once stated that this sketch represented Don Quixote, whom he had portrayed earlier, on 12 November 1908, as a cover drawing for the *Mirror* (fig. 12). In addition, the drawing bears an obvious relation to several drawings and watercolors of this period by Kandinsky, in which he sketched different ideas of a cover for the *Blaue Reiter Almanac* (fig. 13).[64] At a spiritual level the two subjects — Bloch's and Kandinsky's — complement each other. Indeed, it seems fitting that Bloch's "Blue Rider" should also be a "Don Quixote," since of all the Blue Riders, Bloch was to have the most quixotic of careers. Bloch had, in effect, gone back to his earlier version of the Don Quixote theme, and redrawn it in a more Kandinsky-like manner. When we place Bloch's drawing beside Kandinsky's sketches, it is apparent that Bloch's drawing is in many ways more skillful — at once more academically assured,

As it happens, the date at which Bloch's work began to shift towards this more modern style can be dated with relative precision. Of particular interest are two paintings of the Pierrot theme, *Pierrot* (fig. 14), which is dated October 1911, and *The Three Pierrots No. 2* (pl. 5), which was included in the Blue Rider exhibition that December. The first of these paintings does not betray the influence of Kandinsky or Marc, while the second one clearly does. Perhaps the most striking and significant development between these works is the shift in Bloch's handling of the background. *Pierrot* has an almost flat background, similar to those of Bloch's early still-life paintings and portraits and to his illustrations for the *Mirror*. *The Three Pierrots No. 2*, on the other hand, has a background of abstract color swirls, which clearly relates to the abstractions of Kandinsky. In short, in the space of a few weeks, between October and December 1911, Bloch rapidly began to absorb ideas from Kandinsky and Marc, and to move quite aggressively towards a more modern style.

One major event in Bloch's move towards an alliance with Kandinsky and Marc remains somewhat unclear. At some point shortly after his first meeting with them, Bloch attempted to

14. *Pierrot*, 1911, Mrs. Albert Bloch

national boundaries. Small as it was, the group nonetheless included painters from Russia, Germany, France, Holland, and the United States — from places as distant as Moscow and St. Louis. Yet, even though the Blue Rider exhibition included several paintings on loan from artists in other countries, including Russia and France, the core group of Munich-based artists and their friends was very small, consisting of only six: Kandinsky, Marc, Gabriele Münter, August Macke, Heinrich Campendonk, and Bloch.

It was Kandinsky who visited Bloch's studio early in December 1911 to invite him to join the new group. Bloch readily assented, first expressing surprise and then indicating that he had heard some gossip about the tensions which had been brewing. Why was Bloch included? No documents record the thinking behind the decision. We do know, however, that his name was on the very first list of exhibitors that Marc prepared, which he enclosed in a letter of November 1911, even before the December rejection of Kandinsky's painting which precipitated the final break with the New Artists' Union.

A primary factor in Bloch's selection was that Kandinsky was fascinated by work which stood somewhat outside the mainstream of modern art but which exhibited a spiritual affinity with it, such as the art of "primitive" peoples, of children, or of artists who lacked academic training and were essentially self-taught, such as the French customs officer Henri Rousseau. While Bloch was not a true primitive, since he had some formal training, as a painter he was largely self-taught. His work had a fresh, bold character and he had developed largely in isolation, without much contact with other painters in Munich. In this sense he offered a general parallel with Rousseau and served as a sort of natural primitive and outsider.

Bloch showed six paintings in the first Blue Rider exhibition, more than any other artist except for Münter, Kandinsky's mistress, who also showed six. Bloch's paintings included two city scenes, religious works, and subjects from the *commedia dell'arte*. Although the city scenes cannot now be identified, the two religious scenes, *Procession of the Cross* (pl. 9) and *Head [of Christ]* (Mrs. Albert Bloch), can be identified and located, as can the two scenes of figures from the *commedia dell'arte*, *Harlequinade* (pl. 4) and *The Three Pierrots No. 2* (pl. 5).

The question of whether Bloch was truly an integral member of the Blue Rider group or was only included through a series of happenstances is a delicate one. Arguments can be produced on either side. In a late interview discussing her years with Kandinsky, Gabriele Münter described Bloch as "one of our closest friends," and Bloch also clearly became very close to Marc and his wife, whom he sometimes visited at their country home.[65] On the other hand, Bloch never even met Macke, and he later recalled of the Blue Rider group that "I took very little part in their activities, preferring to remain withdrawn with my work, showing it when I could, and spending what leisure I allowed myself with a very few friends."[66]

In his later writings, Bloch took particular pains to stress his differences with Kandinsky, placing himself in the role of a traditionalist and characterizing Kandinsky as one who had pushed abstraction to the point of absurdity. In 1911, however,

show his work with the New Artists' Union but was rejected. In his Denver lecture, Bloch declared that his work was supported by Kandinsky and Marc but was voted down by the membership, and that his rejection played a role in causing Kandinsky and Marc to secede from the Union. Other records of the New Artists' Union, however, do not support this statement, and in fact Bloch's application was probably never submitted to a general vote. It appears that Bloch applied to exhibit his work in the group's next exhibition, but was rejected by the President of the Union, Adolf Erbslöh, because he was not a member. Thus, Bloch's "rejection" was probably made on procedural grounds rather than artistic ones. In any case, the fact that he was not associated with Erbslöh or with the New Artists' Union became a point in his favor when the Blue Rider group was formed.

Although Bloch did not know it at the time, the studio visit from Kandinsky and Marc occurred at a key juncture. The pair was becoming increasingly frustrated by the New Artists' Union, and their annoyance came to a head early in December 1911, when the membership voted to reject a painting by Kandinsky from their coming exhibition because it was too abstract. Marc and Kandinsky promptly withdrew from the group and began organizing an alternative show, more in line with their own goals for the course of modern art. They chose to call the group "The Blue Rider," after their projected almanac, which had been in the works since June 1911. Significantly, rather than choosing work in a single style or expressive of a single point of view, they chose work of varied approach, which was linked only by its underlying sincerity and independence. They also chose work by artists of varied nationalities, to demonstrate that the "new art" was a world-encompassing movement, unfettered by these issues of modern versus traditional, and realistic versus abstract, were probably less apparent, and Bloch apparently did not see his disagreements with Kandinsky in such severe terms.

MUSIC AND MOOD

Not surprisingly, around the time of the first Blue Rider exhibition, Bloch began producing work that surpassed his earlier efforts. In general, he moved away from literal realism towards greater freedom of expression. The dramatic shift in his approach was noted as early as 1919 by Arthur Jerome Eddy, who had organized the first showing of Bloch's work in the United States four years before. Assessing Bloch's productions of the period from 1909 to 1915, Eddy declared that they "showed astonishing developments always in the direction of greater freedom and abstraction. For instance, *Factory Chimneys*, painted some years ago is so realistic that it might hang in any exhibition and attract little attention save for a certain simplicity and strength. At the other extreme his *Night I* is almost a pure creation of the imagination as well as a beautiful composition of line and color."[67]

Bloch's rapid development in this period away from literal realism followed the central tenet of the Blue Rider movement — a stress on the "spiritual." Thus, in the preface of the *Blaue Reiter Almanac*, Kandinsky and Marc declared that, "We are standing at the threshold of one of the greatest epochs that mankind has ever experienced, the epoch of spirituality."[68] Precisely what was meant by this word "spirituality" is sometimes difficult to make out, for as used by Kandinsky and Marc — and for that matter by Bloch himself — it was a diaphanous concept which embraced a variety of ideas. At the time of the Blue Rider exhibition it encompassed a particularly heady mix, including an interest in rhythm, in music, in mysterious shifts of mood, in intensified color, in simplified form, and in correspondences with other expressions of primitive and modern art.

Later in life, Bloch reacted against some of these precepts, and in his 1934 Denver lecture he explained at some length the impossibility of creating musical effects on canvas. Around the time of the Blue Rider exhibition, however, he seems to have been entranced by these ideas, as is confirmed by a piece on him written for the *Mirror* in 1913 by Murray Sheehan, a young student in Paris who visited him in Munich. Sheehan was immediately struck by the swirling rhythms of Bloch's work, which made his figures look "misshapen" and "embryonic." In addition, Bloch used color not literally, but for emotional effects. Consequently, "his figures vary in color from infra-red to ultra-violet." The reason for these odd effects, Sheehan reported, was that Bloch sought to present "the feelings which are provoked by a certain subject," but to do so without resorting to literal representation. In fact, he strove to achieve "an absence of materiality," and "to strip off all flesh and blood to present pure spirit." Of particular interest, Sheehan's report confirms that in this early period, Bloch sought inspiration for his paintings in music. "In one of Bloch's own favorite phrases at present, he is trying now to 'sing his pictures onto canvas.'"[69]

16. First Blaue Reiter exhibition, Thannhauser Gallery, Munich, 1911/12, Photo: Gabriele Münter, Gabriele Münter- und Johannes Eichner-Stiftung, Munich

It is striking, in fact, how many of Bloch's paintings of this period allude to music and dance. Bloch's two major entries in the first Blue Rider exhibition, for example, *Three Pierrots No. 2* and *Harlequinade*, both portray dancing figures. What is more, *Harlequinade* was evidently inspired by a specific piece of music, Beethoven's C-Minor Symphony, for in a drawing of the composition, produced in 1913, Bloch included some bars of Beethoven's symphony at the bottom of the composition (fig. 17).

Along with an interest in music, Bloch was clearly interested in capturing extremes of emotional mood. Sometimes, in fact, he seems to have planned paintings in deliberate opposition to each other. A case in point is two works from the time of the first Blue Rider exhibition, the *Piping Pierrot* of late 1911 (pl. 13) and *The Duel* of 1912 (pl. 15). The two works occupy facing pages of Bloch's scrapbook, and seem to have been painted approximately in succession, but they express two nearly opposite states of feeling. *Piping Pierrot* shows a solitary Pierrot in white, playing a flute. He stands beside a solitary tree, against a brilliantly colored landscape of red and green. Like so much of

15. First Blaue Reiter exhibition, Thannhauser Gallery, Munich, 1911/12, Photo: Gabriele Münter, Gabriele Münter- und Johannes Eichner-Stiftung, Munich

17. Cover illustration for the *Mirror*, 11 April 1913, State Historical Society of Missouri, Columbia

Bloch's work, the painting is subtly tinged with melancholy, yet nonetheless its essential spirit is hopeful and optimistic: it forms a poem of spring and rebirth after the leafless time of winter. *Duel* on the other hand, creates a deliberately jarring effect, and forms a kind of visual analogue to a migraine headache. In the background on the left, a figure with a white Pierrot-like face lies prostrate on the ground. He has clearly just been shot and is being attended by two friends. On the right, the man who has shot him and his second, holding a top hat, stand coolly, remorselessly, like fashion plates. In the left foreground, a distended face looks anxiously out at the spectator. Thus, Bloch has compressed into one image a variety of horrible things: physical pain, psychological suffering, man's cruelty to his fellow man, and the senseless suddenness of death. Notably, he used a variety of visual techniques to accentuate the uneasy mood. The outlines of the forms, for example, are distorted and distended, which creates a generally queasy feeling. In addition, the coloring of the piece emphasizes a distinctly sickly tone of yellow, a color which Kandinsky associated with insanity. "If we were to compare it with human states of mind," Kandinsky wrote of yellow, "it might be said to represent not the depressive but the manic aspects of madness. The madman attacks people and disperses his force in all directions, aimlessly, until it is completely gone."[70] In short, *Piping Pierrot* is hopeful: *Duel* is anxious and despondent. Indeed, in many of Bloch's paintings of this period, his intention seems to have been not so much to represent figures or physical things as to capture some lyric mood of joy or sorrow.

INFLUENCES

Bloch was strongly resistent to having his work grouped with that of other radical modernists, or placed in stylistic cubbyholes. "One thing I *beg*," he wrote to Arthur Jerome Eddy.

"Don't if you can help it, allow the papers to treat the exhibition as a sensation. Don't, *please*, let them call me Futurist, Expressionist, or any other kind of 'ist.'"[71] Similarly, in a letter published in the *Mirror*, Bloch protested that Reedy once inaccurately applied stylistic labels to his work.[72] In statements such as this, Bloch stressed his desire to have his work judged on its purely spiritual and emotional qualities, without reference to stylistic influences.

In fact, however, Bloch's work of this period often reveals obvious debts to the work of other modern artists. Indeed, many of his paintings seem to relate directly to works which were shown in one of the Blue Rider exhibitions, or were reproduced in one of the Blue Rider publications. The variety of these influences is suggested by the two paintings discussed above, *Piping Pierrot* and *Duel*. *Piping Pierrot* clearly alludes to the work of Matisse, specifically to Matisse's *Music* (1910; The Hermitage, St. Petersburg), which was reproduced in the *Blaue Reiter Almanac*.[73] (The mask-like face of the piper is particularly close to Matisse.) *Duel* on the other hand, has a strong affinity with the work of Edvard Munch, and in fact the distended, anxious face in the foreground seems to have been directly inspired by Munch's famous painting *The Scream* (1893; Najonalgalleriet, Oslo). In short, right around the time of the Blue Rider exhibition, Bloch went from being virtually isolated from new artistic developments to being able to draw from a great range of varied artistic sources, according to the emotional effect he wished to produce.

Interestingly, it seems to have been only in this period, not earlier, that Bloch became aware of the work of the artists associated with the group known as Die Brücke (The Bridge). Richard Green, for example, has correctly noted that Bloch's untitled painting of two seated nudes (pl. 1) "seems to show some kinship with the Dresden painters in its vigorous slashing brushwork, heavy outlines, and sharp colors."[74] Green, however, erroneously supposed that Bloch's painting was an early one, from about 1910. Instead it seems to date from about 1912, as is suggested both by a 1911 drawing, which likely preceded it, and by the Kandinsky-like background. In fact, the painting may well have been inspired by a specific work, *Bathers* by Otto Müller, a print which was reproduced in the exhibition catalogue of Die Brücke when the group showed at the Galerie Commeter in Hamburg in 1912.[75] While the two works are certainly not identical, there are many striking parallels, particularly in the treatment of the nude seen from behind.

An artist of Die Brücke seems also to have inspired one of Bloch's most successful compositions, *The Green Domino* of 1913 (pl. 20). One of Bloch's strongest designs, it bears an obvious relation to the street scenes of Ernst Ludwig Kirchner. It is strikingly similar, for example, to Kirchner's famous painting *The Street* (1913; Museum of Modern Art, New York). Bloch's painting depicts a street parade very similar to that of the Kirchner painting, which is dominated by a fashionably dressed woman. Moreover, his composition is structured in a similar way, from clearly defined triangular units.

Of course, in addition to these new influences, Bloch continued to draw on earlier sources of inspiration. *In the Forest* (fig. 18), for example, clearly alludes to Cézanne, who had influenced Bloch's still-life paintings as early as 1910. The archlike shape of the trees recalls Cézanne's *Bathers* (1899-1906; Philadelphia Museum of Art), which Kandinsky reproduced in *Concerning the Spiritual in Art*, while the volumetrically rendered figures (including one smoking a pipe) resemble Cézanne's famous painting *The Cardplayers* (1890-92; The Metropolitan Museum of Art, New York).

On occasion, also, Bloch went back to themes he had explored years before, in his own early work. The marvelous drawing *Home Run Cigars* (fig. 19), for example, although executed around 1913, clearly alludes to Bloch's American experience, since baseball was not played in Europe. It refers back to Bloch's illustrations for the *Mirror*, such as the spirited study of a baseball player which he published on 19 April 1906, in which the vigorous draftsmanship recalls the work of George Bellows.

WASSILY KANDINSKY AND FRANZ MARC

A range of modern influences swirl through Bloch's paintings of this period, but the central figures of the Blue Rider were Kandinsky and Marc, and not surprisingly, they influenced Bloch's painting of his German period most profoundly. Assessing Bloch's response to both men presents a real challenge. Kandinsky's influence on Bloch's paintings of the German period is more pervasive. In his writings, however, Bloch eulogized the work of Marc and severely criticized Kandinsky.

18. *In the Forest*, 1914, Mrs. Albert Bloch

Since Bloch's writings were produced roughly a quarter of a century after the first Blue Rider exhibition, at first it is tempting to suppose that they do not reflect his early views, and that by the time he settled in Kansas his opposition to Kandinsky had hardened. To some extent this may have been the case, but the best explanation for this seeming contradiction between word and deed is probably somewhat more complex. In fact,

Bloch seems to have rejected Kandinsky's ideas about abstraction while imitating many of his pictorial effects; at the same time, he seems to have admired Marc's ideas while finding it difficult to imitate his work. The reasons for this complex reaction become apparent when we assess Bloch's relationship to Kandinsky and Marc in its totality, considering his response to three distinct factors: their personalities, their cultural backgrounds, and their artistic styles.

19. *Home Run Cigars*, 1913, Mrs. Albert Bloch

When Bloch first met Kandinsky and Marc, Kandinsky, the more extroverted of the two, made a stronger impression. "Never had I listened to such inspired and inspiring talk upon the subjects which interested me most," Bloch later wrote. "He was bursting with ideas, and his work between 1909-14 showed this in every canvas, every scrap of paper. He had thought long and earnestly, often fruitfully, upon all aspects of the subject which so engaged my own thought. How could a receptive hearer, sixteen years younger, fail to learn from a man like that, who was not trying to teach."[76]

Almost from the first, however, Bloch seems to have felt "critical reservations regarding the actual *work* of Kandinsky," feeling that it pushed too far towards pure abstraction.[77] In 1911, when Bloch met him, natural appearances were becoming increasingly camouflaged in Kandinsky's work, and he was standing on the verge of pure abstraction. The members of the New Artists' Union clearly thought as much, when they rejected one of Kandinsky's non-figurative paintings and triggered the creation of the Blue Rider group. Kandinsky, on the other hand, was probably giving a backhanded complement when he praised Bloch's drawing. It seems likely that he felt that Bloch's work was too realistic. A number of Bloch's paintings clothe Kandinsky's abstract compositions with more realistic subject matter, and it seems likely that Bloch made these paintings in part as a critique of Kandinsky's approach. From Bloch's standpoint this use of recognizable figures provided the designs with greater spiritual and humanistic significance.

Bloch responded somewhat differently to Marc. Marc had originally intended to study theology, and like Kandinsky, had a mystical bent and saw painting as an escape from the materialism of modern life. While he defended Kandinsky's abstract work, however, Marc himself was not so interested in pursuing pure abstraction. Instead, he found solace in the spiritual innocence of animals, which became the major subject of his colorful canvases. In his letter to Edward Maser, Bloch wrote:

> As for Marc, my first experience of his work, a large one-man show at *Die moderne Galerie* in Munich early in 1911 before ever I had met the man himself, took me captive at first sight, even though I recognized immediately that Marc's external gift (though not his genius) was essentially decorative. Here at last I found painting which fed in full measure my need and my longing. Here was the *new voice* — something never yet heard — the authentic new voice, yet speaking throughout in the revered, *traditional* mode. Less vocal, surely less tolerant than Kandinsky, who was his senior by fourteen years, there was yet a profundity in his rather reticent talk, in the man's silences and very bearing, in his often half-humorous *obiter dicta*, which the Russian, for all his more obvious charm, lacked entirely.[78]

Perhaps Bloch also found Marc easier to accept than Kandinsky because of his more similar cultural heritage. Both Marc and Bloch came from essentially German backgrounds, whereas Kandinsky's background was more mystical and Russian.

Bloch's paintings from about 1911 to 1914 show a progressive assimilation of modern ideas, particularly from Kandinsky. One of the most striking developments of this period is the gradual integration of the figure with the background. His earliest paintings, such as the plant against the yellow background or the head against the red, treat foreground and background as two entirely separate entities. By the time of the Blue Rider exhibition, however, in paintings such as *Harlequinade, Head*, and *The Three Pierrots No. 2*, Bloch had shifted to a background of swirling ribbons of color, which responded more sympathetically to the foreground element and is reminiscent of Kandinsky's paintings. By 1914, however, in paintings such as *Harlequin with Three Pierrots* (pl. 21), Bloch had developed a style of handling in which both foreground and background are entirely interwoven. *Harlequin with Three Pierrots*, for example, is very close to Kandinsky's *Composition IV*, which was reproduced in the *Blaue Reiter Almanac*, even to the black lines of the trees. But whereas Kandinsky's paintings shows unrecognizable squiggles and blobs, Bloch's paintings, for all the visual fireworks, nonetheless show recognizable figures in dramatic relation to each other.

Bloch's foreground figure, in his checked costume, is Harlequin, the tumbler, with his magic wand. To the left, three Pierrots watch him perform. Interestingly, the figural scheme is borrowed from religious painting — it is the same configuration that we find in renderings of Christ appearing to the three Marys after his Resurrection. Just what Bloch meant by using a religious image in this unorthodox way is hard to define — and he himself surely would have refused to explain. But in some way we are clearly meant to see this magical harlequin as a Christ-like figure that will transport us to heaven through the magic of his art. Unlike Kandinsky, Bloch never ventured into pure abstraction, although sometimes he came right up to the verge. Some of his most remarkable paintings are those of night in the city, such as *Night II* (pl. 24), in which only the black outline of a figure ties the painting to the real world. Arthur Jerome Eddy, who owned one of these night paintings, described the series as a "synthesis" and "summary" of Bloch's impressions of Munich by night. "It is vision on vision, dream on dream," Eddy wrote, "a composite of a hundred glimpses, the fusion of a hundred impressions; it represents no part of the city, but *is* the city by night."[79]

Although they are somewhat less frequent than such parallels with the work of Kandinsky, we find qualities in Bloch's paintings which recall Marc as well. Striking in its similarity to Marc is a recently discovered figure composition of 1912, *Untitled (Infernal Figures)* (pl. 16). Bloch chose to paint figures from the *commedia dell'arte* rather than the animal subjects that Marc favored. Nonetheless, the bold faceting of the forms in Bloch's painting, in cubist shapes, recalls Marc's example, as does the bold, unnaturalistic, and probably symbolic use of color. Once again, Bloch seems to have merged the theme of the carnival with Christian symbolism. His painting is at once a carnival of clowns and a scene of the Last Judgment, with dead Pierrots, Harlequins, and Columbines rising from their graves. Significantly, both Kandinsky and Marc were fond of such eschatological themes. Here Bloch translated their millennial concerns into his own characteristic type of subject matter.

CITYSCAPES

Bloch's city scenes of 1911 and 1912 show, with particular clarity, how he moved in this period from a fairly realistic manner to a more visionary, mystical approach. His first cityscape, of April 1911, shows a view from an upstairs window over a nondescript urban landscape of houses, vacant lots and billboards (pl. 2). A hunched figure walks along in the foreground, and in the lot behind, some children are playing, their shapes rapidly indicated with a few blurry strokes. The painting combines two conflicting tendencies. In its unflinching focus on urban "ugliness," the picture recalls canvases by American painters of the "Ashcan School," such as George Luks, John Sloan, and George Bellows. Indeed, the composition is strongly reminiscent of works by Bellows, such as *The Lone Tenement* (1910; National Gallery of Art, Washington), which also shows a vista across a vacant urban lot.[80] Bloch's handling of form and color, however, differs from that of his American contemporaries, for he more radically reduced the scene to flat shapes, and made more obvious use of clear black outlines. In fact, Bloch's formal language in this untitled cityscape is close to that of two members of the New Artists' Union of Munich, Adolf Erbslöh and Alexander Kanoldt, both of whom painted architecture in a somewhat similar fashion, with simplified geometric shapes and black outlines.

By late 1911, in *Houses at Night* (pl. 8), Bloch's abstract restructuring of form had taken on a new expressive life. One of his most remarkable paintings, and perhaps his first *bona fide* masterpiece, *Houses at Night* portrays two hunched foreground figures, who are silhouetted against a row of tenements. Everything about the painting is twisted and sinister, from the bent shapes of the foreground figures to the irrational, twisted forms of the windowless buildings behind them. Significantly, we are no longer dealing with realism but with an imaginative vision. Indeed, the two figures in the foreground appear to be symbolic, for one of them resembles Mephisto, whom Bloch portrayed in an earlier etching, and the other hooded, skeletal man resembles the devil/death figure that appears in his *Harlequinade*. Thus, moving away from literal transcription, Bloch transformed the modern city into a scene of hell or purgatory reminiscent of Dante.

The ominous qualities of the city are also the subject of a remarkable work on paper, *Figure Between Houses* (pl. 61), which Bloch exhibited in the second Blue Rider exhibition of 1912. This drawing juxtaposes a harlequin in a black mask with an ominous city of swaying buildings to create a powerful symbolic portrait of the forbidding structures of the modern city and the strange class of sinister tricksters that inhabit the bleak streets below them.

Bloch concluded this city series with his most fanciful portrayal, *Impression Sollnhofen* (1912), which shows house facades packed together into a decorative pattern. As in a cubist painting, some of the houses are transparent, and reveal the buildings behind them. In addition, some of the houses have anthropomorphic qualities. Windows and doors suggest eyes, mouths, and noses, and facades are bent to create oval faces or even Pierrot-like crouching figures. Bloch's sources for this remarkable conception are not clear. Sadly, *Impression Sollnhofen* was later destroyed, although fortunately Kandinsky and Marc admired it enough to reproduce it in the *Blaue Reiter Almanac*.[81]

Later in life, Bloch occasionally returned to urban themes, for example in the series of drawings collectively titled "The Black City," which he produced from about 1918 into the late 1930s. Buildingscapes, however, never became the central focus of his art. Instead, he put his major effort into religious and carnival scenes, both subjects that he began painting around the time of the first Blue Rider exhibition.

RELIGIOUS THEMES

Although he painted portraits, still lifes and landscapes, two subjects dominate Bloch's German work: Christian subjects and comic figures from the circus or the *commedia dell'arte*. Very often, however, these two subjects blend together, since he used both to symbolize the alienation of the artist. The suffering figure of Christ provides a model for the sufferings of the artist, who is humiliated and scorned by the common crowd; while sad clowns or the *commedia dell'arte* figures of Pierrot and Harlequin also exemplify the artist's suffering, they present his dilemmas as comical — as something too pathetic to regard in a completely tragic fashion. Interestingly, both these subjects first appear in Bloch's work only shortly before the first Blue Rider exhibition.

The spiritual intensity of Bloch's art derives in part from the fashion in which he transformed and slightly scrambled his subjects. Throughout Bloch's early work one finds traditional poses and motifs, most often lifted from time-worn religious traditions. Kneeling saints and apostles, Christ rising from the dead or lying prostrate in prayer in the Garden of Gethsemene, the three Marys at the tomb — these are only a few of the motifs which appear in Bloch's paintings. Yet they always appear in a slightly unfamiliar, slightly unusual guise, which short-circuits our attempt to reduce them to a familiar meaning. Rather than Christ being entombed we find Pierrot; rather than Christ being levitated toward heaven, we find a leaping Harlequin. As a result of this process, we cannot reduce the meaning to something routine — we must grope more broadly for its deeper spiritual significance.

Bloch's first known religious paintings were the two he exhibited in the 1911 Blue Rider exhibition. The first, *Head*, a relatively modest work, in an El Greco-like style, shows Christ displaying his wounds. The second, *Procession of the Cross* (pl. 9), which is more ambitious, has dark outlines like those of an early German woodcut, and the way the design is divided into two zones brings to mind late medieval art, such as the early German religious paintings held by museums in Munich. At the top Christ and Mary Magdalene lead a mob of hostile figures, many of whom brandish staves or whips. At the bottom, the Virgin Mary stands beside a solitary tree, with an apostle in yellow seated beside her. Significantly, the painting contains a number of motifs which appear repeatedly in Bloch's later work, both in paintings and poetry — for example, a rocky hillside, a lone tree, a cross, the figure of Christ, the path of pilgrimage or suffering, and a shrouded figure. The painting thus is an important one in establishing Bloch's imagery and narrative interests.

Bloch's interest in painting such religious themes, in a primitivist manner, can be traced to both French and German sources. The French tradition of creating such works can be traced back to Gauguin. In paintings such as *The Yellow Christ* (1889; Albright-Knox Art Gallery, Buffalo, New York), Gauguin paid homage to the medieval calvaries he encountered in Brittany and deliberately strove to create a primitive effect, with bold, flat colors and strong outlines. Some of Gauguin's followers, such as Maurice Denis, concentrated chiefly on creating such religious paintings; and at least one French artist who worked in this mode, Pierre Girieud, made his way to Munich, where he exhibited his paintings of the life of Christ at the New Artists' Union exhibition.

Curiously, however, while in Munich, Bloch made relatively few paintings which are purely religious in nature — it was not until his return to the United States that he began to focus on such subjects. For the most part, during his German period, he conflated religious imagery with other subjects. For example, in 1912-13 Bloch painted a lamentation, which in composition is similar to innumerable religious paintings — but he dressed his figures in the costumes of Pierrot, and titled his work *The Death of Pierrot* (location unknown; formerly Koehler Collection, Berlin). Similarly, his ambitious *Entombment* of 1914 (pl. 23) is ambiguous. It is unclear whether it represents the burial of Christ or the burial of Pierrot.

These lapses from traditional subject matter and traditional rendering, however, are clearly deliberate: they transform the painting from a topical vignette into a more generalized and universal statement of the human condition. As Arthur Jerome Eddy wrote of *Lamentation* (pl. 18), which he once owned: "The figures convey the feeling of lamentation far more strongly than if they more literally resembled human beings; they are sorrowing masses as distinguished from mere weeping men and women. Besides they are fine harmonies of line and color, decorative as well as significant."[82]

Religion deals with the question of human meaning; mime and pantomime are forms of expression that go beyond words, to deal with the essential character of the human condition. Moreover, in both cases, Bloch was interested in what are essentially forms of popular art: the popular folk art of Christian Europe and the popular entertainment of cabarets.

CLOWNS, HARLEQUINS AND PIERROTS

Even more significant than these religious subjects are the figures of Pierrot, Harlequin, and other grotesques and clowns from the *commedia dell'arte*. These figures appear in about half of the paintings that Bloch executed in Europe and in much of his later work as well.

Bloch's "Italian Comedy" paintings are outgrowths of his earlier renderings of circus acrobats and clowns. He had drawn several clowns for the *Mirror*, and some of the first paintings he executed in Munich deal with such subjects, for example, a rendering of a circus parade, led by a duck, which directly echoes the subject matter of a cover he drew for the *Mirror* on 6 August 1908. Throughout his stay in Germany, Bloch occasionally went back to painting clowns and the circus, for example *Clowns III* (fig. 20), which he showed in the German Expressionist exhibition of 1914 in Dresden.

Around the time of the 1911 Blue Rider exhibition, however, Bloch shifted from clowns to figures of the *commedia dell'arte*, particularly Harlequin and Pierrot. It is hardly surprising that these *commedia* subjects begin to appear only after Bloch's arrival in Germany, since the Italian comedy was popular in Europe but did not exist in the United States. Bloch's fixation on this subject matter, however, was unusual. His intense engagement with it occurred at precisely the same moment that he came under the strong influence of Kandinsky and Marc. But neither Kandinsky nor Marc made paintings of Pierrot and Harlequin, although they were in contact with other artists, particularly writers and musicians, who focused on such themes. Indeed, Bloch's exploration of the tragicomic possibilities of this subject matter was one of his most distinctive contributions to the Blue Rider movement.

In the period surrounding and just following the first Blue Rider exhibition of 1911, many of Bloch's paintings explored different aspects of the Pierrot theme. *Reclining Figure* of 1911 (pl. 12), for example, shows a white Pierrot reclining in a red landscape. The effect of the painting lies in the contrast between the wistful, clown-faced Pierrot, who is meditative, expressionless, and colorless, and the brilliant red landscape, which possesses an oriental splendor. According to the notation in Bloch's scrapbook, the larger version of this painting (now

20. *Clowns III*, 1913, possibly destroyed by the artist, photograph in Albert Bloch's Record Book, vol. I, Mrs. Albert Bloch

lost) once belonged to Kandinsky, although it is not recorded in other listings of Kandinsky's collection.

The Green Domino of 1913 (pl. 20), expresses a variation of this theme. Here the central figure is a female cabaret singer, but her appearance is very similar to that of Pierrot, since she wears a ruffle around her neck and has a painted white face with heavily outlined eyes. Other grotesque figures are placed around her. As in the earlier *Harlequinade*, the central figure is flanked by two somewhat sinister figures: a long-nosed, hunchbacked punchinello in the left foreground, and, on the right, a masked figure in red, like the devil figures in Pernod advertisements. In addition, a man in the background with a monocle peers back at us to take in the spectacle. Thus modern streetlife, with its strangers parading before each other, becomes a kind of carnival.[83]

As the contrast between *Reclining Figure* and *The Green Domino* suggests, between 1911 and 1914 Bloch tended to move from single-figure designs to more complicated arrangements of multiple figures. This tendency towards greater elaboration reached its peak around 1913-14, when Bloch produced his most ambitious multifigured compositions of the Pierrot theme.

The two most ambitious of these are *Frieze for a Music Room* and *Entombment*, each of which contains about twenty figures. Bloch began work on *Frieze for a Music Room* in 1910, completed a first version of the design in 1913, then destroyed it and started a second version, which he completed in 1915 (fig. 21). Thus, Bloch worked on the design for five years. In a brief essay for the *Mirror*, written when he exhibited the piece in St. Louis in 1919, Bloch noted that it was difficult for him to complete a work which had been started at another time and in a different style.[84]

The painting depicts a kind of enchanted garden, inhabited by musical Harlequins, Pierrots, and clowns. It is separated into three sections, each divided from the other by arching trees. Bloch lifted many of the motifs from earlier paintings, and in effect, the *Frieze* forms a kind of grand summation of his varied treatments of Harlequin and Pierrot. In the center three Pierrots play bagpipe, flute, and mandolin; on the left a Harlequin leaps over a Pierrot on all fours; and on the right a seated Pierrot is surrounded by figures both dressed and undressed. Their relationship to each other is not altogether clear, although some of the figures recall the theme of the *fête champêtre* by painters such as Jean Antoine Watteau.

On the whole, however, the mood of the painting is cheerful rather than somber, and in a letter to Eddy, Bloch described the effect as "decorative." His general intention seems to have been to create a pastoral idyll, akin to the effect of soothing music. Because of its decorative purpose, Bloch seems to have deliberately worked towards a tapestrylike effect, with ribbons of color, and scattered decorative accents (like the traditional medieval *milles fleurs*), running through the green background.

Like the *Frieze*, *Entombment* also represents a synthesis, in fact, a kind of *tour de force*, since it contains twenty-six figures, both nude and clothed. In contrast to the *Frieze for a Music Room*, however, the effect is harsh and tragic, and the color scheme is dominated by fierce oranges and reds, against a complementary background of deep blue-green.

These two paintings are a culmination of Bloch's progression towards more complex and elaborate designs. Perhaps more successful than these crowded compositions is *Summer Night* (pl. 19) of 1913, which, although it contains fewer figures and is less elaborate as a compositional machine, conveys both a subtler and more pervasive sense of mood. The painting exudes a kind of bittersweet sadness, like the recollection of a romantic evening with a lover of long ago. In *Summer Night* the figures all express a strongly spiritual quality. Their gestures all seem to allude to religious art from both Eastern and Western sources. Two figures each hold a hand to their chin, a traditional gesture of religious contemplation. Another figure stands with his palm turned upward, like St. Francis about to receive the stigmata. And finally, still another figure in the background sits on the ground with his head turned up towards the sky, as if lost in some kind of mystical ecstasy. While the outlines of the figures are still firm, they have become transparent, and indeed, the background seated figure seems not so much to sit as to levitate. *Summer Night* is the first of what might be called Bloch's "Ghost

Paintings" — paintings in which the figures are no longer material forms, but ghostly apparitions, which evoke the spirit of the human figure but not its physical substance. One of the most effective of Bloch's "Pierrot" paintings, *Summer Night* also anticipates the religious and spiritual themes of his later work.

THE *COMMEDIA DELL'ARTE*

Bloch, of course, was by no means the first artist to make paintings of Harlequin and Pierrot. As with religious subjects, those of the *commedia* had precedents in both French and German art, and Bloch was probably familiar with these national traditions.

As the name suggests, the Italian comedy originated in Italy, but it was imported to France in the seventeenth century. In part because Italian actors generally did not speak very good French, the actors of the Italian comedy relied heavily on mime for their effects. Over time it developed a fixed set of stereotyped characters, in particular those of Harlequin and Pierrot, who competed with each other for the love of the fickle female, Columbine. Broadly speaking, Harlequin was a clown of action, Pierrot a clown of feeling.

The name "Harlequin" is ultimately derived from "King Harl" or "The Herle King," a spirit of the night and air from northern mythology. Harlequin carries a wooden stick, which often functions as a magic wand, giving him the power to disappear, take on fantastic disguises, fly through the air, or transport himself to distant places. On stage, his movements are lively and acrobatic. His costume has a motley pattern, with diamond-shaped lozenges.

Pierrot's character is very different. Rather than having divine antecedents, he originated as a young and untrustworthy valet, and was only gradually transformed into a melancholy and sensitive romantic. He carries no attribute but is closely associated with the moon, which is associated with both love and insanity. Pierrot's costume is generally a single color, most often white.

Bloch's renderings of Harlequin and Pierrot demonstrate that he was familiar with their distinct characteristics. In representations of Harlequin, for example, Bloch repeatedly emphasized his movement and energy, often portraying him leaping. Once or twice Bloch also focused on Harlequin's reputation as a trickster, notably in the remarkable drawing *Figure Between Houses*, in which a masked harlequin symbolizes the sinister tricksters who lurk in the shadows of the dark buildings of the modern city. By contrast, Bloch invariably represented Pierrot as subdued and wistful. Pierrot often looks on in astonishment

21. *Frieze for a Music Room*, 1915, Mrs. Albert Bloch

while Harlequin executes his remarkable leaps. In one important drawing, *Suicide* (pl. 60), which was probably included in the second Blue Rider exhibition, Bloch portrayed Pierrot's tragic melancholy. He showed him as a suicide, hanging from the branch of a tree, no doubt the victim of hopeless love. Silhouetted against a full moon, Pierrot sways in rhythm with the windswept grasses just below his feet.

From Paris, the Italian comedy spread to the rest of Europe. A key figure in its dissemination was Jean-Gaspard Debureau, who in 1830 began acting the part of Pierrot at the Funambule Theater in Paris. By making his costume more like that of real life, he transformed Pierrot into a symbol of modern man. Writers such a Théophile Gautier and Charles Baudelaire wrote enthusiastically about Debureau, and one poet, Jules Laforge, made a kind of specialty of writing about the Pierrot character. Due in large part to the influence of Debureau, Pierrot and Harlequin became frequent subjects in the works of French painters, from Jean-Léon Gérôme to Pablo Picasso.[85]

From Paris the characters of Pierrot and Harlequin made their way to Germany, achieving particular popularity in the Schwabing district of Munich, where artists and students congregated. Thus, for example, Franziska zu Reventlow, an eccentric exhibitionist known as "the queen of Schwabing," wrote of dancing through the carnival festival in Pierrot costume; and Bloch himself, in a piece he wrote for the *Mirror* in 1912, described how during the carnival the streets were filled with "clowns and bumpkins, Harlequin and Columbine, and Pierrot, sorry dog, with Ash Wednesday's shadow already lurking in his great, yearning eyes."[86] Cabarets in Munich, such as "The Eleven Executioners," where the playwright Frank Wedekind performed songs, often featured Pierrot and Harlequin, and Wedekind's famous play, *Lulu*, contains a scene in which Lulu has her portrait painted in Pierrot costume.

A number of artists associated with the Blue Rider group dealt with Pierrot and Harlequin. Thus, for example, August Macke and Alfred Kubin both represented Harlequin, and Alexej Jawlensky painted the Pierrot-like dancer, Alexander Sacharov. Most notably, the composer Arnold Schoenberg, whose music, writings and paintings were prominently featured in the *Blaue Reiter Almanac*, composed a song cycle, *Pierrot Lunaire*, which was first performed in Berlin in 1912. No other artist of the group, however, concentrated so intently on these characters as Bloch did, or explored them in such varied fashion.

Why did Bloch focus on Pierrot and Harlequin? Like other artists of the period, he seems to have seen these characters as exemplars of the artist's ambiguous role. In an early self-portrait, he portrayed himself as Harlequin, and it is tempting to see all his other Pierrots and Harlequins as essentially portraits of his own identity as an artist and as representing his own precipitous shifts of mood.

Like Pierrot, the artist Bloch was an entertainer, subject to the fickle whims of his audience. Like Pierrot, he was eager for applause, but also contemptuous of it. Like Pierrot, he was often forced to conceal his own feelings, to wear a white mask of indifference, in order to perform his part. Like Pierrot, he was tired of the duplicity of words and sought a form of communication which was more spontaneous, more natural, and more authentic. Like Pierrot, he struggled with the serious issues of life, yet found it difficult to do so in a purely heroic fashion. This insight lies at the core of Bloch's achievement: it was his genius to express this fact in visual terms.

Significantly, Bloch's exploration of *commedia* subjects introduced not only a distinctive iconography but also, more profoundly, a distinctive set of emotional chords and of artistic strategies associated with them. Pierrot and Harlequin became an avenue towards exploring tragicomic moods which mixed humor, pathos, and wistful melancholy. Kandinsky and Marc were essentially single-minded in their pursuit of artistic goals. They followed their special spiritual visions straight into the realm of apocalypse and ecstasy. Bloch's vision could also, at times, be ecstatic, spiritual, or apocalyptic. But what was unique about Bloch's subject and his overall approach was its doubleness, its inherent irony, its very modern sense of complexity and contradiction and of deviance from a straight course or single, achievable goal.

Curiously, many of the artists who were fixated on Pierrot and Harlequin — such as Aubrey Beardsley, T. S. Eliot, and Igor Stravinsky — eventually turned to traditional religion for solace. Despite Bloch's obsession with *commedia* characters, he was fundamentally a serious man, and in his later years he, like these other artists, also turned towards traditional religion to provide solace against the cruelties of the modern age.

BLOCH'S LAST COVER ILLUSTRATIONS FOR THE *MIRROR*

Bloch's work of the Blue Rider period was completely radical by American standards — just how radical is revealed in his correspondence with William Reedy. Unfortunately, few of the drawings that Bloch sent back to Reedy in St. Louis survive, but Reedy's correspondence provides intriguing commentary about them. In August 1909, for example, Bloch wrote to Reedy describing a cover illustration that he had prepared, and Reedy urged him to send it, so that he could use it for the September number. When it arrived, however, Reedy was shocked:

> That cover. Are you crazy? Why, the thing is a jumble to my eyes: an indistinguishable complex of uglitude, nothing defined, of nothing suggestive — a what is it? Really, my dear fellow. I *do* wonder if you're getting Wiertized in your ideas. That cover would — oh well. I won't say more than that it won't do. Maybe you're ahead of your time, but it's too far beyond for me, and, if that, what of the hopelessly lagged art crowd. I can't make anything out of it, except an effort at originality gone bug-house. I feel you'll not like what I've said, but I'm terribly in earnest in saying that this work is indicative of a disordered imagination in line and color. As for idea, what in the name of heaven has that sketch to do with St. Louis? Of course, for advanced and outré Munich the thing might do, but for here — never. I'm sorry I've to jump on your work, but you'll understand that I didn't mean to discourage you. All I'd say is that you're too much afraid of convention.... So much for that! Don't be disheartened; if you're right you're right, and you're the artist, not I.[87]

22. "Christmas 1912," Cover illustration for *Mirror*, 19 December 1912, Mrs. Albert Bloch

Reedy did not reproduce the piece and sadly, it has not survived. While Reedy described the effect as "art nouveau," the labels he used for artistic movements were not always accurate. We can only guess at the style of the work, which seems to have preceded Bloch's contact with Kandinsky and Marc by almost two years. Whatever its style, clearly it was far too advanced for Reedy's taste.

By 1912 Reedy had not published any of Bloch's drawings for three years, although he was still occasionally receiving new material. More than ever, he was bewildered by Bloch's latest work, as is apparent from his reaction to a drawing titled "Pantomime," which Bloch sent to him in St. Louis around October 1912. Reedy wrote:

> I am returning this "pantomime" to you simply because I cannot see that it means anything to me, or is likely to mean anything to anybody else. I don't say that it is crazy, or that it is not. All I can trust myself to say is that the great majority of people don't see in colors, and would not be able to understand what you are trying to do.[88]

Around the same time as this rejection, however, Reedy decided to print a Christmas cover for the *Mirror* that Bloch had sent to him. He seems to have thought it would be fun to shock his readers, for in private correspondence he confessed that he was completely put off by the design. In a letter of 17 October 1912, to his friend Thekla Bernays, he noted that "Mr. Bloch has done me an Xmas cover that is a fright."[89]

Bloch's composition (fig. 22) translated the traditional theme of the nativity into the Blue Rider ideal of world fellowship. A bare-backed madonna on the left, who seems to be wearing a strapless evening gown, is worshiped by a procession of international figures, including a kneeling African, a gesticulating Chinese, and a turbaned gentleman from the Middle East. Bloch drew the figures with swirling curves, and sketched a background which explodes into a kaleidoscope of swirling colors, like a Kandinsky abstraction.

Today the work seems tame enough, but nothing so modern had ever been published in the United States. Consequently, to make Bloch's work more understandable, Reedy provided two explanatory texts. The first, titled "Reflections," he penned himself on the magazine's first page. "Well, *that* is the new Art," Reedy exclaimed. "I had it done especially in Munich, the home of Post Impressionism, Expressionism, Cubism, Futurism…." Reedy went on to single out three major qualities of the work — primitivism (although he did not use the word), ugliness, and egotism. Then, after describing Bloch's design as "a flattened-out Joseph coat color hard boiled Easter egg," he noted that in the view of some critics, Bloch's work "is the oriflamme of those who are to be the masters of the future."[90]

In addition, Reedy commissioned an article on the cover from Francis A. Curley, the curator at the St. Louis City Art Museum. Curley, however, was not sympathetic to Bloch's accomplishment. He described his figures as Frankenstein monsters, criticized his lack of feeling for beauty, and noted condescendingly that his work lacked the "finer spirit" of figures like Honoré Daumier and Jean François Millet. As he commented slightingly, "In the present example, the riot of color and chaos kaleidoscopically arrayed, poignantly conjures up vivid scenes from impressionable boyhood life, when such stars were seen under the inspiration of an intercepted baseball bat."[91]

Bloch clearly was not pleased, and in a letter to him Reedy confessed that neither he nor Curley had been able to comment intelligently on Bloch's design. "Don't mind the articles in the Mirror," he wrote. "Confessedly neither Curley nor I knew anything about the art of the cover, but the only purpose in writing was to play the thing up and draw attention to it." In the same letter, Reedy urged Bloch to send him more work, boasting that "I can tackle pretty near anything that the post office will let pass."[92]

Indeed, Reedy published one more cover by Bloch, a drawing of clownlike creatures moving around a leaping Harlequin.[93] Once again, Reedy felt explanation was necessary, and he commissioned a piece about Bloch's work from Murray Sheehan, a writer and educator from Ohio who was studying at the Sorbonne. Sheehan praised Bloch's work, applauding his "steady development in the line of greater assurance." Noting that Bloch was aiming towards a purely spiritual form of expression, Sheehan described the result as "subjective painting." Although Sheehan cautiously approved of Bloch's work, he was wary of the hazards of this approach.

> Of course, the danger then arrives of their giving us all the feelings without giving us the key as to what they are about. That is the trouble with Kandinsky. Too frequently he gives but a puzzle-picture of emotions, and leaves you to figure out what it is all about."[94]

Although not an unqualified endorsement, Sheehan's statement was informative and generally sympathetic — one of the few such reviews that Bloch received in the United States. Nonetheless, after the Harlequin cover, Reedy published no more of Bloch's drawings. Public reactions seem to have persuaded Reedy that, as he once expressed it, Bloch's work was "too elevated for this latitude."[95]

"GERMAN WRITERS IN CARICATURE"

Nonetheless, Reedy did not abandon his protégé. Shortly after this last cover for the *Mirror*, he arranged for George Sylvester Viereck, editor of the *International*, to publish a long article by Bloch, "German Writers in Caricature," which Bloch not only wrote but also illustrated with a group of satirical drawings. Ironically, Bloch had written harshly of Viereck a few years before in the *Mirror*, making fun of his pimples and dismissing him as a "flash-in-the-pan," but evidently that did not stop him from writing an article for Viereck's magazine.[96] Bloch's piece appeared in two consecutive issues of the *International*, in September and October 1913.[97]

Reedy celebrated the publication of Bloch's essay with a brief article, "A Mirrorite Arrives," in which he attempted to evaluate not only the essay but the whole of Bloch's recent work.

> Recently, this paper printed two covers done by him in the post impressionist vein, one done in the manner of Matisse, the other one like Picasso or Picabia. Bloch has a fine, rich line. He disdains other essentials of beauty. He is savage, primordial. He draws and paints the Revolution and throws it in the face of the bourgeoisie with a captivating insolence.[98]

Reedy's purpose was undoubtedly friendly, but as usual his stylistic comparisons were not very accurate, and Bloch was offended. On 30 October 1913, Bloch wrote to protest, and Reedy published his complaint in the *Mirror* on 21 November. Noting that "I only partially approve of Matisse and Picasso," Bloch protested every one of Reedy's characterizations. "Don't, for heaven's sake," he stated, "think of me as having 'arrived,' nor am I 'postimpressionist,' 'Expressionist,' 'cubist,' 'futuristic,' 'orphist,' or whatever else people may chose to label themselves. I am, in all humility, and hope ever to remain nothing more (and surely nothing less!) than Albert Bloch, by the grace of God — artist." Bloch went on to declare that he felt inextricably in Reedy's debt, but it is hard to believe that Reedy did not feel annoyed and frustrated by such a sharp reaction to his attempt to praise Bloch's work.[99]

ARTHUR JEROME EDDY

Fortunately, just as Reedy's support was wavering, Bloch earned the patronage of Arthur Jerome Eddy, who was assembling a major collection of modern art. Eddy learned of Bloch's work from Kandinsky, who wrote an enthusiastic letter describing his work in 1913. "He works most energetically," Kandinsky declared, "accomplishes much, makes fine progress, and constantly gains in the form of his inner expression. Him, too, I really can recommend warmly."[100]

By 1915 Eddy had purchased so many paintings by Bloch that he was able to stage an exhibition of twenty-five of them at the Art Institute of Chicago. The exhibition subsequently travelled to St. Louis, where it opened at the City Art Museum in September. Still supportive, despite his recent slights, Reedy published a favorable review of the show in the *Mirror*, quoting extensively from Eddy's foreword to the catalogue.[101] In the second edition of his book, *Cubists and Post-Impressionism*, published in 1919, Eddy praised Bloch's work in forceful terms. "I have lived with Kandinsky's and Bloch's pictures several years," he wrote, "and like them more and more. They practically line the side walls of a room at one end of which hangs a full length Manet and at the other end a full length Whistler — neither artists nor laymen have ever noted or seemed to feel any conflict. The brilliant canvases make a fine setting for the two more sober, illustrating the fact that *good paintings* of all schools and all times hang well together."[102]

THE STURM GALLERY PERIOD

In addition to Eddy, Bloch found another important patron in this period. Through the mediation of Franz Marc, Bloch had made contact with Herwarth Walden, the owner and manager of Der Sturm Gallery in Berlin, who began energetically promoting his work. A man of prodigious energy and enthusiasm, Walden had an uncanny talent for recognizing new talent. His two chief enthusiasms were the Blue Rider group and the Italian Futurists, but he displayed such diverse figures as Oskar Kokoschka, Paul Klee, Marc Chagall, and Heinrich Campendonk.

Between 1912 and 1917, Walden latched on to Bloch's work, featuring it in seventeen Sturm exhibitions, beginning with the Berlin display of the first Blue Rider exhibition in March 1912. Walden included paintings by Bloch in group shows which traveled throughout Germany, as well as to Norway and Sweden. He also staged one-man shows of Bloch's work in Basel, Jena, and his own gallery in Berlin. In 1916 he staged a two-man show at his gallery which featured the work of Bloch and Klee.

Walden's promotion had significant practical consequences: during this period, for the first and only time in his life, Bloch was able to support himself (barely) through the sale of his paintings. In addition, through Walden's gallery, Bloch was exposed to a great range of artistic styles. Thus, his work of this period has a unique emotional range and variety, as he shifted from one influence to another with seemingly effortless confidence, never losing a distinctive personal quality of his own.

Walden was based in Berlin, a city with a tougher, more brittle quality than Munich, which was more relaxed and easygoing. Something of this harsher spirit seems to be reflected in Bloch's *Portrait of Mr. A. M.* (pl. 11; the man's identity is not recorded), which dates from the time that Bloch first came in contact with Walden. With his close-cropped hair, pronounced eyebrows, red lips, and white face, the man resembles a Pierrot, with his features not smooth and youthful, but sagging and embittered. Although there are still some echoes of Kandinsky, particularly in the background, the painting sets us on edge. It is harsh and biting in a fashion which recalls the work of contemporary Berlin painters, such as George Grosz, Max Beckmann, and Otto Dix.

Indeed, in the period from 1914-16, Bloch's work often contains hints of the artists that Walden promoted — the Italian Futurists, Kokoschka, Kirchner, the members of Die Brücke, and others. Throughout this period, however, the strongest influence on him remained the work of Marc and Kandinsky.

FINAL CONTACTS WITH FRANZ MARC

As World War I approached, Bloch was growing increasingly disenchanted with Kandinsky, whose theories of abstraction seemed to him too abstruse. But he had grown closer to Marc and his wife Maria, and occasionally visited them in the country at Sindelsdorf, not far from Munich, where Marc, who was fond of animals, kept a dog and a pet deer.

Marc was now moving into a new artistic phase and producing work which impressed Bloch as magnificent. As Bloch later reminisced:

> Towards the end — a few months before the coming of the cataclysm — Marc seemed to be feeling his way to something new. These last pictures were not shown until after his death, in a great memorial exhibition; but on my last visit to him, in the early summer of 1914, I saw all of them, some of them finished, some only begun…. He was painting pure abstractions!… Abstractions as only Franz Marc could have painted them. It was the same color, the same feeling, the same atmosphere — form and rhythm even were the same, but intensified, though one could recognize few of the forms objectively. These paintings presented a complete and perfected color lyrism.[101]

Bloch exaggerated somewhat. Marc's paintings of this period are not purely abstract by any means — animals and landscape elements remain plainly visible. Nonetheless, it is curious that Bloch so admired Marc's move towards a more abstract style, when he so deplored Kandinsky's move in the same direction. The distinction is a subtle one, not easily reduced to logic; but at an intuitive level Bloch evidently felt that Marc had retained a connection with the spiritual traditions of the past, whereas Kandinsky was attempting to sever these ties.

Bloch was particularly inspired by Marc's *Tierschicksale* (*Fate of the Animals*), painted in a fractured, cubist style, in which landscape and animals seem to be engulfed in apocalyptic flames or explosions (see Anthology, p. 203). Such a painting would no doubt have left an impact on Bloch due to its artistic merits alone. But *Fate of the Animals* took on even deeper significance after Marc's tragic death. Its ravishing beauty seemed even more poignant after Marc's career was abruptly cut short, while still full of promise. In addition, its violent subject matter seemed like a premonition of the violence of World War I.

Shortly after Bloch's last visit with Marc, the opening of the war, in August 1914, ended the fellowship that had created the Blue Rider group. Kandinsky, an enemy alien, was forced to return to Moscow, while Marc enlisted in the army and departed for the front. Bloch does not seem to have corresponded with Kandinsky. But after Marc left for the war, Bloch kept up a lively exchange of letters, which continued until Marc was killed near Verdun on 4 March 1916. Indeed, Bloch received his last postcard from Marc on the very day of his death. Much of this correspondence concerns Marc's essay, *Das Geheime Europa* ("The European Idea"). Bloch translated the essay into English and sent it off to various magazines in America, but apparently the piece was rejected, and Bloch's translation has since disappeared.

During Marc's last visit to Munich, while on leave in 1915, he attempted to get together with Bloch. But Bloch was spending time with a friend, probably the Munich painter Emmy Klinker, and Marc was unable to locate him.

THE FURTHER INFLUENCE OF MARC AND KANDINSKY

Interestingly, Bloch produced some of his best paintings during the war years and immediately afterwards. As he wrote to Eddy in 1914:

> I feel that I have just turned another corner in my development. My last things (as well as I can judge) seem to mark a great advance over the ones immediately preceding them…. I have half a dozen things in work at present deeper and stronger in vision than anything I have ever had under my hand: if I don't spoil them — We shall see![104]

The paintings dating from 1914-19 feel stylistically continuous with those of the previous period, but they are even freer in their range of style and on the whole more heated in their emotional intensity. These works reveal a range of sources, but as with the works of the previous period it is convenient to divide them into two basic groups, those influenced by Marc and those influenced by Kandinsky.

In this period, for the one and only time in his career, Bloch produced a series of paintings in an essentially cubist idiom. In them, cubic blocks of form are arrayed in energetic patterns, like those of the Italian Futurists, sometimes with surprisingly little reference to recognizable forms. To some extent these works may indeed have been influenced by the work of the Italian Futurists, which Bloch surely had seen by this time, since it was being energetically promoted by Walden. Most likely, however, Bloch was primarily influenced by the late paintings of Marc, which had made such a strong impression on him.

One of Bloch's greatest paintings, for example, was the 1915-16 canvas *Festival of Flags* (fig. 23), which showed tilting, beamlike structures, against a dark sky, filled with planets and stars. In this tilting, uneasy world, a lone, tiny figure is walking across a bridgelike span, the one human element in an otherwise abstract composition. The cubist handling of form, however, and the explosive arrangement of shapes bring to mind Marc's late works, particularly the canvas *Fate of the Animals*, which so profoundly impressed Bloch during his last visit to Sindelsdorf. Probably Bloch was not entirely comfortable producing work that was so close to pure abstraction, for the painting was later destroyed, most likely by Bloch himself.

More commonly, Bloch worked in a flatter, more linear style, more strongly influenced by Kandinsky. A striking example of this influence is *Song I* of 1913-14 (pl. 22), which sums up the human condition and its spiritual struggles. Five figures are arranged on an ascending mountain, made up of triangular peaks of different colors. Some of the triangular units are black (a color of death or suffering), others are red (the color of purifying fire or blood). Linear accents evoke waterfalls, trees, and rays of sunlight and starlight. We need not come up with a precise meaning for each of these elements, but together they clearly symbolize the perils, travails, and ecstasies of life, which the human spirit must confront. Arrayed within this network of triangles are a series of figures, all differently colored and in different postures. A figure in white lies prostrate; one in black is standing, but stopped as if rising from the dead; another in pink is seated in a meditative posture; and still another in blue is standing but covers his face with his arm. The topmost figure, in gold, raises his arms in ecstasy, like a Christ who has risen from the dead. In a general way, the painting clearly portrays various steps towards spiritual transcendence, from death, meditation, despair, and hesitation, towards religious ecstasy.

The fundamental concept of the piece seems pure Kandinsky, for Kandinsky wrote extensively about the triangle as a shape with spiritual significance, whose peak represents the highest point of spiritual development.[105] Bloch, in typical fashion, chose to translate Kandinsky's concepts into human terms. In addition to Kandinsky, Bloch probably was influenced by others as well. For example, he may have been influenced by Oskar Kokoschka, who also was fond of painting figures communing with the clouds and storms on lonely mountain peaks. Kokoschka's work would certainly have been familiar to Bloch, since he was one of the artists promoted by Walden.

One of Bloch's most apocalyptic paintings, *Figures on Dark Ground* of 1915-16 (pl. 27) (the title itself has an ominous sound) is also essentially Kandinsky-like, although it may well have been painted in response to the death of Marc. The painting shows a variety of figures in poses of prayer or prostration — a triangle of figures looking towards us on the left, and two figures shielding their eyes from blinding explosions on the right. The background is filled with lightning rays, exploding stars, crosses, and white falling objects, like fireworks, hail, or Saint Elmo's Fire.

What is the subject matter and meaning of this piece? The poses of these figures recall images of praying saints and mystics, as well as representations of the praying or prostrate Christ at the Garden or Gethsemene. The combination of these figures, however, is confusing, for it cancels out any of these traditional interpretations. The purport of these figures, however, is made plain by a second title for this painting which Bloch penciled over the first in his scrapbook — *The Prophets*. Clearly these terrified figures are prophets who see a terrible punishment coming for mankind, against which there is no protection except prayer.

23. *Festival of Flags (Fahnenjubel)*, 1915-16, Destroyed by the artist, Photograph from the artist's Record Book, vol. I, Mrs. Albert Bloch

From its inception, the artists of the Blue Rider group, particularly Kandinsky and Marc, had been obsessed with the idea of a coming apocalypse, which would signal a new age. With the coming of World War I, this apocalypse was no longer a mystical vision, but an all too terrible reality. Although set in a religious context, it is hard not to see this exploding sky as a reference to the terrible bombardments of the war, which Bloch's friend Marc was experiencing at this time. In fact, the painting seems to have been completed at about the time of Marc's death. It may even, possibly, have been intended as a memorial to that tragedy.

MARC CHAGALL

Towards the end of Bloch's stay in Germany, his work took a more sentimental turn. One of the artists whom Walden represented was Marc Chagall, and Bloch later recalled that he helped Walden install the first Chagall show in Germany. Undoubtedly, Bloch was strongly attracted to Chagall's work, with its cheerful color and its use of cubist devices to create whimsical, often somewhat sentimental narratives. In *Night V* of 1917 (pl. 26), the last of the night series, the apocalyptic imagery which Bloch absorbed from Kandinsky and Marc seems to be combined with various devices lifted from Chagall. The painting shows a winding pathway which leads us to a distant town. Above the town, the sky explodes in color, in a sunset so intense that it might well be an aerial bombardment. Indeed, patches of hot yellow and pink in the left distance make it appear that the town itself may be in flames. While the canvas continues many of the themes of the earlier night paintings, Chagall's influence is evident in the gorgeous intensity of the scarlet and blue in the sky, as well as in the whimsy of the trees in the middle distance, which run and dance like human figures. In addition, the overall mood of the painting owes something to Chagall. Despite the hint of apocalypse, the feeling of the painting is strangely cheerful, like that of Chagall's Russian fantasies.

Chagall's influence is also evident in *Winter* (pl. 29), a 1918 painting which might be viewed as a kind of synthesis of ideas derived from Chagall and Marc. Like other paintings of this period, *Winter* shows a man ascending a mountain, which is evidently intended as a symbol of man's spiritual aspirations. In this case there are a man and a woman at the bottom of the composition and two mountains. As our eye moves upward, magical, strangely-colored animals line the route — two dogs, a pink horse, a yellow deer, and a large, ducklike bird. At the tops of the peaks are a house, a church spire, and an animated snowman, who waves his arms in greeting. The menagerie of animals brings to mind Marc, as do many of the central themes of the painting — for instance, the struggle for spiritual ascent and the need to flee from the defilement of modern cities into the innocence of nature. The visual language of the painting, however, with its sweet, almost candylike combination of yellows and reds, and its flattened space, which is compartmentalized into a series of narrative bubbles, resembles Chagall's scenes of Russian village life. Moreover, the touch of sentimentality in the painting, the overall sweetness of the effect, are derived from Chagall and are very different from Marc's work.

Kandinsky, by this time, had moved away from representation altogether. Chagall, on the other hand, seemed to offer a way to be both human and modern at the same time. But there was a price, which Bloch did not entirely escape: that of sentimentality.

FINANCE

Bloch's productivity during this period is particularly remarkable given his constant financial difficulties. Reedy's subsidy of fifty dollars a month was not sufficient to support him, and Reedy himself constantly urged him to be more practical. In August 1910, for example, Reedy wrote to tell him:

> No heroics about art or refusal to surrender to schools or systems can possibly exculpate you for failure to make continued and satisfactory connections with bread and butter…. You see you are getting up towards thirty and the time of the sad, bad, and glad attitude is passing. You must make a living out of your art, and if you refuse to look at it in that light you must not be surprised if other people fail in sympathy for your extravagant ideals. We would all cheerfully assist you in starving yourself for your principles and ideals, but I'll be damned if we will stand for your starving Hortense and the kid.[106]

Reedy's correspondence with Bloch broke off in 1913, and probably his subsidy ended around that time, if not earlier. During the summer of 1912, Bloch's financial situation reached a crisis state, and he returned to the United States to beg for help from Hortense's family. They reluctantly agreed to support him for two years on terms which Bloch later revealed in a letter to Marc:

> If I am not economically independent by October 1914, it is back to America and — change course!… Every support (inadequate though it is) would be withdrawn, and worse yet in that these people could force my wife and child to leave me here and return to America. This already happened once, as you know; and to live again through such a hell is beyond the endurance of both my wife and myself.

In the same letter, Bloch begged Marc to find him two or three supporters who would provide a subsidy. "What one of us sells occasionally in exhibitions," Bloch complained, "can at best supply him with cigarettes."[107] Marc was unable to locate such patrons, but he did help by mentioning Bloch's work to Herwarth Walden, the director of Der Sturm Gallery in Berlin.[108]

The war, however, again reduced Bloch to a precarious state, since it disrupted transportation, slowed the mails, and frightened off many collectors. He staved off the crisis by selling some paintings to Eddy at reduced prices. "I am in no position to bargain with him," Bloch noted in a letter to Marc in February 1915. "I have no choice — either that or starve. I cannot think only of myself."[109] In June he wrote to Marc in despair: "Money, money, and again money. We are at the point of disaster. I have money coming to me. It does not come. Again a picture sold at a very low price: I am not paid." Meanwhile, his funds were dwindling to almost nothing. "When that is gone, what then? I am pure despair: the thought that wife and child could go hungry. Enough of that! It is too horrible."[110]

In a letter to Walden of 4 May 1916, Bloch expressed his fear that he might become an enemy alien and noted ironically that Walden might have to search for him in some German prison camp or Swiss exile.[111] A year later he was still in emotional turmoil about his plans. In a letter written in February 1917 to Maria Marc, Bloch announced that as an enemy alien he felt he could no longer lay claim to the hospitality of Germany. Consequently, he had requested permission to travel with his family to Switzerland. "You have no idea how heavy-hearted I feel!… My wife is greatly grieved, and as much as she tries to keep me unaware of it, the more heavily her sorrow weighs upon me."[112]

Bloch did not leave Germany but remained in the country throughout the duration of the war. The poor economic situation, however, made survival difficult, and getting paid for the pictures he had supposedly sold remained a problem. In a letter to Walden of 8 August 1917, Bloch mentioned the sale of five pictures from an exhibition in Frankfurt but noted that he had not yet received any money. To make matters still more difficult, in 1916 Bloch's second son, Walter, had been born, adding still another weight to his financial burden.[113]

THE END OF THE WAR

The collapse of Germany at the end of the war was profoundly traumatic for Bloch, for he had seen the conflict from the German standpoint. His correspondence with Marc reveals the extent to which his thinking reflected not American but German attitudes and political views. At the outbreak of hostilities, in fact, Bloch was swept up in the wave of popular emotion and was optimistic about Germany's entrance into the war. In one of his letters to Marc he declared: "Germany will win. Undoubtedly."[114] When Marc first wrote to Bloch about his essay, "The European Idea," Bloch at first expressed reservations that Marc had slurred over those national distinctions which had given rise to the most beautiful creation of European art.[115] "There *is* a Germany," Bloch protested.[116] When he received the full text, however, Bloch was inspired and delighted by Marc's approach, and in a letter of 27 April 1915, he described the piece as "a splendid, passionate appeal with which I can agree wholeheartedly."[117]

Over the course of the war, Bloch grew increasingly confused and disillusioned with German militarism. Yet his viewpoint was still essentially German, and he tended to view the allies as aggressors and oppressors. His distress is evident in a letter he wrote to Maria Marc on 11 November 1918, the evening of the armistice between Germany and the Allied Forces. Describing the "infamous conditions" of the surrender as "a peace worse than war," he went on to complain that:

> Somehow all of this must have a meaning — but I am not able to find it. Faith in mankind, once and for all, is gone…. I torment and torture myself, break head and heart in a search for the *sense* of this horror; for sense it *must* have, there must somehow be one. This belief I clutch as firmly as the drowning man his straw, otherwise one could end by despairing of God himself.[118]

Up until 1918, Bloch probably intended to spend his entire career in Germany. Indeed, not long after his arrival there, Reedy advised him to stay and make a name for himself in Europe. As Reedy wrote in June 1910: "If I told you my full mind I would say, *do not come back to America at all*. Cast around and see if you cannot get in your hooks on the other side…."[119] An indication of Bloch's immersion in German culture is that he generally wrote inscriptions in his scrapbook or on his drawings in German rather than in English.

The harsh conditions at the end of World War I made it impossible for Bloch to remain in Germany. From March through May 1918 he stayed in Ascona, on Lake Maggiore, where the painter Gordon McCouch (whom he had met in Munich around 1910), had found him somewhere to stay. Tall, stalwart, and conventionally handsome, McCouch came from a wealthy Philadelphia family, and reading between the lines, he seems to have been of a temperament very different from that of Bloch — easygoing and good-natured rather than rebellious and fretful. Nevertheless, they formed a lasting friendship, and in Bloch's last will and testament of 1947, McCouch is described as "my old and faithful friend" — the only one of Bloch's early acquaintances, except for Emmy Klinker, to be mentioned.

Bloch's plans at this time were very uncertain. In a letter of 23 November 1918, to Dr. Walter Dexel, the director of the *Kunstverein* (Art Union) in Jena, he noted that he planned to travel to America, but hoped he could return to Europe in the fall.[120] Perhaps he would settle in Switzerland or the Nether-lands. He expected to return to Germany once things returned to normal. In May 1919 Bloch finally made the promised journey to the United States. He seems to have spent a good part of 1919 in St. Louis, probably struggling to work out his financial problems.

No doubt his meetings with his relatives were humiliating, and in a letter of 17 October 1920, to Hans Goltz, Bloch described his one-year stay in the city as a nightmare.[121] The one mitigating circumstance is that Bloch seems to have reestablished his friendship with Reedy, who once again generously allowed him to use the *Mirror* as a forum for his ideas, after a silence of four years.

As if in compensation for the humiliation he was experiencing from his in-laws, in July 1919 Bloch published two powerful assertions of the autonomy of the artist. "From a Painter's Notebook" consists of forty-one aphorisms and a fable titled "Chastity." Without exception the aphorisms deal with the role of the misunderstood artist in a world of philistines. In the same issue, Bloch published an extraordinary statement of his artistic credo, titled "Der Künstler Über Alles" (The Painter Above Everything). Here he expressed his conviction that the artist was the vehicle of higher spiritual truths, and thus, in his view, beyond criticism and above reproach. Those who attempted to defend their work, such as George Bernard Shaw, G. K. Chesterton, and H. G. Wells, were not true artists.

> It is not part of the duty of an Artist to convince or convert other people to a point of view. The Artist need not, indeed cannot, trouble to consider whether he be right or wrong. He knows, insofar as he is an Artist, that a work of Art is, of itself, *right*…. We must accept what he brings, or let it be. We cannot expect him to be a pander of popular vanity, or a purveyor to individual necessity…. He has no duty to the public; only to himself. His offering is a free gift; take it or leave it.[122]

During these months in St. Louis, Bloch arranged to show a group of his paintings at the St. Louis Art Guild, and once again Reedy allowed Bloch to use the *Mirror* as his soapbox. After the bold statements of "Der Künstler Über Alles" it is something of a shock that this final statement, "My Pictures at the Guild," is notably defensive, even cringing in tone. Bloch seems to have known that in St. Louis he would be judged guilty, whatever he said in defense of his art. Long-windedly, Bloch declared of his display that the collection "does offer to the critical observer a fairly authentic glimpse of the artist's development during the last decade or more; and that no single picture but shadows forth in greater or less degree the characteristics of the painter during that particular phase of his progress."[123]

REEDY'S DEATH

Leaving his family in St. Louis, Bloch returned to Europe, with strong forebodings that this visit would be his last — as indeed proved to be the case. He was just about to embark from New York when the news reached him that Reedy had died of angina, while attending the Democratic presidential convention in San Francisco. Thekla Bernays, Reedy's friend who had contributed to the *Mirror*, sent Bloch a copy of the memorial issue of the magazine, and in a note of thanks for her kindness, Bloch complained of the pompous sanctimony of the tributes to his old friend.[124]

Just over a decade later, in 1931, Bloch paid tribute to Reedy in a drawing, *Silenus at Table* — portraying him as he was, both wise and dissolute.[125] Bloch's *Sonnets to the Dead* contains two in homage to Reedy, one of which memorably concludes:

> I'd give it all, if I might still sit by,
> You talking endlessly, I giving heed,
> Your last remaining listener now, spellbound
> Before the heavenly nonsense you expound.[126]

LAST TRIP TO EUROPE

Bloch arrived in Ascona in August 1920, where his friend Gordon McCouch had arranged for him to stay at the Casa Caglione on the quay.[127] Staying in the Ticino, with its beautiful lakes and mountain landscapes, must have been idyllic, particularly with the company of the good-natured McCouch. Yet the unsettled political situation, financial worry, and the sheer uncertainty of the future must have cast a pall of desperation over the whole experience.

It is tempting to see Bloch's 1920 painting *Veranda* (pl. 32) as a response to this curious situation. The painting shows two friends chatting at a café, while a waiter stands by expectantly. One of the pair, who seems to represent McCouch, is animated and gesturing; the other, who resembles Bloch, is more withdrawn and holds his head in his hand. In the distance stand two figures who seem more allegorical, more symbolic. One faces towards us with a wistful expression, the other turns his back on us, and gazes out at the deep, indigo lake and the twinkling stars. Through these figures, Bloch seems to pose the questions which so troubled him at the time. How would he support himself? What would the future bring? What is the meaning of human existence?

As *Veranda* illustrates, at the time of these moves and financial difficulties, Bloch's art changed quite dramatically in style, no longer resembling the work of Kandinsky or Marc, but taking on a look quite similar to the German village scenes of Campendonk, one of the artists in the wider circle of the Blue Rider whom Bloch had befriended. Now he began painting the people and settings around him generally with a touch of social criticism and commentary.

To some extent, one might say that Bloch's work grew more "realistic," although it did not do so in a conventional sense. It was still tinged with aspects of fantasy, which were expressed both in the often unusual, often slightly whimsical juxtaposition of figures, and in the flattened, somewhat cartoonlike drawing, which, like the work of Campendonk, distorts, flattens, and rearranges elements in a fashion reminiscent of Cubism.

Undoubtedly, this shift in style seems to directly reflect the disruption of Bloch's life. No longer working in familiar surroundings, he was forced to paint in unfamiliar settings and places, in brief snatches of time. In addition, his concentration of poverty and human suffering undoubtedly reflected his own

24. *Highway*, 1920, The Saint Louis Art Museum, Bequest of Morton D. May

desperate financial situation, as well as the social disruption of the war, which had left many people homeless. In the United States, this phase of Bloch's career has attracted little interest. Curiously, however, in Germany these paintings of the late teens and early twenties, with their social themes, are the aspect of his work that is best known. His paintings of the economic and other hardships that followed World War I — the paintings of beggars, blind men, cripples, and destitute workers — particularly appealed to the East German communist regime, and were several times reproduced and displayed.

Highway of 1920 (fig. 24) is characteristic of Bloch's work in this period. It shows a procession of poor people — two women, a child, a man with a stick who may be blind, and several other straggling men. They make their way down a little road, past the barns, houses, and church of a country village, but do not stop, for there is no welcome for them there. The color scheme is muted and sad: dull greens, browns, and yellows, without dramatic accents. The painting contains some echoes of Bloch's painting of Christ bearing the cross, which he showed in the first Blue Rider exhibition. In a very similar fashion, the design is divided into two bands, and it contains a similar motif in the lower zone of a veiled woman standing by a tree. In this case, however, the procession of sufferers is not one of apostles and saints, but of homeless people of the sort found all over Germany at the time. Wherever he looked, it seems, Bloch saw not happiness, but misery and sorrow. Few places are more beautiful than Ascona on the Italian lakes. But Bloch's *Souvenir, Ascona* (pl. 33) reveals the human suffering underneath the facade. In the foreground of the painting is a coachman ready to give a ride, standing before a café. But in the distance are a seated beggar with his hat beside him, a famished stray dog, and a homeless man and child.

DEPARTURE

In September 1920 Bloch obtained permission to return to Munich, but through most of October he was ill, although he managed to read and accomplish a little work. By 30 November he was in Munich, where he again became ill. Undoubtedly, the experience of collecting his paintings and possessions, and saying his final farewell to his intimate friend, Emmy Klinker, was a painful one. After about a month in Munich, he returned to Ascona, making a side trip to Vienna to attend a reading conducted by the poet Karl Kraus. He then spent a few more weeks in Ascona, and returned to the United States in the last week of April.

Throughout the course of this last trip, in his letters to Thekla Bernays, Bloch confided that he no longer planned to live in Germany and gradually reconciled himself to this decision. The housing situation in Munich had become desperate; feelings against foreigners were running high; and a wave of reaction was sweeping over Bavaria, placing power in the hands of the Center Party Monarchists and the extreme right wing.[128] Though he was convinced that his future struggles would be "bitter and heartbreaking," he assured Bernays that, "I feel that I *ought* to be in the United States; and in a way the fight there is going to be an interesting one."[129] In an undated letter of 1919 to the English sculptor Eric Gill, Bloch confided, "The expatriate is rather a pathetic figure, after all, and he can't fight his fight in a foreign land — insofar as an artist can fight it at all."[130]

RETURN TO THE UNITED STATES

When Bloch arrived in New York in May 1921, he had no clear idea of where he would settle or how he could support his family. To boost his spirits, Thekla Bernays wrote an encouraging letter declaring, "Why should *you fail*, where *others, so much less endowed, have succeeded.*"[131] But Bloch responded bitterly that "any success I must achieve must be a sheerly artistic one" since he lacked "the ability to flatter snobbish taste or bourgeois prejudices. I simply don't see how I am going to get on in the open market!"[132]

Despite this complaint, Bloch soon established contact with Charles Daniel, of the Daniel Gallery in New York, who in November staged a show of forty-one canvases that Bloch had painted in Europe over the previous twelve years. The show received a brief review in *Arts*, and Bloch sold several paintings, as well as a few drawings.[133] Around this time he also sold an article, "Portraits and the Painter," which he had written some years before, to *The Smart Set*, edited by H. L. Mencken. The proceeds from these ventures netted him enough to survive through early summer 1922.[134]

By late summer, however, Bloch was completely destitute and had nowhere to turn. Reprieve came unexpectedly thanks to a writer friend in Chicago, Eunice Tietjens, who got him an appointment to the Chicago Academy of Fine Arts. For the next year Bloch taught painting in Chicago, living there alone, and sending most of his money back to his wife and children, who stayed with relatives in St. Louis. A humorous drawing by him from this time shows him on his knees with a dustpan cleaning up his apartment (fig. 25).

While in Chicago, he learned of an opening for a Professor and Head of the Department of Drawing and Painting at the University of Kansas, in Lawrence, and he immediately applied

The Happy Housewife
Goes Gaily about the morning's Duties

25. *The Happy Housewife Goes Gaily About the Morning's Duties*, 1922, Mrs. Albert Bloch

for the position. Asked for an account of his "academic and artistic training," he provided a seven-page letter about his life, which remains an important and almost unique document, although it contains startling omissions. Evidently afraid that he would be viewed as a dangerous radical, he never mentioned Kandinsky, Marc, Klee, or the Blue Rider group, although he cited his friendship with such academic figures as Oscar Berninghaus and Richard Miller, whom he had known in St. Louis.[135]

With the help of some strong letters of support from painter friends in Chicago, Bloch was hired from a distance, and in July 1923, he made his first visit to Lawrence to meet with Chancellor Ernest Hiram Lindley and Dean Harold Butler. He arranged to rent a small house on the north side of the campus which would soon become his home for the remainder of his life. In August he moved to Lawrence permanently, and, after about a year of separation, finally regathered his wife and children with him under one roof. In September 1923 he wrote to thank the Chancellor for the loan of twenty-five dollars. Probably this was the initial downpayment for his rent, and the fact that Bloch needed to borrow the money suggests that he was broke at the time.[136]

LAWRENCE, KANSAS

Bloch's house in Lawrence, at 1015 Alabama Street, is still occupied by his widow, Anna, and remains today very much as it was at the time of his death. It is somewhat startling to discover how modestly a veteran of epochal events in the history of modern art lived for his last thirty-eight years. Nothing about the structure is impressive or distinctive: one can find similar wood-frame houses in the working-class neighborhoods of any American city. But for Bloch this retreat was all he wanted. He was clearly grateful for the income he received as a teacher, which allowed him this modest shelter and with it the freedom to pursue his work without distraction.

Bloch's two creative laboratories were his small bedroom study, with just room for a bed, a desk, and a few shelves of books, and the attic which served as his studio, an utterly modest room with unpainted wooden beams and woodwork. His easel still stands just as he abandoned it, along with his brushes and colors.

Bloch had become a celebrity for his caustic caricatures in the *Mirror* when he was still in his early twenties; and he was not yet thirty when he showed his paintings in the Blue Rider exhibition in Munich. Arthur Jerome Eddy, in his book *Cubists and Post-Impressionism*, considered Bloch the most important American artist working abroad. "His progress in the few years he has worked in Munich has been little short of marvelous," Eddy stated. "I have the feeling that he is by long odds the strongest American painter on the other side who is working in the modern vein."[137]

Yet early on, even at the most blazing moments of his success, Bloch often proved reluctant to reveal himself. As has been noted, he did most of his writing for the *Mirror* under a pseudonym, and for the first three years of his correspondence with Karl Kraus, he refused to divulge his identity. As early as 28 January 1918, when he was still living in Germany, Bloch declared, in a letter to Walter Dexel, that if it were not for the money he needed so badly, he would never again appear in public, never allow anyone to write about him, and only paint for those few who understood and appreciated his work.[138]

Proud words! But after Bloch had taken his teaching job in Kansas, in 1923, he was able to adopt these principles and pursue what he described as a life of "oyster-like concentration." For the last thirty-eight years of his career, he cut off all his ties with art dealers and art critics, and sent his work to art exhibitions only when specifically invited. "Let you come find me, the mouse-trap maker," he once wrote. While from time to time he sold a painting, he made no effort to drum up new business and, as he stated later, he "never made a point of mentioning, let alone advertising [his] connection with Marc and Kandinsky."[139]

As a young man in St. Louis and Munich, Bloch had showed an astonishing responsiveness to the latest happenings, not only in painting but in music and the theater. By the time he settled in Lawrence, however, his views were set, and he no longer was interested in keeping up with current trends. "I am not sure that you are well placed in your isolation out there in Kansas," the collector Duncan Phillips wrote to Bloch in 1928. "Your efforts to educate may be uphill work."[140] Nonetheless, Bloch made no effort to expand his circle of contacts. During the 1930s, Bloch was working within forty miles of two of the major American Regionalist painters: Thomas Hart Benton, in Kansas City, Missouri, and John Steuart Curry, who was painting murals for the Kansas State Capitol in Topeka. Bloch, however, made no effort to meet either artist, and in one of his essays of the early 1930s he condemned Regionalism in the strongest terms.

Anna Bloch has noted that Bloch's colleagues and neighbors tended to look on him with suspicion. "Their fears," she confesses, "in some ways were justified: he certainly did not 'fit in' with a conservative administration and faculty, and its individual members, and those townspeople he came into contact with either valued him as a unique and intellectually

exhilarating personality or feared him as an unknown but suspect eccentric."[141]

KARL KRAUS (1874-1936)

Two events of the period 1914-16 reshaped the course of Bloch's career and led to the creation of his later style. One of these was the death of Franz Marc near Verdun, on 4 March 1916. For Bloch, Marc represented all that was most pure and noble about the Blue Rider enterprise, and his senseless death filled Bloch with a profound sense of spiritual loss. While Bloch had initially supported Germany's entrance into the war, from this time forward he felt only loathing towards the forces of militarism, mob psychology, and materialism which had destroyed his friend. No doubt the blow was particularly hard because it came at a time when his own family affairs and financial situation were becoming extremely difficult. In later years, he recalled this period as one of emotional darkness, of almost overwhelming pessimism. After Marc's death, Bloch's paintings never again expressed the brash exuberance of his early work. While his later works are sometimes quietly hopeful, they seem to express this hopefulness somewhat dimly, through a veil of suffering and sorrow.

26. *Posthumous Portait* (Karl Kraus), 1955, Private collection

The second great event of this period was Bloch's discovery of the writings of Karl Kraus, the Viennese poet and critic. Bloch's almost religious reverence for Kraus was undoubtedly connected with the emotional devastation he felt at this difficult time. Kraus seemed to provide a beleaguered voice of honesty and independence in a world which Bloch perceived as completely false, hypocritical, and rotten.

In tribute to these two figures, Bloch decorated his study in Lawrence with a photograph of Marc and two woodcuts by him as well as with a group of photographs of Kraus. In his art he expressed his devotion to Marc through several compositions of birds and animals, which translate Marc's favorite themes into his own highly personal late style. He expressed his devotion to Kraus through a remarkable posthumous portrait of 1955 (fig. 26) — one of his very few tributes to a specific individual. Bloch outlined Kraus not in shadow but in white, like the negative of a photograph, and through this device suggested that he intended not a physical likeness but a kind of "spirit portrait." Kraus's nervous, delicate hands suggest his sensitivity. A splash of light on his forehead emphasizes his intellectual aspect.

Bloch's immense admiration for Kraus is difficult for an American to grasp, for Kraus's use of German has often been described as "untranslatable," and his work is little known in the United States. Poet, critic, and polemicist, Kraus circulated his work chiefly through a monthly magazine, *Die Fackel* (*The Torch*) which he wrote almost entirely himself. For Bloch a strong part of Kraus's appeal was a moral one, for during World War I, Kraus was the only writer of note or consequence in Germany or Austria to oppose the conflict, which he denounced in each successive issue of *Die Fackel* with unrelenting fury. Kraus's revulsion for the war reached its peak of creative expression in a long stage-poem, *The Last Days of Mankind*, which appeared in special issues of *Die Fackel* and was collected as a book in 1922. Clearly intended to be read rather than staged, the book has hundreds of scenes and characters and no coherent plot. Nonetheless, through haunting images of murdered children, frozen soldiers, forests of dead trees which have been shattered by shellfire, and other similarly ghastly scenes (which he often learned about from notices in the daily newspaper), Kraus described the horror of war. In a letter to Kandinsky, Bloch praised Kraus as the teacher "to whom I owe *everything*." (see Anthology, p. 187) In an introduction to Kraus's poetry, Bloch described Kraus as "the greatest ethical force in the world today…. His is the voice today crying in the wilderness of our foul corruption," Bloch wrote of Kraus in the "Translator's Foreword" of his edition of Kraus's *Poems* in 1930.[142]

Interestingly, however, Bloch was not an instant convert to Kraus: he was initially put off by the poet's admirers. In 1913 Bloch wrote somewhat sarcastically of Kraus's work and around the time of the article's publication he deliberately avoided an opportunity to meet Kraus in person when he visited Munich.[143] Several months later, however — on 7 March 1914, to be exact — Bloch picked up a copy of *Die Fackel* while waiting for a friend at a café.[144] He quickly found himself captivated, for Kraus's voice seemed like the perfect confirmation of his own deeply buried feelings. Bloch later described this moment of discovery in verse:

> How should I be so blest
> That I should find you in the very hour
> When most I needed you?…
> I idly turned
> The pages of the red brochure that burned
> Bright on the table, as, resigned
> to waiting on a tardy friend,
> Bored at the very thought of *you*
> I picked up and read that *Fackel* through
> Until the very end.[145]

Soon afterward, Bloch joined the subscription list of *Die Fackel* and with brief interruptions received the magazine regularly until it folded at the time of Kraus's death in 1936. Although out-of-print copies of *Die Fackel* were hard to find, Bloch tracked them down through friends, book-dealers, and fellow Kraus enthusiasts, so that by the time of his death his set of *Die Fackel* was complete. During the terrible war years — "that damnation of four years," as Bloch later described it — Kraus's writings were a source of almost daily spiritual comfort to Bloch, and he spent hours reading from the magazine to Klinker. An insomniac, Bloch often read and reread *Die Fackel* on sleepless nights, making marginal notations beside the most striking passages, marking typographical errors, and noting the fine points of word choice and grammatical usage. Both Marc and Bernays confessed in letters to Bloch that they were unimpressed with Kraus's writing, and found it difficult and mannered. But Bloch was undeterred by their skepticism, and continued to praise Kraus in the strongest possible terms.[146]

Bloch's admiration for Kraus is psychologically peculiar, since on other occasions he was strongly resentful of authority figures. Bloch's father seems to have been a remote, inadequate figure, and a psychologist might well propose that the artist spent much of his life trying to find a father in such figures as William Reedy and Wassily Kandinsky, who served both as mentors and as figures to rebel against. Karl Kraus was the last and most satisfying of these substitute fathers — the one whom Bloch most profoundly revered.

Remarkably, Bloch's admiration for Kraus had none of the critical edge of his relationship with Reedy or Kandinsky. Ordinarily critical and rebellious, Bloch accepted Kraus as a godlike figure and regarded his words with unwavering reverence. Significantly, however, Bloch deliberately avoided actual contact with Kraus but instead always kept him at a godlike distance. Bloch's closest contact with Kraus came in 1921, when he had returned to Europe to clear out his apartment in Munich and made a side trip to Vienna to attend one of Kraus's public readings from Shakespeare. He vividly described the event in 1937, in an article for *Books Abroad*.[147]

Shortly after settling in Lawrence, Bloch began corresponding with Kraus, in letters that have a strong quality of psychological obeisance, since they focus on the most minute questions of language and style. One letter, for example, inquires about Kraus's use of the apostrophe, another about his use of "zu" in infinitive construction.[148] In this correspondence, Bloch also expressed his support for Kraus's battles with other writers. In 1926, for example, Kraus published a letter from Bloch applauding the war he was waging against Imre Bekessy, a Viennese journalist. To start with, Bloch deliberately signed only his initials, but Kraus knew the source of the letters from the postmark, and began referring to him as "Der Leser aus Kansas" (the reader from Kansas). In a prefatory note to the letter on Bekessay, Kraus commented on the irony that "local idiots" were not interested in the matter, but that his "Bekessiade" was understood and appreciated on the American prairie.[149]

Although Bloch guarded his privacy, in 1926, in seeming emulation of Kraus's Shakespeare reading, he made a public appearance before the University of Kansas German Club to give a reading of the poetry of Kraus. The psychological importance of this event to Bloch is suggested by the fact that later the same evening he penned a letter to Kraus describing the event — and for the first time signed the letter with his whole name. Kraus published the letter in the March number of *Die Fackel*, adding the sarcastic comment that if he were ever to attempt to read his verse at the University of Vienna, the authorities would probably deny him entrance.[150]

This disclosure of his identity clearly marked an important rite of passage for Bloch. The following year he staged another public reading of Kraus's work in St. Louis, to about fifty invited guests. This time, however, he read not the German text but his own translations into English of thirty-eight of Kraus's lyrics. As he reported enthusiastically to Kraus, the response was favorable: the audience applauded and made interested comments.[151]

All this was leading up to the dramatic question — would Kraus allow Bloch to publish his translations and become the first to introduce Kraus's work to an American audience? Over a period of ten months, from spring to fall of 1927, Bloch translated more than a hundred poems by Kraus as well as a section of *The Last Days of Mankind*. In October Bloch wrote to Kraus requesting permission to publish these translations in America.[152]

Kraus's publishing company, however, had granted translation rights to a young writer from Vienna, Karl Wickerhover, who had already translated several poems. In a cordial note to Bloch, Wickerhover proposed that they collaborate on a collection.[153] But Bloch had already translated some of the very same verses, and in a long letter, he minutely dissected the manifold faults of Wickerhover's renderings, forcefully arguing that his own were immensely superior.[154] The ruthlessness of Bloch's critique, however, which contains not a single complimentary note about Wickerhover's work, suggests something deeper than an interest in linguistic issues; it suggests that he did not wish to share the honor of introducing Kraus to American audiences, preferring to undertake the project on his own.

Wickerhover never answered Bloch's letter and he seems to have disappeared as a rival. Not long afterwards, Bloch sent his translation to Theodor Haecker in Munich for a critical assessment. Haecker seems to have scrutinized it closely, since he held the manuscript from December 1927 until July 1928. His response, however, was strongly positive. While he questioned specific lines, and felt that at times Bloch's language was too cumbersome and Germanic, he described the overall effect as "beautiful and noble."[155]

In the summer of 1928 Bloch wrote a foreword to his translations, extolling Kraus's importance in the strongest terms. He had considerable difficulty, however, finding a publisher interested in the work. In January 1929 he approached Edmund R. Brown, President of the Four Seas Company in Boston, who agreed to publish an edition of five hundred copies, if Bloch would make a prepayment of four hundred dollars and guarantee the sale of two hundred copies. Such a sum clearly represented a fortune to Bloch, but in his eagerness to produce the book he agreed to make a down payment of $125 and to pay the rest in eleven monthly installments of twenty-five dollars.[156]

Over the course of the next nineteen months, the book was gradually set in type, with many delays owing to Bloch's incessant changes and to the fact that the Four Seas Company was taken over by Bruce Humphries, Inc., in the spring of 1930. But in July 1930 the book was bound and printed, and Bloch finally received the fruit of his many years of work.

Rather than being pleased, however, Bloch was horrified. His first step was to send a telegram to Brown asking him not to send the book to reviewers and to recall any copies already sent out. He followed with a letter describing, in minute detail, a series of "unrivalled masterpieces of negligence and casual incompetence" and accused Brown of "deliberate sabotage." To prevent the book from circulating further, Bloch recalled the copies that remained with the publisher.[157]

Several review copies, however, had already been sent out, and shortly afterwards Bloch was pained by a sarcastic review by H. L. Mencken in the *American Mercury*, in which he made fun of Bloch's effusive statements about Kraus's importance. What particularly galled Bloch was that Mencken clearly had not bothered to read the poems, but had simply skimmed Bloch's introduction. "What a poisonous burden of spite," he commented, "can be packed into a dozen casual lines of ostensibly detached criticism."[158] Even favorable reviews provoked Bloch's ire, and when a writer from Milwaukee sent him one, Bloch replied with a letter protesting the "slovenly and irreverent" fashion in which he had quoted the poems.[159] Thus, rather than being the triumph he had hoped for, the publication of the book was an emotional disaster for him.

One can partly sympathize with Bloch's distress, for the Four Seas printing of his text was undoubtedly botched. Yet Bloch himself was partly at fault, since he created much of the confusion himself with last-minute changes. In fact, it seems unlikely that any publication would have fully satisfied him. Probably no book could have met the standards of perfection that he felt his revered master deserved, nor was it reasonable to suppose that American readers would ever respond enthusiastically to a writer whose sensibility was so arcanely bound up with specifically Austrian concerns. Kraus remains essentially unknown in the United States, except to specialists in German culture. Despite this major setback, Bloch's reverence for the master remained unshaken. Although he never again attempted a public reading of Kraus's work, he continued to revise and correct his translations and in 1947 published a few of them in a collection of his own poetry, *Ventures in Verse*, which opens with a sonnet in praise of Kraus. He also prepared a translation of Kraus's aphorisms and submitted it to the poet W. H. Auden, who made only minor corrections and recommended the work for publication. Despite Auden's support, however, the manuscript was never printed.[160]

The richest intellectual stimulation of Bloch's later years came not from painters or art historians, but from a scattered cadre of Kraus enthusiasts. After Kraus's death, Bloch exchanged roughly a hundred letters with Sidonie Nádherný von Borutin, who had been Kraus's supporter and mistress and had entertained the poet at her castle in Janowitz. Bloch also formed an intense friendship with Michael Lazarus, a scholar of Kraus's work.[161]

How should one evaluate Bloch's efforts on behalf of Kraus? Certainly, they had none of the popular impact that he must have hoped for, but while little known, they should not be dismissed as entirely ludicrous. For one thing, specialists in German poetry have given Bloch high marks. Vincent Kling, for example, has written that "it is most unlikely that any translator of Kraus's poems could ever equal the splendid, brilliant versions done by Albert Bloch." Declaring that they "throw all other versions into the shade" he has rated Bloch among "the very first rank of translators."[162] Similarly, Harry Zohn, who has written on the "untranslatability of Kraus," has nonetheless written that, "If there is one man who could claim to be the English translator of Kraus, it was the late Professor Albert Bloch."[163]

Equally significant, Bloch's immersion in the work of Kraus provides the key to understanding the sensibility of Bloch's later work. It is striking, for example, the degree to which Kraus shaped the entirety of Bloch's literary taste. In his later years, when Bloch made translations, he focused exclusively on the poets that Kraus promoted, such as Paul Zech, Georg Trakl and Else Lasker-Schüler, or on passages by earlier writers whom Kraus had published — such figures as Matthias Claudius, Immanuel Kant, Johann Wolfgang von Goethe, and Eduard Mörike. The style of Bloch's later writing, also, was clearly modelled very directly on Kraus. Altogether different from the lean directness of his early articles for the *Mirror*, it is essentially Germanic in structure, with clauses piled on top of each other like cumulus clouds building to a thunderhead and the verb pushed as far as possible to the end.

For Bloch, Kraus became a true doppelgänger — another self. Indeed, one gets the sense that it was through becoming Kraus, by stepping into the soul of another artist, that Bloch found a new artistic center for his own creative work. It appears that Bloch's late paintings are attempts to put Kraus's moral and spiritual viewpoint into visual form. Of course, since Kraus himself rarely commented on the visual arts, this was not a literal exercise. In a fundamental way, however, Kraus's poetry was the principal influence on Bloch's later work.

The question of why Bloch chose to identify with Karl Kraus, out of the great mass of European writers and poets, is an intriguing one. In an unpublished preface to a collection of translations of Kraus, Bloch stated that Kraus's views came to him as a confirmation of ideas he had already formed. To a remarkable degree, in fact, Bloch and Kraus came from similar backgrounds and had similar life experiences. Like Bloch, Kraus's ancestors were Bohemian, he grew up in the city, and his mother died when he was relatively young. Like Bloch, Kraus was involved in journalism. Like Bloch, in poetry Kraus preferred lyric forms, with a tone of bittersweetness. Like Bloch, Kraus sought to promote spiritual values. Like Bloch, Kraus saw himself as standing above the vulgarity and materialism of modern life. Perhaps the most intriguing of Bloch's affinities with Kraus is that of their common Jewish background. Bloch's Jewishness, however, raises a host of sensitive questions — all the more so because he never sought to affiliate himself openly with Jewish traditions, and in fact seems to have deliberately avoided doing so.

The imagery of Bloch's paintings generally avoids the Jewish themes of the Old Testament and focuses on the Christian themes of the New. Indeed, according to his widow, Anna, Bloch even considered converting to Catholicism, although he was ultimately put off by the rigidity of Catholic dogma.[164] Bloch seems to have steered clear of specifically Jewish groups.

Certain key aspects of Bloch's approach, however, suggest a strong connection, if only an unconscious one, to his Jewish background — his willingness to work as an outsider, his pursuit of the spiritual above all other goals, and his devotional attachment to a writer of Jewish background, Karl Kraus, whose writings and whose reverence for the word as a sacred thing seem connected to his Jewish heritage. The man of wisdom, particularly of spiritual wisdom, that is to say the rabbi or reader of the Torah — the man connected with the inscrutable word of God — is a central figure of the Jewish tradition. Thus, as Walter Musch has suggested, Kraus's concern with the debasement of the holy word was ultimately rooted in his Jewish heritage. "The word came to be for him a holy weapon," Musch has written of Kraus, "and the critique of the desecrators of the word, a profession of faith."[165] While outwardly Bloch rebelled against his Jewish background, in essential ways he remained true to its central spirit.

In this willingness to break down racial and national barriers, the Blue Rider group had been far ahead of its time. Indeed, today one cannot look at Bloch's paintings of Dachau, then a favorite locale for landscape painters, without thinking of the unspeakable horrors which were later perpetrated on Jews and others persecuted there, at the Dachau concentration camp. The mournful subjects and tortured surfaces of Bloch's later paintings reflect an attempt to somehow hold on to the ideals of his early life, in a world which could perpetrate such horrors.

THE LATE STYLE

In terms of numbers, Bloch produced about half his lifetime's production in the eight fertile years stretching from 1910-18, when the defeat of Germany in World War I forced him to return to America. The difficult years from 1919-23, when he finally settled in Lawrence, mark a clear divide in his work, a chasm dividing two distinct styles. During the remaining thirty-eight years of his life, he produced more fitfully, more slowly, and more reluctantly, and his work stood even farther outside of any prevailing fashion or trend. For Bloch, himself, however, it was the work of these later years that represented his finest achievement, the fulfillment and culmination of his early strivings.

Bloch's late paintings inspire very different reactions. Several art dealers and museum curators have expresssed to me their intense distaste for these works, and their unwillingness to exhibit or handle them. Some enthusiasts like Richard Green, David Cateforis and Anna Bloch, on the other hand, have judged Bloch's late paintings to be the high point of his achievement and far superior to anything he produced in Europe.[166] Such divergence of response certainly points to the fact that Bloch's style changed dramatically after he returned to the United

States, and that the two phases of his career call upon distinct emotional and aesthetic qualities. Paradoxically, however, the major themes and underlying spirit of Bloch's later work grew directly out of the earlier period, even to the point of echoing early motifs and compositions.

The close connection between the two phases is apparent from a practice which Bloch adopted at the time he made the transition between the two — that of extensively repainting and reworking some of his earlier paintings. Throughout his later years, Bloch occasionally reworked paintings that he had started some years earlier, but this practice was particularly common during the early 1920s. Thus, Bloch's later work both directly pays homage to, and also very consciously reformulates, his early approach.

This process of reworking is particularly well documented in Bloch's canvas *Pilgrims in the Snow*, which he first painted in 1917 and reworked in 1925 (see Cateforis, pp. 79-80, figs. 1, 2). Since Bloch made a photograph of the first painting, it is possible to compare the two versions. The first version was considerably bolder in effect, with sweeping, clearly defined lines. The second adopts a more finicky and tentative stroke, which hovers over the forms like a halo or aura. Paradoxically, the later painting is both more sculptural, since Bloch more thoroughly worked over the internal areas of the form, and also more intangible, since the flickering brushstrokes never seem to quite reduce anything to a definite physical substance. While the first painting has a stronger overall pattern, the second more subtly differentiates the individual figures.

The subject matter in Bloch's late paintings is considerably more desolate than that of his early work, focusing as it does on such things as leafless trees, dark birds perched ominously on dead branches, and wintry solitudes. Not all his later work is gloomy, of course. He certainly sometimes painted joyful subjects, such as a group of luminous floral still lifes. Yet even these "happy" paintings are touched by a mood of something ghostly and fragile.

One subject, in particular, dominates much of Bloch's later work — that of shrouded figures wandering upon the landscape. Notably, Bloch translated "A Song of War" by the German romantic poet Matthias Claudius, in which the slaughtered victims of war rise up from the dead to haunt the poet, and certainly it is tempting to interpret these figures as the ghosts of war and other terrible misfortunes.[167] To be sure, Bloch himself would probably have resisted such a straightforward explanation and insisted that his intention was more ambiguous and more complex. It is not far off the mark, however, to propose that all Bloch's later work was colored by the terrible destructions of the two world wars and by the rise of the Nazis in Germany. He clearly felt that all of human civilization was threatened. His paintings at once record the sickness he was witnessing, and, simultaneously, seek to preserve and pass on the great spiritual truths of the Western tradition.

Bloch's use of color also experienced a fundamental change. The color of the late paintings are distinguished by his extensive use of white, which he used to soften every other color on his palette. Kandinsky once wrote of white that it provides

"a symbol of a world from which all colors as material attributes have disappeared."[168] Bloch clearly used white as a way of evoking the spiritual. Indeed, in a revealing letter to Sidonie Nádherný, he stated that his goal in his paintings was to achieve "a total fusion of matter with spirit, blurring the remnants of the tangible object." As he added, "I paint still-life pictures, landscapes, compositions with figures — just like everyone else. But with me the result is inescapably a total spiritualization of the object."[169] In Bloch's hand, this use of white gives the forms in his late pictures an evanescent quality, as if they were not real things, but spiritual essences, or perhaps, elusive memories.

Bloch's palette in his later years was very limited. Each of his colors seems to have possessed a definite symbolism, so that in using them he was not simply representing forms but conducting a kind of spiritual alchemy. Conceptually, they divided the world into four elements: earth colors (such as raw and burnt umber or burnt sienna) for earth and flesh; earth green for foliage; ultramarine blue for sky; and white for pure spirit. At their most fundamental level, they express a basic polarity between the heaviness of the earth colors, which seem to pull downward towards the earth and wish to blend with it, and the spiritual lift of the sky colors, the ultramarine and the white, which lift heavenward. (In his poem, "To My Palette," he characterized blue as a spiritual color "fetched out of heaven" to vitalize the more material "earth clods.") His use of color was thus a direct expression of the interplay between physical and spiritual, the theme which became the central concern of his work.

THE THIRTIES

By the 1930s, Bloch had shifted to a more forceful and vigorous manner of painting, almost always dominated by the color blue. His first paintings in this manner retain the spiritual and religious overtones of the work of the 1920s, although perhaps with a somewhat chillier quality.

Winter of 1931 (fig. 27), for example, shows a man, a woman, and a donkey, apparently the holy family, seated on a small hillside, looking down on a village of little houses. The subject is not strictly traditional, being neither a "Flight Into Egypt," nor a "Nativity," nor an "Annunciation to the Shepherds," but a curious hybrid of all three. Bloch also updated the narrative, bringing it into his own time and place, for the little village, with its wooden houses, is clearly based on Lawrence, Kansas. In contrast to the works of the 1920s, with their delicate, even tentative brushwork and fractured compositions, the effect is both more confident and more unified. The cloudswept night sky is rendered boldly, in great sweeping strokes of blue and white, and the whole scene glows in a kind of magical, nocturnal half-light.

A subtle undercurrent of anguish becomes the dominant note in *Winter in the Dead Wood* (pl. 36), a canvas which Bloch worked on from 1934-38. This shows a dead wood in the deep snow of winter, with some crows sitting on the branches of the leafless trees, and a red sun setting over two distant snowcapped hills. While no human figures are present, the various trees and stumps have a strongly human quality. The dark line of broken trees in the foreground resembles a line of bystanders, like beggars watching a parade; the limbs of the trees behind them reach up imploringly, like anguished hands; and the two stumps look strikingly like people who have fallen in the snow. In its imagery, the painting relates to the poetry of Karl Kraus, whose poems frequently describe lonely dead trees, often shattered by the violence of war.

By this time, Bloch was clearly aware that a new world war was inevitable. Indeed, his trees have the quality of innocent human sufferers, for whom night and winter are approaching, and for whom spring is still distant. Nonetheless, despite the overall feeling of bleakness, the painting contains elements of hopefulness. The gestures of the trees stretch heavenward, for example, and two of them on the left combine to form an arch, thus suggesting both a loving couple and the vaulting of a church or cathedral.

Somewhat less optimistic is *Autumn Night* of 1934, which shows a hooded man, standing beside a tree, looking out towards the spectator with sorrowful, frightened eyes (see Anthology, p. 188). Behind him stretches an expansive, almost

27. *Winter*, 1931, Mrs. Albert Bloch

featureless landscape, on which a mysterious white horse grazes and distant white trees gesture skyward, like inverted streaks of lightning. The ominous gray sky suggests an approaching storm. With his saucerlike round eyes, the central figure has an exaggerated, sentimental quality, like the posters of large-eyed children produced in the 1960s by Keane. Nonetheless, Bloch himself considered this painting one of his most important productions, and in 1936 he sent a photograph of it to Kandinsky, to demonstrate the progress of his most recent work.

More subtle in approach, and consequently more effective, is *The Garden of Asses* of 1938-39 (pl. 37), a work which clearly pays homage to the animal paintings of Franz Marc. Marc's animals, however, generally evoke spiritual freedom, and express a state of nature towards which humans should aspire. Bloch's animals, on the other hand, are emblems of patience and dumb

suffering. Bloch once commented that the painting was inspired by the donkeys which he saw mistreated as beasts of burden during World War I. His goal was to create a Garden of Eden for these abused creatures. Significantly, the four asses on the right are painted with more earthy colors — black, yellow, purple, and dull red — while the two on the left are rendered in white. The ones on the left also have a white dove — the symbol of the soul or holy spirit — placed between them. Thus, Bloch transported these dumb beasts of burden from an earthly into a spiritual realm.

TEMPLETON

Bloch's helpmate and soulmate during much of this later period was a young woman from Kansas City, Kansas, Anna Francis, who came to Lawrence, after two years of junior college, to attend the University of Kansas. She first met Bloch when she took a painting class, where he appeared from time to time to provide criticism. She also attended many of Bloch's lectures. "We would all tremble," she recalls of his weekly painting critiques, adding "his demand for the best that mind was capable of could be painful."[170] By spring the Depression had deepened and Anna's parents could no longer afford to pay her rent. At this time the Blochs offered to take her in and provide her meals.

After graduation, Anna moved back to Kansas City, but after working there two years she returned to Lawrence to get a master's degree in English. For a while she lived in an apartment with a friend, but when the house was sold the Blochs both invited her to move back in. By now, the Blochs' younger son, Walter, had left home and Hortense felt lonely. Around this time, Anna was also hired as secretary of the art department and was allowed to paint in the portrait class when there was no other work to do. Thus, she both lived and worked with Bloch, and her involvement with him became a full-time commitment.

This new relationship left a residue in Bloch's work. In 1934 Bloch produced the most romantic works of his career, a series of twenty drawings which he titled "The Templeton Vignettes," after a village in western Massachusetts that had struck him as the ideal country retreat.[171] Most of these sketches portray two lovers in a romantic paradise. One drawing shows them embracing, in another they stand together on a hillside, looking out at the sky and the stars. In *Summer Night II* of 1935 (fig. 28), Bloch also produced a strikingly romantic painting of two lovers in a nocturnal summer landscape, the man seemingly naked, the woman clad only in a filmy gown. Stars sparkle in the sky, and foliage and water glimmer in the starlight. The woman is sleeping and the man looks down on her with thoughtful concern.

LETTERS TO MARIA MARC AND KANDINSKY

By 1936 Bloch was again painting with confidence, and in that year he penned two letters explaining his new approach. With the exceptions of his Denver lecture of 1934, and his letter to Edward Maser of 1955, they are Bloch's only extended statements of his artistic goals.

28. *Summer Night II*, 1935, Mrs. Albert Bloch

It is striking that Bloch chose to phrase these first extended statements about his art to the two key father figures of the Blue Rider group, Marc and Kandinsky — Marc himself, of course, being absent, and thus addressed through the surrogate of his widow, Maria. This suggests the degree to which Bloch always felt more connected with the Blue Rider group than with current trends in American painting. At the same time, both letters indicate that he saw his recent work as a new departure, something which was significantly different both from his own earlier paintings and from the work of his early mentors. In particular, he now saw himself at odds with the abstract tendencies of Kandinsky.

In a letter to Maria Marc, written in January 1936, Bloch noted that his current progress was a form of deliberate "regress" which eschewed all "modern trends," and which "has led me back, in a great arc, to the point of departure of my artistic development." Noting that his subject matter still treated "masks and carnival figures," as well as "the shrouded figures or mourners and the wretched," Bloch boasted that his work now achieved a "somber monumentality" derived from "an intensity for which I was then far from mature enough.... I believe with the greatest confidence that finally I have found my destined way."[172]

Bloch voiced similar sentiments to Kandinsky in a letter of 22 June 1936, but expressed himself somewhat more contentiously, noting that he could not view Kandinsky's work "with such uncritical enthusiasm as twenty-five years ago," and that he had immersed himself in the poetry of Kraus, who had become the central force in his life and work. Since Bloch enclosed some photographs of his recent paintings, he did not bother with long descriptions. He pointedly commented, however, that unlike Kandinsky, "I continue to paint 'objectively,' as you call it; more objectively than before."[173] His primary goal, however, was a spiritual rather than a material one. He was interested in the spiritual aspects of man, rather than the material aspects, and his art was rooted in his Christian faith in the Resurrection.

Such spiritual convictions are difficult to argue with, and they make artistic criticism extremely difficult. In his response,

Kandinsky did not comment on Bloch's pictures, and Bloch wrote back, suggesting that he did not like them. This was probably correct, since Bloch's new approach was utterly at odds with the direction of Kandinsky's work. Nonetheless, on 4 April 1937, Kandinsky wrote back very politely, for the most part avoiding outright criticism. Noting that he himself had dispensed with "literary themes," Kandinsky confessed that he did not wish to exclude such themes "on a rigid principle." Nonetheless, "even in painting that uses the 'incidental theme' I prefer the cooler expression."[174]

Despite this expression of open-mindedness on Kandinsky's part, Bloch was apparently annoyed by his failure to appreciate his work. Bloch's later writings not only consistently attack Kandinsky's view on modern art, but describe him as rigid and doctrinaire, despite Kandinsky's many assertions to the contrary, both in his correspondence with Bloch and in his published statements.

THE FORTIES

Bloch's paintings of the early 1940s, when Nazi armies were overrunning Europe, are the blackest and most despairing of his career. The artist's pessimism reached a peak in *Ultimate Night* (1940; private collection), which shows a naked corpse lying in the mud, amidst a landscape of blasted trees and shattered fences, while a wolflike dog hovers over him, and an apelike figure in the background strides forward into a cloud of black mist.

Through the Night of 1942 (see Cateforis, p. 82, fig. 5) portrays a similar, apocalyptic world, although Bloch's unhappiness is expressed in quieter terms, with a delicate undercurrent of hope. The painting shows five shrouded figures, who sit waiting in a dungeon, cave, or bombshelter. Their draped, rounded forms recall the contemporary "Tunnel Drawings" of the sculptor Henry Moore, showing figures sleeping in the London Underground shelters, during the German blitz. Bloch's figures, however, are not people sketched from contemporary life, but figures drawn from the art of the past, such as seated Madonnas. Thus, they are not simply individuals waiting for the terror outside to pass, but bearers of artistic and religious accomplishment, who represent the heritage of Western civilization.

Bloch's oddest painting of this period, *March of the Clowns* of 1941 (pl. 39), provides a hysterically comical response to this same atmosphere of tension. Although painted at a time when victory over the Nazis was far from certain, Bloch conjured up a parade of clowns to celebrate Hitler's defeat. The foremost of them holds up for ridicule a Nazi swastika and a puppet figure of Hitler. Looking on approvingly are a variety of cartoon characters lifted from the comics of the 1920s, including Krazy Kat, Ignatz Mouse, Popeye the sailor, Olive Oyl, Wimpy the hamburger man, Lord Plushbottom, and Ball Popper. In the air, various stars and symbols glow like apparitions, including a cross and a Star of David. All is folly in Bloch's sarcastic vision, but nonetheless he sharply contrasts the evil folly of Hitler and his minions with the lovable folly of his beloved funny paper characters and clowns.

GEORG TRAKL (1887-1914)

Bloch had discovered the work of Karl Kraus during the dark days of World War I, and the dark days of World War II brought him a second literary interest — the poetry of Georg Trakl. The son of a prosperous storekeeper in Innsbruck, Trakl flunked out of school and then studied pharmacy at the University of Vienna, where he became addicted to cocaine. At this time he began publishing his first poems, which were praised by Kraus. During World War I, Trakl was drafted into the medical corps, where he witnessed unspeakable horrors. This led him to a nervous breakdown, and after a failed suicide attempt he was sent to the military hospital in Cracow for observation. There he took an overdose of cocaine, apparently deliberately.

Trakl's lyrics are filled with images of decay and death, and in his mature work he abandoned logical connections in favor of a succession of visual images which float one after another, not so much for their narrative or symbolic significance as for their evocation of mood. Bloch later confessed that initially he was bewildered by Trakl. In some mysterious fashion, Trakl's poems conjured up images and conveyed a mood, but their grammar was peculiar and difficult, and the exact nature of the logical connections often unclear.

Bloch began making translations as a means of attaining a fuller understanding of their purport, and before long he became intensely engaged in the project. As Bloch once wrote:

> Trakl is rarely palpable, never explicit; it all seems to come to nothing more tangible than an aura of mood and melody, an emanation of dim light from deep shadow, a nebula of atmosphere and color, most tenuous when seeming most compact and solid — to a series of vanishing images perhaps, one might even venture to call them impressionist pictures: the jotting down, one after the other, of phenomena not so much observed as just caught sight of in passing.[175]

Thus Trakl not only challenged Bloch's ability as a translator, but stimulated his visual imagination as well.

With their inherently visual approach, Trakl's poems have an obvious appeal to a painter. His imagery strikingly resembled the subject matter of Bloch's paintings, even before Bloch's discovery of his verse; Trakl was even fond of the same range of cold colors that appealed to Bloch, such as blue, silver, purple, dark velvet green, and black.

Thus, Trakl reinforced, stimulated, and encouraged a series of existing tendencies in Bloch's work. In his later paintings, while not exactly an illustrator in the usual sense, Bloch became to some extent a representor of the world described in Trakl's poems — a world of shadows, crumbling stone walls, cathedrallike avenues of trees, ominous birds, abandoned cemeteries, and mysterious shrouded figures.

FALLS VILLAGE

Of course not all of Bloch's paintings of the 1940s were intensely gloomy, in part because he spent several happy summers on the east coast. These vacations with Anna inspired a group of lyrical landscape paintings in which, despite stormclouds and other emblems of gloom or emotional turbulence, he powerfully expressed his intense love of nature and the cosmos.

Bloch learned of Falls Village, Connecticut, through his correspondence with Lyonel Feininger. Bloch had known Feininger slightly when they lived in Europe, and shortly after Feininger returned to the United States (after being branded by the Nazis as "degenerate"), Bloch began corresponding with him. When Bloch sent on photographs of his work, Feininger responded sympathetically, remarking that they were both "Spätentwickler" (late developers). "You have the love of dead trees and bare hill forms that obsess me," Feininger wrote, "and which express the inner lonesomeness of life on this planet."[176] Bloch arranged a small show of Feininger's watercolors at the University of Kansas, and when this produced no sales, he bought some pieces himself, and donated them to the museum, although he could ill afford to do so.

Feininger rented a cottage in Falls Village from a family named Parsons, and there was a second cottage on a ridge just above the one he rented, which was available for the summer at modest cost. Conditions were too primitive for Hortense. There was only a kerosene stove for cooking and an outdoor cold shower for bathing. Bloch had no car and the general store was located a mile away. Anna, however, accompanied Bloch there for several summers, and they both found the place idyllic. Some of Bloch's most pleasing paintings of these years were the works which were inspired by his summers in Falls Village.

Gulls (pl. 38), painted in 1941, shows a rocky inlet on the seashore, and is a turbulent expression of the romantic spirit.[177] Dark rocks and trees tower on the left, while to the right the sea tears away at the beach and at a dead, bent tree, in the center of the painting, which is engulfed by a breaking wave. Driftwood litters the foreground; in the sky, a flock of gulls wheels amidst the wind and dark clouds — a passage of painting which resembles the late bird paintings of Marc but is darker in palette and more brooding in spirit.

Old Graveyard (pl. 40), which is more gentle in mood, was inspired by old New England cemeteries, which are often lost in the woods, overgrown and neglected. The imagery of the painting also recalls the poems of Trakl, who dealt with similar subjects. Anna Bloch recalls that the old cypress tree in the center was based on a real tree in Falls Village, and that one day Bloch borrowed her sketchbook to make a drawing of it. The rest of the composition he concocted from his imagination, and it is one of his most striking designs, based on the subtle interplay between the inverted V of the tree and the sideways V of the curving path.

The Falls Village idyll ended when the Parsons family sold their farmhouse and moved into the cottage which Bloch had rented. After that, he and Anna took a house closer to the village itself for two summers, then tried nearby Lakeville, and finally, for one summer, rented a cottage in New York state, in the Catskill Mountains. After 1951, however, as Bloch's health declined, they made no more trips east.

RETIREMENT

The theme of death which plays such a role in Bloch's work took on a new pertinence in 1947, when he suffered a severe heart attack. His frail health after this blow put an end to his teaching career. No doubt he had been growing tired of his teaching duties in any case, and with the support of his doctors he arranged to go into early retirement. Not long afterwards, in 1949, his wife, Hortense, died after suffering a series of heart attacks. Anna Francis was already living in the house and had been his helpmate and companion for the previous seventeen years. In 1951 he married her. Bloch's own near brush with death, his retirement, the death of his first wife, and his marriage to Anna Francis all set the stage for his later style, in which he sought to be spiritually at peace in preparation for his impending death.

Over the next few years, Bloch's work went through a gradual shift, slowly becoming more colorful and luminous. He continued to paint shrouded figures, but the sense of misery and despair that pervaded his work of the 1940s gradually softened. *The Grieving Women* of 1950 (pl. 44), for example, shows a series of draped, grieving figures in a barren landscape of rocks and deathly white trees. Set at sunset, the effect is profoundly desolate, but the fact that some of the figures embrace and comfort each other marks a new note of optimism. These figures seem like survivors from a terrible catastrophe, but survivors nonetheless. Their worst suffering seems to be behind them.

Figures in Silver Light (pl. 45), painted the following year, is even more hopeful, even cheerful. In this case the shrouded figures are not so much sufferers as solemn philosophers. Figures confer together, gather on a bench, or stroll in a garden. The scene is illuminated by moonlight, and the color has a cold, silvery beauty, like that of Bloch's romantic paintings of the early 1930s. During this period, Bloch returned to painting Harlequins and clowns, and as with the shrouded figures, there seems to be a general progression from a more bitter, disillusioned quality, to a kind of wistful romanticism.

Conference of 1951 (pl. 46) is still bitterly satirical. In it Bloch wrought a terrible revenge on the bureaucracy of warmongers and satirized the endless conferences which marked the Cold War diplomacy of the 1950s. A group of clowns, arranged in a band across the canvas, have been reduced to skeletons and scarecrows. Their garments lie in tatters and their faces are grotesque and horrible, with putrefying flesh.

Four years later, Bloch's mood had changed. *Blue Eclipse* of 1955 (pl. 48) is very different in spirit, and betrays a mood of poetic wistfulness that had not appeared in Bloch's work for decades. A Harlequin on the left and a clown on the right stand on a winding yellow road that leads through a dense forest to a pale yellow house in the distance. In the sky is the "Blue Eclipse" of the painting's title, a blue moon which is beginning to overlap a yellow one. Once in a blue moon, apparently, one can witness such romantic scenes.

Perhaps even more poignant in their effect are Bloch's last religious paintings, which focus on the image of the spiritual pilgrim. While very different in effect from the early work, they clearly go back to concepts which Bloch had absorbed during his Blue Rider period. Kandinsky, for example, wrote extensively about the spiritual qualities of the color blue. This notion provided the essential theme of Bloch's *The Blue Bough* of 1952 (pl. 47), in which blue is used symbolically, to evoke a spiritual quality which can bring dead things to life.

Impromptu of 1959 (pl. 49) deals even more directly with the theme of death and with the hope of overcoming death through spiritual faith. In the foreground is a fence behind which stands a dense thicket of trees and branches. We might interpret these elements as emblems for the distractions of daily life, which cut us off from spiritual concerns. In the upper zone of the painting, on a tree-topped hill, two figures are striding forward, a stopped figure who enters a green door on the right, and a red, Christ-like figure, who moves upward and heavenward up the hill. Both these figures clearly portray aspects of death, which is likened both to entering a dark cave and to climbing skyward towards eternal life. Perhaps the great surprise of the painting is its brilliance of color, with its bright blues, reds, yellows, and greens. The effect is eerily psychedelic, but also excited, even exuberant. Death is thus portrayed not as fearful but as a curiously joyful experience.

A conscious summation of Bloch's life journey, *Impromptu* also proved to be his last painting.[178] After completing it, Bloch would sometimes go up to his studio and play with the colors on his palette, like a child moving food around his plate. But he never again could summon up the energy to put brush to canvas and create a full painting.

DEATH

Bloch's death came two years later, on 9 December 1961, after a long slow decline. His will provides stark evidence of the modesty with which he lived. Bloch clearly specified how his funeral should be carried out, making it clear that he wanted the ceremony to be as simple as possible, that he wished to be placed in a simple wooden box, and that he desired that "*no eulogy*" (he underlined these words) should be delivered. Thus, even after his death, Bloch preferred to remain invisible. In a touching clause, he asked for his clothes to be given to the Salvation Army and added: "Bury me in my *oldest clothing* — not necessarily in the paint-stained rags I wear in the studio — , so that what remains of decent and serviceable apparel may be of use to someone who needs it."[179]

Bloch's one sign of vanity was his concern for his literary remains, for he asked Anna to work with his old friend Michael Lazarus to prepare them for publication. Unfortunately, however, nothing came of this proposal, both because of the time and labor involved and the lack of interest from any publisher. In 1996, thirty-five years after Bloch's death, the bulk of his poetry and writings remained in manuscript form. The one exception is a useful anthology of his translations of German poetry, *German Poetry in War and Peace*.[180]

Bloch's "disappearing act" after he settled in Kansas was a brilliantly successful one, so much so that he disappeared not only from living history but from most accounts of the past as well. An inherent paradox of the present exhibition is that in bringing Bloch's work to wider attention it must also penetrate the veil of secrecy, of invisibility, with which he so carefully surrounded himself.

Bloch's artistic achievement is clearly remarkable, although a variety of factors make a final assessment of its importance very difficult. At the highpoint of his career, Arthur Jerome Eddy praised Bloch as a giant in American art, believing that he was a major figure, whose work could stand comparison with such artists as Whistler and Kandinsky. Even today, Eddy's assessment is by no means ridiculous, for it is hard to think of another American painter who so fully assimilated modern ideas, not simply as a gifted imitator but as an active participant in the modern movement. Bloch's late work, however, seems to veer away from the main course of twentieth-century art and remains difficult to assess. The best of the late paintings, such as *The Blue Bough* or *Passing Train* (pl. 42), certainly rank with the best of the early work, but it is hard to say to what stylistic category they belong.

To call Bloch a member of the Blue Rider group does not quite do justice to his views, for in his later work he proudly diverged from the example of Kandinsky and even from that of his revered Marc. In significant ways, however, he remained true to the goals of these early years. He always kept a photograph of Marc beside his desk, and his work continued to be a dialogue, although sometimes an argumentative one, with the work of Marc, Kandinsky, Macke, Klee, Chagall, and the other figures whom he had befriended during his years in Germany. Bloch's late work, for all its unusual features, is much more an expression of the Blue Rider group than of the Americans that surrounded him, such as the Regionalists, whom he so despised. To be sure, in Bloch's final, densely textured paintings, the goals of his early work have been transformed through sorrow and suffering, study of the old masters, and an intense involvement and commitment to the poems and criticism of Karl Kraus. But in them, the spiritual ideals of the Blue Rider group also found a kind of second life.

1 Bloch to Maria Marc, January 1936, translated by Mrs. Albert Bloch. Courtesy of Mrs. Albert Bloch.

   I owe special thanks to Scott Heffley, who first introduced me to the work of Bloch, and has become a good friend in the course of working on this project. My deepest thanks also go to Anna Bloch, who has been remarkably generous in making available most of the primary documents on which this essay is based. Her vivid recollections of the late master have made him seem a living presence.

   Margaret Conrads, Samuel Sosland Curator of American Art at the Nelson-Atkins Museum of Art, deserves much of the credit for organizing this book and exhibition, one of several monumental projects which she has guided to fruition over the last year. Julie Aronson, the Nelson-Atkins's Assistant Curator of American Art, has kindly helped with fact-checking, obtaining photographs, and other similar matters. Two scholars at the University of Kansas, Frank Baron and David Cateforis, have been extremely generous in sharing their ideas and research. In addition, Sally Metzler, Curator at the Cummer Museum of Art, Jacksonville, Florida, and my wife, Marianne Berardi, have provided important support in a great variety of ways. I owe special thanks to my in-laws, James and Anne Berardi, who very generouly gave up their dining room table so that I could write this piece.

   In the notes that follow I have focused on primary sources, but in composing this essay I have drawn very frequently on the work of two previous scholars, Richard Green and Werner Mohr, and the fundamental importance of their research needs to be acknowledged. Richard Green was the first writer to clearly lay out the principal facts of Bloch's career. Two pieces by him were particularly helpful to me: "Albert Bloch, His Early Career: Munich and Der Blaue Reiter," *Pantheon*, 39 (January-March 1981), pp. 70-76 and "Introduction," *Albert Bloch (1882–1961): Paintings*, exh. cat. (New York: Sid Deutsch Gallery, 1988), n.p. More recently, Werner Mohr has gone through Bloch's papers very systematically, and has worked out the course of his career in greater detail. A great deal of the material in this essay is drawn from Mohr's voluminous study, "Albert Bloch as Caricaturist, Social Critic and Authorized Translator of Karl Kraus in America," Ph.D. diss., University of Kansas, 1995.

   Annegret Hobert, Curator at the Lenbachhaus in Munich, one of the foremost experts on the artists of the Blue Rider, has been the single most helpful person in getting this essay into publishable form. Words cannot express my gratitude for her careful corrections and above all, for her willingness to let me expand this piece far beyond the length originally allotted to it.

2 Albert Bloch, "Statt einer Autobiographie (Auszüge aus einem Brief)," *Der Ararat — Glossen, Skizzen und Notizen zur neuen Kunst*, no. 2 (1920), p. 137.

3 Albert Bloch, "Letter to Edward A. Maser," 20 June 1955 in *Albert Bloch: A Retrospective Exhibition of His Work from 1911-1955* (Lawrence: The University of Kansas Museum of Art, 1955), n.p.

4 Courtesy of Mrs. Albert Bloch.

5 James Neil Primm, *Lion of the Valley: St. Louis, Missouri* (Boulder: Pruett Publishing Company, 1981), pp. 345-47.

6 Herman Salinger to Anna Bloch, 12 October 1982. Courtesy of Mrs. Albert Bloch.

7 C. A. Macartney, *The Habsburg Empire, 1790-1918* (New York: Macmillan, 1969), p. 517.

8 Salinger to Anna Bloch, 12 October 1982; Ruth Kestenberg-Gladstein, "The Jews between Czechs and Germans in the Historic Lands, 1848-1918," in *The Jews of Czechoslovakia — Historical Studies and Surveys* (The Jewish Publication Society of America, 1968), vol. 1, p. 27.

9 Albert Bloch, "My Father," in "Sonnets to the Dead," in "Ventures in Verse," III, unpublished typescript. Courtesy of Mrs. Albert Bloch.

10 Albert Bloch, "Beside the Still Waters," in *Ventures in Verse: Selected Pieces* (New York: Frederick Ungar, 1947), pp. 19-31.

11 Bloch to Bernays, 30 November 1920, Thekla Bernays Papers, Missouri Historical Society, St. Louis.

12 Bloch to Butler, 23 June 1923, Archives, University of Kansas, Lawrence. See Anthology, pp. 197-99

13 Anna Bloch, "Albert Bloch's Silent Spirit," *Art and Antiques*, October 1987, p. 89.

14 "Kindly Caricatures No. 3: Halsey C. Ives," *Mirror*, 8 June 1905, Bloch's drawing on p. 5, Reedy's text on p. 3.

15 Bloch to Wuerpel, 5 May 1925, Spencer Library, University of Kansas, Lawrence. See also "Kindly Caricatures No. 90: Edmund H. Wuerpel," *Mirror*, 10 January 1907, p. 5.

16 Albert Bloch, "American Painting in Germany," *Mirror*, 9 June 1910, pp. 4-6.

17 The best account of Reedy and the *Mirror* is that of Frank Luther Mott, *A History of American Magazines* (Cambridge: Harvard University Press, 1957), vol. 4, pp. 101, 652-56. The only full-scale biography of Reedy is that of Max Putzel, *The Man in the Mirror: William Marion Reedy and His Magazine* (Cambridge: Harvard University Press, 1963).

18 "His Master's Voice," *Mirror*, 30 March 1905, p. 1.

19 Bloch owned a copy of Aubrey Beardsley's famous illustrated edition of Sir Thomas Malory's *Le Morte D'Arthur*, which remains in his study in Lawrence.

20 William Marion Reedy, "Caricaturist Albert Bloch Abroad," *Mirror*, 18 February 1909, p. 3.

21 In a letter of 29 August 1908 to Bernays, Reedy also declared that Bloch "devours" copies of *Jugend*. Reedy Papers, Missouri Historical Society, St. Louis.

22 Albert Bloch, "German Writers in Caricature," *International*, October 1913, p. 294. Bloch also mentioned Gulbransson in passing in this essay.

23 "Sara," *Mirror*, 1 March 1906, illustration and text, p. 1.

24 For an account of Boardman Robinson and Robert Minor, see Rebecca Zurier, *Art for the Masses* (Philadelphia: Temple University Press, 1988), p. 134. Bloch clearly knew Minor: he painted a portrait of him, which he exhibited in St. Louis in 1919.

25 William Marion Reedy, "A Mirrorite Arrives," *Mirror*, 17 October 1913, p. 2.

26 Albert Bloch, "Gotham Comment and Caricature," *Mirror*, 19 December 1907.

27 Albert Bloch, "The Work of Henri Matisse," *Mirror*, 14 May 1908, p. 9.

28 See "Kindly Caricatures No. 169: Benjamin Altheimer," *Mirror*, 10 September 1908, p. 5.

29 Reedy to Dreiser, 16 September 1915, Dreiser Collection, University of Pennsylvania Library; quoted in Mott, *History of American Magazines*, p. 653.

30 Putzel, *Man in the Mirror*, p. 135. These financial arrangements are reported indirectly in Reedy's letters to Bloch, for example, Reedy to Bloch, 22 February 1911.

31 Reedy to Bloch, 28 May 1909, Reedy Papers, Missouri Historical Society, St. Louis.

32 Albert Bloch, "Kandinsky, Marc, Klee: Criticism and Reminiscence," no. 4 in typescript "Pictures and People: From a Painter's Point of View," lecture at the Denver Art Museum, 13 December 1934, p. 89 (hereafter Denver lecture). See Anthology, pp. 199-205.

33 Cited in Peg Weiss, *Kandinsky in Munich* (Princeton: Princeton University Press, 1979), p. 3.

34 Bloch to Arthur Jerome Eddy, n.d., quoted in Arthur Jerome Eddy, *Cubists and Post-Impressionism*, 2nd ed. (Chicago: A. C. McClurg and Co., 1919), foreword.

35 William Marion Reedy, "Caricaturist Albert Bloch Abroad," p. 3.

36 See *Mirror*, 8 April 1909, p. 22; 15 April 1909, p. 14; 22 April 1909, p. 14; 29 April 1909, p. 14.

37 Reedy to Bloch, 12 December 1909; 18 January 1910; 29 January 1910, Reedy Papers.

38 Bloch published the following cartoons in *Lustige Blätter*: "Rotundelein," 22 December 1909, p. 6; "Philosophie," 16 February 1910, p. 10; "Termingeschäft," 23 March 1910, p. 18; "Frühlingsdüfte," 4 May 1910, p. 12; "Der Autor auf der Probe," 18 May 1910, p. 3; "Uraufführung bei Max Reger," 16 November 1910, p. 6; "Früchtchen," 11 January 1911, p. 8; "Die Schauspielerin," 15 March 1911, p. 18; "Der Sportsmann," 17 May 1911, p. 3; "Polizeistunde am goldenen Sonntag," 9 December 1911, p. 20.

39 Albert Bloch, "The *Elektra* of Strauss," *Mirror*, 6 May 1909, pp. 5-7.

40 The title of Bloch's essay is confusing, but in fact this was simply a show of work by American painters, not the work by artists living abroad. It was dominated by American Impressionists such as John H. Twachtman and Childe Hassam. The one artist Bloch singled out for praise was Winslow Homer.

41 Albert Bloch, "American Painting in Germany," pp. 4-6.

42 Mohr, "Albert Bloch as Caricaturist, Social Critic and Authorized Translator of Karl Kraus in America," p. 118.

43 Joseph Strong, pseud.,"The Beggar: A Street Corner Story," *Mirror*, 16 December 1910, pp. 32-35.

44 Joseph Strong, pseud., "Derelicts: A Conversational Fragment," *Mirror*, 23 June 1910, pp. 32-35.

45 Reedy to Bloch, undated letter, July 1910, Reedy Papers.

46 Joseph Strong, pseud., "Curtain Speech: An Afterthought," *Mirror*, 30 June 1910, p. 5.

47 Joseph Strong, pseud., "An Ambition," *Mirror*, 10 November 1910, p. 3.

48 Reedy to Bloch, 29 June 1910, Reedy Papers.

49 Joseph Strong, pseud., "Wehmut," *Mirror*, 7 March 1912, p. 5.

50 Joseph Strong, pseud., "Compositions in Monochrome," *Mirror*, 15 February 1912, pp. 6-7.

51 Joseph Strong, pseud., "Prophecy," *Mirror*, 23 May 1912, p. 11.

52 Joseph Strong, pseud., "Where is Sanctuary?," *Mirror*, 23 May 1912, p. 7.

53 Reedy to Bloch, 8 January 1913, Reedy Papers.

54 Bloch, with commentary by Reedy, "Kindly Caricatures No. 99: Dawson Watson," *Mirror*, 14 May 1907, p. 7, text pages 7-8; Bloch to Butler, 23 June 1923. See Anthology, p. 197-99.

55 Bloch to Butler, 23 June 1923.

56 Denver lecture, 1934, p. 90.

57 Ibid.

58 Ibid., p. 91.

59 Weiss, *Kandinsky in Munich*, p. 172, note 103.

60 Private collection, Kansas City, Missouri. Bloch's fondness for roughly

finished work may have gotten its start in New York, where he was exposed to the work of the Ashcan School.

61 Denver lecture, 1934, p. 89.

62 Ibid.

63 My dating differs from that of Werner Mohr, who places the meeting only a year after Bloch's arrival in Munich. See Mohr, "Albert Bloch as Caricaturist, Social Critic and Authorized Translator of Karl Kraus in America," p. 38.

64 A series of these sketches are in the collection of the Städtische Galerie im Lenbachhaus, Munich.

65 Edouard Roditi, "Interview with Gabriele Münter," *Arts Magazine*, 34 (January 1960), p. 41.

66 Bloch, "Letter to Edward A. Maser."

67 Eddy, *Cubists and Post-Impressionism*, p. 201.

68 Wassily Kandinsky and Franz Marc, *The Blaue Reiter Almanac*, edited and with an introduction by Klaus Lankheit (New York: The Viking Press, 1974), p. 250.

69 Murray Sheehan, "The New Art: Apropos the Work of Albert Bloch," *Mirror*, 11 April 1913, pp. 5-6.

70 Wassily Kandinsky, *Concerning the Spiritual in Art*, edited by Robert Motherwell (New York: Wittenborn, Schultz, 1947), p. 58.

71 Eddy, *Cubists and Post-Impressionism*, p. 204.

72 Albert Bloch, "Mr. Bloch Protests," *Mirror*, 21 November 1913, p. 9.

73 *The Blaue Reiter Almanac*, p. 116.

74 Green, "Introduction," *Albert Bloch (1882-1961): Paintings*, n.p.

75 Peter Selz, *German Expressionist Painting* (Berkeley and Los Angeles: University of California Press, 1957), p. 134.

76 Bloch, "Letter to Edward A. Maser."

77 Ibid.

78 Ibid.

79 Eddy, *Cubists and Post-Impressionism*, p. 201.

80 William Reedy's writings confirm that Bloch was aware of the work of the Ashcan School painters. He once noted that Bloch "gives an exotic, sensual twist even to the realism of such American artists as John Sloan and George Luks" ("Caricaturist Albert Bloch Abroad," p. 3).

81 Bloch wrote "destroyed" beside the photograph of this painting in his Record Book. Possibly he destroyed this and other works when he emptied his apartment in Munich in 1920.

82 Eddy, *Cubists and Post-Impressionism*, p. 202.

83 Hans Konrad Roethel, former director of the Lenbachhaus in Munich, has suggested that this painting may have been inspired by the dancer Marie Delvard, who performed at the Elf Scharfrichter cabaret in Munich.

84 Albert Bloch, "My Pictures at the Guild," *Reedy's Mirror*, 11 March 1920, pp. 178-80.

85 For an account of the influence of the *commedia dell'arte* on modern art, see Martin Green and John Swan, *The Triumph of Pierrot* (New York: Macmillan, 1986). See also Janice McCullagh, "Albert Bloch's Clowns," *Albert Bloch: Artistic and Literary Perspectives*, eds. Frank Baron et al., (Munich: Prestel-Verlag, 1997), pp. 41-54.

86 Strong, "Wehmut," p. 5.

87 Reedy to Bloch, 27 September 1909, Reedy Papers. The word "Wiertized" refers to the Belgian historical painter Antoine Joseph Wiertz (1805-65).

88 Reedy to Bloch, 9 November 1912, Reedy Papers.

89 Reedy to Bernays, 17 October 1912, Bernays Papers.

90 William Marion Reedy, "Reflections," *Mirror*, 9 January 1913, p. 2.

91 Francis A. Curley, "The Adoration of the Magi," *Mirror*, 9 January 1913, p. 21.

92 Reedy to Bloch, 17 January 1913, Reedy Papers.

93 *Mirror*, 11 April 1913. This design repeated the composition of *Harlequinade*, 1911 (pl. 4).

94 Sheehan, "The New Art: Apropos the Work of Albert Bloch," pp. 5-6. The evidence that Sheehan visited Bloch in Munich, while circumstantial, is compelling. In his text, Sheehan quotes Bloch on several occasions, apparently drawing not from letters but from a face-to-face meeting. In addition, he refers to recent paintings by Bloch which he could only have seen in Munich.

95 William Marion Reedy, "A Mirrorite Arrives," p. 2.

96 Bloch, "Gotham Comment and Caricature," pp. 33-35.

97 Bloch, "German Writers in Caricature," *International*, September 1913, pp. 264-65, and October 1913, pp. 293-96.

98 Reedy, "A Mirrorite Arrives," p. 2.

99 Bloch, "Mr. Bloch Protests," p. 9.

100 Eddy, *Cubists and Post-Impressionism*, p. 203. For an account of Eddy's

collection, see Paul Kruty, "Arthur Jerome Eddy and His Collection: Prelude and Postscript to the Armory Show," *Arts Magazine*, 61 (February 1987), pp. 40-47.

101 William Marion Reedy, "Albert Bloch," *Mirror*, 6 August 1915, pp. 16-17.

102 Eddy, *Cubists and Post-Impressionism*, p. 205.

103 Denver lecture, 1934, p. 117.

104 Eddy, *Cubists and Post-Impressionism*, p. 204.

105 Kandinsky, *Concerning the Spiritual in Art*, p. 27.

106 Reedy to Bloch, 17 August 1910, Reedy Papers.

107 Bloch to Marc, 18 July 1913. See Anthology, pp. 163-64.

108 Postcard from Marc to Bloch, 4 August 1913. See Anthology, p. 164.

109 Bloch to Marc, 26 February 1915. See Anthology, p. 168.

110 Bloch to Marc, 21 June 1915. See Anthology, pp. 169-70.

111 Bloch to Walden, 4 May 1916. Staatsbibliothek, Berlin.

112 Bloch to Maria Marc, 6 February 1917. Courtesy of Mrs. Albert Bloch.

113 Bloch to Walden, 8 August 1917. Staatsbibliothek, Berlin.

114 Bloch to Marc, 16 November 1914. See Anthology, p. 166.

115 I have used Bloch's translation of the title of this essay. While far from literal, it seems to me to capture the essence of Marc's idea. The German words Marc employed, "Das Geheime Europa," are not easily rendered into English, but a more literal translation would be "The Hidden Europe."

116 Bloch to Marc, 6 December 1914. See Anthology, p. 167.

117 Bloch to Marc, 27 April 1915. See Anthology, pp. 168-69.

118 Bloch to Maria Marc, 11 November 1918. Courtesy of Mrs. Albert Bloch.

119 Reedy to Bloch, 29 June 1910, Reedy Papers.

120 These letters belong to Dexel's sons but copies were provided for Mrs. Albert Bloch by Maria Schuchter of Innsbruck.

121 Bloch to Hans Goltz, *Der Ararat*, December 1920, p. 137.

122 Albert Bloch, "Der Künstler Über Alles," *Reedy's Mirror*, 31 July 1919, p. 333.

123 Albert Bloch, "My Pictures at the Guild," pp. 178-80.

124 Bloch to Bernays, 15 September 1920.

125 Collection of the Missouri Historical Society, St. Louis.

126 Albert Bloch, "Sonnets to the Dead," in "Ventures in Verse," III, unpublished typescript. Courtesy of Mrs. Albert Bloch.

127 Bloch to Bernays, 4 August 1920, Bernays Papers.

128 Bloch to Bernays, 15 September 1920, Bernays Papers.

129 Bloch to Bernays, 30 January 1921, Bernays Papers.

130 Albert Bloch, undated letter in "Ishmael's Breviary," typescript, p. 138. Courtesy of Mrs. Albert Bloch.

131 Bernays to Bloch, quoted in Mohr, "Albert Bloch as Caricaturist, Social Critic and Authorized Translator of Karl Kraus in America," p. 72.

132 Bloch to Bernays, 30 January 1921, Bernays Papers.

133 *Arts*, November 1921, p. 112. For an account of Charles Daniel, see Hilton Kramer, "Daniel Gallery Days," *New Criterion*, 12 (February 1994), pp. 84-85.

134 Anna Bloch, "Albert Bloch in Kansas: An Introduction," *Kansas Quarterly*, 24 (1993), p. 7.

135 Bloch to Butler, 23 June 1923. See Anthology, pp. 197-99.

136 Bloch to Ernest Lindley, undated (September 1923), Archives, University of Kansas, Lawrence.

137 Eddy, *Cubists and Post-Impressionism*, p. 200.

138 Bloch to Dexel, 28 January 1918. See Anthology, p. 175.

139 Bloch, "Letter to Edward A. Maser."

140 Phillips to Bloch, 30 April 1928. Courtesy of Mrs. Albert Bloch. As a young man, Bloch was probably aware of reclusive American artists, such as Winslow Homer and Albert Pinkham Ryder. They may have, to some extent, served as a model for his later retreat from the public sphere.

141 Anna Bloch, "Albert Bloch in Kansas," p. 6.

142 Albert Bloch, "Translator's Foreword," *Karl Kraus, Poems: Authorized Translations from the German* (Boston: The Four Seas Press, 1930), pp. 9-21.

143 Albert Bloch, "German Writers in Caricature," p. 296. See Mohr, "Albert Bloch as Caricaturist, Social Critic and Authorized Translator of Karl Kraus in America," p. 193 and note 5, p. 202.

144 The date is inscribed on Bloch's first copy of *Die Fackel*, which bears his marginal note on page 1. Bloch's copies of the magazine are now in a private collection.

145 Albert Bloch, "Epistle to Weidlingau," unpublished manuscript, April-May 1938. Courtesy of Mrs. Albert Bloch.

146 Marc to Bloch, 17 December 1914. Bloch defended Kraus against the criticisms of Bernays in a letter of 16 April 1921, Bernays Papers.

147 Albert Bloch, "Karl Kraus's Shakespeare," *Books Abroad*, 11 (1937), pp. 21-24.

148 Bloch to Kraus, 27 August 1924 (*Die Fackel*, 668-75, December 1924, p. 1010); Bloch to Kraus, 1 February 1925 (*Die Fackel*, 679-85, March 1925, pp. 107-8).

149 Bloch to Kraus, 1 February 1926, published in *Die Fackel*, 717, March 1926, pp. 33-34, with an introductory comment by Karl Kraus.

150 Ibid.

151 Bloch to Kraus, 19 December 1927. Courtesy of Mrs. Albert Bloch.

152 In Bloch to Theodor Haecker, 3 January 1928, copy in the possession of Mrs. Albert Bloch, he refers to this request.

153 Wickerhover to Bloch, 26 January 1928. Courtesy of Mrs. Albert Bloch.

154 Bloch to Wickerhover, no date, probably February 1928, draft in the possession of Mrs. Albert Bloch.

155 Haecker to Kraus, 7 July 1928, copy in the possession of Mrs. Albert Bloch.

156 Bloch to Brown, 14 January 1929; Brown to Bloch, 18 January 1929; Brown to Bloch, 5 February 1929; Bloch to Brown, 9 February 1929. Courtesy of Mrs. Albert Bloch.

157 Bloch to Brown, September 1930.

158 Bloch, "Literary Adventures," typescript, p. 17. Courtesy of Mrs. Albert Bloch.

159 Ibid., p. 15.

160 Mohr, "Albert Bloch as Caricaturist, Social Critic and Authorized Translator of Karl Kraus in America," p. 255.

161 See Heinrich Fischer and Michael Lazarus, editors, *Karl Kraus: Briefe an Sidonie Nádherný von Borutin 1913-36* (Munich: Fischer, 1984), pp. 19-20, 59-61, 691-93.

162 Vincent Kling, "Review of *Karl Kraus* by Harry Zohn," *Modern Austrian Literature*, 12 (1979), pp. 188-92.

163 Harry Zohn, "The Translation of Satire: Kurt Tucholsky and Karl Kraus," *Babel*, 14 (1968), pp. 201-05.

164 Conversations with Mrs. Albert Bloch, 1995.

165 Leonard S. Klein, ed., *Encyclopedia of World Literature in the 20th Century* (New York: Frederick Ungar, 1989), vol. 2, p. 236.

166 Richard Green, *New Themes in Albert Bloch's Art after his Return from Europe*, typescript, n. 1; David Cateforis, "Albert Bloch's Visionary Landscapes," in *Albert Bloch: Literary and Artistic Perspectives*, pp. 121-28.

167 Albert Bloch, *German Poetry in War and Peace: A Dual-Language Anthology*, ed. Frank Baron (Lawrence, Kansas: Max Kade Center for German-American Studies, 1995), pp. 2-3.

168 Kandinsky, *Concerning the Spiritual in Art*, p. 59.

169 Bloch to Nádherný, 10 June 1948, Brenner-Archiv, Innsbruck.

170 Anna Bloch, "Albert Bloch in Kansas," p. 7. For the information in this section I am indebted to a two-page typscript provided to me by Mrs. Bloch as well as to conversations with her.

171 Bloch apparently passed through the town of Templeton, but never lived there. Thus, the "Templeton Vignettes" portray the ideal, and were not intended as a documentary record.

172 Bloch to Maria Marc, January 1936. See Anthology, pp. 181-82.

173 Bloch to Kandinsky, 22 June 1936. See Anthology, pp. 186-87.

174 Kandinsky to Bloch, 4 April 1937. See Anthology, pp. 189-90.

175 Albert Bloch, "After the German of Georg Trakl," unpublished postscript to a translation of 34 of Trakl's poems, spring 1943. Courtesy of Mrs. Albert Bloch.

176 Lyonel Feininger to Bloch, 7 March 1939, Munson-Williams-Proctor Institute, Utica, New York. See Anthology, pp. 196-97.

177 Falls Village is in the western part of the state, several hours from the coast. This painting, therefore, does not portray Falls Village, although Mrs. Bloch has identified it as a Connecticut landscape.

178 While Bloch's late paintings do not seem to reflect specific influences so frequently as his early work, his late work does reveal a general affinity with that of other artists of the 1950s, such as Rico Le Brun or Abraham Rattner, who tried to find a compromise between a figurative approach and the new abstract styles which were then coming into vogue.

179 Bloch's will, 1 January 1947. Courtesy of Mrs. Albert Bloch.

180 Bloch, *German Poetry in War and Peace: A Dual-Language Anthology*.

Annegret Hoberg

THE BEGINNINGS

Furnished with a small monthly allowance by William Marion Reedy, the editor of the St. Louis *Mirror*, the twenty-six-year-old Albert Bloch arrived in Munich at the beginning of 1909, aiming to further his artistic training. He had started his career as an illustrator and caricaturist in St. Louis, and in the previous four years had worked almost exclusively for Reedy's satirical weekly. Consequently, as in the case of Lyonel Feininger, his early work was decisively affected by this early emphasis on drawing and caricature.

Bloch initially intended — partly at the request of his sponsor Reedy — to pursue a full course of study at the Academy of Art in Munich. However, he turned first to the portraitist Leo Samberger and the etcher Hans Volkert, neither of whom taught at the Academy.[1] It is still not clear why he chose these two particular teachers. As a caricaturist who had been intensely preoccupied with the presentation of the human figure and face, Bloch made an obvious choice by selecting a portrait painter as a teacher. However, Samberger was even then an extremely traditional artist, who, as a direct successor to Franz von Lenbach, produced commissioned portraits in an Old Master fashion, in a darkly-toned studio painting style. He had not embraced the innovations in Munich painting that had taken place since around 1900 — Impressionism, Naturalism, the open-air painting of the Leibl circle, the Dachau School of Painting, the "Scholle," or the Munich Secession.[2]

Hans Volkert was a figure of little significance in Munich art. His work, with the exception of a few of his sheets for the "Verein für Originalradierung München" (Munich Association for Original Etching), has remained unknown up to the present day. However, Volkert introduced Bloch to the technique of etching. The young artist was soon a master of it, as some ten etchings dating from around 1909 demonstrate. Their subjects are mostly closely related to his own prose texts — short stories, usually with bitter or satirical but sympathetic descriptions of street scenes, which Bloch continued to send along with his drawings to the *Mirror* in St. Louis.[3] On his etching *Seated Blind Beggar*, Bloch noted, "The first plate I ever etched Sept. 4 1909."

The scattered notes he made in later years show that — as he admitted without any pride on several occasions — he was then completely ignorant of recent modern art in Europe. Among other things, he walked through a room full of works by Paul Cézanne at the spring exhibition of the Munich Secession without noticing what sort of art he had before his eyes. His first encounter with the latest avant-garde work was in New York in 1908, when he saw an exhibition by Henri Matisse at Alfred Stieglitz's gallery, "291," and reviewed it for the *Mirror*. In the so far rather imprecise art-historical scholarship on Bloch, it is only the positive nature of his review that has been noted. However, this positive response referred only to Matisse's graphic work, the quality of which Bloch, as a draftsman, immediately recognized. The young artist apparently had no comprehension of the paintings, for which he was completely unprepared.[4]

On the other hand, Bloch's correspondence with Reedy shows he was well aware of the illustrated magazines *Simplicissimus* and *Jugend*, which were founded and published in Munich and included the work of the outstanding illustrators Thomas Theodor Heine, Olaf Gulbransson, Bruno Paul, Ferdinand von Reznicek, and Erich and Rudolf Wilke. The worldwide renown of these magazines, then at the height of their fame, was apparently one of the reasons why Bloch chose to stay in Munich, rather than in Paris or Berlin.[5]

In any case, Bloch was apparently only too willing to listen to Samberger's and Volkert's advice not to continue his academic studies, since his style had already become too independent and individual. Like many young artists of the emerging avant-garde after the turn of the century, Bloch preferred to continue his work on his own, free of the shackles of traditional training. His development as a painter in this voluntary isolation apparently progressed rather slowly, and only a few paintings dating from his first two years in Munich, 1909 and 1910, have survived or are documented.[6] Instead — and much to the annoyance of his sponsor, Reedy — he seems to have spent his time mainly reading, writing, and visiting museums, and in the summer of 1910 had even reached a point at which he was considering an early return to America.[7]

It was apparently in the winter of 1910 that Bloch traveled to Paris, hoping to find some new artistic stimuli. There, the works that impressed him most included those of Vincent van Gogh, as well as the early Pablo Picasso, Paul Gauguin, and Odilon Redon.[8] The first large-scale paintings that Bloch produced, such as *The Dancer (Ragtime)* (pl. 7) and the circus scene *Slack-Wire* (Spencer Museum of Art, Lawrence), show an expressive application of the paint with impasto influenced by Van Gogh. However, at the same time, they have a characteristic exaggeration in the faces and movements, betraying Bloch's origins in caricature drawing.[9]

1. *Untitled (Housetops and Wall)*, 1911, Mrs. Albert Bloch

THE NEUE KÜNSTLERVEREINIGUNG AND THE BLUE RIDER

After Bloch's visit to Paris, an unexpected turn of events left a lasting impression on his subsequent artistic career. On his return to Munich, he quite by chance came across the catalogue of the second exhibition of the Neue Künstlervereinigung München or NKVM (New Artists' Union of Munich), which had been held in September 1910; the catalogue included a number of small illustrations. As he looked at the reproductions, Bloch immediately sensed an affinity between them and his own artistic approach. Although Bloch's reminiscences of this initial encounter with the NKVM in Munich, recorded in his 1934 Denver lecture are interesting (see Anthology, pp. 199-205), until recently they caused a certain amount of confusion for those attempting to reconstruct his artistic biography. In the lecture, he dates his visit to Paris as 1909–10, adding,

> But while I was away in Paris that first time, I missed an event of the greatest importance that had taken place in Munich, and which was to have a very marked effect upon the painting of many of the younger men throughout Germany as well as in other countries. This was the first exhibition of the Münchner neue Vereinigung, the New Society of Munich, whose leading spirit was Wassily Kandinsky, although he was not nominally the head of the organization. When presently I saw an illustrated catalog of this exhibition, I was immediately interested, and regretted that I had not been in town to see the show; for I recognised, even from the inadequate little black-and-white reproductions, that here was [sic] a few people—Germans, Russians, Frenchmen, Italians —, some of whom were striking out in a direction which seemed entirely sympathetic to the zigzag development which I was then undergoing myself, and that there was a certain kinship between some of this work and the groping experiments I was making independently and without previous knowledge of the existence of these others.

There is a great deal of evidence, however, to show that Bloch cannot have been referring here to the first NKVM exhibition held in the winter of 1909, and that he must have meant the second, which was held one year later and which was expanded to include the foreign artists from France and Italy to whom he refers. He himself mentions Picasso, Georges Braque, Georges Rouault, and others, all of whom were first represented at the second exhibition.[10] That Bloch was confused after a lapse of nearly thirty years becomes particularly clear in a subsequent passage which outlines how Franz Marc joined the NKVM. He refers to the sharp attacks in the press, which were even stronger for the second exhibition than for the first — for example, in the *Münchner Neueste Nachrichten* on 10 September 1910, the critic M. K. Rohe wrote of "incurably mad" and "shameless bluffers." Bloch wrote about a well-known moment in Blue Rider history, however mistaking the exhibition with which it was associated: "During this first exhibition of the group, the newspapers … had been so scathingly abusive that Marc, who at that time was still quite unknown, felt moved to write a letter of protest to the leading daily of Munich…." It was through this letter to the newspaper that Marc first made contact with the New Artists' Union in Munich, becoming a member in January 1911. Thus, Bloch's reference is clearly to the second exhibition in the fall of 1910.[11]

In any case, Bloch felt immediately attracted to the works reproduced in the catalogue. The striking immediacy and simplicity of the depictions, which broke with pictorial tradition in what was then a revolutionary fashion, certainly provided a special parallel to his own autodidactic efforts to achieve an

2. *View of a Factory*, 1911, Present location unknown, Photo courtesy of Mrs. Albert Bloch

anti-academic, simple style of painting. From the spring of 1911, Bloch experienced his first period of tremendous artistic productivity. His works included a series of urban landscapes, first depicting his immediate surroundings in Schwabing, as seen in *Untitled (Cityscape)* (pl. 2). During his visit to Dachau in the early summer of 1911, he portrayed the precise, completely unadorned view, behind a wall, of the roofs of two houses, drawn with simple outlines (fig. 1).

His larger composition *View of a Factory* (fig. 2) is also astonishingly close to contemporary paintings of the New Artists' Union, such as the urban landscapes of Adolf Erbslöh, Alexander Kanoldt, and Gabriele Münter. There are the same apparently accidental, unspectacular and cropped views of the urban environment, seen in the building site in Erbslöh's *Street* of 1910 — in its own day a provocative work with a novel effect

3. Adolf Erbslöh, *Street*, 1910, Wallraf-Richartz-Museum, Cologne

(fig. 3); the walls and roofs of Alexander Kanoldt's *Houses in Greenery* (fig. 4) — a view of Nikolaiplatz in Schwabing, where Kanoldt lived in 1910–11; and Gabriele Münter's extremely reduced *Buildings in Schwabing* (fig. 5), with its geometrical outlines and the bare fire-wall on the street corner. Bloch's paintings show a very similar use of black contours, with the delineation of detail through shortened brushstrokes, and a two-dimensional style of painting, with strong solid colors lacking any modeling or atmospheric interruption of the sort that Impressionist and Naturalist painting required.

Bloch's portraits of 1911 also benefit from a newly won sense of assurance in his handling of provocatively simple formal means — means which at the same time serve to intensify the expression. The impressive *Portrait of a Boy* (pl. 6) has the rather typical mid-brown tones of Bloch's early paintings, although there is nothing academic about it. Rather it has a raw, emphatically "ugly" quality. The artist showed the painting in the first German exhibition in which he took part — at the twenty-second exhibition of the Berlin Secession in the spring of 1911, where it appeared alongside works by Max Beckmann, Lovis Corinth, André Derain, Ferdinand Hodler, Braque, Feininger, Picasso, and others.[12]

Prior to his stay in Dachau, north of Munich, in the summer of 1911, Bloch had already seen an exhibition of the work of Franz Marc and Pierre Girieud in May at the

Thannhauser Gallery, which had made a deep impression on him.[13] In deciding to spend the summer in Dachau, he was following the still-popular fashion among younger generation

4. Alexander Kanoldt, *Houses in Greenery (Nikolaiplatz Schwabing)*, 1910-11, Private collection

Munich artists: producing open-air paintings in the painters' colony there, free from academic constraints. Like a similar painters' colony at Worpswede in northern Germany, the so-called New Dachau school of painting had developed during the 1890s, its principal figures being Adolf Hölzel, Ludwig Dill, and Arthur Langhammer. Adolf Hölzel, in particular, became an influential teacher there, and he was not without some

5. Gabriele Münter, *Buildings in Schwabing*, 1910, Private collection

influence on Kandinsky's early work, of around 1903–04.[14] Impressed by Gauguin and the subsequent "Nabis" school, Hölzel developed his own technique of "cloisonnism," meaning the inclusion of bold areas of color between dark outlines —

achieving a new two-dimensional style and a "synthesis" of the pictorial structure. Hölzel thus created a "cautious avant-garde" style, which was moving in its own way towards the abstraction

6. Page from the artist's Record Book, vol. 1, with photographs of *Factory*, *Procession of the Cross*, and *Harlequinade*, 1911, Mrs. Albert Bloch

of the pictorial object. One of the few — although important — paintings by Bloch that clearly shows Hölzel's influence is his ambitious composition *Procession of the Cross* of 1911 (pl. 9), which is closely related to Hölzel's *Golgotha (Sketch of a Burial)* (fig. 7) and other religious paintings by him. The theme and composition remained unique in Bloch's early work; however, the painting was so important to him that in the winter of 1911 he showed it at the first Blue Rider exhibition.

The events that led Albert Bloch to the NKVM, and soon afterward to the Blue Rider group, came with increasing frequency in the fall of that year. In the 1934 Denver lecture, Bloch noted: "About a year later a visitor to my studio suggested that I invite Kandinsky and his associates to have a look at my work. This I was reluctant to do, for various reasons; but after some persuasion, I consented to see Kandinsky and ask him round to my place, if he would only come. As it turned out, Kandinsky

was glad to come...." The visit must have taken place in early October 1911 at the latest. Kandinsky and Marc apparently recognized at once in the plain — that is, "unspoiled" and, in the best sense, "primitive" — quality of Bloch's painting the pioneering element necessary for the new form of art which they were then trying to identify in a variety of places, in part for the *Blaue Reiter Almanac*, which they had been planning since June 1911. The immediacy of effect in Bloch's painting may have been due to some extent to his lack of prior assumptions, a certain lack of encumbrance by the cultural traditions of Europe.[15] Kandinsky and Marc apparently decided soon after their visit to invite Bloch to take part in the planned third exhibition of the New Artists' Union.

Until recently, the only evidence of these events was in the published correspondence between Kandinsky and Marc; however, some recently discovered letters from Adolf Erbslöh to Franz Marc now allow us to follow the course of events in more detail.[16] Since the NKVM had decided at one of its meetings in the spring of 1911 to organize its next exhibition without inviting outside guests, Erbslöh was unable to accede to Marc's suggestion of inviting Bloch to participate.[17] Along with a number of other factors, particularly the long-simmering artistic opposition between the progressive thinkers of the NKVM and its more moderate membership, the rejection of Bloch as a participant may well have triggered Kandinsky and Marc to start to give more concrete shape to their plans for their own separate exhibition. The 4 November 1911 postcard from Marc to Kandinsky, so important in the formation of

7. Adolf Hölzel, *Golgatha (Sketch of a Burial)*, 1908, Collection Bahlsen, Hannover

the Blue Rider group, reads, "L.K., got a separate room at Thannhauser for second half December, in addition to the Association, where we can show anything we want.... My program: Burljuk, Campendonk, August [Macke], a few glass paintings, Schönberg, Bloch, and Rousseau if at all possible (not too big). Then Delaunay and possibly two or three old things (rice paintings, glass paintings, votives). *It has to be something fine.* Yours, Fz. M."[18]

However, the actual break with the NKVM only took place on 2 December 1911, when the jury rejected Kandinsky's *Composition V* for the third exhibition with the flimsy excuse that it was "too big." Kandinsky, Marc, and Münter then resigned from the Union and immediately began feverish preparations for their own counter-exhibition, which included sending an express letter to the Austrian artist Alfred Kubin to persuade him to resign and join them as well. Probably only one day later, Kandinsky visited Bloch to encourage him to participate. On 4 December 1911, he wrote to Marc, "Was at

8. First Blue Rider Exhibition, Thannhauser Gallery, Munich, 1911, Photo: Gabriele Münter, Gabriele Münter- und Johannes Eichner-Stiftung, Munich

Bloch's. He was wide-eyed. But he said, 'It's not completely unexpected.' Will join us."[19]

The now legendary "First Exhibition by the Editorial Board of the *Blaue Reiter*" was held from 18 December 1911 to 1 January 1912 at the same time as the NKVM exhibition, also at the Thannhauser Gallery in Munich. Six paintings by Bloch were shown, a considerable total only matched by Gabriele Münter. Apart from the painting entitled *Hamlet Composition*, all of the works listed in the catalogue can be identified: *View of a Factory* (fig. 2), *Procession of the Cross* (pl. 9), *The Three Pierrots No. 2* (pl. 5), *Head [of Christ]* (Mrs. Albert Bloch), and *Harlequinade* (pl. 4).[20] The latter was also illustrated in the small catalogue of the exhibition. In the photographs which Gabriele Münter took at the Thannhauser Gallery, several of Bloch's paintings can clearly be seen alongside her own works and those of August Macke (figs. 8, 9).

The jovial postcard which the new Blue Rider group sent from the exhibition's opening party on 18 December at the

famous Schottenhamel hotel in Munich to the absent Robert Delaunay in Paris proves that Albert Bloch was also present that evening.[21] A photograph taken by Münter around the same

9. First Blue Rider Exhibition, Thannhauser Gallery, Munich, 1911, Photo: Gabriele Münter, Gabriele Münter- und Johannes Eichner-Stiftung, Munich

time shows several friends from the Blue Rider circle on the balcony of the apartment she shared with Kandinsky in Schwabing: Franz and Maria Marc, Kandinsky, Heinrich Campendonk, the Russian composer Thomas von Hartmann, and, standing at the center, the Berlin factory-owner Bernhard Koehler (fig. 10). Koehler, an uncle of August Macke's wife Elisabeth, was to become an important patron of the Blue Rider group and in 1913 purchased two of Bloch's paintings for his own collection.

After closing in Munich, the Blue Rider group's first exhibition toured for several years, first to Cologne and, in March 1912, to Herwarth Walden's newly founded Der Sturm Gallery in Berlin, one of the leading avant-garde galleries in Germany before World War I. Franz Marc made the initial preparations for this tour as early as the beginning of 1912, and on 2 January 1912 he wrote to Kandinsky from Berlin, "More than ever I regret now that Bloch had his *Harlequinade* reproduced [in the catalogue]."[22] Looking at Bloch's painting, which is strongly marked by a graphic drawing style, with figures moving in a rather forced, pantomime fashion, and particularly the slightly sentimental deportment of its principal figure, one may be able to appreciate why Marc did not regard *Harlequinade* as entirely appropriate to the endeavors of the Blue Rider group. At the beginning of March 1912, Marc continued, "Could Bloch's *Harlequinade* not be replaced by his picture of houses (reproduced in bl. Rider)?" — referring to Bloch's *Impression Sollnhofen*, illustrated in the *Blaue Reiter Almanac*. In fact, Bloch later recorded in his Record Book, started during his first years in Munich with photographs of his works, that he withdrew *Harlequinade* from the tour and added *Impression Sollnhofen* to it.

10. On the balcony of Kankinsky's Ainmillerstraße apartment, Schwabing, 1911. From left to right: Maria and Franz Marc, Bernhard Koehler, Heinrich Campendonk, and Thomas Hartmann; Seated: Wassily Kandinsky, Photo: Gabriele Münter, Gabriele Münter- und Johannes Eichner-Stiftung, Munich

And it was precisely this latter painting that subsequently met with harsh and even destructive criticism at several of the tour's stops. During the guest showing at Walden's Der Sturm Gallery, the illustrated supplement to the Berlin newspaper *Der Tag* reproduced *Impression Sollnhofen* on 26 March, along with works by Burljuk, Kandinsky, and Marc (fig. 11), commenting, "Apparently the town of Lilliput is being shown at the precise moment when Mr. Gulliver has just finished having his midday nap on top of it. Or perhaps it is a town that has just become ill due to an earthquake." Equally lacking in comprehension, and even more sharp in tone, the *Leipziger Tageblatt* of 27 March 1912 wrote, "A. Bloch is exhibiting a painting, *Impression from Sollnhofen*…. This type of art is certainly Impressionism … the fact that in terms of drawing the buildings depicted are impossible needs attract no further attention; however, the fact that the proportions are apparently really not supposed to hit you in the face demands a considerable amount of blind faith in the reforming mission of the new art."[23] Even in a review of the exhibition during its later stop at the Folkwang Museum in Hagen, in which Bloch's paintings are discussed in detail, and somewhat positively, *Impression Sollnhofen* was given a negative reception.[24]

With these press reviews it should be remembered that Kandinsky, Marc, Jawlensky, and others did not receive any better treatment, and sometimes received worse. The height of these attacks, directed mainly at Kandinsky, occured when the Blue Rider exhibition was shown in September 1912 at the Kunstsalon Ludwig Bock in Hamburg. Here and at subsequent stops on the tour, Bloch had altered his selection considerably; he showed *Impression Sollnhofen*, *Piping Pierrot* (pl. 13), *Dance*, *Figural Composition*, and *Serenade* (fig. 12). The newspaper *Altonaer Nachrichten* wrote on 7 September 1912:

> Albert Bloch, the group's figure painter, has developed a fabulous skill in designing people who look as if they have been made out of cake dough. A few years ago we saw a stall at the Hamburg Fair, with the last remnants of the now almost extinct Aztec tribe. They were exactly the same kind of pointed creatures, looking like larvae without blood, juice, or spine, that Bloch is showing us here on a large canvas…. There seem to be half a dozen of these unhappy people here having a real boxing-match with each other to the accompaniment of music. Will the sack of white flour in the middle manage to throw down the brown apprentice pushing forward against him so impetuously? Their hot-tempered eagerness for the fray has apparently encouraged the others to assiduous work, as they are winding their way round them in eel-like coils like rubber men.[25]

Albert Bloch must have been particularly hard hit by such criticism, since in his Harlequin and dance paintings he was attempting, among other things, to express pure emotion through the moving human figure by the rhythm of line and form — and for this purpose, precisely in the phase around

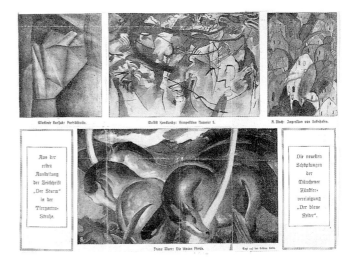

11. Illustration from the Berlin newspaper *Der Tag*, 26 March 1912, Gabriele Münter- und Johannes Eichner-Stiftung, Munich

1912–13, had largely abstracted all the details from his Pierrots and clowns to reduce them to the simplest body types and robed figures.

In the meantime, other important exhibitions had been taking place. From February to April 1912, the second exhibition, "Blue Rider: Black and White" was shown, including more than three hundred pieces of graphic work exclusively, and for the first time presenting the work of Paul Klee. Bloch participated with eight drawings, which are described in the exhibition catalogue simply as "Studies I–VIII," so that only some of them can now be identified. *Figure Between Houses* (pl. 61) was illustrated in the catalogue, and the stylistically similar and impressive black-and-white drawings *Dance* and *Suicide* (pl. 60) can be assigned to the group on the basis of old labels or inscriptions.[26]

In the spring of 1912, the final preparations for another important exhibition were also being made: the great "Sonderbund" exhibition, held in Cologne from May to September 1912, which was the most important exhibition of international avant-garde art in Europe during this period. A number of commissioners, museum officials, and gallery owners organized the exhibition with the assistance of the participating artists; August Macke, who was from the Rhineland area around Cologne, acted as mediator for the Blue Rider group. Several disagreements took place between the organizers and the Blue Rider group in advance of the exhibition; the Blue Rider artists did not feel that they were being adequately represented. At the end of May, a hasty decision was made to put together a small show of the paintings that had been refused for the Sonderbund exhibition. The exhibition was once again held at Walden's Der Sturm Gallery, this time in July 1912. The first letters from Marc to Bloch that survive refer to these events. Bloch had submitted his large new painting *Duel* (pl. 15) to the Sonderbund, along with others, and Marc was using his influence with Bernhard Koehler to persuade him to buy it, although without success. At the end of May 1912, when Bloch was traveling via Cologne and Bremerhaven to America for a few months to ask for financial assistance from his wife's relatives, Marc gave him the addresses of three of the Sonderbund commissioners — the museum directors Richard Reiche and Alfred Hagelstange from Barmen and Cologne, respectively, and the Düsseldorf gallery owner Alfred Flechtheim. Bloch did in fact have a meeting with at least Reiche and Hagelstange during his journey, and attempted to mediate in the matter of the "refused" paintings.[27] After some hesitation, Bloch also took part in the protest exhibition in Berlin, after the Sonderbund only accepted *Duel* from among the paintings he had submitted. It appears from the catalogue that the painting was shown in the same hall as works by Kandinsky, Marc, Macke, Jawlensky, and Erbslöh.

Duel appears, at first sight, to be slightly out of place in Bloch's oeuvre, in terms of both its theme and its formal qualities. It shows figures in elegant contemporary dress. The victorious marksman is in the right foreground in shirt and dress trousers with his pistol lowered. His second stands next to him in a coat with a top hat, and in the background a group gathers around the man who has been shot. At the front, on the edge of the painting, a figure with a pale face looks at the viewer, turning away from the scene like an embodiment of bad conscience. A small version of *Duel* (fig. 13), with fewer figures and a summary treatment of the landscape background, dated as early as September 1911, still shows a style resembling the "cautious" cloisonnism of the *Procession of the Cross* (pl. 9), which was probably produced at around the same period. In

the larger version, Bloch introduced the figure in the foreground, among other changes. As Henry Adams has rightly noted, this was surely influenced by Edvard Munch's similar use of figures to convey jealousy or psychological terror.[28]

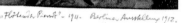
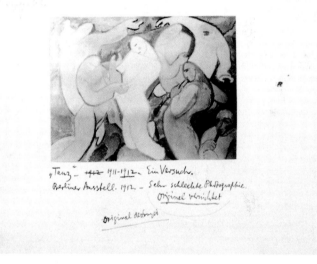

12. Page from the artist's Record Book, vol. I, with photographs of *Piping Pierrot*, *Impression Sollnhofen*, and *Dance*, 1911-12, Mrs. Albert Bloch

Bloch carried out some further elaboration of the costumes, as well as the landscape background, using fanned-out fields of color. It is possible that Bloch may have been inspired to produce this unusual depiction by a work by his fellow artist Gordon McCouch, which, with its Cubist formal language, was probably produced around 1910–11 (fig. 15).[29] McCouch, born in Philadelphia in 1885, flourished in Munich during the same period as Bloch, but soon moved to Porto di Ronco, near Ascona in Switzerland, where he lived and worked until his death in 1956; Bloch repeatedly referred to him as his oldest artist friend from the Munich period.[30] Another indication of possible connections between their depictions of duels is that

Bloch's *Duel (First Small Version)* of 1911 was formerly owned by McCouch in Ascona. Moreover, this idea was clearly not the only one they shared; for example, Bloch noted in his Record Book alongside the photo of his painting *Row of Houses* (1916; location unknown, formerly Kunstverein, Jena): "After a water-color, taken from a sketch by G. M. McCouch." Bloch's later drawing *The Bearer of Burdens* also seems to be based on a painting by McCouch. Bloch created a fine tribute to his friend in his poem *Gordon Mallet McCouch of the Casa Stella*, written in Lawrence at the end of the 1920s.[31]

In the spring of 1913, through the mediation of Marc, Bloch held his first large one-man exhibition at Max Dietzel's Munich gallery — an important event in any artist's life. Along-side older paintings from 1911 such as *Ragtime* (pl. 7), *Houses at Night* (pl. 8), and *The Three Pierrots No. 2* (pl. 5), he also showed some portraits he had painted during his visit to America in 1912, as well as new larger-format paintings — particularly the outstanding work *The Green Domino* (fig. 14, pl. 20). A variety of interpretations have been given to this depiction of a figure dressed in green, who stands at the center of the painting, facing the viewer frontally. She is placed against a prismatically splintered red and yellow background and is surrounded by a masked Harlequin, a red devil, and the hunchbacked, crooked-nosed figure of the "doctor" from the Italian *commedia dell'arte*, who often appears in Bloch's Harlequin paintings. The painting has been connected in particular with a famous contemporary Munich cabaret group, "The Eleven Executioners," and with the singer Mary Delvard. The painting does seem to assemble a specifically Munich cast of characters. However, it is more probable that the central figure with the ruff, the white-painted face, and the dark-ringed eyes is the Russian dancer Alexander Sakharoff, who also belonged to the NKVM and Blue Rider circles. Sakharoff, famous for his brilliant dancing and andro-gynous appearance, was a close friend of Jawlensky and von Werefkin, as well as Kandinsky, with whom he collaborated on the drafts of plays. In Jawlensky's well-known *Portrait of the Dancer Alexander Sakharoff* (fig. 16), the model, already made up and dressed to go on stage, is gazing out at the viewer from

14. *The Green Domino*, 1913, Mr. and Mrs. Elliot Goldstein

darkly made-up eyes in a similarly frontal fashion. Bloch's painting *The Dancer Sakharoff*, listed in Max Dietzel's exhibition catalogue of May 1913, shows that he also knew Sakharoff.[32] While the *commedia* types around the central figure are drawn from the familiar stock of figures in Bloch's paintings, the massive shape of a completely red devil with little horns, cropped at the right edge of the painting, is quite unusual. However, every

13. *Duel (First Small Version)*, 1911, Horst Kollman

15. Gordon McCouch, *Duel*, c. 1910-11, Mrs. Albert Bloch

16. Alexej Jawlensky, *Portrait of the Dancer Alexander Sakharoff*, 1909, Städtische Galerie im Lenbachhaus, Munich

17. Thomas Theodor Heine, *Simplicissimus as a Well-Wisher*, c. 1905, Städtische Galerie im Lenbachhaus, Munich

contemporary Munich viewer of the painting would instantly have identified the figure as the famous red *Simplicissimus* devil, which Thomas Theodor Heine sketched for the first *Simplicissimus* poster in 1896, and which had been the magazine's emblem, along with its red bulldog, ever since (fig. 17). As late as 1919 the figure was still to be seen aggressively in action on the *Simplicissimus* cover: *The Kiss of Peace*.

Over the next few years Bloch became increasingly better known and worked on improving his image as an artist. In February 1916 he even wrote in a letter to Herwarth Walden: "I would like to ask you to note the hyphen between my first name and my surname. Whenever my work is being discussed, I would like my name written as Albert-Bloch. There are many others with similar names who also work with brushes and paints. There has frequently been some confusion and this is always somewhat embarrassing. In this manner I would like to ensure that the public and the gentlemen of the press consider both of my names as one entity."

HERWARTH WALDEN AND OTHER PATRONS, 1913–16

It was not only his first one-man exhibition that made the year 1913 a decisive milestone in Bloch's career. As early as March, Marc had used his influence with Herwarth Walden, the director of Der Sturm Gallery in Berlin, to hold a separate exhibition of Bloch's work there.[33] During the year, Bloch's valuable affiliation with Marc deepened into friendship. During the spring, Marc and Kandinsky successfully arranged to have Bloch included in the planned large-scale "First German Autumn Salon" at Walden's Der Sturm Gallery. Marc was to become the central link between Bloch and the Blue Rider group in the following years until his early death in 1916. In his memoirs, Bloch himself emphasized that his personal contact with the individual artists in the group was not very extensive, and that he did not even know some of them — Macke, for example.[34] Marc increasingly became the one to whom Bloch turned to discuss both artistic and personal cares and worries.

In July 1913 Bloch wrote a long letter to Marc asking for his assistance in finding a long-term patron, such as Herwarth Walden or Bernhard Koehler, and mentioned that he would visit Marc in Sindelsdorf in Upper Bavaria. The visit must have taken place shortly afterward, and Bloch was able to see Marc's famous painting *Fate of the Animals* (see p. 203) almost finished on the easel, as he recalls in a long passage in his Denver lecture — as well as other large-scale works that Marc had finished that summer, such as *The Unfortunate Land of Tyrol* (fig. 23). As a souvenir of the visit, Bloch gave Franz Marc an untitled drawing (pl. 63). The drawing shows an original combination of personal and humorous references in a tangle of lines, with the Bavarian landscape in the background. Among other things, Bloch himself can be seen on a bicycle, with the tall figure of Marc at his easel. The hand covered in rings and holding a cigarette is that of the Berlin poet Else Lasker-Schüler, the divorced wife of Herwarth Walden; she was

18. Sketch for *The Death of Pierrot*, 1912-13, Present location unknown, Photograph from the catalogue of the "First German Autumn Salon," Berlin, 1913

another frequent visitor of Franz and Maria Marc during that year.[35] Marc thanked Bloch in a letter on 4 August 1913: "Your wonderful drawing has given us tremendous pleasure."

The fall and winter of 1913 brought two of the highlights of Bloch's period in Germany. First he participated in the "First German Autumn Salon" in Berlin, which united numerous younger artists from twelve different countries and took stock for the first time of the developments of Expressionism, Cubism, and Futurism. In it, Bloch was able to show three of his paintings and two drawings,[36] and both *Still Life I* and *The Death of Pierrot* were purchased directly from the exhibition by Bernhard Koehler (fig. 18).[37] Shortly before the closing of the Autumn Salon came the second triumph. Bloch traveled to Berlin to be present at the hanging of his own large one-man exhibition, which followed immediately in December 1913. In addition to the many paintings by his colleagues of the Autumn Salon such as Marc, Campendonk, and Klee, he was also able to see several works by Feininger and, for the first time, three paintings by Marc Chagall. There were also a number of large, astounding compositions by Kandinsky, the suggestive power of which this time even the press was unable to resist. Bloch also received for the first time a remarkable and positive response to his work. On 19 September 1913 the *Berliner Zeitung am Mittag*, for example, wrote that Macke, Feininger, and Bekhtejeff belonged to a moderate group, along with the "Munich artist Albert Bloch, who in his painting *The Death of Pierrot* presents an immediately effective vision."[38]

Bloch was impressed by the panorama of work represented at the Autumn Salon, and was given a very warm welcome by Herwarth Walden and his wife Nell, who introduced him to Lyonel Feininger and Hans Arp.[39] On returning to Munich, Bloch wrote to thank them for, among other things, a musical evening at the couple's home: "I haven't seen Kandinsky yet; nobody so far. I'll have a lot to tell them: about the Autumn Salon, Koehler's collection, your music, the fine collection that your ladyship has!"[40] For Bloch, Walden's encouragement was decisive during the subsequent years; by 1917, the dealer had shown Bloch's works at more than a dozen individual and group exhibitions in his gallery in Berlin, as well as in other cities, both in Germany and abroad. The fact that Bloch was — alongside Chagall and Kokoschka — one of the most frequently exhibited artists in the Sturm circle has been largely forgotten today.

Bloch's very first Der Sturm exhibition in December 1913 met with a positive reception. The *Berliner Börsenkurier* wrote on 25 December 1913, "The twentieth exhibition at the Sturm mainly presents a large number of paintings by the previously unknown artist Albert Bloch, whose name will be one to remember...." It continues, mentioning, among other things, "the shadowy ghost world of his *Summer Night*" (pl. 19).[41] In fact, this new painting, which Bloch had added to this collection — which was mostly identical to that shown at Max Dietzel's gallery — represents a new achievement in his work. The painting, in remarkably cool, icy violet and green-tinged tones, with its mute and mysterious figures scattered across a flowing landscape, is another of his works that demands interpretation. *Summer Night* is also one of the few paintings by Bloch in which he eschews the narrative accessories of his Harlequins and clowns. The artist reduces the bald-headed figures to a basic physical schema with emphatic hand gestures, while at the same time achieves an increased degree of spiritualization. According to tradition, the painting was based on a poem by the Symbolist writer Otto Julius Bierbaum, who at that time had moved with his famous journal *Die Insel* from Berlin to Munich, and was a friend of Franz Blei, Max Halbe and Karl Wolfskehl. This interpretation is based on a 1922 entry in the catalogue of the Arthur Jerome Eddy collection in Chicago, although it was later disputed by Bloch.[42] Positive evidence that it is indeed correct, however, may be provided by a note in Bloch's own handwriting on one of his drawings from 1913: "Summer night, dream summer night.... Bierbaum."[43]

It would certainly be rewarding to examine the extent to which other compositions by Bloch from the period around 1913–15, such as *The Heights* (pl. 68), *Song I* (pl. 22), and *Kneeling Figures* (private collection), are related to the German Expressionist poetry of those years — such as that of Paul Scheerbart, Paul Zech, Frank Wedekind, and Alexander von Bernus. The explicitly conceptual content of these unusual pictorial inventions appears to suggest that Bloch's own imagination meshed in a unique way with the poetry of others. The fact that Bloch was intensely preoccupied with contemporary German, and particularly Munich, literature is shown, among other things, by his series "German Writers in

Caricature," produced in the winter of 1912–13 and published in fall 1913 in two successive issues of the New York magazine *International: A Review of Two Worlds.* In brief comments, Bloch provides characterizations of Maximilian Harden, Hermann Bahr, Frank Wedekind, Hermann Sundermann, Max Halbe, Gustav Meyrink, Edgard Steiger, Karl Ettlinger, Arthur Schnitzler, Max Liebermann, Franz Blei, Thomas T. Heine, Ludwig Thoma, Friedrich Freska, Ernst von Wolzogen, Erich Mühsam, Heinrich Mann, and Karl Kraus.[44] The sale of these pieces to the *International* must have eased Bloch's financial difficulties slightly, particularly from 1913 on. At the beginning of the year, Reedy had ceased to pay his stipend. Even before this, Bloch had supplied caricatures to the *Lustige Blätter* in Berlin, nine of which were published between 1910 and 1912. In 1913 Bloch also produced a series of etchings, all taken from favorite larger paintings of the previous three years, such as *Houses at Night* (pl. 78), *Duel* (pl. 79), and *The Three Pierrots No. 2* (pl. 5).[45] The etchings were probably produced for sale, like the numerous drawings in pen and ink, watercolor, or colored pencil, with "after my own painting" listed again and again in Bloch's exhibition catalogues between 1913 and 1919.

Under these circumstances, Kandinsky again provided Bloch with tremendous assistance when, in the fall of 1913, he turned to the American collector Arthur Jerome Eddy with "enthusiastic" words for him.[46] At this time, Eddy had already purchased works by Kandinsky himself, Marc, and Münter. Eddy then became the most important collector of Albert Bloch's work, and during the following years purchased at least twenty-five paintings and twenty-four etchings from him.[47] As early as the first edition of his book *Cubists and Post-Impressionism* in 1914, Eddy mentions Bloch in a very positive, although rather general way, introducing him with the words, "A. Bloch is a young American living in Munich, who has allied himself with the Blue Knights and made an impression by his very personal expressions." In 1915, Eddy initiated a large one-man exhibition of Bloch's work in Chicago, and the collector wrote an introduction that was as full of praise as it was verbose and superficial. However, despite this very substantial encouragement from Eddy, Bloch apparently felt that the collector had not shown him appropriate appreciation either financially or artistically — the latter probably causing him more bitterness than the low selling prices. Looking back, he wrote to Kandinsky in 1936, "I will never forget the way in which you did everything possible for me and for my work whenever you could. Eddy was a pathetic exploiter as a collector (and an even more pathetic illiterate as a writer about art), but how glad I was at the time to let myself be exploited by him: he kept my head above water for a couple of years!"[48] In a poem written in the late 1930s in the *Sonnets to the Dead* Bloch settled the score with his former patron Arthur Jerome Eddy in no uncertain terms.[49]

Bloch again was stimulated by Kandinsky's art around this time, as seen, for example, in the background design of his *Three Pierrots No. 2* of 1911. The impression made by Kandinsky's large, almost totally abstract *Improvisations* and *Compositions* at the "First German Autumn Salon," and probably also by studies

seen in Kandinsky's Munich studio, is apparent in several of Bloch's works created around 1913–14. For example, Bloch's *Working Drawing for a Picture* of 1913 (fig. 19) shows dissolving, semi-abstract landscape forms in Kandinsky's style, although the impression of floating color zones is still emphasized by

19. *Working Drawing for a Picture*, 1913, Mrs. Albert Bloch

the broad, ink borders around the individual shapes. In addition, Bloch even marked the areas with handwritten color notations, a process developed by Gabriele Münter, which she maintained throughout her life, and which Kandinsky was using precisely in the period around 1912–13 in the complex compositional sketches for his large paintings.[50] With the subject of the three Pierrots, however, Bloch preserved particular elements in the background that belonged to his own thematic world, and left the human figure untouched. The same is true of Bloch's ambitious painting *Harlequin with Three Pierrots* (pl. 21), the largest painting he produced in his entire artistic career; the work has justifiably been compared on many occasions with Kandinsky's large *Composition IV* (fig. 20) since Ernst Scheyer first drew attention to the connections between the two paintings in 1963.[51] The dissolving zones of color with the use of yellow, orange, red madder, white, and black are unusual for Bloch and are borrowed from Kandinsky, as are the three large black lines cutting through the center of the painting. The lines are a reminiscence of the spears of the "Guardians," stylized into graphic ciphers, and a veiled motif based on Kandinsky's *Composition IV.* Bloch's study drawing for the painting (pl. 67) — with its color specifications given in German describing the

20. Wassily Kandinsky, *Composition IV*, 1911, Kunstsammlung Nordrhein-Westfalen, Düsseldorf

quality of the colors and transitions with words such as "bright," "coldly quiet," "becoming deeper," and "delicate" — is incomparably closer in technique to Kandinsky than to the work of any other artist in the Blue Rider circle.

The painting of a white clown resting in a colored space, *Reclining Figure* of 1911 (pl. 12), which Bloch later incorporated into a composition with several figures (fig. 21), had already reflected the influence of Kandinsky, although in a more timid fashion. Bloch gave Kandinsky the oil study for *Reclining Figure* as a present, while he, in turn, owned a watercolor sketch for Kandinsky's *Composition VII*.[52] However, the large version of *Reclining Figure* of 1914 (formerly Eddy Collection, Chicago), with its Symbolist mood and the Pierrot in an expressive dancing posture at the center, "hunted" or "enchanted" by a Harlequin, seems to lack any compelling sense of coherence, either in content or form. Bloch himself seems to have noticed that he had reached a point of ossification in his Harlequin and clown paintings.

The last paintings of this type were produced in 1915, with the final version of the much reworked *Frieze for a Music Room* (see p. 19) and a repetition of his *Harlequinade*, which he had produced in a number of variations and media (pls. 4, 50). Bloch noted in his Record Book about *Frieze for a Music Room*: "The first attempts, 1910–11–12– 13 — all destroyed. Finally completed *1915*. Exhib. 'Sturm,' Berlin 1916." The last note refers to Bloch's two-man exhibition with Paul Klee at Der Sturm Gallery in 1916. When his *Frieze* received special praise in the press, while Paul Klee was criticized, Bloch protested: "If the month wasn't so far advanced, I would prefer to withdraw the *Frieze for a Music Room* from the exhibition, as I did before with a painting on a similar occasion. I suppose it is good, although it represents a phase of my development that is already over." Bloch recognized that it was time to reorient himself, and new influences can be seen in his paintings around 1915.

Kandinsky's artistic influence on Bloch is obvious in the period around 1913–14 — in his memoirs Bloch emphasizes Kandinsky's inspirational power, in spite of his later serious

reservations about his art and that of other "Modernists"[53] — although their personal contacts during the Blue Rider years remained only haphazard.[54] By contrast, Bloch's relationship with Franz Marc intensified in its intimacy. After the outbreak World War I in August 1914, Bloch's personal relationship with Marc, who had been drafted and sent to the Western front, became more rather than less intense; it was maintained through an active correspondence. Among other things, Bloch sent parcels with food, cigars, and German newspapers to his friend in the trenches. In the spring of 1915 Marc sent him an essay, "The European Idea," that he had written at the front. Bloch immediately suggested translating it into English for an American newspaper. Surprisingly, Marc eagerly took up this suggestion, and commissioned Bloch to carry out the difficult task of translation.[55] When Marc, on leave from the front, returned to Sindelsdorf in July 1915 he visited Bloch in Munich; during his second and last period of leave in November of the same year he also went to see Bloch, but he missed him — a

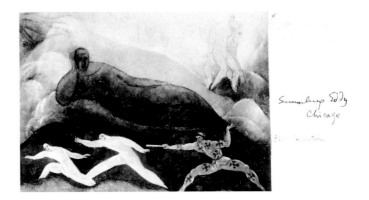

21. *Reclining Figure*, 1913, Present location unknown, Photograph from the artist's Record Book, vol. I, Mrs. Albert Bloch

fact that brought back painful memories to Bloch even decades later.[56]

Marc's artistic work, unlike Kandinsky's, appears at first glance to be of little significance for Bloch's painting. On closer examination, however, it becomes apparent that Marc's art not only left its mark on Bloch's early expressionistic work, but also had lasting influence — both in concrete formal elements and as an "intellectual message." In fact, it had a more lasting influence on him than that of any other artist's work. A painting such as Bloch's *Mountain Village* of 1915 (fig. 22) — with its division into turbulent zones of landscape, its scattered houses, its mountain peaks soaring up with a relieflike quality, and its three crucifixes on the hill at the left — irresistibly calls to mind one of Marc's major works, *The Unfortunate Land of Tyrol* of 1913 (fig. 23).

Marc's painting attracted attention at the "First German Autumn Salon" and Bloch had certainly seen it earlier, during his visit to Sindelsdorf. The link between the two paintings is particularly emphasized by the three backlit crucifixes, which Bloch, with his own special pathos, intensifies into an allusion to Golgotha. In Marc's work their arrangement transforms the entire landscape into a graveyard and makes it into a metaphor for existential suffering.

One reason why the influence of Marc's formal language is less noticeable than that of Kandinsky's is that Bloch's reception of Marc's painting was apparently mediated in part through Heinrich Campendonk. A contemporary of Bloch's, born in 1889, Campendonk had moved to Sindelsdorf in 1911, along with Helmuth Macke, a cousin of August Macke, and became a close neighbor of Marc's. The relationship of Macke and Campendonk toward the older and more mature Marc, to whom they looked up so much, was like that of students toward a respected teacher. Bloch naturally also took his place in this network of adulatory relationships with Marc, and particularly during 1916–18 grew closer to Campendonk.[57] There is a great deal of evidence of close personal contact between Bloch and Campendonk; for present purposes, we need refer only to a letter from Bloch to Walden from the spring of 1917: "Last

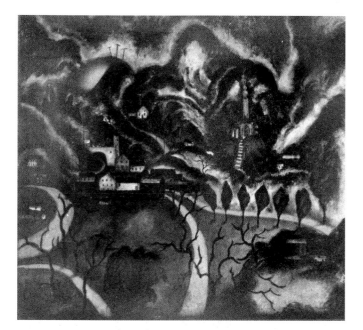

22. *Mountain Village*, 1915, Present location unknown, Photograph from the artist's Record Book, vol. I, Mrs. Albert Bloch

week I visited Campendonk at Seeshaupt for a break. He's been painting some very fine things again recently."[58] Without going into a detailed discussion of Campendonk's painting, it can be said that during this phase of his work, Campendonk was transforming Marc's pictorial inventions into softer, lyrical, often fairy-tale-like and even sometimes folkloric elements, usually by transferring them to Bavarian landscape scenery. This pleasing style, without the strong ruptures that distinguish every genuine invention in art, may have been particularly suited to Bloch's more moderate approach. A painting such as his *Monastery* of 1916–17 (fig. 24) clearly reflects these influences. Beside the photograph of it in his Record Book, Bloch notes, "I print for Campendonk." He added the same note to the photograph of his painting *Mountain* (pl. 28), which with its prismatically

splintered, transparently luminous, colored landscape forms once again directly reflects the influence of Marc.

As early as December 1916, Bloch and Campendonk presented a joint exhibition at the Kunstverein in Jena. Their correspondence with the director of the Kunstverein, the painter and art historian Walter Dexel, indicates that a further joint exhibition was planned in the art building "Das Reich" (The Empire) in Munich, recently founded by the Schwabing

23. Franz Marc, *The Unfortunate Land of Tyrol*, The Solomon R. Guggenheim Museum, New York

poet and art patron Alexander von Bernus. However, in the spring of 1918 Bloch exhibited his collection there without Campendonk.[59]

Bloch had been put in touch with Walter Dexel by another increasingly important fellow artist in Munich, Paul Klee.[60] In March 1916, Bloch and Klee had a two-man exhibition in Walden's Der Sturm Gallery in Berlin, which added the final touch to 1916 as the most successful exhibition year in Bloch's career.[61] Bloch received such positive commentary in the Berlin press, in contrast to that given Klee, that he felt compelled to write a letter of protest to Walden: "I find it unbearable to be praised in this way as a contrast to Paul Klee," he wrote. "I should like to protest against this publicly. Not in any way in order to give myself personal satisfaction, however. What the critics write about me is generally of no importance — only not in this context. The only considerations that hold me back are an inhibition about stepping forward in such a personal matter and a fear of creating the impression that Paul Klee needs anyone else's help."[62] Walden reacted immediately, printing Bloch's letter, along with a short reply, in an April issue of his journal, *Der Sturm*.[63]

In the following years, Bloch became closer to Klee, visiting him and exchanging works with him. Klee's art was to be the final decisive artistic influence on him from the Blue Rider circle. His relationship with Klee may have been all the more important to Bloch when, in March of 1916, Marc's death in action affected him so deeply.

THE YEARS 1917–21

In the spring of 1917 Bloch and Campendonk were present at the reburial of Franz Marc's remains in the cemetery in Kochel.[64] Since Marc's death, Bloch had kept in touch with his friend's widow, Maria, mainly by letter, and he had helped her to organize the large-scale commemorative exhibition for Marc that was held in the Münchner Neue Sezession in the fall of 1916.[65]

Unfortunately, Albert Bloch destroyed a particularly large number of the paintings he produced during 1917–18. From the contemporary photographic documentation in his second Record Book, which begins at this time and ceases during his visit to Ascona in 1921, it can be seen that practically all of the works produced in the first half of this period were in a style resembling that of *Deserted Village* of 1917 (fig. 25). Now often in long, oblong formats, they mostly show imaginary landscape spaces, often nocturnal, with intersecting zones. Scattered through the landscapes are plant motifs — graphically drawn trees or stylized plants — and architectural elements — small houses and churches with illuminated windows. In their style, in the fusion of organic and inorganic elements, with symbolic shorthand for plants and architecture, as well as in their subject matter, these paintings are extraordinarily close to Klee's painting of the same period. This is seen even in the use of titles, such as *Deserted Village, Deserted Villa,* and *Night in the Valley.* Klee's *Marsh Legend* of 1919 (fig. 27) can serve here as one example of his painting and work on paper during this period.

In 1918, as an *Homage to Klee,* Bloch painted a landscape with two men, two houses, and a cow, signed "AB to Paul Klee" (fig. 26).[66] The two men with hats probably represent a self-portrait of Bloch on the left and a portrait of Klee. Bloch is apparently trying to hold back the small, striding figure of the dark-bearded Klee, who turns away from him. Here, too, the transparent white silhouettes of the houses and the suggestion of trees strongly recall the work of Klee.

While 1916 brought Bloch a painful loss with the death of Marc, it also brought him an enriching personal encounter. Since 1915, for financial reasons, Bloch had been giving private art lessons. In 1916 Emmy Klinker, a young woman from Barmen in the Rhineland, became one of his students (fig. 28).[67] Bloch and Klinker soon developed a close relationship, which is reflected both in their later correspondence and in documents from the period when they were both in Munich.[68] Emmy Klinker's father, legal counselor Richard Klinker, became an enthusiastic purchaser of Bloch's paintings; Bloch's second Record Book lists numerous paintings in Klinker's possession, almost all of which were destroyed by fire in Barmen during World War II.[69] In June 1917 Bloch approached Walden to see whether it would be possible for Emmy Klinker to exhibit at Der Sturm Gallery, and the following year a joint exhibition

24. *Monastery,* 1916-17, Present location unknown, Photograph from the artist's Record Book, vol. I, Mrs. Albert Bloch

25. *Deserted Village,* 1917, destroyed, Photograph from the artist's Record Book, vol. I, Mrs. Albert Bloch

of her work along with that of Bloch, Elisabeth Niemann, and Kurt Schwitters did in fact take place.[70] Bloch wrote to Walden on 17 June 1917 in this connection: "Klinker's works are strong and very independent, and there's something tremendously *self-sufficient* about them." A glance at a work such as Klinker's *View of Schwabing* (fig. 29), a photograph of which has survived in Bloch's estate, confirms this assessment.

While the overriding influence of Klee ebbed for Bloch after 1918, his work remained linked to that of Campendonk;

26. *Untitled (Landscape with Two Men, Two Houses, and a Cow, Homage to Klee)*, 1918, Kunstmuseum Bern, Paul Klee-Stiftung

27. Paul Klee, *Marsh Legend*, 1919, Städtische Galerie im Lenbachhaus, Munich

Bloch's *Woodland Idyll* of 1918, which was illustrated in the second edtion of the Munich art historian Fritz Burger's book *From Cézanne to Hodler*, once again reflects a phase that had passed (figs. 30, 32).

Another central impulse of this period can only be touched on briefly here: that of Marc Chagall's extremely unconventional and inspiring early work, which Bloch was able to see on several occasions at Walden's Der Sturm Gallery.[71] The strengthened color forms, often with a sweet, reddish-yellowish palette, in Bloch's still lifes from 1916 on are the first signs of Chagall's influence, as are the introduction of animals such as doves, and the motif of the dog, which hereafter appears again and again. In essence, it may have been Chagall who showed Bloch the way back to a clear form of figurative objectivity, which at the same time could incorporate fairy-tale and naïve elements.

There is an obvious quotation from Chagall in Bloch's ambitious painting *Sunday Afternoon* (fig. 31), which successfully demonstrates this new style. The violin player in hat and coat, here placed in an elevated position at a window, is a reference to Chagall's then already famous painting *The Fiddler* of 1912–13 (fig. 33), in which the figure is seen in the same hat and coat, floating large and upright over a landscape of houses.[72]

Bloch subsequently explored in greater depth the naïve quality gleaned from this new source of influence. In his depictions of childlike wooden figures — which towards the end of the war clearly include a sociocritical component — between toy houses, or in flowering landscapes with butterflies and dogs,

28. Emmy Klinker on an excursion near Munich, c. 1917-19, Courtesy of Mrs. Albert Bloch

29. Emmy Klinker, *View of Schwabing*, c. 1918-20, Present location unknown, Courtesy of Mrs. Albert Bloch

31. *Sunday Afternoon*, 1918, destroyed during World War II, Photograph from the artist's Record Book, vol. II, Mrs. Albert Bloch

Bloch went so far that in 1920 the well-known Munich critic Leopold Zahn described him in the journal *Der Ararat* as belonging to a new trend in art, "corresponding to a pure infantilism … a childlike quality of perception and experience" (fig. 34).[73]

Der Ararat was published by the art dealer Hans Goltz at the end of 1918, initially as a political leaflet, but it soon continued as an avant-garde art journal. In it, three drawings by Bloch were published in 1918–19: for the first leaflet issue, he produced the cover, showing a broken Ark with two pairs of noisy donkeys and pigs as a satire on the "peace politicians," and the drawing *The Hand of the Entente* (fig. 35), in which two intimidated German "academic socialists" in the new democratic government after the German capitulation are being held captive.[74] All of these drawings have a markedly stiff, naïve style; Bloch had abandoned the elegant line art of the *Mirror* caricatures.

In the dense pen drawing *The Black Street (Barmen-Ruhrdistrict)* (fig. 36), new possibilities arose in which Bloch

30. *Woodland Idyll*, 1918, destroyed, Photo from the artist's Record Book, vol. II, Mrs. Albert Bloch

32. Heinrich Campendonk, *Family Picture*, c. 1914, Städtische Kunsthalle, Bielefeld

using themes and stylistic means that were also being developed by Campendonk (fig. 38).[76]

In 1919 Hans Goltz organized at his gallery the last, and also the largest, one-man exhibition in Germany of Bloch's work during his lifetime. This show also served to take stock of his creative work during the Munich period. To accompany

33. Marc Chagall, *The Fiddler*, 1912-13, Stedelijk Museum, Amsterdam

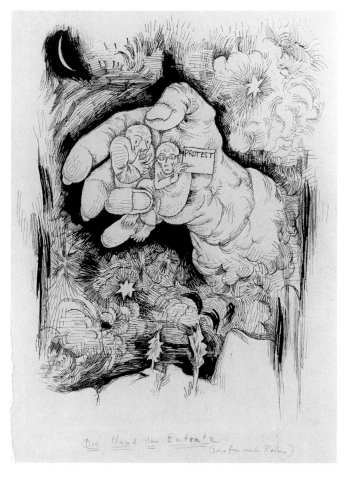

35. *The Hand of the Entente*, 1918, sketch for *Der Ararat*, Städtische Galerie im Lenbachhaus, Munich

further developed this style.[75] Here, and in the 1920–21 paintings, his last two years in Germany, emerge the sociocritical topics which other artists were also trying to address in the face of the misery of the postwar period, with war cripples, poverty, and mourning. In paintings such as *Interior* (pl. 30), painted after his return to Munich from Ascona at the end of 1920 and dedicated to Emmy Klinker, Bloch succeeded convincingly,

34. *Adoration*, 1917-18, destroyed, Photograph from the artist's Record Book, vol. II, Mrs. Albert Bloch

the exhibition, the December 1920 issue of *Der Ararat* was dedicated to Bloch and included a series of illustrations, among them the interesting painting *Sleepwalker* (1918; private collection, formerly owned by Hans Goltz). As was the procedure with all of "Goltz's" artists (Goltz had taken over the artistic representation of Bloch's work after the disagreement with Walden in 1918), Bloch was invited to provide an autobiographical statement in his issue of the journal. Bloch's one-page note, "In Place of an Autobiography," is very revealing with regard to his growing unwillingness to participate in the art business, the way in which he was increasingly distancing himself from the art of his own time, and his tendency towards withdrawal and isolation. It anticipates attitudes that would make a mark on his late work.[77] At the same time, with its closing statement of thanks to Goltz terminating their business relationship, it was marked by a mood of farewell. Bloch was

36. *The Black Street-(Barmen-Ruhrdistrict)*, 1921, Mrs. Albert Bloch

already embarking on his final departure for home. He had only returned to Munich from Switzerland one last time to put his affairs in order, and he spent the months up to March 1921 with Emmy Klinker.

One of the first important paintings Bloch produced in America is the strange picture *Group of Three* (fig. 37, pl. 31), with two silent women and a man in a claustrophobically small room with a wooden floor and walls. Here again, the painting might be compared with one by Chagall, his *Sabbath* of 1910 (fig. 39), which shows a group of three figures, arranged differently in a box-like, wooden room, and similarly viewed from above. Bloch's and Chagall's paintings share, above all, their

mood of silent expectation and vague uncertainty. The subject of *Group of Three* preoccupied Bloch for a long period; in 1935 he made a watercolor of it, and in 1942 a second version in oils. In his personal anthology of texts, "Ishmael's Breviary," which he continued with determination in the United States, Bloch wrote a passage about this painting as well as, around 1932–33, a poem over three pages long, *Group of Three*. With their suggestive undertow effect, the lines are among the most impressive lyrics that Bloch wrote, and at the same time provide a fascinating insight into potential ways of interpreting his art:

The stillness cries above the silence,
the room is clamorous with its hush…
The clock there on the wall behind them—round face, flat face,
face scarred in numerals,
numerals for features, features heedless, helpless, blank—
unexpectant…
It must be afternoon—you cannot know,
but it must be afternoon, some time in the afternoon.
You feel that it is afternoon,
late afternoon bending toward evening…
Do you hear that the clock ticks—do you hear?
Its ticking is loud, the stillness is louder,

it drowns the ticking of the clock…
There is no air. The window is closed, the window is open—
you cannot know. They do not know
there is no air …
Hearken unto me ye nations
and give ear unto my words thus
saith the Lord God of Israel
behold I shall smite—
there is no air…[78]

37. *Group of Three*, 1921, Michael Hasenclever Galerie, Munich

38. Heinrich Campendonk, *The Poor*, 1918, Kaiser Wilhelm Museum, Krefeld

39. Marc Chagall, *Sabbath*, 1910, Wallraf-Richartz-Museum, Cologne

40. Albert Bloch's study and bedroom, 1961; above the chest of drawers are four Hinterglas paintings depicting religious scenes, Courtesy of Mrs. Albert Bloch

With its variation of forms, *Group of Three* presents a concluding assessment of Bloch's "interior" style during the postwar years in Germany. At the same time, it heralds a transformation to a different type of popular pictorial language, which, to some extent, was to characterize his work on his return to America.

In the discussion of Bloch's early Expressionist work during the period from 1909 to 1921, much has been said about the various influences on him of his fellow artists, whose work Bloch was constantly assimilating into his own style in unconventional ways. In spite of all his success, however, Bloch during this period of his creative work obviously remained dissatisfied by these outside influences. He destroyed more than half of his early work. In addition, by 1930 at the latest, he had clearly dissociated himself from his "modern" past in Munich, henceforth declaring himself a traditionalist and preserver of declining values.

Bloch's late thinking and creative work from the 1930s to the 1950s, with its marked cultural pessimism, admiration for Karl Kraus, and very noticeable orientation toward the art of the Old Masters, particularly those of early Renaissance Italy, is worthy of separate investigation. However, an important aspect of Bloch's work created after his return to America is an attitude still entirely shaped by the tradition of German idealism, and with which Bloch continued to uphold the spiritual message of the Blue Rider movement as he lived in what he often described as the cultural "desert" of his American surroundings (figs. 40, 41).

41. Albert Bloch's study and bedroom, 1961; above the head rest of his bed are portraits of Karl Kraus, and on the very top are two photos of Kraus's grave, Courtesy of Mrs. Albert Bloch

1. Bloch to Butler, 23 June 1923, Archives, University of Kansas, Lawrence. See Anthology, pp. 197–99.

2. See also Annegret Hoberg, ed., *Leo Samberger*, exh. cat. (Munich: Neue Pinakothek, 1986). Bloch himself, in his essay "Portraits and the Painter" written in Munich in 1916, classifies Franz von Lenbach as belonging to "this poor dead art [which] would, by now, be definitely at rest" (in the *Smart Set*, 69 [October 1922], p. 92).

3. Compare with his etchings of 1909–12, for example, Bloch's written contributions to the *Mirror*: "The Beggar," 16 December 1909, "Derelicts," 23 June 1910, "Compositions in Monochrome," 15 February 1912, and "Compositions in Monochrome," 7 March 1912.

4. Albert Bloch, "The Work of Henri Matisse," *Mirror*, 14 May 1908, p. 9. Bloch's verdict on one of the oil paintings is: "a small square of cardboard, covered over with crude, raw paint, making a most amazing jumble of color, and giving us no hint of what it is all about." He concludes, "In sharp contrast to these things in color are the drawings, etchings and lithographs on the farther side of the partition. Here we have Henri Matisse doing clearly the things he knows best how to do." I am grateful to Werner Mohr, Cologne, for generously providing copies of all of Bloch's written contributions to the *Mirror*, which he copied from the originals held by the Missouri Historical Society, St. Louis, for the purposes of his dissertation. See also Werner Mohr, "Albert Bloch as Caricaturist, Social Critic and Authorized Translator of Karl Kraus in America," Ph.D. diss., University of Kansas, 1995.

5. For example, Reedy writes to Bloch on 16 June 1909, "If as a matter of exercise in language you feel like translating a story from *Jugend* once in a while, I would be pleased to have it." (Letters from William Marion Reedy to Albert Bloch, Missouri Historical Society, St. Louis; Bloch's replies have unfortunately not survived.) On 2 August 1909, Reedy writes that Bloch's caricatures are good enough "to make a strong attack upon the citadel of *Simplicissimus*." Cited in Werner Mohr, "Albert Bloch: Caricaturist and Critic," *Albert Bloch: Artistic and Literary Perspectives*, eds. Frank Baron et al. (Munich: Prestel-Verlag, 1997), p. 40, note 21. Numerous further quotations from the correspondence between Reedy and Bloch are given in Mohr, "Albert Bloch as Caricaturist, Social Critic and Authorized Translator of Karl Kraus in America."

6. The earliest paintings surviving are *Man in Derby*, a still rather caricaturelike work signed "July 1909," and *Still Life, Geraniums*, "May 1910." Mrs. Albert Bloch.

7. Reedy to Bloch, 29 June 1909: "Now as concerns your return: do not jump at things too hastily. You know that when you departed the understanding was you were to be gone two years.... Cast around and see if you cannot get in your hooks at the other side — Munich, Berlin, Dresden, Paris, London, anywhere. That is what I would do if I had your gift, taste and twist in my art.... You say another year of study, leisurely reading and thinking would find you much better equipped than now. Agreed. But you can study and think and read even while you are working." Reedy Papers.

8. Unfortunately, only very sparse and vague details have been preserved from Bloch's various journeys to other German and European cities. In his later art historical lectures, Bloch mentions on one occasion that he had seen the paintings of the Italian Old Masters in museums "in New York, in Paris, in London, in Munich, Cologne, Frankfurt, in Berlin & Vienna."

9. Albert Bloch, "Kandinsky, Marc, Klee: Criticism and Reminiscence," no. 4 in typescript "Pictures and People: From a Painter's Point of View," lecture at the Denver Art Museum, 13 December 1934, p. 89 (hereafter Denver lecture). In the Denver lecture, Bloch mentions the influence of several French artists on the initial stages of his painting, including the statement, "Vincent van Gogh I loved at first sight." See Anthology, pp. 199–205.

10. The New Artists' Union was founded in January 1909 by Wassily Kandinsky, Alexej Jawlensky, Adolf Erbslöh, Alexander Kanoldt, Gabriele Münter, Marianne von Werefkin, and others, and in December 1909 presented its first exhibition at the Thannhauser Gallery. At the time of the second exhibition in 1910, Kandinsky — as Bloch correctly notes — was no longer the chairman of group; he had already resigned as chairman due to several disagreements.

11. Bloch goes on to describe in detail how the *Neue Münchner Nachrichten* refused to print Marc's statement of support, and how Marc then sent a copy of his letter to the group's secretary Adolf Erbslöh (i.e. not to Kandinsky). The NKVM then decided to print Marc's letter "in a folder" alongside the scandalous article by Rohe, and insert it in the catalogue.

12. It remains a question who enabled Bloch to participate in the exhibition. It could not have been the NKVM artists, with whom Bloch came into personal contact only later in the year, and who did not exhibit at the Berlin Secession themselves.

13. Bloch to Maser, 20 June 1955: "I got to know him [Franz Marc] through his work before I ever saw him personally, at an exhibition of his work at 'Die moderne Galerie' in Munich in early 1911. I was captivated by it

immediately, although it was clear to me that his talent, not his genius, was principally decorative. This was a painting that met my own needs and desires. Here was the new voice — something never heard before — the authentic new voice that was nevertheless constantly speaking with the respected traditional modulation." See Anthology, pp. 205–07.

14. See Wolfgang Venzmer, *Adolf Hölzel, Leben und Werk* (Stuttgart, 1982); Peg Weiss, *Kandinsky und München: Begegnungen und Wandlungen 1896-1914*, exh. cat. (Munich/Los Angeles: Prestel-Verlag, 1982), particularly pp. 54–55.

15. Kandinsky and other NKVM artists welcomed Bloch at the time as a fellow traveler, although Bloch recalled in his Denver lecture, "And it was while I was thus more or less helpless bumbling about that Marc and Kandinsky came upon me and found in me what they regarded as a promising recruit."

16. Frank Baron, "Albert Bloch, The Blue Rider and the Failure of the European Idea," *Albert Bloch: Artistic and Literary Perspectives*, pp. 23–30.

17. See also the first mention of Bloch by Franz Marc, in a letter of 11 October 1911 to Kandinsky: "Erbslöh has written off Bloch, Epstein and Bolz — I'll write to him about it." In Klaus Lankheit, ed., *Wassily Kandinsky, Franz Marc: Briefwechsel, mit Briefen von und an Gabriele Münter und Maria Marc* (Munich: Piper 1983), p. 66. Bloch himself had written to Erbslöh about this on 5 October. See Baron, "Albert Bloch, the Blue Rider and the Failure of the European Idea," note 15.

18. Lankheit, ed., *Wassily Kandinsky, Franz Marc: Briefwechsel*, p. 74. In his Denver lecture, Bloch suspects that he may have been one of the immediate reasons for the break with NKVM and the formation of the Blue Rider; he writes, "... quite innocently and unwittingly, I was indirectly responsible for the breaking up of the New Society of Munich." See Anthology, pp. 199–205.

19. Lankheit, ed., *Wassily Kandinsky, Franz Marc: Briefwechsel*, p. 81.

20. *The Three Pierrots No. 1* was formerly owned by Franz Marc, and is now in the Franz Marc Museum, Kochel.

21. The card includes a short note in French in Kandinsky's hand, signed by himself, Münter, Bernhard Koehler, Franz and Maria Marc, with Bloch adding "A votre santé Albert Bloch" underneath; postmarked 19 December 1911. Reproduced in *Delaunay und Deutschland*, exh. cat. (Munich, 1985), p. 485, Document 11/19.

22. Lankheit, ed., *Wassily Kandinsky, Franz Marc: Briefwechsel*, pp. 99–100.

23. This and all other press comments cited below, unless otherwise indicated, are from the Press Documentation held by the Gabriele Münter and Johannes Eichner Foundation, Munich. The Leipzig press notice on Bloch began, "The basic concept underlying the most recent modern painters emerges slightly more clearly in Bloch and Franz Marc, where it means not reproducing the individual impression of what is seen, but summing up the total of a series of observations of one and the same object in various situations."

24. *Zeitung Hagen*, 6 July 1912: "A. Bloch (Munich) places *The Three Pierrots* in moving lines, in which an effort to achieve the value of simplification can be sensed, on a gray-blue ground, with a very modest use of bright color providing a sensitive emphasis on the clown's dual existence. The sense of artistic measure is also revealed to some extent in the *Houses with Chimneys*." With *Impression Sollnhofen*, however, the review speaks of "childish drawing" and "moods that produced such confusion."

25. Bloch's *Serenade* and *Sketch of a Composition* are described in the same tone. On 24 September 1912, the *Altonaer Nachrichten* continued its offensive with a pamphlet attacking the "hare-brained future painting," and warning of the day "when people will start to like rubber men with triangular gallowslike faces like the ones that Gimmi [the Swiss artist Wilhelm Gimmi] and Bloch are producing in masses before our eyes..."

26. Mrs. Albert Bloch suspects that the drawings *Carnival Sketch, Sheep, Houses*, and *Harlequinade* (cat. no. 52) were "possible candidates" for the second Blue Rider exhibition. In the case of the watercolor *Harlequinade*, this was also suspected by Klaus Lankheit. The sheet derives from Paul Klee's estate, and was probably exchanged for Klee's own pen drawing *Horse Race* of 1911, which was also shown at the second exhibition in 1912, and was in Albert Bloch's possession until 1954 (now in the Miyagi Museum of Art, Senai, Japan).

27. This emerges from a long letter from Marc replying to Bloch on 7 June 1912. Marc closes by wishing Bloch "Much luck on your journey and for your years in America; hopefully you'll let us hear from you now and then, and you can be sure that this will always give us a great deal of pleasure." Collection of Mrs. Albert Bloch.

28. Evidence of Bloch's attention to the work of Edvard Munch is provided by his poem *The Deathbed Watchers: after a Lithograph of Edvard Munch*, written around 1932–33 for his collection of poems, *Ventures in Verse*. Bloch's painting *Deathbed* of 1915–16 (see Anthology, illustration on p. 173) also responds to the motif from Munch, although it makes it into an imaginary vision.

29. Location unknown; photo in the collection of Mrs. Albert Bloch.

30. They knew each other by 1910 at the latest, when Bloch etched *Profile of McCouch* and signed the plate "18-2-10 Mac."

31. "Portraits and People, No. 3" in "Ventures in Verse," I, unpublished manuscript, n.p., n.d. Courtesy of Mrs. Albert Bloch. The poem bears the epigraph "Your last letter brought back to me so vividly our Noctes Ambrosianae. I shall be writing soon. Meanwhile here this," and it begins with the lines:

> You call my name and rise with glass in hand.
> I sit here thirsting in an arid land.
> I dream your laugh as fancy's cup I drain,
> and — Looking at you! — drink to you again.

See also the long poem "Bread and Wine" in "Ventures in Verse," III.

32. In an article in his series "German Writers in Caricature" Bloch even mentions "the mimetic genius of Alexander Moissi [Sakharoff], the dancing of Clotilde van Derp." (Sakharoff's beautiful wife and dancing partner.)

33. In a card dated 6 March 1913, Marc tells Bloch, "I'll be writing to Walden today again about your collection."

34. Bloch, "Letter to Edward A. Maser," 20 June 1955 in *Albert Bloch: A Retrospective Exhibition of his Work from 1911-1955* (Lawrence: The University of Kansas Museum of Art, 1955), n.p. "In principle, the group as such did not really interest me at all, although I had a feeling that it, or rather Marc and Kandinsky, would make European art history. I took relatively little part in the group's activities, preferring to be alone with my work, exhibiting it when I was ready to, and spending the leisure time I allowed myself in the company of friends who had little connection with painting or the other arts. It was only with Franz Marc that the acquaintance deepened into friendship." See Anthology, pp. 205–07.

35. On the relationship between Marc and Lasker-Schüler, see Peter-Klaus Schuster, *Der blaue Reiter präsentiert seiner Hoheit sein Blaues Pferd: Cards and Letters* (Munich: Prestel-Verlag, 1987). That Bloch also knew Else Lasker-Schüler at this time is indicated by the fact that around 1913–14 during a visit to Munich she had already wanted to personally introduce him to Karl Kraus. She described Kraus as a writer from the Sturm circle. In his later *Ventures in Verse*, Bloch translated a few poems by Lasker-Schüler.

36. *Still Life I, The Death of Pierrot, Harlequin* as well as a *Portrait Study* and *Sketch of a Wrestling Match.*

37. Unfortunately, a large part of the Koehler Collection was lost in Berlin in 1945, or was transported to Russia and lost; Bloch's paintings are recorded in his Record Book, v. I, Mrs. Albert Bloch.

38. On the same day, the *Vossische Zeitung* wrote, "... Albert Bloch's *Harlequin* is not without graceful talent." The *Allgemeine Zeitung Berlin* of 20 September 1913 also emphasized that, among the many extremists, the more moderate figures of Macke, Feininger, "and the very lively Albert Bloch" were pleasant to note.

39. Bloch to Marc, 18 December 1913: "I found it an unusually fine and powerful representation of the new direction." See Anthology, p. 165.

40. Bloch to Walden, 3 December 1913. Further on, he writes, "McCouch sends his greetings and thanks you again. He is completely delighted." See Anthology, p. 171. Bloch does in fact appear to have enabled his friend to take part in the "Autumn Salon" through Marc; see the note from Marc to Bloch of 18 August 1913, stating that "a small landscape" by "your friend" had been accepted. McCouch's *Thunderstorm* is listed in the appendix to the "Autumn Salon" catalog as the final item, no. 366.

41. I am grateful to Frank Baron for drawing attention to this press comment.

42. "Exhibition of Paintings from the Collection of the Late Arthur Jerome Eddy," The Art Institute of Chicago, 1922, "Inspired by a poem by the late Max Bierbaum." In his copy of the catalogue, Bloch corrected the name in a handwritten note: "the name is Otto Julius B." (Eddy had called him "Max Bierbauer" in the foreword to the catalogue of Bloch's one-man exhibition in Chicago in 1915, adding "but the picture was *not* 'inspired' by his poem."

43. Now private collection.

44. Bloch's comments are distinguished not only by their being very well-informed, but also by their well-aimed judgements, which Bloch formulated in his typical style of criticism, which was sometimes biting. Eight original drawings from the series "German Writers in Caricature" are preserved in the collection of Mrs. Albert Bloch. The discovery of the publication of the series in the *International* was first made by Werner Mohr. See Mohr, in "Albert Bloch: Caricaturist and Critic," pp 33–34, note 5.

45. A copy of *Arabesque* (Estate of Gabriele Münter) is held by the Städtische Galerie im Lenbachhaus, Munich, Inv. No. GMS 672. Bloch copied his own compositions for this purpose, such as the pen drawing

Memorandum for an Etching, The Duel, 1913 (Dr. and Mrs. Nathan Greenbaum). A 1913 etching of two clowns entitled "Clowns von 1913" leads to the assumption that Bloch was also considering the publication of a portfolio.

46. In the second edition of his *Cubists and Post-Impressionism,* Eddy goes into more detail: "In October, 1913, Kandinsky wrote me a very enthusiastic letter regarding the work of Albert Bloch ... saying 'He works most energetically, accomplishes much, makes fine progress, and constantly gains in the form of his inner expression. Him, too, I really can recommend warmly.'" Arthur Jerome Eddy, *Cubists and Post-Impressionism,* 2nd ed. (Chicago: A. C. McClurg Co., 1919), p. 200. The quotation has been used by various writers about Bloch since it was first republished by Donald Humphry in the foreword to *Albert Bloch: A Retrospective Exhibition of His Work from 1911 to 1956,* exh. cat. (Tulsa: Philbrook Art Center, 1961), n.p.

47. See Paul Kruty, "Arthur Jerome Eddy and his Collection: Prelude and Postscript to the Armory Show," *Arts Magazine,* 61 (February 1987), pp. 40-47. Unfortunately, a substantial part of the Eddy collection was sold at auction by his heirs in Chicago in 1937, including seventeen paintings by Bloch, e.g. *Prize Fight, Entombment,* and *The Green Domino* (pls. 17, 23, 20).

48. Bloch to Kandinsky, 20 November 1936. See Anthology, pp. 187–89.

49. The poem *Arthur Jerome Eddy* in "Sonnets to the Dead" in "Ventures in Verse," III, unpublished manuscript, reads:

> Your exposition of the newer painting
> and your defense of "modernistic" trends,
> your well intended efforts at acquainting
> Philista with strange methods and their ends,
> showed up a quite illiterate Philistine
> explaining what he never understood
> still, your bad taste, consistent with our pristine
> native bad taste, worked neither harm nor good.
> And all in all, your indoor sport: collecting
> and talking up young painters, helped to keep
> some few from want; and one, who, not objecting
> that you should take such care to get him cheap,
> might for such benefit have been more grateful,
> had he not found your shallowness so hateful.

50. The color specifications in English are frequently "yellow," both for the background and for outlined color zones — another similarity with Kandinsky's technique — as well as "white" and "white to rose to purple to black."

51. Ernst Scheyer, "Albert Bloch: an American Blaue Reiter," in *Albert Bloch (1882-1961): An Exhibition of Watercolors, Drawings, and Drypoints,* exh. cat. (Lawrence: The University of Kansas Museum of Art, 1963), n.p.

52. *Reclining Figure,* 1911, was still in the Nierendorf Gallery, Berlin, in the 1960s. Presumably Kandinsky gave it to gallery during his period at the Bauhaus. His watercolor *Composition VII* was in Bloch's possession until 1954. See Anthology, p. 186, for illustration.

53. Even in his old age, when Bloch clearly described himself as a "traditionalist" which he provided for Maser, he also wrote, "I must point out that, in spite of my critical remarks about Kandinsky's work, I have never known anyone who could speak in a more inspired and inspiring way about the subjects that interest me than he did, and that I always found his work extraordinarily exciting then as well." In statements made closer to the time, Bloch was much more clearly on Kandinsky's side than in his later ones; for example, in his "German Writers in Caricature" in 1913, he introduced the writer and art critic Franz Blei with the words, "The possessor, probably, of the keenest aesthetic perception in Germany, despite the fact that he refuses to take the art of Kandinsky seriously." And in a handwritten note in the 1922 Eddy catalogue, he noted from an acquaintance alongside Kandinsky's *Improvisation 30 (Sea Battle),* "I wish you could realize its beauty. Even such a reproduction as this should give you *some* idea. Don't think of 'objects' — but try to concentrate upon the wonderful balance of color, line and form."

54. The remark by the more-than-eighty-year-old Gabriele Münter that Bloch was one of her "best friends," which has been persistently repeated since Eduard Roditi, "Interview with Gabriele Münter," *Arts Magazine,* 34 (January 1960), p. 36, certainly requires qualification. The fact that their personal contact in Munich was not all that close is shown, for example, by Kandinsky's question in a letter to Bloch of 2 April 1937, "Were you already married when we met in Munich?" See Anthology, pp. 189–90.

55. "The European Idea" was one of three essays that Marc wrote while he was at the front in 1914–15, along with "In the Purgatory of War" and "The Supreme Type." The German version was published in *Das Forum,* 1 (1914–15), pp. 632–38. Unfortunately, Bloch's translation was never published, and the manuscript has been lost. See Klaus Lankheit, *Franz Marc, Schriften* (Cologne, 1978), pp. 163–67, 225–26. See Baron,

"Albert Bloch, the Blue Rider and the Failure of the 'European Idea'" pp. 23–32.

56. For example, in a letter to Maria Marc of August/September 1935. See Anthology, pp. 178-80.

57. "Letter to Edward A. Maser:" "For a while I also saw a good deal of Campendonk. He visited me when he came to Munich, and I visited him in the country."

58. Bloch to Walden, 19 March 1917. Campendonk moved from Sindelsdorf to Seeshaupt on the Starnberger See in 1916. In a draft of a letter to Maria Marc of January 1937, Bloch recalls Campendonk much more critically.

59. See Bloch to Dexel, 6 January 1917. The exhibition that was already being planned for the spring of 1917 only took place a year later.

60. This emerges from a letter of 20 January 1963 from Grete Dexel to Bloch, who had died in the meantime. Courtesy of Mrs. Albert Bloch.

61. Twelve more paintings were sent to Arthur Jerome Eddy from this exhibition in the fall of 1916, and he purchased most of them.

62. In the accompanying letter introducing the letter of protest, probably written on 29 March 1916, Bloch wrote, "Dear Mr. Walden I have read the reviews of my paintings in the Berlin press. However, they gave me no pleasure. Would you be prepared to print a small response of mine to the Berlin critics in *Sturm*?" The same letter includes Bloch's remarks about his *Frieze for a Music Room*, 1915.

63. *Der Sturm*, 7 (April 1916), p. 11.

64. On Easter in 1918, in a letter to Maria Marc, he once again recalled the death of his friend: "It was just two years, and it's a year now since the few of us stood in the cemetery in Kochel. But I could not write. I was ill for nearly the whole month." Courtesy of Mrs. Albert Bloch.

65. See the letter from Maria Marc to Gabriele Münter of 15 July 1916, in which she complains of difficulties with the "Münchner Neue Sezession": "The loyal and enthusiastic friends, Campendonk, Bloch — would probably like to help, but they are not members." in Lankheit ed., *Wassily Kandinsky, Franz Marc: Briefwechsel*, p. 282.

66. The Paul Klee Foundation, Bern, also has Bloch's watercolor *For Clown Painting IV*, 1914 (pl. 51). In addition to the drawing *Horse Race*, mentioned above (note 26), Bloch also owned Klee's gouache *Mountain Landscape*, 1917, the watercolor *Small Park Landscape*, 1920, and an untitled wax crayon drawing of 1920 (all sold in 1954).

67. Emmy Klinker studied initially in Karlsruhe, and then with Lovis Corinth in Berlin. "In 1916, during the war, I came to Munich. Here I kept in touch with the trends that are today exemplary of modern art, through the youngest member of the Blue Rider, Albert Bloch (now in the USA). Among the acquaintances I made there was the stimulating company of Paul Klee." See Emmy Klinker, in *Rundschau: Die Welt der Frau*, 5 August 1956, n.p. She had also met Alexej Jawlensky in her father's house in Barmen, a town that was very active artistically at the time.

68. For example, as early as 6 February 1917, when Bloch was writing to Walden that he was thinking of leaving Germany for a time because of the chaos of the war, he mentions that "A student of mine will take over my studio and represent me in Germany so far as necessary." See Anthology, p. 173.

69. The catalogue of the Sturm exhibition "Albert Bloch — Harald Kauffmann," May 1917, cat. no. 22, lists *The Monastery* as "Owner: Legal Counselor Dr. Klinger/Barmen." In a letter of 20 October 1946, after the devastating bombings of 1943, Emmy Klinker, who continued to be active as a painter in Munich until her death, wrote to Bloch in Lawrence, "The works of yours that have survived are *Interior*, end of 1920 (pl. 30) [later purchased by the Städtische Galerie im Lenbachhaus from the collection of Emmy Klinker], *Street*, 1921. *Regular Guests*, February 1921 and undated a small house in a garden composed in red-green." Letters from Emmy Klinker to Bloch 1934–61 courtesy of Mrs. Albert Bloch. In his "Sonnets to the Dead," Bloch dedicated a grateful and affectionate poem to Richard Klinker, beginning "Yes yes, that old ass Klinker."

70. Unfortunately there is no catalogue of this 64th Sturm exhibition. In the National Gallery in Berlin, however, there is a small watercolor by Bloch, *Imaginary Composition* of 1918, which he painted on the back of an invitation card to the exhibition's opening for the Berlin writer and art critic Walter Mehring (See also exh. cat., Berlin 1961, no. 53).

71. According to Mrs. Albert Bloch, Bloch helped with the hanging of an exhibition of Marc Chagall's work at Der Sturm Gallery: "He once told me that he helped put up the first Chagall show in Germany — and I am confident that this was at Der Sturm." (Mrs. Albert Bloch to Maria Schuchter, 1 March 1987). It is unlikely that this refers to the first Chagall exhibition in the summer of 1914. For that installation Chagall himself traveled to Berlin from Russia, and therefore must have met Bloch. However, it could well be a reference to one of the many other presentations of Chagall's work at Der Sturm.

72. The fiddler is one of the earliest fundamental motifs in Chagall's work, already appearing in paintings produced in Russia such as *The Dead Man*, 1908, *Russian Wedding*, 1909, and *The Fiddler* of 1911.

73. Leopold Zahn, "Über den Infantilismus in der neuen Kunst," in *Der Ararat*, January 1920, pp. 5–7. The article includes the statement, "A number of northern artists feel particularly close to his [Henri Rousseau's] style and his approach: above all Chagall, Albert Bloch and Davringhausen." The December 1920 issue of *Der Ararat* published a pen drawing, *Worship*, p. 137.

74. On the lower edge of the drawing, Bloch noted: "(very freely adapted from Rodin)." The third drawing, "Michel, are you him … or him?" was published as the cover in *Der Ararat* no. 2, 25 January 1919; see Martin Lindner, "Illustrierte Zeitschriften der Revolution," in *Süddeutsche Freiheit. Kunst der Revolution in München 1919*, exh. cat. (Munich 1993–94), pp. 81–82, with illustration.

75. The title refers to the French occupation of the Ruhr district up to 1923, where conditions were particularly miserable in postwar Germany.

76. See also Heinrich Campendonk's *Interior*, 1919, Kunsthalle, Basel.

77. *Der Ararat*, December 1920, nos. 11 and 12, p. 137. Bloch refuses to give any information about himself, and with deliberate polemicism describes "people who proudly call themselves Cubists, Futurists or Expressionists" as "dice-chuckers, star-gazers and articulators [Würfler, Zukünftler oder Ausdrückler]." In his verbose style he responds to Goltz's request for a few impressions of artistic life in America (Bloch had spent nearly a year in the United States from May 1919) negatively: "Because from the long, long months of my last visit to my home country, what has remained with me is more of a nightmare [Alpdruck] than an impression [Eindruck]; and if there is any artistic life there at all, it must have scurried past me very cautiously and without me noticing. The whole time there I lived just about as withdrawn as an oyster in its shell, except that my sensations must have been less pleasant than those of an oyster, since it is known not to have any."

78. "Ventures in Verse," II, 1932–33. A rejected version of this is found in the earlier first volume under 29a. In the poem, Bloch describes the "hymnbook" on the table, the plant and the dog. The long stanzas about the dog — "he is part of all the stillness! And all its parts are part of its parts" — support the unlikely supposition that the dog that appears in Bloch's paintings (as well as H. M. Davringhausen's) at this period is used to convey emotion, as a kind of substitute for the harlequin motif. The Jewish subject matter discernible in *Group of Three* cannot be discussed here in detail. Statements by the artist, as well as by his widow Anna Bloch, confirm that he was not a practicing religious Jew, and behaved indifferently toward his Jewish heritage. This attitude is also seen in many of Bloch's statements in his correspondence with the Karl Kraus circle during the 1930s and 1940s. Nevertheless, his Jewish origins may have played a role for Bloch. Even in his Munich period, he gave his extensive collection of personal texts the remarkable title "Ishmael's Breviary." A kind of self-characterization may be seen in the motto which Bloch placed at the head of his ambivalent poems about Jews, The Chosen People, in "Ventures in Verse," II, 1934–37: "Hear, O Israel, your self-outcast half-brother Ishmael!"

PAINTER'S PROGRESS:
THE LATER WORK OF ALBERT BLOCH

David Cateforis

On the whole ... I am an impossible creature, quite willing to remain an obscure, rough-hewn square peg, if only I may keep my inward freedom.

Albert Bloch[1]

Despite the historical significance of his association with the Blue Rider during his years in Europe, and notwithstanding the quality of his subsequent painting in the United States, Albert Bloch remains an inconspicuous figure in the history of American art. He himself is largely responsible for this situation, for, following his definitive return to America in 1921, he refused to promote himself or his art, seeking neither critical attention nor financial success in the art market. After a large solo exhibition at the Daniel Gallery in New York in November 1921, Bloch kept his work out of commercial galleries and exhibited elsewhere by invitation only. The modicum of financial security afforded by his faculty position at the University of Kansas enabled Bloch to establish his independence from the commercial art world and the various artistic fashions that it promoted. "I have not become very 'famous,'" he wrote to Kandinsky in 1936, "I am one of the painters who is, so to speak, 'known,' but not, thank God, one of great celebrities of the day…. I want nothing but my peace, and here, in this pleasant little university town … I have finally found it."[2]

Bloch maintained his independence as a matter of principle, for he did not see art as a means of achieving fame or fortune but rather as an elevated calling. The sole function of art, he declared, "*has always been and must always remain the deepening of the human perception and consciousness*: to bring to mankind a clearer idea of itself in its relation to its temporal environment."[3] But beyond and above that, Bloch continued, art was meant "to give to the human race some sense of the dependence … of our life here on earth, upon a state of being higher than our present one: to bring to us a profounder feeling of our inextricable union with the Infinite."[4] It followed that, for Bloch, the fundamental problem of art was not technical, but spiritual. "Hand, eye, pigment, brush, canvas" he proclaimed to be "the enemies of vision: the obstacles, the hindrances, beyond which the spirit must pass before vision becomes fulfillment."[5]

Bloch collected a number of his aphorisms and other brief texts on art under the title "Painter's Progress." In thus alluding to John Bunyan's famous Christian allegory, *The Pilgrim's Progress*, Bloch avowed that he conceived of his artistic life as a form of pilgrimage or spiritual journey. But whereas Bunyan's

Christian moved inexorably forward in his quest to reach the Celestial City, Bloch saw his own progress as a paradoxical movement *backward* — a turning away from the present in the search for more ancient and enduring truths. "Our few truly devoted painters of the modern chaos," Bloch observed,

> are not mad with modernity; they are not running insanely after new, false gods, but rather feeling and groping their way back to the old, true One. And if a kindly light will lead them through the encircling gloom: though they don't know where they're going, still are they filled with an abiding faith that they are on their way.[6]

Images of pilgrimage appear repeatedly in the paintings of Bloch's American years, from the mysterious procession of *Pilgrims in the Snow* (fig. 1) to the lone pilgrims of *The Blue Bough* (pl. 47) and *Impromptu* (pl. 49) of the 1950s. So, too, do explicitly Christian images, such as the roadside crucifix in *The Blue Bough* and the figure of Jesus in *Jordan* (pl. 41). While these latter paintings are overt expressions of Bloch's deeply Christian faith, a more generalized engagement with spirituality animates his entire body of work. The grinning clowns, leaping Harlequins, and dreamy Pierrots that populate so many of his paintings exist in an otherworldly state, far removed from the materialistic concerns of the modern world, as do the robed and hooded figures that

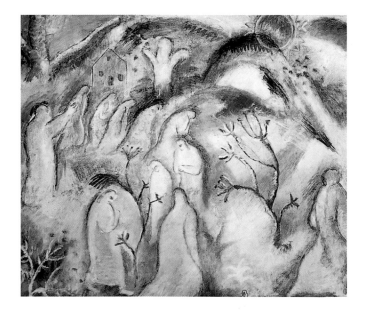

1. *Pilgrims in the Snow (Prozession im Schnee)*, 1917, Courtesy of Mrs. Albert Bloch

A closer consideration of some of the key works painted by Bloch during the nearly four decades that he worked in the United States following his return from Europe will make clear the ever-increasing technical accomplishment and visionary intensity of his art. Bloch's paintings of the 1920s are transitional, extending the formal and thematic concerns of his European work, while gradually moving toward a style of greater simplicity and monumentality. This shift is particularly noticeable in his reworkings of canvases that he had painted in the previous decade. For example, Bloch painted over the 1917 *Pilgrims in the Snow (Prozession im Schnee)*, known from a black-and-white photograph (fig. 1), to create *Pilgrims in the Snow* in 1925 (fig. 2). The 1917 canvas depicted several hooded figures winding through

2. *Pilgrims in the Snow*, 1917-25, Mrs. Albert Bloch

constitute a distinctive leitmotiv in Bloch's art. While clearly inspired by the heavily draped figures in biblical paintings by the Old Masters, Bloch's shrouded personages ultimately transcend specific visual sources and codified narratives. They manifest his own singular vision of spiritual existence and embody a full range of emotions, from grief to exaltation.

Although Bloch's painting was nourished by his study of older art and by his observation of the world around him, he did not seek to reproduce what he saw. "The art of painting," he wrote, "is not imitation; it is divination." Bloch worked from memory and imagination, enriched by visual discoveries that he made during the actual process of painting. Even his depictions of such everyday subjects as flowers, houses, and landscapes appear to have been transformed by the artist's fantasy and elevated from the ordinary to the extraordinary, as in *The House Next Door* (pl. 34), *Garden Glimpse* (pl. 35), and *Gulls* (pl. 38).

Bloch himself often described his paintings in spiritual terms. In a 1936 letter to Kandinsky he attributed metaphysical values to his colors:

> You must think of the palette as cooled down and restrained. The cadmiums, vermillions, madders and the like are now gone. White and blue play an extremely important part in the formation of almost every color-chord: *earth colors* have become *essential* — formerly I had at most light ochre on my palette; through the white and blue they can become so *ethereal* and so spiritualized, so deepened and disembodied, that raw and harsh Indian red, for example, can seem to sing like the angels.

Writing twelve years later to Sidonie Nádherný von Borutin, Bloch emphasized the degree to which reality appeared dematerialized and transfigured in his paintings. "I paint still lifes, landscapes, and compositions with figures, just like everyone else," he observed, "only with me the result is inescapably a complete spiritualization of the object.... A total fusion of matter with spirit, blurring the remnants of the tangible object."

3. *Impromptu*, 1926, Private collection

a highly abstracted landscape. These pilgrims appear flat and insubstantial, their dark outlines blending with the undulating contours of the surrounding hills. The space of the landscape itself is indeterminate. By contrast, the pilgrims of the 1925 version appear to have real mass and volume, and the snowy landscape they traverse recedes convincingly into depth. Richard Green remarks that "the emotional content has been altered by a shift from a generalized patterned statement to an expression that is centered in humanity." He further points to the similarity between the 1925 pilgrims and the robed figures of Giotto and suggests that "perhaps there is a parallel between Giotto's development from highly stylized Italo-Byzantine painting and the growth of *Pilgrims in the Snow* from the semi-abstract style which [Bloch] developed in Europe."

Impromptu (fig. 3), a painting from the following year, offers a more ethereal vision, closer in spirit to Bloch's "semi-abstract" style of the previous decade. Here, a single white-draped figure stands quietly in a secluded glade. A gentle vernal atmosphere permeates the sylvan environment, which is delicately rendered in soft shades of blue and lavender, warm green and pale yellow. The robed figure, with head slightly bowed, stands in mystical communion with the beneficent natural world. We, as viewers, are invited to identify with, and project our own emotions onto, this figure — anonymous, ageless, and sexless — and to share in the state of communion.

Bloch envisions a very different world in *Winter in the Dead Wood* (pl. 36). In this bleak hinterland, the harmony between man and nature has been destroyed, and all signs of human presence erased; only a pair of crows remains to haunt the cold and desolate forest. The hilly, snow-covered terrain is littered with the frozen trunks of blasted trees. Above them, a damp gray sky hangs like a pall. The dull red sun, sinking feebly below the horizon, is powerless to dispel the preternatural chill. The title of Bloch's picture echoes that of the Karl Kraus poem "Der tote Wald" ("The Dead Wood") from *Die letzten Tage der Menschheit* (*The Last Days of Mankind*), an epic drama of protest against World War I. "Der tote Wald" was among several poems from the epilogue of Kraus's drama that Bloch translated into English.[12] In this epilogue the shades of the war's victims come forward to condemn their murderers. The wasted forest cries out: "Your hellish power has won the day./ I once was green./ Now I am grey./ Behold the place where I once stood./ I was a wood! I was a wood!"[13]

Bloch himself had lived in Germany during World War I and had suffered the loss of his close friend Franz Marc in the fighting. For the rest of his life he recalled bitterly the "grisly butchery and insane cruelty of those four years."[14] Memories of the "Great War," mingled with a grim awareness of another approaching worldwide conflict, shaped an obsession with mortality and waste that haunted much of Bloch's art and poetry of the 1930s and 1940s. But his world view during these years was by no means wholly despairing. Alongside desolate landscapes, such as *Winter in the Dead Wood*, he created hopeful visions of a natural paradise — a warm and bountiful world of grace, peace, and concord. *The Garden of Asses (II)* (pl. 37) offers one such vision, in which six gentle asses, each of a different hue, roam freely through a rocky landscape, accompanied by fluttering birds and butterflies. The landscape sparkles with brightly blossoming plants and glowing trees, nourished by phosphorescent streams and waterfalls. The painting's composition is complex and faceted, like a diamond. Strong diagonal lines coax the eye through rich and ambiguous spaces and suggest dynamic forces of growth and life. The sonorous palette of earth colors, whites, and blues is vivid and robust.

The Garden of Asses, like *Winter in the Dead Wood*, grew out of Bloch's experience of World War I some two decades earlier. While living in Munich during the conflict, he witnessed the harsh treatment of asses employed as munitions carriers, and came to conceive of the ass as a symbol for all the exploited creatures of the earth. Bloch painted the first version of *The*

4. *The Garden of Asses*, 1918 (1st version), location unknown, Courtesy of Mrs. Albert Bloch

Garden of Asses in 1918, providing the asses with an imaginary sanctuary from suffering and oppression and, perhaps, paying tribute to Franz Marc, who had devoted so much of his own art to animals and had provided a natural paradise for some of them at his country home. The 1918 canvas entered the collection of the Munich dealer Hans Goltz and today is known only from a black-and-white photograph (fig. 4). Sometime during the 1930s the photograph attracted Bloch's interest and he was inspired to make a pen drawing after it. He then began to work on the second *Garden of Asses* and, at the same time, composed a long, five-part poem, "The Garden of Asses: A Fantasy." In Bloch's poem the ass is intimately associated with the life of Christ, who plays with a loving ass as a child, rides an ass into Jerusalem on Palm Sunday, and is mourned by a braying ass at the Crucifixion. Christ promises to repay the ass for his faithfulness and, in the final section of the poem, that promise is fulfilled through the creation of a garden sanctuary for the asses and all kindred animals. The poet calls out to them:

> Come, beasts that perish! all who labor and
> are heavy laden; there you shall have peace!
> Forevermore be free of all command
> over you; and be yours the land's increase.
> For you this warm sunlight and pleasant shade,
> yours the bell-clear and flower-scented air,
> yours the green pastures and still waters fair,
> for you alone this Eden shall be laid.[15]

The outbreak of World War II displaced such utopian visions as *The Garden of Asses* and reinforced Bloch's tragic obsession with themes of mortality and loss. In *Old Graveyard* (pl. 40) of 1940-41 a dead cypress hangs over an abandoned cemetery amidst glowing paths that meander among leaning headstones and stunted trees. The frayed brushstrokes and spectral palette of whites, grays, and browns intensify the painting's mournful atmosphere of death and decay. In *Through the Night* (fig. 5) the tragic aura becomes almost overwhelming, as the powerfully modeled figures of shrouded mourners loom like mountains in a brooding and mysterious netherworld.

While clearly resonating within the context of World War II, *Old Graveyard* and *Through the Night* seek to communicate on a more universal level. The desolate burial ground in the former picture exists outside any particular time or place, while the grieving figures in the latter painting represent the primal sorrow of the bereaved at all times and in all places. By contrast, the 1941 *March of the Clowns* (pl. 39) is a more overt response to the war itself. As a large crowd watches, an endless

5. *Through the Night*, 1942, Munson-Williams-Proctor Institute Museum of Art, Utica, New York, Gift of Mr. and Mrs. James Penney

parade of brightly costumed clowns issues from a distant archway. The lanky leader of the procession toots on a smoke-belching bassoon. A squat clown marching immediately behind him hoists aloft a pole crowned by a wooden swastika. Dangling helplessly from the swastika is a doll of the Führer.

March of the Clowns may be interpreted as a premature celebration of the defeat of Hitler — a fantasy painted to release the incredible tensions Bloch felt in the midst of the war. Religious symbols play an important role in conveying the painting's meaning. Balancing atop the swastika is a shining Star of David, doubtless standing as a hopeful symbol of the Jewish people's eventual triumph over the Nazi threat. A Latin cross surmounts the archway in the background, transforming the parade of gleeful clowns into a triumphant Christian procession. This Christian presence in the midst of a carnivalesque mass of humanity recalls James Ensor's epochal *Entry of Christ into Brussels in 1889* (1888; J. Paul Getty Museum). But even as it alludes to the work of the Belgian painter, whom Bloch greatly admired, *March of the Clowns* strikes a distinctly American note through its inclusion of characters from comic strips such as *The Katzenjammer Kids*, *Popeye*, *Krazy Kat*, and *Moon Mullins*, anticipating by some twenty years the appropriation of American comic book characters by such Pop artists as Roy Lichtenstein, Andy Warhol, and Mel Ramos.

In *The Blind Man* (pl. 43), another wartime picture, the boisterous atmosphere of *March of the Clowns* gives way to an aura of solemn mystery. The setting is a dense and icy forest whose bare trees rise in a nearly impenetrable mass that all but obliterates the dark sky above. In the center of the painting the thick stand of trees opens onto a mysterious green stream that flows downward to a small outcrop of rocks in the lower foreground. Amidst these rocks, clusters of colorful plants blossom in miraculous defiance of the cold season, offering fresh life that flourishes even in the depths of winter. The titular blind man, a dark figure in a hat and heavy coat, emerges from the forest near the right edge of the stream and feels his way forward with a slender cane.

Set off visually from the surrounding trees as a blackish-brown shape among luminous whites, the blind man seems isolated from the energies of the surrounding forest. But while he may be isolated, he is not alone. Above and to the left of him is a ghostly, white-shrouded figure, hovering along the bank of the stream at the exact center of the painting. Further up is another, smaller apparition, glimpsed in the distance amidst the branches of the trees. If the blossoming plants in the foreground represent new life, these spectres among the barren trees seem just as clearly to stand for death. The forest itself may symbolize the ultimate mystery that lies before every living human being, while the blind man is, in Anna Bloch's words, "Everyman, feeling his way along an unmade path that he cannot see ... in the midst of the beauty and mystery of his lonely, unknown quest."[16]

In the dreamlike intensity of its imagery *The Blind Man* epitomizes the powerful visionary quality of much of Bloch's later painting, which often seeks to express spiritual content through the rich and complex forms and colors of an imaginary landscape. One such landscape is the setting for Bloch's highly personal interpretation of the Baptism of Christ, the magnificent *Jordan* (pl. 41). Jesus appears at the lower center of the picture, a slight, translucent figure, standing at the edge of the shallow blue river. He seems at first sight to be alone, but closer inspection reveals the outlines of several semi-transparent figures hovering in the background behind him. These apparitions suggest the souls of the many who came to Jordan to confess their sins and be baptized by John, as was Jesus himself, or the millions who would be baptized in Jesus's name in the centuries to follow.

Set within a diamond-shaped spatial recess framed by leaning trees and sloping rocks, *Jordan*'s Christ occupies a privileged place in the composition. Light and energy appear to radiate outward from this point, coursing through the wild, rocky landscape, which seems to quake with the sublime spiritual import of the Baptism. From the hard desert ground, fantastically decorated with a motley checkerboard pattern, spiky trees thrust dynamically toward the sky. Above them, craggy masses of rock surge heavenward along steep diagonals. Densely modeled in ochre and umber hues, the dominant forms of the landscape swell with rugged and agitated power. But traversing and overlaying them are spidery black ray-lines and delicate white traceries that vibrate on a finer, more subtle wavelength, to suggest a pervasive spiritual presence.

Similar in feeling to *Jordan* but larger and more ambitious iconographically is *Passing Train* (pl. 42), one of Bloch's most impressive canvases. Under a brooding, moonlit sky stretches a rocky, labyrinthine landscape, inhabited by glowing plants, twisting trees, and ghostly human figures. The picture is rendered intricately in a tawny palette of earth tones, enriched by blues and aerated by whites that cast a gossamer web of spectral illumination over the entire scene. Standing near the left foreground are two gently embracing lovers, clothed in brown and enveloped in a shining aura of white and gold. Their backs are turned to the viewer, who is invited to share in their world, to absorb the sights and sounds of the night and the passing train that traverses the landscape in the distance. Below their feet flows a narrow stream, coursing in a diagonal that divides the couple from the landscape stretching before them. In a clearing across the stream from the lovers, near the center of the canvas, rise the transparent figures of a draped woman and an infant, strongly suggestive of the Madonna and Child. Down and to the right, seated by the edge of the stream, is the ghostly figure of a round-headed, hollow-eyed man, who cradles a cluster of flowers.

Whereas *Jordan* was inspired by the Gospels, *Passing Train* was based on Bloch's personal recollections of summer nights spent on a hillside in Falls Village, Connecticut, where the train called out as it passed nightly through the valley on the other side of the Housatonic River.[17] The glowing lovers may stand for the artist and his companion, joined in rapt contemplation of the magic of the summer night and the music of the distant train. But the painting can also be seen as an elegy for transitory earthly pleasures, as fleeting as a passing train. Bloch began painting *Passing Train* following a severe heart attack that forced him to retire from his teaching position at the University of Kansas; every stroke of his brush must have carried with it an awareness of his own mortality. The ghostly personage seated by the stream may be read as a figure of the ailing artist, who contemplates his approaching death while he holds his own memorial bouquet.[18] The painting is made Bloch's personal *memento mori* by the appearance of his monogram, "AB," on a tombstonelike rock slightly to the left of the apparitional mother and child, next to another, similar rock, inscribed with the Latin epitaph *hic jacet* ("here lies"). In this context the mother and child may represent the Christian hope of resurrection and eternal life, in which Bloch placed great faith.

Bloch's imaginary landscapes, often peopled by robed and hooded figures, give expression to a wide variety of emotional and spiritual states. Something of that expressive range is revealed by comparing two paintings from 1950, *Figures in Silver Light* (pl. 45) and *The Grieving Women* (pl. 44). The latter canvas depicts a tranquil nocturnal landscape, bathed in the lambent atmosphere of a silvery moon. Standing or sitting among the rocks and foliage are numerous figures in shining robes, who, like the draped personage in the 1926 *Impromptu*, appear immersed in contemplation. The darkly robed *Grieving Women* are, by contrast, deeply racked by sorrow. With bowed heads and heavy gestures they mourn together, united in their grief before a desolate terrain stretching back to a grim horizon.

Whereas *Figures in Silver Light* is a warm and welcoming picture that invites us, through its open foreground, to project ourselves into its world, *The Grieving Women* is cold and confrontational, shutting us out through its frontal massing of monumental mourners. While the one picture dreams of an earthly paradise for humans, similar in spirit to the one envisioned for animals in the second version of *The Garden of Asses*, the other acknowledges the terrible tragedies that have befallen humanity by giving concrete expression to the tremendous grief and desolation left in their wake.

The greatest of those tragedies in Bloch's lifetime had been the two world wars. The failure of international diplomacy to prevent these wars and other modern conflicts left Bloch deeply pessimistic about political solutions to human problems. That pessimism finds mordant expression in two works from 1951, the ink drawing *American Statesman* (fig. 6) which caricatures its subject as a marionette, and the oil painting *Conference* (pl. 46), which satirizes political discourse as a colloquy between clowns and dummies, scarecrows and skeletons. In a mockery of open and efficacious communication, *Conference*'s principal "negotiators," arrayed in masks, tattered motley, and crumpled top hats, extend outsized hands to persuade their grinning but inanimate listeners. Echoes of James Ensor, noted previously in Bloch's *March of the Clowns*, are again present, with the arrangement of masked figures surrounding a skeleton recalling a number of the Belgian's pictures (for example, *Masks and Death*, 1899; Musée d'Art Moderne, Liège). But *Conference* is hardly an imitation of Ensor; the style and figural types are Bloch's own, and Bloch's distinctive sensibility reveals itself in numerous details, such as the disturbingly large hands of the top-hatted conferees and the darkly humorous provision of a skull cap for the skeleton.

"American Statesman"

6. *American Statesman*, 1951, Mrs. Albert Bloch

Far from the caustic satire of *Conference* is the image of spiritual pilgrimage presented in *The Blue Bough* (pl. 47), a visionary landscape of remarkable depth and resonance. The ragged scarecrow in the background of *Conference* is replaced in *The Blue Bough* by a roadside crucifix, approached from below by a climbing, robed figure. In the foreground, balancing this background pilgrimage scene, are two substantial yellow-brown tree trunks, which slice diagonally upward and cross to form an "X." While appearing to be solid at their bases, the trees become transparent at their point of intersection, and then issue in a complex of overlapping diagonal limbs of varying degrees of opacity. In this upper left section of the painting the tawny limbs mingle with blue ones that echo the hue of the titular blue bough. That magical blue limb, compact and powerfully modeled, rises from the lower right foreground and winds upward in sinuous counterpoint to the straight shafts of the yellow-brown trunks to the left. Twisting energetically and blooming with colorful flowers, the blue bough seems literally to be a tree of life; it is surely under the influence of the blue limb that a white flower blossoms from the juncture of the yellow-brown trees, which appear otherwise barren.

The striking juxtaposition of earth colors and blue in the foreground of *The Blue Bough* finds a telling literary parallel in Bloch's poem "To My Palette," in which he characterizes blue as a spiritual color, "fetched out of heaven" to vitalize the material "earth-clods."[19] The association of blue with spirituality was, of course, deeply rooted in the German Romantic tradition, to which Bloch was heir; it can be traced back to the symbolic use of blue in Novalis's novel *Heinrich von Ofterdingen* (1802), whose hero dreams of a mystical quest for a blue flower.[20] Kandinsky also saw blue as a profoundly spiritual color. In *On the Spiritual in Art* he observed:

> The inclination of blue towards depth is so great that it becomes more intense the darker the tone, and has a more characteristic inner effect. The deeper the blue becomes, the more strongly it calls man towards the infinite, awakening in him a desire for the pure and, finally, for the supernatural. It is the color of the heavens, the same color we picture to ourselves when we hear the sound of the word "heaven."[21]

In *The Blue Bough* Bloch, like Kandinsky, associates blue with a call "towards the infinite" by positioning the hooded pilgrim directly above the twining limbs of the blue bough. With bowed head and heavy step, this weary traveler nears the end of a long trek, like the poet in Bloch's "And My Feet Were Set on the Road," who journeys on a similar spiritual quest, summed up in the final stanza:

> Strait is the road was set for my feet,
> and my feet still set on the road,
> limping and halt, somehow facing the goal,
> all but beaten, yet no retreat.
> Bent my back beneath the load,
> but song still ashout in my soul.[22]

In Bloch's painting the climber is a spiritual pilgrim, journeying toward the crucified Christ. In this context the blue bough takes on a specifically Christian meaning, connoting Christ as the living tree who offers the promise of resurrection and eternal life.

Significantly, the motif of the climbing pilgrim reappears in Bloch's last painting, *Impromptu* (pl. 49), completed in 1959 less than two years before his death. The vertically oriented composition of *Impromptu*, remarkably similar to that of *The Blue Bough*, again features prominent trees in the foreground and, in the background, a steep mountain landscape ascended at the upper right by a hooded figure. There are, however, significant differences between the two paintings. *Impromptu's* colors are, on the whole, brighter and of higher value. The dark and brooding sky of *The Blue Bough* is replaced by a vivid blue one and indications of burgeoning vegetation and new growth spread throughout *Impromptu's* landscape in springlike profusion.

While richly suggestive of new life, *Impromptu* at the same time alludes to death, through the shrouded figure who moves silently toward a dark portal at the right side of the canvas, just slightly down from the climbing figure, who faces in the opposite direction. While the mountain pilgrim nears the end of his earthly quest, the shrouded figure turns his back on the world and withdraws into a tomblike enclosure. The juxtaposition of these two figures, one still striving through life toward a goal, the other departing from the earthly struggle, suggests the ambivalent attitude toward death that Bloch expressed some two decades earlier in a poem, also entitled "Impromptu," whose final stanza concludes:

> Can not Death wait at least for *me*?
> I am not ready to depart
> and there is all eternity.
> I have but just begun to see
> a little glimmer of light ahead,
> though I must question still the gleam
> and, groping on in very dread,
> doubt if the vision be but dream.
> How can I, dare I, die before
> I know what may the light portend,
> whether it guide me to the door
> I seek my life long to the end?
> Let me but find the door, and I
> could beckon Death and welcome him.
> No more then would his mien be grim,
> and I could lay me down to die.[23]

That Bloch should at the end associate death not with winter but with spring, the green season of rebirth and regeneration, is entirely appropriate, for he believed, as he wrote to Kandinsky, in the "certainty of an all-pervading eternal life."[24] That belief most certainly finds expression in his final painting.

The artistic pilgrimage that Albert Bloch made during the last four decades of his life was a highly personal one, undertaken without regard for the changing fashions of the art world and with no expectation of public recognition. "Such seclusion, such independence, such silence is phenomenal in our vociferous period," wrote James Gilbert of Bloch in 1956.[25] "And yet," Gilbert continued, "this very quality of isolated independence has been rather characteristic of many of our best American artists in every period."[26] Bloch understood and accepted the obscurity that his independence insured him and contented himself in the pursuit of his own vision. In his poem "The Gardener" we sense that he is writing of himself:

> Here's a man lives in a garden
> In the garden he shall live his life,
> yet he leaves it now and then, to harden
> heart and mind in healthful strife
> with the heedlessness and willfulness
> of this world of rushing men.
> Soon, quite whole and cured of all distress,
> he is home again.[27]

Bloch's progress as a painter always brought him back to his own garden. At his easel, exploring worlds of his own imagining, guided by his own spiritual light, Bloch was most truly at home.

1 Albert Bloch, "Painter's Progress", in "Ishmael's Breviary," unpublished manuscript, n.d., n.p. Courtesy of Mrs. Albert Bloch.

2 "Nicht allzusehr 'berühmt' bin ich geworden, ich gehöre zu den Malern, die man halt so 'kennt', doch Gott sei Dank nicht zu den Tagesgrößen.... Ich will nichts als meine Ruhe, und hier in diesem lieblichen Universitätsnestchen ... habe ich sie endlich gefunden." Albert Bloch to Wassily Kandinsky, 22 June 1936. Photocopy courtesy of Mrs. Albert Bloch.

3 Albert Bloch, "Lecture No. 1: General Introduction," unpublished typescript lecture notes for a course in the history of art taught at the University of Kansas, 1923-24, n.p. Courtesy of Mrs. Albert Bloch.

4 Ibid.

5 Bloch, "Painter's Progress," n.p.

6 Ibid.

7 Ibid.

8 "Sie haben sich dabei die Palette sehr abgekühlt und zurückhaltend zu denken. Die Cadmiums, Zinnober, Krapplack u. dgl. fehlen jetzt. Weiß und Blau spielen eine ungeheure wichtige Rolle in der Entstehung von fast jedem Farbklang. Die *Erdfarben* sind mir *wesentlich* geworden — früher hatte ich höchstens Lichtocker auf der Palette —, durch das Weiß und das Blau lassen sie sich so *entrücken* und vergeistigen, so vertiefen und entkörpern, daß sich z.B. das rohe und herbe Indischrot geradezu als Engelssang wahrnehmen läßt." Bloch to Kandinsky, 22 June 1936.

9 Bloch wrote: "[Ich male] Stilleben, Landschaften, Figurenkompositionen...wie jeder andere: nur aber, daß das Resultat — weil ich halt nichts dafür kann — eine vollkommene Vergeistigung des Dargestellten darstellt." ("I paint still lifes, landscapes, figure compositions, just like everyone else: only the result — simply because I cannot do anything about it — is a complete spiritualization of the depicted object.") His explanation of "complete spiritualization of the object" ("a total fusion") is given in a marginal note to the word "Vergeistigung": "Durchgeistigung der Materie, das greifbar Gegenständliche verwischend." Bloch to Sidonie Nádherný von Borutin, 10 June 1948. Photocopy courtesy of Mrs. Albert Bloch. I am grateful to Frank Baron, Mrs. Albert Bloch, and Elke Champion for their suggestions regarding the English translation of this passage from Bloch's letter.

10 Richard C. Green, "Introduction," *Albert Bloch (1882-1962): Paintings,* exh. cat. (New York: Sid Deutsch Gallery, 1988), n.p.

11 Ibid.

12 See Karl Kraus, *Poems: Authorized Translations from the German,* trans. Albert Bloch (Boston: The Four Seas Press, 1930).

13 "The Dead Wood," ibid.; reprinted in Albert Bloch, *German Poetry in War and Peace: A Dual-Language Anthology,* ed. Frank Baron (Lawrence, Kansas: The Max Kade Center for German-American Studies, 1995), p. 107. Kraus's original German appears there on p. 106.

14 Bloch, introduction to Karl Kraus, *Poems,* p. 12.

15 Albert Bloch, "The Garden of Asses: A Fantasy" (December 1938-March 1939), in "Ventures in Verse," III, unpublished manuscript, 1937-41, p. 42. Courtesy of Mrs. Albert Bloch.

16 Mrs. Albert Bloch to the author, 16 October 1995.

17 Mrs. Albert Bloch in conversation with the author, July 1994.

18 Mrs. Bloch recalls the painter saying, in reference to this figure, "You see that he's sick, don't you?" The comment is highly significant because Albert Bloch rarely offered interpretive remarks about his paintings. Conversation with the author, 15 August 1995.

19 Bloch, "To My Palette," in "Ventures in Verse," II, 1934-37, n.p. Courtesy of Mrs. Albert Bloch.

20 See John Gage, "Mood Indigo: From the Blue Flower to the Blue Rider," in *The Romantic Spirit in German Art, 1790-1990,* ed. Keith Hartley, Henry Meyric Hughes, Peter-Klaus Schuster and William Vaughan (New York: Thames and Hudson, 1994), pp. 122-30.

21 Kandinsky, *On the Spiritual in Art,* 2nd ed. [1912], in Kandinsky, *Complete Writings on Art,* ed. Kenneth C. Lindsay and Peter Vergo, (Boston: G. K. Hall & Co., 1982), v. 1, pp. 181-82.

22 Bloch, "And My Feet Were Set on the Road," in "Ventures in Verse," I, unpublished manuscript, early 1930s-37, n.p. Courtesy of Mrs. Albert Bloch.

23 Bloch, "Impromptu," in "Ventures in Verse," II, n.p.

24 In the letter Bloch quotes Franz Marc's biographer, Alois Schardt: "'In der Zukunft hat nur *diejenige Gegenstandsmalerei* ein Recht auf Symbol und Glaubhaftigkeit, *die durchleuchtet ist von der neuen Gewißheit eines sich gegenseitig durchdringenden ewigen Lebens*'!" (Bloch's emphasis.) ("In the future, only *that representational painting* can rightfully lay claim to symbolic meaning and truthfulness *which is illuminated by the new certainty of an all-pervading eternal life!*") Bloch then adds: "Diese Gewißheit glaube ich zu besitzen ...". ("This certainty I believe I have ...") Bloch to Kandinsky, 22 June 1936.

25 James Gilbert, "Foreword," *A Retrospective Exhibition of the Work of Albert Bloch,* exh. brochure (Chicago: The Renaissance Society at the University of Chicago, Chicago, 1956), n.p.

26 Ibid.

27 Bloch, "The Gardener," in "Ventures in Verse," II, n.p.

1. Untitled (Two Seated Nudes)
Ohne Titel (Zwei sitzende Akte)

c. 1911, cat. 1

2. Untitled (Cityscape)
Ohne Titel (Stadtlandschaft)

April 1911, cat. 2

3. Cityscape with Tower
Häuser mit Turm

September 1911, cat. 3

4. Harlequinade
Harlekinade

1911, cat. 4

5. The Three Pierrots No. 2
Die drei Pierrots Nr. 2

1911, cat. 5

6. Portrait of a Boy
Knabenbildnis

1911, cat. 6

7. The Dancer (Ragtime)
Der Tänzer (Ragtime)

1911,   cat. 7

8. Houses at Night
   Häuser bei Nacht

   1911,   cat. 9

9. Procession of the Cross
   Kreuztragung

   1911,   cat. 8

10. Untitled (Portrait of a Man)
Ohne Titel (Porträt eines Mannes)

1911, cat. 11

11. Portrait of Mr. A. M.
Porträt des Herrn A. M.

1914–15,   cat. 25

12. Reclining Figure
   Liegende Gestalt

   1911, cat. 10

13. Piping Pierrot
   Flötender Pierrot

   1911, cat. 12

14. Untitled (Four Pierrots)
Ohne Titel (Vier Pierrots)

1912, cat. 13

15. Duel
Duell

1912,   cat. 14

16. Untitled (Infernal Figures)
Ohne Titel (Höllenszene)

1912, cat. 15

17. Prize Fight
Boxkampf

1912-13, cat. 17

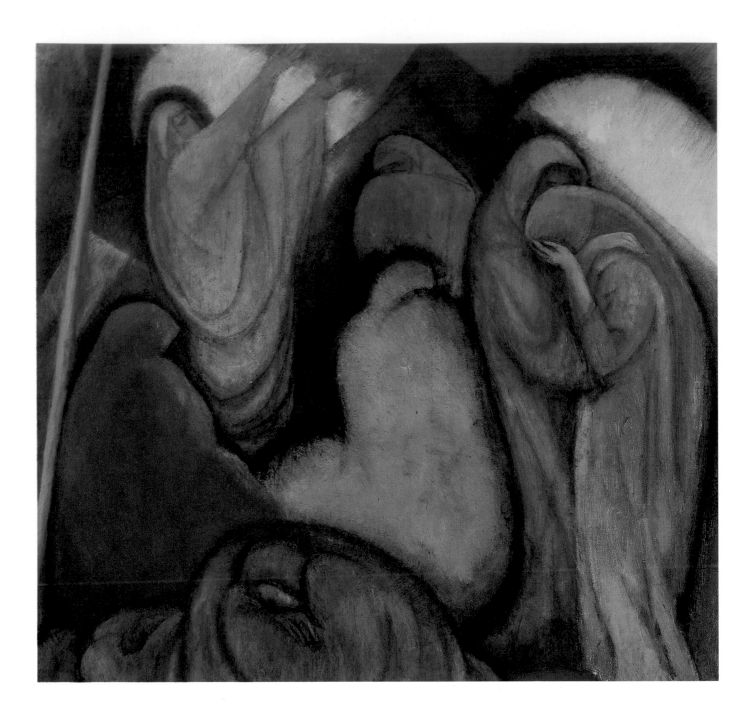

18. Lamentation
Klagelied

1912-13,   cat. 16

19. Summer Night
Sommernacht

1913,   cat. 20

20. The Green Domino
Das grüne Gewand

1913, cat. 19

21. Harlequin with Three Pierrots
Harlekin mit drei Pierrots

1914,   cat. 21

22. Song I
Lied I

November 1913-April 1914,   cat. 18

23. Entombment
Begräbnis

1914, cat. 23

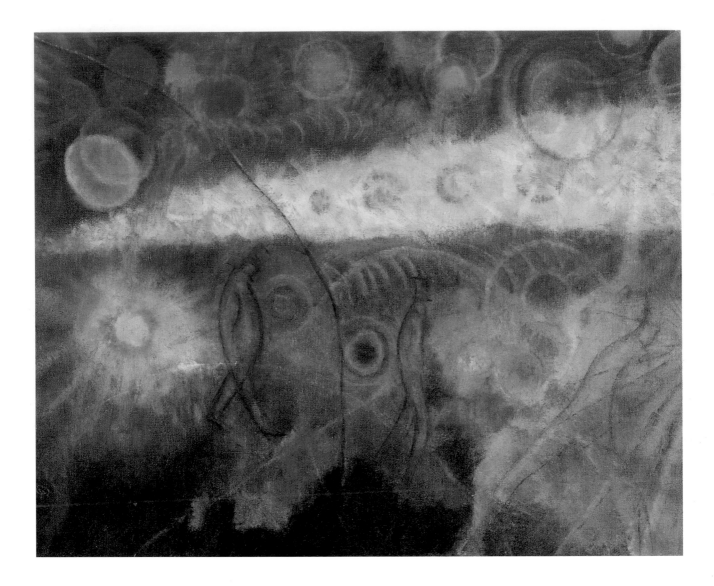

24. Night II
Nacht II

1914, cat. 24

25. Still Life III
Stilleben III

April 1914, cat. 22

26. Night V
   Nacht V

   1917, cat. 28

27. Figures on Dark Ground
   Gestalten auf dunklem Grund

   1916,   cat. 27

28. Mountain
Gebirg

1916, cat. 26

29. Winter
Winter

1918, cat. 29

30. Interior
    Interieur

    1920, cat. 30

31. Group of Three
    Dreiergruppe

    1921, cat. 32

32. Veranda
Veranda

1920,   cat. 31

33. Souvenir, Ascona
Erinnerung, Ascona

March–April 1921, cat. 33

34. The House Next Door
Das Haus nebenan

1934,   cat. 35

35. Garden Glimpse
   Gartenecke

   1936,   cat. 37

36. Winter in the Dead Wood
Winter im toten Wald

1934-38,   cat. 36

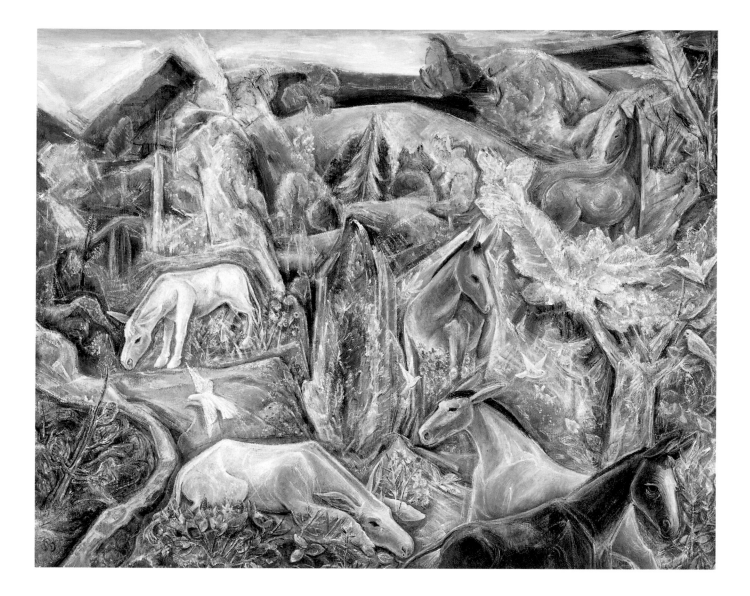

37. The Garden of Asses (II)
Der Eselsgarten (II)

1938-39, cat. 38

38. Gulls
Möwen

1941, cat. 40

39. March of the Clowns
Der Marsch der Clowns

1941, cat. 41

40. Old Graveyard
Alter Friedhof

1940-41, cat. 39

41. Jordan
   Jordan

   1946,   cat. 43

42. Passing Train
Vorbeifahrender Zug

1947-48,   cat. 44

43. The Blind Man
Der blinde Mann

1942, cat. 42

44. The Grieving Women
Klagende Frauen

1950/57, cat. 46

45. Figures in Silver Light
Gestalten in silbernem Licht

1950, cat. 45

46. Conference
Konferenz

1951, cat. 47

47. The Blue Bough
Der blaue Ast

1952, cat. 48

48. Blue Eclipse
Blaue Dämmerung

1955, cat. 50

49. Impromptu
Impromptu

1959, cat. 51

50. Harlequinade
Harlekinade

1911, cat. 52

51. For Clown-Picture IV
Zum Klownbild IV

1914,   cat. 53

52. Scherzo
Scherzo

1912/26,   cat. 54

53. Form and Color Study, No. 9: Railway Bridge
Form- u. Farbenübung, No. 9: Eisenbahnbrücke

1913,   cat. 55

54. Blue Waterfall
Blauer Wasserfall

1932,   cat. 56

55. Blue Ravine
Blaue Schlucht

1939,   cat. 57

Rodin

58. Rodin

n.d., cat. 60

J.S. METCALFE OF "LIFE"

59. J. S. Metcalfe of "Life"

n.d.,   cat. 61

1911

60. Suicide
Selbstmörder

1911, cat. 62

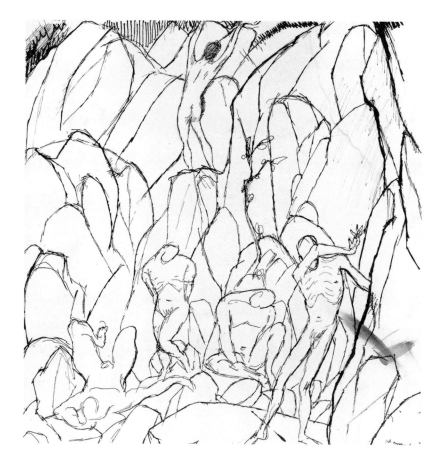

61. Figure Between Houses
   Figur zwischen Häusern

   1911,   cat. 63

62. First Movement (Study for *Song I*)
   Erste Bewegung (Studie für ›Lied I‹)

   May 1912,   cat. 67

63. Untitled
Ohne Titel

1913, cat. 71

64. Untitled (Hofbräu Nightmare)
Ohne Titel (Hofbräu-Alptraum)

c. 1911,   cat. 64

65. Notes for 3 Cityscapes
Notizen zu 3 Stadtbildern

1911, cat. 65

66. Study for Wrestling Match
Studie für Ringkampf

1912-13, cat. 70

67. Working drawing for *Harlequin with Three
Pierrots*
Studienzeichnung für ›Harlekin mit drei Pierrots‹

1913, cat. 69

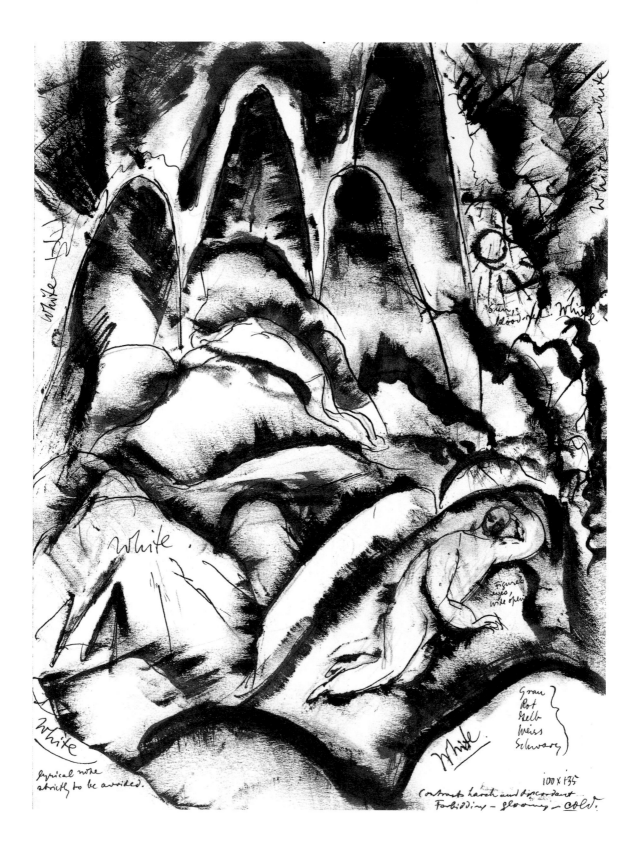

68. Ink Study for *The Heights*
   Studienzeichnung für ›Die Höhen‹

January 1914,   cat. 66

69. Self-Portrait
Selbstbildnis

1918, cat. 73

70. Untitled (Buildings with Clock Tower)
Ohne Titel (Gebäude mit Uhrenturm)

1917, cat. 72

71. In the Beginning. For a Cycle of the Creation
Am Anfang. Für einen Zyklus der Schöpfung

1922, cat. 74

72. Untitled (Landscape)
Ohne Titel (Landschaft)

1924, cat. 75

73. Night in the Black City
Nacht in der schwarzen Stadt

1931,   cat. 76

74. Templeton Vignettes I, House on the Terrace
   at Night
   Templeton-Vignetten I, Haus mit Terrasse bei
   Nacht

   1934, cat. 77

75. Untitled
   Ohne Titel
   1936,   cat. 78

76. Untitled
   Ohne Titel
   1940,   cat. 79

77. Continuation of a Drawing Begun by A. F.
Fortführung einer von A. F. begonnenen
Zeichnung

1946,   cat. 80

78. Houses at Night
Häuser bei Nacht

1913, cat. 82

79. Duel
Duell

1913, cat. 83

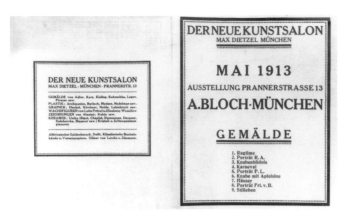

Brochure for the solo exhibition "Albert Bloch," Kunstsalon Dietzel, Munich, 1913, Courtesy of Mrs. Albert Bloch

Broschüre der Einzelausstellung ›Albert Bloch‹, Kunstsalon Dietzel, München 1913, Mrs. Albert Bloch

– Ich habe das Ausgehalten- und Geduldetsein endlich satt. Ich muß irgendwie Verbindungen anknüpfen, Verbindungen meiner Kunst willen, und nicht blos [sic] wegen einer zufälligen Schwägerverwandtschaft, die mir es ermöglichen würden meine Arbeiten fortzusetzen und mit meiner Familie hier in Europa friedlich weiter zu leben. – Sie wissen ja daß mir eine Äusserstfrist auferlegt worden ist: bin ich bis Oktober 1914 noch nicht wirtschaftlich selbstständig, heisst es dann, zurück nach Amerika und – umsatteln!

Natürlich kann mich niemand dazu <u>zwingen</u>, doch wird es unausbleiblich dazu kommen, im Falle einer Verweigerung meinerseits mich darin zu fügen, daß uns jegliche Unterstützung (so ungenügend sie auch schon ist) entzogen wird, und schlimmer noch daß die Leute meine Frau und Kind zwingen mich hier allein zu laßen und nach Amerika zurückkehren. So ist es schon einmal geschehen wie Sie wissen; und wieder so

Drawing by Franz Marc in letter of 26 October 1913 to Albert Bloch, Courtesy of Mrs. Albert Bloch

Zeichnung von Franz Marc im Brief vom 26. Oktober 1913 an Albert Bloch, Mrs. Albert Bloch

eine Hölle durchzumachen hält weder meine Frau noch ich aus. – Die Leute drüben (meine Schwiegerverwandten) betrachten die Sache vom reinen kommerziellen Standpunkt aus: man kann's ihnen ja nicht einmal verdenken – doch macht diese Einsicht mir die Sache nur noch peinlicher.

Es handelt sich also um eine gewissermassen <u>dauernde</u> Unterstützung von Seiten eines wirklichen Kunstfreundes, der mir <u>nur wegen meiner Kunst</u> beistehen würde, und nicht aus Gründen der Pflicht, Freundschaft oder Verwandtschaft. Es fragt sich nur, wo sich eine solche Persönlichkeit findet. Was tun? Vielleicht können Sie mir Rat geben – oder mich mit solchen Leuten in Verbindung setzen die dafür Interesse hätten. Könte Walden irgendwie für mich eintreten? Er schreibt mir immer sehr freundlich und nett, doch kennen wir uns kaum. Meine Ausstellung bei Dietzel war vollständig ohne Erfolg, was bei einer so naivschlampigen Geschäftsleitung nur zu erwarten war. Auch weiß ich daß München für unsereins keine besondere Stätte ist, und daß überdies die Zeiten sowieso ungünstig sind. – Hoffentlich geht's mir im Herbstsalon und bei Walden im Dezember besser: der versteht wohl die Sache viel besser wie der arme Dietzel, und wird sich obendrein auch persönlich bemühen, um doch einen kleinen Erfolg zu sichern. Dietzel tat absolut nix! – Doch darum ist mir am wenigsten zu tun, und Dietzel ist trotz allem ein anständiger, netter Mensch.–

Auch an einzelne [sic] Verkäufe liegt mir nicht viel. Was unsereiner gelegentlich in Ausstellungen verkauft, dafür kann er sich höchstens mit Zigaretten versorgen: zum Leben reichts lange nicht aus. – Die Lage ist verteufelt ernst, wie Sie sehen. Findet sie keine Abhilfe so kann weiß Gott was daraus werden. Wenn ich nur zwei, drei Leute finden könte die mir monatlich so und soviel zu schiessen, und sich dann mit Bildern entgelten! Das wär's: der einzige Ausweg.–

Der Brief wird lang, merk' ich. Also, Schluß!
Bitte grüßen Sie mir Ihre Gattin; auch die meine läßt grüßen. Ich hoffe bei Ihnen eine Menge neue Sachen zu sehen, und freue mich schon darauf. Die »Verzauberte Mühle« bei Dietzel ist ein herrliches Dingchen!
Also, auf Wiedersehen,

Ihr Bloch

FRANZ MARC AN ALBERT BLOCH

Sindelsdorf [4. August 1913]

Lieber Bloch,

mit Ihrer wunderschönen Zeichnung haben Sie uns eine riesige Freude gemacht; sie ist so famos, ich möchte sie am liebsten im Herbstsalon austellen [sic]. Wir besuchen Sie Donnerstag 4 Uhr im Atelier. Wiedersehn und Grüsse von uns beiden

Ihr F. Marc

FRANZ MARC AN ALBERT BLOCH

Berlin [18. August 1913]

Lieber Herr Bloch,

ich stecke hier in so unglaublicher Arbeit, daß ich keine Zeit bisher fand, Ihren lieben Brief zu beantworten. Von Ihrem Freund hingen wir die kleine Landschaft auf, mehr war nicht möglich – es hielt zu wenig stand. Aber das Kleine ist recht fein. Von Ihnen wurde das Ölbergbild zurückgestellt. Gratuliere zum Verkauf an Koehler. Ich komme hier schon mit manchen Leuten zusammen und versuche was nur möglich ist, aber die Berliner sind spröd und trocken in all diesen Dingen. Wir sind gegen Ende Sept. (ca. 26.) wieder in Sindelsdorf. Ich bringe ein süsses, zahmes Reh mit!
Herzl. Gruss von uns beiden Ihr

Fz. Marc

FRANZ MARC AN ALBERT BLOCH

Sindelsdorf, 26. Oktober 1913

Lieber Bloch,

Dank für Ihren lieben Brief; die Bitte betreff des Pferdes amüsiert mich; Sie werden es sicher nicht brauchen können, was ich Ihnen da zeichne; erstens zeichnen Sie genauso gut wie ich. (Pferdebeine sind doch auch nicht anders als Menschenbeine!) und dann können hundert Menschen jeder ein springendes Pferd zeichnen ohne dass eins dem anderen gleicht.

Eben fällt mir ein, dass im Tierbuch von Piper ja eine Menge Pferde sind, vielmal besser als ich es Ihnen demonstriren kann, so hör ich mit der Zeichnerei auf und schicke Ihnen das Buch, dazu 2 Photos, die sehr orginelle Momente eines Pferdes zeigen. Buch Seite 53, 156, 103, 74, 57.

Rechnen Sie für Fracht der Sicherheit halber 10 Tage; Die Sendung erfolgt auf Kosten des Sturm, der die Bilder austellt [sic]; Rücksendung natürlich auf Ihre Kosten, ausser wenn Walden, wie ich vermute, die Collection noch in andere Städte schickt; dann trägt jeweils der Austeller [sic], der die Collection empfängt, die Last der Sendung. Die 1. Fracht München-Berlin haben Sie jedenfalls nicht zu tragen.

Wenn wir wieder nach München kommen besuchen wir Sie sicher. Herzlich von Haus zu Haus

Ihr F. Marc

ALBERT BLOCH AN FRANZ MARC

München, 18. Dezember 1913

Lieber Marc!

Eben fällt mir ein daß Sie das letzte mal Ihr Taschenmesser hier vergessen haben. Soll ichs Ihnen zuschicken, oder wollen Sie lieber warten bis Sie

Catalogue for the solo exhibition "Albert Bloch," Herwarth Walden's Der Sturm Gallery, Berlin, 1913, Courtesy of Mrs. Albert Bloch

Katalog der Einzelausstellung ›Albert Bloch‹ in Herwarth Waldens Galerie ›Der Sturm‹, Berlin 1913, Mrs. Albert Bloch

wieder zu mir kommen? – Leider werde ich Ihnen kaum was neues zeigen können, da es in letzter Zeit ziemlich schlimm mit der Arbeit ging, und war ich ausserdem mit allerlei Nebensächlichen [sic] beschäftigt. Auch war ich inzwischen in Berlin meine Bilder bei Walden zu hängen. Den Herbstsalon erwischte ich noch gerade vor seinem Schluss. Das war eine außerordentlich starke Ausstellung, was mich eigentlich überraschte, da mir der Katalog eine Enttäuschung war. Mit einigem war ich absolut nicht einverstanden (wie Sie wohl auch nicht, wie ich annehme), aber im großen Ganzen fand ich es eine selten schöne, kräftige Vertretung der neueren Richtung. – Auch die Köhler Sammlung hab ich gesehen. Die glaube ich, steht wohl einzig da. Durand-Ruel ist nicht mal damit zu vergleichen. – Wie froh ich bin das [sic] die zwei Sachen von mir drin hängen werden, und Ihnen bin ich vor allem dankbar, daß Sie's bewirkt haben. –

Mit meiner Ausstellung im Sturm bin ich eigentlich ganz zufrieden. Die Räume sind gediegen und die Bilder hängen ganz günstig. Ich glaube kaum daß ich verkaufen werde, obwohl mir Walden schon versicherte ein Bild wäre bereits so gut wie verkauft. Ich aber kenne meinen unausbleiblichen [sic] Pech, und muss nur immer damit rechnen. Zwei Bilder davon gehen nach Dresden, zur Reiche Ausstellung, schreibt mir Walden. Reiche wäre bei ihm gewesen und habe sie dort ausgesucht. Dass ich sonst keine persönliche Einladung bekommen habe, wundert mich. –

Hoffentlich gehts Ihnen nach Wunsch – und der Erfolg bleibt auch nicht aus. – Bitte grüßen Sie mir die Gnädige Frau; auch meine Frau möchte grüßen lassen. –

Herzlichst

Bloch

FRANZ MARC AN ALBERT BLOCH

[Feldpostkarte] La Croix au mines, September 1914

Lieber Freund,

einen herzlichen Gruß aus dem Krieg. Gestern waren wir schon im Feuer. So ein Artilleriekampf ist etwas fabelhaft mystisches und grossartiges. Es geht mir ganz gut; es ist unglaublich, woran sich der Körper gewöhnen kann. In den ersten Tagen hatte ich stets an die 40 - 50 klm zu reiten und selten mehr als 3 Stunden Schlaf im Freien Feld. Aber schön ist es! Herzl. Händedruck von Ihrem

F. Marc

FRANZ MARC AN ALBERT BLOCH

[Feldpostkarte] Hageville, 9. XI. 1914

Lieber Bloch,

Gestern kam ein lieber Cigarrengruß von Ihnen. Es ist immer so schön zu fühlen dass man unser Soldaten draussen so freundlich gedenkt. So gut die deutsche Sache steht, so wird es doch mit dem Heimkommen noch eine gute Weile haben, – mit dem Malen auch! Aber an Malerei und an das neue Europa, das wir haben werden und das kommen muss, denke ich immerwährend. Dass der gute August Macke gefallen ist, werden Sie wohl schon wissen; er wurde am 26. IX, als er französ. Gefangene machte, schwer verwundet; seine Leute konnten ihn nicht mehr holen, seitdem fehlt von ihm jede Spur und Nachricht. Wäre er nur verwundet und Kriegsgefangener, hätte er wohl Gelegenheit gehabt, irgendwelche Nachricht zu geben. Ich leide bitterlich an diesem Verlust. Er hatte kurz zuvor das eiserne Kreuz bekommen. Nun brennt der Orient auch schon, – wie viele Staaten wird es noch ergreifen. Schicken Sie mir doch zuweilen Blätter od. interess. Ausschnitte der Frankf. Zeitung; bayr. Zeitungen bekomme ich hier ohne Mühe.

Leben Sie wohl, mit herzl. Gruss Ihr

Fz. Marc

ALBERT BLOCH AN FRANZ MARC

München, 16. November 1914

Lieber Marc!

Ihre Karte aus Hageville vom 9. XI, freute mich wie immer wenn ich Nachricht von Ihnen bekomme.

Ich weiß nicht was ich Ihn1en zu den Feiertagen schreiben soll, außer den üblichen Gruß und die herzl. Wünsche für Ihr ferneres Wohlergehen. – Ich werde dafür sorgen daß Sie die Frankfurter Ztg. [Zeitung] mit ziemlicher Regelmäßigkeit bekommen. Hoffentlich hat Sie daß Paket welches ich Ihnen kürzlich sandte in guter Ordnung erreicht. Ich mußte es zur Max II Kaserne hinaus tragen, da es die Post nicht annahm. Bitte schreiben Sie mir ungeniert was Sie brauchen können: es ist mir immer eine Freude wenn Sie es mir möglich machen einen Wunsch zu erfüllen.

Ich hörte nur zufällig daß Macke gefallen sein soll; jedoch wurde es bestritten. Es heißt nur daß er in Fkrch. schwer verwundet gefangen ist, und daß jede Nachricht fehlt. Es ist ja möglich daß er durch seine Verletzung nicht in der Lage ist Wort von sich zu geben. Klee soll durch einen Schweizer Freunde, der in Paris eine Untersuchung der Lazaretten in die Wege geleitet haben. Hoffentlich ist seine Mühe nicht umsonst. Obwohl ich den Macke nicht persönlich kenne, würde ich sein [sic] Tod aufs tiefste bedauern; denn allem Vernehmen nach ist er ein wirklich feiner Mensch; und überdies wäre sein Ableben ein Verlust für die jüngere Malerei. Ich halte an der Hoffnung fest, daß er noch lebt.

Kampendonck [sic] ist wohl längst im Felde. Wissen Sie seine Adresse? Ich möchte ihm auch mal einen Gruß schreiben. –

Von Kandinsky habe ich nie was gehört. Daß ihn Klee in der Schweiz besucht hat, wissen Sie wohl. K. sitzt in irgend einem kleinen Nest, und – schreibt wieder ein theoretisches Werk über Malerei!! Mir unbegreiflich: doch messe ich mir kein Urteil bei.

Mir ist nichts übrig geblieben als mich der Arbeit wieder zuzuwenden. Allerdings kann ichs nicht verantworten wenn ich an Euch alle im Felde draußen denke: es will mir nicht anders als ein triviales Handwerk erscheinen, wenn ichs mit dieser Riesengegenwart vergleiche. Doch kann ich nichts dafür; und in der Tat bin ich so allmählich wieder ins Malen hinein gekommen, dass mich meine Arbeit jetzt, ebenso wie früher, völlig in Anspruch nimmt. »Wozu«, darf ich mich aber nicht fragen! – Fleißig bin ich in letzter Zeit gewesen, sage ich Ihnen. Zwei Sachen fertig gemacht, und noch <u>sieben</u> andere unterwegs: darunter eine 2 Meter Schwarte!

München ist ganz ruhig. Vom Krieg ist kaum was zu merken. Theater, Konzerte, allabendlich. Die Theatinerstraße, Kaufingerstr., sind belebt wie früher. Im Café Luitpold u. Café Odeon täglich Musik: der reinste Faschingsrummel. Das Stefanie bleibt der gleiche Saustall wie früher. Der Krieg hat manches Übel für uns Zurückgebliebenen: z.B., Ganghofer kackt täglich ein patriotisches Gedicht in den Zeitungen; Goltz gibt eine künstlerische Kriegsmappe heraus (Neue Sezession: finster, sag ich Ihnen!); jeder Kollege der zu wenig Begeisterung aufbringt um auf jeden Preis ins Feld hinauszukommen, treibt umso eifriger in den Caféhäuser [sic] Weltpolitik; die Aktion erscheint unentwegt weiter; und die Mnchnr. Neuesten [Münchener Neueste Nachrichten] sind noch nicht vom Zensor aus der Welt geschaffen. […] Deutschland wird siegen. Zweifellos. Mit dem Feind wird es schon fertigwerden. Aber wie wird es mit dieser schleimigen Patriotenbrut einstmals abrechnen?

Ja, lieber Freund, Ihr da draußen im Felde habens [sic] in mancher Hinsicht besser als wir in der Stadt. Was sind eure Strapazen gegen die täglichen Ausspeiungen eines einzigen journalistischen Stimmungmachers? Eure Gefahr ist gross: es geht ums Leben. Uns gehts um den Geist; nur um den Geist – sonst laufen wir keine Gefahr; haben auch keine Strapazen. Wir schlafen warm, essen gut und reichlich, spazieren wenn die Sonne scheint; hocken im Café oder in die geheizte Stube, wenn das Wetter schlecht ist. Es geht uns brillant; und ihr blutet draußen auf dem Felde. Wenn ich nur körperlich imstand wäre <u>einen kleinen teil</u> der Strapazen zu ertragen: ich weiß nicht – ich wäre versucht mich naturalisieren zu lassen, meine Familienpflichte [sic] zu vergessen, und auf gut Glück die Sache da draußen mit euch zu probieren. – Wenn Sie mich kennen,

werden Sie mir gerne glauben daß ich das alles in einer Großsprecherischen Absicht nicht gesagt habe. – Und da ich nicht irrsinnig werden will habe ich mich kopfüber in die Arbeit geworfen. Ich komme mit Niemanden mehr in Berührung: diese dumme anmassende [sic] Kriegsgespräche und weltpolitische Meinungsäußerungen von Menschen, bei dem ich immer ein gewisses Quantum von Intelligenz voraussetzte, weiter anzuhören ist mir unmöglich. – Ich bleibe tagsüber im Atelier, gegen Abend gehe ich ins Café, um die Zeitung ganz flüchtig durchzusehen, und dann nach haus. Wenn Sie hier wären, würden Sie's verstehen. Sie dürfen meinem Verhalten einem Mangel an Interesse nicht zuschreiben. Das ist es auf keinen Fall. – Übrigens will ich Sie mit meinem »Geisteszustand« nicht weiter langweilen. Ich wollte Ihnen nur ein wenig von München erzählen, und bin ganz unwillkürlich von meiner harmlosen Absicht abgerutscht.

Wie geht es Ihrer Gattin? Ich habe sie seit Ihrem Ausrücken nicht mehr gesehen. Sie hatte sich einmal bei uns zum Tee angemeldet, wurde aber im letzten Augenblick verhindert. Grüßen Sie sie mir bitte auf diesem Umweg. Ich schreibe ihr in den nächsten Tagen einen Gruß. Schreiben Sie mir wieder recht bald, wenn Sie Zeit bekommen, wie's Ihnen geht.

Von uns beiden seien Sie herzlichst gegrüßt,

Ihr Bloch

FRANZ MARC AN ALBERT BLOCH

Hageville, 22. November 1914

Lieber Bloch,

Ihr langer Brief vom 16. XI hat mich sehr gefreut und interessirt – gefreut, da mir Ihre Haltung in dieser unheimlichen Stunde die einzig würdige scheint, und interessirt, da Sie das dumme München, das ich so kenne aber heraussen doch wieder oft ganz vergesse, mir wieder so famos vormalen. Die neue Secession ist schon sehr übel, – Maria sandte mir 2 Nummern des Zeit-echo, das vor allem in seiner Graphik schon Trostlos ist, so eine Art Wohltätigkeits-ausgabe für notleidende malende Nicht-Combatanten, unter dem scheinheiligen Deckmantel von moderner Kunst. Mich ärgert nur, dass Klee bei der Gesellschaft mittut, die seine Gutmütigkeit, sein »weites Herz« nur ausnutzt; denn er gehört mit keinem Strich seiner Arbeit dahinein. – Der Verlust von August Macke war für mich ein furchtbarer Schlag. Wir wussten wohl kaum, wie ich an diesem Freunde, an seinem ganzen Menschen hing. Es war etwas Unlösbares, unzertrennliches zwischen uns, das auch der Tod nicht zerreissen konnte, – so ging einfach ein Stück von mir mit in seinen Tod, – zum ersten Mal in meinem Leben, das ich das Gefühl hatte, dass ich etwas Wirkliches, Unersetzliches verlor, – dass ich ärmer wurde. Alle andern Verluste wie der für mich sehr schmerzliche Tod meines Vaters hat mein Wesen eher bereichert und gestärkt. Dass er noch als französ. Kriegsgefangener lebt, halte ich für gänzlich ausgeschlossen. Er fiel am 26. Sept, als er im Begriff war, französ. Gefangene zu machen, wahrscheinlich irrtümlich von seiner eigenen Truppe beschossen. Er rief noch zurück und wurde im Wirrwarr des Moments aus den Augen verloren und ist seitdem gänzlich verschollen. Er war wohl tödlich getroffen und von den Franzosen kurzerhand eingegraben, so wie es bei uns in den Vogesen auch gemacht wurde. Man hat nicht Zeit, lange nach Brieftasche und Namen zu suchen. Dass er nach 2 Monaten noch keine Möglichkeit gehabt haben sollte, ein Lebenszeichen nach Deutschl. zu geben, ist nicht denkbar. Die Ungewissheit über seinen Tod ist für seine arme Frau doppelt schrecklich und quälend. Er war Leutnant u. Kompanieführer und hatte wenige Tage zuvor das eiserne Kreuz bekommen. Er hat die grauenvollsten Schlachten mitgemacht. Mir ist weh, wenn ich an ihn denke. – Denken Sie sich: Campendonk ist zu faul od. zu energielos, um sich als Soldat zu melden! Er hält seine Malerei offenbar für wichtiger. Ein junger Mensch wie er und kerngesund; er wurde seinerzeit militärfrei, da er sich durch eine Hungerkur krank stellte. Gottlob sind solche Typen eine Ausnahme! – Wir sind momentan ganz aus dem Gefecht gezogen; ich finde sogar Zeit für mich zu arbeiten und manches zu schreiben und meine Arbeit, wenn ich wiederkomme, aus tiefem Grunde vorzubereiten. Aber ich denke und schreibe lieber im Sattel als in einer Schweizer Retraite. Kandinsky schrieb mir letzthin sehr nett. Gruss Ihrer Frau u. Ihnen

Ihr F. M.

<u>Glück zur Arbeit!</u>

ALBERT BLOCH AN FRANZ MARC

München, Kurfürstenstr. 59/IV, 6. Dezember 1914

Lieber Marc!

Ihr schöner Brief und die beiden Karten, kamen schon vor einigen Tagen: ich freute mich darüber sehr. Ich wollte am liebsten gleich antworten, doch kam so manches dazwischen, sodaß ich erst heute Abend in der Lage bin. [...]

An Neuem wäre nichts zu berichten. Ihre liebe Gattin war gestern bei uns zum Tee: wir waren herzlich froh, sie willkommen zu heißen. – Sie erzählte von Ihrem Aufsatz, der in der Frankf. Zeitung gedruckt werden soll. Einiges zitierte sie aus dem Gedächtnis: sehr wenig – nur genügend um mir einen Begriff von Ihrem Gedankengang zu geben. Ich möchte sehr gern das Manuskript sehen: sollte der Aufsatz wirklich gedruckt werden, so werde ichs schon zu lesen bekommen. Aber ich glaube kaum daß eine Tageszeitung in dieser Stunde sowas erscheinen läßt. Für anderes als gangbare Patriotismusware werden die Blätter wenig Interesse haben. Auch wenn zufällig in der Redaktion einer sitzen sollte der für derartiges Geist und Sympathie hätte (was ich für sehr fraglich halte), müßte er doch sofort einsehen daß so ein Artikel für das große Publikum gänzlich unverständlich, oder wenigstens ungeniessbar ist.

Die Aufgabe der Tagespresse oder die Aufgabe die sie sich stellt ist eine Aufhetzung des Volkes. Sie läßt nicht nach den Hass zu schüren den sie in erster Linie selbst angefacht hat. Aufwiegelei, Verleumdung und Entstellung sind die Werkzeuge womit sie den Banausen-patriotismus und die Hurrastimmung erzeugt die ihr Not thun. So wird ein Artikel wie dieser wenig Aussicht haben dürfen. Sicher ist die Frankf. Zeit. die am wenigsten Verachtungswerte die gegenwärtig in Deutschland erscheint; doch muß ich sehr zweifeln ob auch diese Platz für solche Äusserungen zu Verfügung [sic] hätte. Es gibt natürlich, außer Tagblätter, auch verschiedene bessere Zeitschriften, die gerne bereit wären, so einen Aufsatz zu drucken (z.B. »Das Forum«) doch werden sie eben nicht von sehr vielen gelesen. Da wäre für diesen Zweck <u>»Die Neue Zürcher Zeitung«</u> am allerbesten. Sie hält sich streng neutral; ist sehr zuverläßig, höchst anständig, und mit ihrer Meinung sehr zurückhaltend. Seit Anfang des Krieges wird sie eifrig von allen jenen gelesen die von den Ausschreitungen der Heimatsjournalen angeekelt sind. Ich glaube sicher daß sie den Artikel annimmt und Ihnen auch das gewünschte Publikum (qualitativ, wie quantitativ) geben könnte. Ich würde mich zuerst dorthin wenden. –

Ihr Gedanke, daß mit diesem Kriege die Völker Europas ein gemeinsames Blutopfer darbringen, ist erhaben = schön. – Das zeugt mir von Ihrer Erkenntnis daß dieser Krieg eine unerbittliche <u>geistige Notwendigkeit</u> ist. Das habe ich nun immer gewußt, aber so überraschend die Tatsache auch [*Wort unleserlich*] mag, es scheinen sehr, sehr wenig andere das zu wissen. Ich habe diesen Gedanken hie und da aufgeworfen (es waren wirklich intelligente, »aufgeklärte« Leute), wurde aber, so oft ich nur davon anfing, mit Entrüstung zurückgewiesen. Man wollte absolut nichts davon wissen; der Standpunkt war immer der eines eng begrenzten Patriotismus. Russland hat angefangen; England hat angestiftet u.s.w. – Auch gut; aber diese Menschen begreifen nicht dass das alles nur <u>äusserlich</u> ist. Von diesem Gesichtspunkte aus ist der Krieg sicher eine Notwendigkeit. Die Natur schert sich ein Dreck [sic] um Anlässe. [...] – Käme einer daher und predigte von einer inneren Notwendigkeit; oder vom geistigen Reinemachen; oder von einer philiströs bequemen Zeit oder von Siechtum des Ideals, oder was weiß ich: – was wäre sein Teil? Gelächter oder Gleichgültigkeit. – [...] Ich kenne den Zustand. Anfangs

schwebte auch ich in Deutschlandsbegeisterung, wie's sich ein Hofbräuhaus (oder Stephanie) Stratege nicht besser wünschen könnte. Das war natürlich, und ich schäme mich dessen keineswegs. Ich war von den Ereignissen so gepackt, mein Kopf war so erhitzt daß ich einfach nicht imstande war die Sache anders als vom Pöbelstandpunkt aus zu betrachten. Am liebsten wäre ich gleich mithinausgezogen: was mir dennoch nicht möglich war. Erst nach eine [sic] Woche oder noch länger kam ich wieder zur Besinnung. Dann sah ich diesen Krieg für daß [sic] was er wirklich ist: dann erst wurde mir anschaulich, daß ich eigentlich schon lange von der Notwendigkeit eines solchen Weltbrandes überzeugt war. Jüngst schrieb ich nach Hause an einen Freunde, den Herausgeber einer pazifistischen Wochenschrift, mein sehnlichster Wunsch sei, daß die Vereinigte [sic] Staaten auch in diesen Kriege hineingezogen wären. Das wird aber kaum verwirklicht sein. Erst später kommt die Reihe an uns; aber dann werden wir viel zu sühnen haben. –

Mit Ihrem Gedanken, die Grenzen zwischen Land und Land gänzlich zu verwischen muß ich mich streiten. (Oder hat Ihre Frau nicht richtig zitiert?) Denn erstens; sind Grenzen einfach nicht aufzuheben. Es <u>gibt</u> ein <u>Deutschtum</u>; es gibt ein <u>Russischen</u> Geist [sic]; es gibt eine <u>Französische</u> Malerei; und solange diese alle bestehen bleiben, ist jedes künstliche Beiseiteschaffen der Grenzen einfach nicht auszudenken. Auch gibt's ein <u>Volksbewußtsein</u> (das einzig Schöne – wenigstens in Deutschland – das der gegenwärtige Krieg bisher hervorgebracht hat). – Doch, vielleicht habe ich Ihre Frau misverstanden, oder hat sie nicht ganz richtig zitiert; so will ich diesen Gegenstand lieber nicht weiter berühren. –

Was ich da alles sagte, scheint mir beim Durchlesen ziemlich dumm und unzulänglich. Aber Sie werden mir viel nachsehen müßen, und wenn Sie mich kennen, werden Sie wissen wie Sies aufzunehmen haben. Mir fehlt eben vollständig die Gabe mich klar und richtig auszudrücken; so bin ich meistens still. Manchmal laß ich mich trotzdem hinreissen – und das vorhergehende ist das diesmalige Resultat. – Ich werde Sie künftig verschonen.

Was Sie mir von Kampendonck [sic] erzählen ist interessant. Ich glaube aber nicht dass es sich da um Faulheit oder Mangel an Energie handelt. Weiß Gott, so faul wie ich bin, könnte er kaum sein! Ich habe wenig Gelegenheit gehabt, bei K. zu beobachten; aber mir scheint daß seine Frau in deren Menage das Hauptwort führt. Vielleicht hält sie ihn ab. –

Meine Arbeit scheint langsam Vorwärts zu wollen. Bin ziemlich fleißig; doch muß ich mich dazu zwingen. Bin ich schon mal in der Arbeit drin, dann gehts immer gut: dann bin ich <u>ganz</u> dabei. Krieg, Probleme, Tagsrummel, alles weg! – Wohin es führen wird? Was nachher kommen wird, wenn der Krieg vorbei ist? Mit vielem wird aufgeräumt werden – vielleicht auch mit meiner Malerei – doch darüber kann ich nicht nachgrübeln. Ich muß arbeiten, meinen Weg gehen und kann mich darin nicht um Probleme kümmern. Ist der Weg falsch, dann helfe mir Gott – ich weiß keinen anderen. – Wenn's Sie interessiert sende ich Ihnen mal Photographien meiner Arbeiten vom letzten Jahr (Sie waren schon solange nicht mehr bei mir!) –

Jetzt muß ich diesen langen Brief schließen, ohne Ihnen das Geringste erzählt zu haben. – Schreiben Sie mir mal wieder: es ist mir immer eine Freude von Ihrem Wohlergehen zu erfahren. – Meine Frau läßt vielmals grüßen, auch ich.
Herzlichst

Ihr Bloch

FRANZ MARC AN ALBERT BLOCH

[Feldpostkarte] 29. Dezember 1914

Lieber Bloch,

Ihren langen guten Brief zu beantworten finde ich jetzt nicht Zeit; wir sind wieder in der Feuerstellung, riesig interessant und grossartig. Ich habe leichten Dienst, so dass ich dem Ganzen mit grosser Ruhe zusehen kann. – Ich weiss nicht, in welchem Sinn Sie den Artikel von Kraus ansehen. Mir geht es bei der Lektüre wie immer bei Kraus: ich lese immer sehr viel Gutes heraus, muss es mir aber mit Mühe aus dem gekünstelten Rederausch herauslesen; das Ende vom Lied ist immer, dass ich ihn nie zu Ende lesen kann, es kommt immer ein Punct, wo er mich ödet. Über die völkische Grenzverwischung denke ich »zunächst und vorderhand« wie Sie, aber das Problem hab ich auch anders gestellt, als Sie es von m. Frau aufnahmen, vor allem in einer zweiten Sache, die ich jetzt schreibe zwischen Auf- u. Absatteln! Für das Unterbringen des Manuskripts lass ich Wolfskehl sorgen; Ich dachte auch an den Merkur, nannte m. Frau auch die Züricher Zeitung. Ich bin wohlauf und hoffe mit Ihnen allen u. für uns alle auf ein gutes besseres neues Jahr.

Ihr F. Marc

ALBERT BLOCH AN FRANZ MARC

München, 17. Januar 1915

Lieber Marc!

Die Paar Zeilen eigentlich nur um mein langes Schweigen zu entschuldigen. Ich war krank, hatte ausserdem den Kopf voll Sorgen, und war nie zum Schreiben aufgelegt. Sie begreifen ja. Keine Vernachlässigung – im Gegenteil: ich denke viel und oft an Sie, und möchte immer wissen daß Sie wohlauf sind, und daß es Ihnen in jeder Hinsicht gut geht. […]

Ich will ein Paar Sachen von Ihnen nächstens mit an Eddy schicken. Er hat sich neulich erkundigt. Vielleicht ist etwas da auszurichten. Wir wollen versuchen und hoffen. Aber verlassen Sie sich nicht darauf. Er war von jeher ein arger Knicker: jetzt scheints noch schlimmer zu sein. – Lassen Sie bald wieder Nachricht kommen.
Herzlichst

Ihr B.

ALBERT BLOCH AN FRANZ MARC

München, 26. Februar 1915

Lieber Marc: –

Ihre liebe Postkarte aus Bollweiler, kam kürzlich an, und freute mich wie immer, sehr. – Wie kommen Sie wieder nach Deutschland? – Waren Sie beurlaubt? oder liegen Sie etwa im Lazarett? […]

Ich glaube auch daß es für Sie am ratsamsten war, mit dem Versandt der Bilder an Eddy zu zögern. Zwar ist der Weg nach Amerika über Italien noch immer ganz gefahrlos (die Versicherungsprämien sind noch ganz gering), doch wenn Ihnen an einem Verkauf nicht viel liegt, ist es doch besser zu warten bis sich die Zeiten etwas gelegt haben, denn Eddy war ja von jeher ein arger Knicker, und jetzt scheint er die Konjunktur ausnützen zu wollen, und mit dem Zahlen wirds noch schlimmer als zuvor. Leider zwangen mich meine Verhältniße seinem Ansinnen nachzukommen (ich zehrte eben an dem allerletzten Rest) und nun hat er mir anständigerweise einen Vorschuß gewährt, der mich eine Zeitlang über Wasser halten wird. – Was ich für Preise bekomme, weiß der Teufel. Ich bin außerstande mit ihm zu handeln: bin eben gezwungen jeden beliebigen Angebot [sic] zu acceptieren; ich habe keine Wahl – entweder das, oder hungern. An mich allein darf ich ja nicht denken.

Was das mit Amerika ist möchte ich auch gerne wissen. Man kann nur hoffen, und meine Hoffnungen werden immer schwächer. – Das [sic] es den Amerikanern absolut am Verständnis mangelt ist klar. Der Wille ist gut, aber die ganze kulturelle Tradition (soweit sie überhaupt existiert) Englisch. In der letzten »Zukunft« ist übrigens ein Aufsatz von einem Deutsch-Amerikaner, betitelt »Germans – be fair« der diesen Zustand klar beleuchtet. Es ist das vernünftigste was ich bis jetzt über die Haltung des amerikanischen Volkes gelesen habe. –

Neues gibts nicht. München bleibt München – auch im Krieg. Dumm, selbstzufrieden, harmlos, und leichtgläubig. An G'müatlichkeit fehlts selbstverständlich auch jetzt nicht. Die Neuesten Nachrichten walten ihres Amtes! –

[…] Die Neue Sezessions Ausstellung habe ich nicht gesehen. Ich gehe auch nicht hin; aber da der Ostini sie ziemlich günstig »beurteilt« weiß ich von vornherein, daß es ein hervorragender Mist sein muß. –

Die eigene Arbeit? – Nichts zu sagen. Ich arbeite was ich kann, und habe weder Mut noch Hoffnung verloren. Übrigens war ich fast den ganzen Winter über krank. –

Jetzt Schluß! – Bitte schreiben Sie bald wieder – wenn nur eine Karte und seien Sie recht herzlich von uns beiden gegrüßt,

Ihr Bloch

FRANZ MARC AN ALBERT BLOCH

[Feldpostkarte] 5. März 1915

Lieber Bloch,

Dank für Ihren lieben Brief; wir stehen auf deutschem Kriegsboden im Elsass. Schicken Sie mir doch gelegentlich die No. d. Zukunft »Germans – be fair« Für derartige Zusendungen bin ich immer sehr dankbar. Maria hat jetzt zu wenig Gelegenheit, derlei für mich zu finden. Über die neue Secession hab ich in den Neuest. Nachr. gelesen, – es ist immer dasselbe, – es nimmt höchstens noch dümmere Formen an als vor dem Kriege. Vive la bagatelle! – Dass Sie so viel krank gewesen sind, thut mir sehr leid, ich wünsche Ihnen von Herzen ein besseres Frühjahr. Im Sommer kommen wir wieder! Gruss Ihnen beiden

Ihr Fz. Marc

ALBERT BLOCH AN FRANZ MARC

München, 27. April [1915]

Lieber Marc:

Es ist jetzt lange seitdem ich Ihnen schrieb. Verzeihen Sie mir meiner scheinbaren Vernachläßigung. Das wars wirklich nicht; sondern schlechte Stimmung, schwankende Gesundheit und fehlender Anlaß. Jetzt scheint die Sonne wieder (vielleicht nur vorübergehend), mit der Gesundheit gehts leidlich, und den Anlaß haben Sie mir selber in die Hand gelegt. »Das Geheime Europa« ist ein herrlicher, brausender Aufruf, dem ich rückhaltlos beistimmen kann. Nach dem patriotischen Hurrahgeheule der Tagespresse und der Schweissfussenthusiasten, und dem seichten Gefasel der Pacifisten kommt mir der wahre Posaunenschall Ihrer Stimme wie ein Freudengruß. Auch bringt mir diese Stimme einen langersehnten Trost. Denn sie bestätigt meine langgehegte Überzeugung daß auch wir Nichtbeteiligten an diesem ungeheuren Ereignis einen engen und wahren Anteil haben. Daß wir nicht bloße Müßiggänger sind, die wir während dieser Zeit unsere Stunden in Ateliers und Studierstuben verbringen. Das [sic] auch wir im Feindeslande kämpfen. –

[…] Zuerst dachte ich, ich möchte gern Ihren Aufsatz ins Englische übersetzen; doch wozu? Amerika kennt noch keine solche Fragen, würde sie auch nicht im mindesten zu würdigen wissen. Der Weckruf wäre dort nicht am Platze. Man hat keine Zeit für derlei »Spekulationen«, oder, Hirngespinste wäre der geeignete Ausdruck. Wohl könnte ich das Essay unterbringen: ich wüßte einige Zeitschriften die es sehr wahrscheinlich annehmen würden. Aber kaum zwanzig Menschen würden darauf achten. Amerika hat eben ganz andere Probleme, und auch in England dürfte die Zeit noch fern sein, da Ihre Gedanken einen irgendwie vernehmbaren Widerhall erfahren. –

Glauben Sie nicht, daß Sie die Idee des Geheimen Europas weiter ausarbeiten könnten? Sicher haben Sie noch nicht alles dazu gesagt? Denn schon bei der Lektüre war mir manches eingefallen, woran sicher auch Sie gedacht haben dürften. Vielleicht wollen Sie für diesmal nur das allerwesentlichste berühren; und behielten sich vor ein anderes mal darauf zurück zu kommen. Ich hoffe es. –

Von mir nichts neues. Heute schien die Arbeit wieder mal vorwärts gehen zu wollen: Gottlob!! Meine Frau war letzthin sehr krank (hätte sehr leicht in Lungenentzündung ausarten können) – auch der Junge war eine Woche lang unwohl. Jetzt sind beide wieder hergestellt; und nun dürfte es bis zum Sommer ohne besondere Schwierigkeiten weitergehen. Bis zum Sommer! – Und wann sehen wir uns wieder? Bald ists ein Jahr! – Schreiben Sie mir doch dann und wann eine Karte, einen Brief verlange ich ja nicht. Grüßen Sie mir Ihre Frau auf diesem Umweg: wir haben seit einiger Zeit nichts mehr von ihr gehört. Herzlichst von uns beiden

Ihr Bloch

FRANZ MARC AN ALBERT BLOCH

[Feldpostkarte] 4. Mai 1915

Lieber Herr Bloch,

Dank für Ihren lieben Brief; es freut mich sehr, daß mein kurzer Artikel einen solchen Widerhall bei Ihnen gefunden hat. Ich hab meine Ideen seither freilich noch weit ausgebaut, auch schriftlich; Maria hat alles in Händen; nur mag ich jetzt nichts in Druck geben. Ich muss erst alles langsam ausreifen lassen und überarbeiten, wenn ich einmal Distanz sowohl zur Kriegstragödie als auch zu meinen eigenen geistigen Erlebnissen gewonnen habe. Es eilt nichts im Leben und darf nie eilen. Und manches was ich zu sagen habe und sagen möchte, kann gar nicht spät genug gesagt werden. Wenn Sie sich der Mühe unterziehen wollen und Freude daran haben, den Artikel in's Englische zu übertragen u. in America unterzubringen, freut es mich persönlich sehr. Wenn 3 Menschen in America damit etwas geweckt werden, – oder auch nur einer, – so wäre es nicht umsonst gewesen. Ich gebe Ihnen völlig freie Hand darin. Meine Gesundheit ist jetzt sehr gut, ich möchte Ihnen gern ein bischen was von ihr abgeben. Seien Sie und Ihre Gemahlin herzlich gegrüsst von Ihrem

F. Marc

ALBERT BLOCH AN FRANZ MARC

München, 8. Mai [1915]

Lieber Marc!

Ihre Karte vom 4ten habe ich bekommen.

Da Sie trotz meines Bedenkens den Wunsch haben das »Geheime Europa« ins Englische übertragen zu sehen, so will ichs gern versuchen. Hoffentlich gelingt mir die Arbeit. Ihre Gedanken glaube ich vollauf begriffen zu haben: d.h. ich glaube, mit ihnen auch im innerlichsten Sinne vertraut zu sein, doch fehlt mir ganz und gar die schriftstellerische Begabung wie ich meine und es gibt in [*Ihrem Aufsatz*] eine große Menge auf der Hand liegenden [sic] begriffliche Wendungen, die sich überhaupt nicht verenglischen lassen. Schon der Titel »Das geheime Europa«: das Wort »Geheim« hat im Englischen drei oder vier Äquivalenten, von welchen sich keiner mit dem deutschen Wort in Ihrem Sinne völlig deckt. Wie wäre also »Europa Incognita« als Titel für die Englische Übersetzung? So müßte die Übersetzung, und dürfte sie, keine Wörtliche sein, sondern möglichst frei und geschmeidig, damit die Gestaltung der Idee für den Leser immerhin genießbar würde.

Jedenfalls mache ich den Versuch, und seien Sie versichert daß der Gute Wille dabei ist. Ich kann nur hoffen daß ich etwas Anständiges zustande bringe denn ich möchte Ihnen aufrichtig diese kleine Freude bereiten. –

Sollte ich nicht vielleicht auch die Erlaubniß des Forum einholen? [...] Für die Amerikanische Aufnahme der Arbeit kommen nur ein oder zwei Zeitschriften in Betracht: »The Independent«, »The Atlantic Monthly«, höchstens noch, »The Forum« alle ganz achtenswerte Publikationen. Außerdem käme noch die Samstagabend Ausgabe der New Yorker »Evening Post« in Erwägung: eine wirklich hervorragende Tageszeitung: vornehm, anständig, ohne den geringsten Hang zum Sensationellen. Ich glaube wir werden die Arbeit schon unterbringen. Wenn ich sie nur nicht verpatze! –

Neues gibts nicht. Ich sehe niemanden. Jetzt ist der Bub krank. Die Wohnung ist seit Monaten ein Spital.
Seien Sie von uns beiden herzlichst gegrüßt,

Ihr Bloch

FRANZ MARC AN ALBERT BLOCH

[Feldpostkarte] 14. V. 1915

Lieber Herr Bloch,

es freut mich sehr, dass Sie sich zu der Übersetzung entschlossen haben. Ich bin auch sehr einverstanden dass sie dem Geist nach und nicht nur wörtlich gemacht wird. Der Titel ist schwer übersetzbar, das fühle ich auch. »Eur. incognita« scheint mir nicht möglich; es klingt zu sehr an »terra incognita« an, das einen ganz anderen Ideenkreis wachruft. Das »geheime Eur.« bedeutet eher: der unsichtbar arbeitende europaeische Gedanke; das Bewusstsein, dass es eine tiefere europaeische Formel gibt, zu der sich alle guten Europ. bekennen; »the unspoken Europe idea« – so was ähnliches; eine Art »europäischer Generalbass«. Sie werden schon das richtige finden. – Was ist nur mit Ihnen, dass in Ihrem Hause immer der Krankheitsengel umgeht: Ich sage mit Absicht »Engel«, – ich verdanke meinen Kinderkrankheiten die geistigsten Epochen meines Kinderlebens, – ich freute mich auch immer, wenn ich krank sein durfte.
Herzl. Gruss

Fz. Marc

ALBERT BLOCH AN FRANZ MARC

München, 21. Juni 1915

Lieber Marc: –

Nun ist die Übersetzung endlich und glücklich fertig. Sie glauben gar nicht, wie gut es sich auf Englisch ließt. Eine Mordsarbeit sage ich Ihnen aber! Ich habe mich für »The European Idea« als Titel entschlossen. (Etwaige Einwände natürlich gerne berücksichtigt!) – Dem Artikel selbst müsste ich eine kurze Einleitung vorangehen lassen, um Sie Ihrem amerikanischen Publikum gewissermaßen vorzuführen. Jetzt muß an dem ganzen herumgeschliffen werden, und dann folgt die letzte Abschrift. Schade, daß ich keine Tipp-maschine habe! – Unterbringen werde ich die Sache totsicher: nur fragt sich, ob irgend ein Honorar herauszuschlagen ist. Die Paar Zeitschriften die überhaupt in Betracht kommen, haben infolge ihrer ziemlich abseitsstehenden Interessensphäre eine nur beschränkte Leserzahl. [...]

Soll ich Ihnen die Übersetzung zugehen laßen ehe ich sie wegsende oder halten Sie das (wie ich) für unnötig? Wenn ich nur Geld hätte es mit der Schreibmaschine machen zu laßen: doch das wäre etwas zu kostspielig. So müßte ich selbst einige Abschriften anfertigen: eine langwierige Prozedur. –

Einiges Bedenken habe ich auch wegen der Kriegs-Zensur. Es sind ja stellenweise eben nicht gerade schmeichelhafte Bemerkungen die Sie über Ihre Landsleute machen: doch diese Stellen irgendwie herabzudämpfen hielt ich für unangebracht, und übersetzte getreu Ihrem Sinn nach. Hoffen wir daß die Zensur in diesem Falle ein Auge zudrückt. Was die Übersetzung selbst angeht: so habe ich mir sehr große Freiheiten mit Ihrem Wortlaute gestatten müssen. Überall war ich bedacht Ihre Gedanken möglichst genau wiederzugeben: so war ich oft gezwungen im weiten Bogen umzuschreiben; stellenweise sogar zu ergänzen u.s.w. [...] – Trotz alle dem glaube ich den ganzen Esprit Ihrer Sprache beibehalten zu haben, und das freut mich sehr; denn das beweist mir daß ich die Sache doch ziemlich gut gemacht habe. Wo es nur irgend anging ohne Weiteres dem Worte nach zu übersetzen, tat ich dies natürlich. – Ich will nur hoffen daß meine Arbeit Ihnen ein wenig Freude machen wird. –

Sonst wäre nichts von Interesse: uns gehts gesundheitlich besser – sonst aber miserabel. Geld, Geld, und wiederum Geld. – Wir stehen vor dem Debacle. Ich hab Geld zu bekommen. Es bleibt aus. Verkaufte wieder ein Bild zu einem sehr guten Preis: ich kriege das Geld nicht. Ich hätte mindestens ein paar Tausend M zu erwarten. Habens die Engländer mit der übrigen Post gekapert, ists erst unterwegs, oder noch nicht weggeschickt? Ich weiß nicht – höre nichts – habe nichts als den allerletzten Rest woran wir noch zehren. Wenn das aus ist: was dann? Ich bin in heller Verzweiflung: Der Gedanke Frau und Kind könnten Hunger leiden! Genug davon. Es ist zu entsetzlich! – Schreiben Sie mal wieder und seien Sie uns Beiden herzlichst gegrüßt,

FRANZ MARC AN ALBERT BLOCH

[Postkarte] 25. Juni 15

Lieber Bloch,

Dank für Ihren lieben Brief und die Nachricht der gut beendeten Übersetzung. Schicken Sie dieselbe natürlich gleich ab, ohne auf meine Kenntnisnahme zu warten, – aber die Abschrift senden Sie mir bald tunlichst, denn ich bin sehr neugierig, wie sich das alles in einem englischen Gewand ausnimmt. Sie müssen ja in allem, besonders in der Wahl der Zeitschrift ganz selbst entscheiden; ich bin recht neugierig. Bitten Sie jedenfalls um <u>mehrere</u> Belegexemplare. Ich bin ein bischen skeptisch. Die Hypocrisie in Amerika scheint mir in grösster Blüte; Die ruchlosesten Geschäfte werden unter dem moralischsten Deckmantel geführt; es ist kein guter Geist in America, – am wenigsten bei Bryan, – alles um den Sündenapfel der Praesidentschaft; schliesslich sind erbliche Königsrechte doch sittlicher und dem Staatswohl zuträglicher.

Herzlichst Ihr Fz. Marc

Ich komme ca. Mitte Juli in ganz kurzen Urlaub; ich benachrichtige Sie dann.

ALBERT BLOCH AN FRANZ MARC

München, 30. Juni 1915

Lieber Marc!

Ihre Karte vom 25. tat mir weh. Was Sie da alles über Amerika sagen klingt genau wie das Urteil irgend eines Zeitungslesers. Daß Sie nicht ohne weiteres wißen daß <u>alles</u>, was Sie jetzt in Deutschen Zeitungen über meine Heimat u. Landsleute lesen in allen Punkten sehr tendenziös gefärbt ist trifft mich Wunder. Daß Sie die allgemeine <u>Anglo</u> =amerikanische Verständnißlosigkeit für alles Deutsche nicht begreifen, ist nicht erstaunlich; ebensowenig wie mich die Deutsche Verständnislosigkeit für Amerikanisches Wesen nicht erstaunt. Die <u>Ausgangspunkte</u> der Auffassung über ethische Fragen der beiden Länder sind so grundverschieden, daß alle Annäherungsversuche (was Meinungen anbetrifft) nur in eitlem Aneinander=<u>vorbei reden</u> ausarten. Ich verstehe die Deutsche (Kontinentale) Auffassung in Sachen der Ethik. Sie ist sachlich, anständig und vernünftig. Die Amerikanische Auffassung ist sentimental=idealistisch, <u>unsachlich</u>, aber aufrichtig im höchsten Grade: immerhin unvernünftig. Ich verstehe sie ebenso gut wie die Deutsche, nur mundet sie mir nicht: ich kann es zu Hause nicht aushalten – meistens deshalb. Sonst könnte ich <u>vielleicht</u> ebenso gut drüben malen wie hier. Wenn Sie also sagen daß die Hypocrisie in Amerika in größter Blüte zu sein scheint; befinden Sie sich in einem großen Irrtum. Das Amerikanische Volk ist gerade das Gegenteil von Heuchlerisch; das scheint Ihnen natürlich Paradox, doch glauben Sie mir getrost. Es ist ein Volk von Kinder [sic]: tatsächlich. – Und schließlich sind die Journalisten bei uns keinesfalls korrupter als bei Euch oder bei den Franzosen: nur vielleicht <u>noch</u> ungebildeter. – Sie sind also ziemlich falsch informiert. Aber wozu die Gegensätze aufzeichnen und auf alle einzelne eingehen? Ich bin, weiß Gott nicht dazu berufen. Wenn Sie aber sagen »es ist kein guter Geist in Amerika« so muß ich wirklich bitten. Erstens: was wißen Sie vom <u>Amerikanischen</u> Geist. Dann: wer den Amerikanischen Geist nicht selbst, am eignen Leib, an der eignen Seele erlebt, <u>erlitten</u> hat, darf nicht, <u>kann</u> nicht über ihn urteilen. Die

Gegensätze <u>innerhalb</u> dieses Geistes sind zu groß, zu erschreckend. Ich weiß, ich weiß: dieser Geist hat mich aus meiner Heimat vertrieben. Der Künstler will Ordnung; dort gährts noch zu sehr. Aber was gewaltiges, <u>schönes</u>, steckt doch in diesem Geist. Eines Tags steht er da ruhig, erhaben. Aber dann ists für mich zu spät: ich selbst werde es nie mehr erleben können. – [...]

Bin hoch erfreut daß Sie Urlaub bekommen, und daß ich Sie wiedersehen werde. Bitte versuchen Sie mir einen ganzen Tag zu reservieren; u. benachrichtigen Sie mich bitte sobald Sie den Urlaub antreten. Bin ich zu anspruchsvoll?

FRANZ MARC AN ALBERT BLOCH

[Feldpostkarte] 3. Juli 1915

Lieber Bloch,

dass ich betreff America »vorbeigedacht« habe, beruhigt mich förmlich. Ich weiss über America <u>nichts</u> als was in deutschen Zeitungen zu erfahren ist, die im Grunde nur die Thaten der Herrn Wilson & Bryan berichten, die dem <u>Ernst</u> der gegenwärtigen Weltsituation einfach nicht gewachsen sind. Ist es so, dass die Americaner »literarisch« denken u. handeln? Die grossen Diletanten [sic] des Weltkrieges? – Sehen werden wir uns <u>bestimmt</u>, aber voraussagen <u>wann</u> kann ich heute nicht. Ich fahre wahrscheinlich sofort hinaus, ich muss ein paar Tage absolute Ruhe haben im Eigenen, – dann will ich meinen Freunden Nachricht geben. Seien Sie darob ja nicht böse.

Gruss F. Marc

Mein Urlaub wird vom 8. bis 17. Juli sein.

FRANZ MARC AN ALBERT BLOCH

[Feldpostkarte, 17. August 1915]

Lieber Bloch,

wie lange ist schon der Urlaub her und der freundliche Nachmittag bei Ihnen, für den ich Ihnen nochmals Dank sage. Empfehlen Sie mich herzlich Ihrer Frau. – Ihr Tabak schmeckt famos; wenn Sie je wieder solchen schicken lassen, bestellen Sie für mich mit, ja? Kürzlich wurde ich mit dem eisernen Kreuze ausgezeichnet. Immer im gleichen Feldleben, bei leidlicher Gesundheit. – Was macht mein Aufsatz?

Gruss Fz. Marc

FRANZ MARC AN ALBERT BLOCH

[Feldpostkarte] 31. August 1915

Lieber Bloch,

Ihre Übersetzung ist famos; so weit ich sie überhaupt beurteilen kann, scheint mir das meiste darin sehr glücklich, im Sinn praezis und dabei doch für amerikanische Ohren verständlich. Wie gehts Ihnen und Ihrer Familie? Von mir nichts Neues. Beachten Sie anstehend die etwas veränderte Adresse.

Herzlich Ihr Fz. Marc

ALBERT BLOCH AN FRANZ MARC

München, 25. Februar 1916

Lieber Marc!

Ich schreibe nur weil ich mir nicht vorstellen kann was mit Ihnen ist! Sehr kurz nach Ihrem letzten Urlaub, als ich erfuhr daß Sie bei mir waren ohne mich anzutreffen, schrieb ich Ihnen einen Brief, und sandte Ihnen in denselben Tagen ein Paket Tabak. Ich nehme an das [sic] Brief u. Paket fehlgegangen sind, oder haben Sie mir doch geschrieben? Denn es ist ja auch möglich daß ein Brief oder eine Karte aus dem Feld nicht ankommt.

Ich wollte eigentlich nichts weiter: – nur wissen wie's Ihnen geht, u. ob Hoffnung besteht Sie bald wieder auf Urlaub zu begrüßen. –

Diesen, d. h. nächsten, Monat (März) stelle ich zu gleicher Zeit mit Klee bei Walden 16 Bilder aus. Die meisten ganz neue Sachen, Einiges darunter wirklich gut. –

In letzter Zeit habe ich auch mehrfach verkauft, zu meinem nicht geringen Erstaunen. Im letzten Jahr fast 6000 M. –! Was sagen Sie dazu? Das kam alles so unerwartet, das meiste fast alles auf ein mal! So daß es uns jetzt wenigstens vorübergehend erträglich geht. –

Ihre Frau sah ich einige Male im Morgenkonzert im Odeon. Klee traf ich zufällig gestern auf der Straße. Sonst sehe ich so gut wie niemanden. –

Schreiben Sie mir bitte ein mal wieder eine Zeile, wenn Sie Zeit haben. –

Gruß von meiner Frau u. auch von mir,

Ihr Bloch

FRANZ MARC AN ALBERT BLOCH

[Feldpostkarte] 29. Februar 1916

Mein lieber Bloch,

mit mir ist weiter nichts als dass ich seit 8 Tagen im dicksten Kriegsgetümmel bin u. nichts als diesen kurzen Gruss in einem französischen Unterstand schreiben kann. Ihren Tabak hab ich allerdings leider nicht bekommen. Da hätte ich mich schon bedankt, trotzdem ich sehr schreibfaul geworden bin, — es ist nicht zu ändern! Gratuliere zu Ihren Erfolgen. Diese Nachricht hat mich wirklich <u>herzlich</u> gefreut.
Mit Grüßen an Sie u. die Ihren

Ihr Fz. Marc

II. ALBERT BLOCH – HERWARTH WALDEN 1913-17

ALBERT BLOCH AN HERWARTH WALDEN

München, 3. Dezember 1913

Lieber Herr Walden; Liebe gnädige Frau! –

Empfangen Sie nochmals meinen allerherzlichsten Dank für Ihre Liebenswürdigkeit und Güte: ich kann es nicht vergessen, wie Sie sich beide mit dem langweiligen Fremdling abgegeben haben! – Hoffentlich kann ich mich eines Tages revanchieren: wenn Sie nach München kommen. –

Ihre Musik machte einen sehr starken, nachhaltigen Eindruck, Herr Walden. Verzeihen Sie, daß ich es wieder erwähne: vielleicht ist es Ihnen nicht angenehm solch Laienlob zu hören. – Die Daphnislieder, die ich mittlerweile sorgfältig durchgesehen habe sind ganz einfach famos! – Das [sic] sie keine Aufführung erhalten bleibt mir ein Rätsel. – Doch genug davon: ich werde Ihnen übertrieben vorkommen. –

[…] Die Zeichnungen wovon wir sprachen werden Sie demnächst bekommen: es sind deren zwanzig. Hoffentlich werden Sie was damit anfangen können. Die Preise sind alle hinten angegeben: Brutto oder Netto; wie's Ihnen praktisch erscheint. – Um Gottes willen aber, verkaufen Sie mir doch ein Paar Bilder, wenns nur irgendwie zu machen ist! Es brennt; es brennt! –

Kandinsky habe ich noch nicht gesehen; – niemand bis jetzt. Ich werde da viel zu erzählen haben: vom Herbstsalon, Koehlers Sammlung, Ihre Musik, – die schöne Kollektion der gnädigen Frau! –

Wenn Sie den Herrn Arp wieder sehen grüßen Sie ihn von mir und geben Sie ihm meine Adresse: er soll es nicht versäumen mich in München aufzusuchen. –

McCouch läßt grüßen und nochmals danken. Er ist ganz entzückt überhaupt. –

Mit herzlichsten Grüßen an Ihnen [sic] Beide,

Ihr Albert Bloch

ALBERT BLOCH AN HERWARTH WALDEN

München, 29. Februar 1916

Lieber Herr Walden! –

Vielleicht können Sie die Paar Aufzeichnungen in den Sturm unterbringen. Ich fand sie in einem Notizbuch, und habe sie teilweise aus meinem Englischen übertragen. Das Deutsch werden Sie wohl ziemlich einwand-

Herwarth and Nell Walden, Berlin, 1916, Gabriele Münter- und Johannes Eichner-Stiftung, Munich

Herwarth und Nell Walden, Berlin 1916, Gabriele Münter- und Johannes Eichner-Stiftung, München

frei finden, aber wenn Sie irgendwo grammatikalische Fehler entdecken sollten, bitte korrigieren Sie sie mir. –

Dann, im Falle der Verwendbarkeit, senden Sie mir einige Belegexemplare der betreffenden Sturmnummer, nicht wahr? –

Für die schöne Einladung zu meiner Ausstellung, besten Dank. Ich freue mich sehr daß ich mit Klee zusammen ausstelle.
Die besten Grüße an Sie und an die gnädige Frau.

Ihr Albert Bloch.

Ich lege Wert darauf die Daten der Bilder im Kataloge auszuführen. Auch möchte ich Sie bitten den Bindestrich zwischen meinen Vor- und Familienname [sic] zu beachten. Wo immer die Rede von mir ist, den Namen so drucken zu lassen: Albert-Bloch. Es sind verschiedene »Namensvetter« [sic] die sich des Pinsels bei der Arbeit bedienen. Verwechslungen sind öfter vorgekommen, die mir immer peinlich waren. So möchte ich das Publikum und auch die Hrn. Kritiker zwingen meine beiden Namen als ein Ganzes anzusehen. –

Catalogue for the exhibition "Albert Bloch – Paul Klee," Der Sturm Gallery, Berlin, 1916, Courtesy of Mrs. Albert Bloch

Katalog der Ausstellung ›Albert Bloch – Paul Klee‹, Galerie ›Der Sturm‹, Berlin 1916, Mrs. Albert Bloch

ALBERT BLOCH AN HERWARTH WALDEN

München, 18. März 1916

Lieber Herr Walden!

Vielen Dank für die Belegexemplare des »Sturms«.

Ihr Nachruf auf unseren lieben Freund [Franz Marc] gefiel mir sehr. –

Was tun wir jetzt? Wo hinaus? Wie lange noch wird dieser Himmelschreiende Skandal des Sinnlosen Mordens andauern? Er musste fallen, aber dafür dürfen die Hans von Hajeks und wie sie sonst heissen, ihre »Kriegsbilder« in aller Gemütsruhe weiterpatzen. Es ist trostlos – trostlos!

Das einzige das mich im Hinblick auf Marcs Tod aufrecht hält ist nur die Tatsache daß ich es noch gar nicht fassen kann.

Viele Grüße,

Ihr Bloch

ALBERT BLOCH AN HERWARTH WALDEN

München [undatiert, März 1916]

Lieber Herr Walden!

Die Zeitungsausschnitte sind heute angekommen. Ich danke Ihnen. Allerdings haben sie mir keine Freude gemacht. Würden Sie bereit sein von mir eine Verwahrung gegen die Berliner Kritik im Sturm abzudrucken? Es ist mir unerträglich so im Gegensatz zu Paul Klee gelobt zu werden. Ich möchte mich dagegen öffentlich auflehnen. Nicht etwa um mir persönliche Genugtuung zu verschaffen. Was die Kritik über mich schreibt kann mir im Allgemeinen gleichgültig sein, nur in so einem Zusammenhang nicht. Die einzige Rücksicht die mich hier hemmt, ist die Scheu mich in einer so persönlichen Sache hervorzutun. Das werden Sie wohl verstehen. Bitte raten Sie mir. Auch will ich mit Klee hierüber sprechen. –

Wenn der Monat nicht schon so vorgerückt wäre, möchte ich am liebsten den <u>Fries zu einem Musikzimmer</u> von der Ausstellung zurückziehen.

Wohl ist er gut, wenngleich er eine überstandene Phase meiner Entwicklung darstellt; aber diesen Leuten hat er nicht zu »gefallen«. Daß er gut ist, können sie am allerwenigsten ahnen, geschweige denn; warum er gut ist: so kann er ihnen höchstens gefallen, so peinlich mir das, unter den Umständen, auch ist.

Mit besten Grüßen,

Ihr Albert Bloch

P.S. – Vielleicht wäre die Angelegenheit am besten damit abgetan, indem Sie einfach obigen Brief (mit Weglassung dieses Postscriptums) abdrucken. Er enthält schliesslich auch eine Verwahrung, und erspart mir die lästige Notwendigkeit mich mit den Leuten näher einzulassen; dann vermeide ich zu gleicher Zeit den Schein der Unbescheidenheit. Wenn sie wollen können Sie dem Brief ein Paar Worte vorausschicken, um zu motivieren warum er an Stelle einer eingehenderen Verwahrung erscheint.

ALBERT BLOCH AN HERWARTH WALDEN

München, den 29. März 1916

Lieber Herr Walden!

Gewiss können Sie nach Ihrem Gutdünken drei oder vier der Bilder in Berlin einstweilen zurückbehalten. –

Ich danke Ihnen für die Abschrift der zwei Briefe, die anbei mit ein Paar Korrekturen an Ihnen [sic] zurückgehen. –

Klee lehnt selbstverständlich jeden Protest im Sinne einer Verteidigung seiner Kunst, ab, wie mir ein Brief den ich soeben empfing eindringlich klarlegt. In diesem Sinne wollte ich garnicht protestieren: das ersehen Sie aus der beigelegten Korrektur. So scheint mir auch daß der Titel vielleicht nicht »Für Paul Klee« lauten sollte. <u>Ihm</u> ist die ganze Sache ja schnuppe: <u>mir</u> aber nicht; und ich will am allerwenigsten den Klee kränken.

Mit diesem einen Vorbehalt, bin ich sonst mit Ihrer Auffassung der Angelegenheit ganz einverstanden.

Entschuldigen Sie bitte daß ich Sie in einer so rein persönlichen Sache in Anspruch nehme, und empfangen Sie meinen besten Dank für Ihre Liebenswürdigkeit.

Herzlichsten Gruß, auch an der [sic] gnädigen Frau,

Ihr Bloch

Invitation for Albert Bloch to the opening of his exhibition with Paul Klee, Der Sturm Gallery, Berlin, 1916, Courtesy of Mrs. Albert Bloch

Einladungskarte für Albert Bloch zur Eröffnung seiner Doppel-Ausstellung mit Paul Klee in der Galerie ›Der Sturm‹, Berlin 1916, Mrs. Albert Bloch

ALBERT BLOCH AN HERWARTH WALDEN

München, 12. April 1916

Lieber Herr Walden: –

Ich weiß nicht recht wie das mit dem <u>Gelben Bild</u> u. dem <u>Sterbezimmer</u> ist. Man ist ja selbst am allerwenigsten seinen eignen Sachen gegenüber kompetent; aber gerade bei diesen beiden Bildern (erst nach dem ich sie nicht mehr im Atelier hatte) stiegen in mir allerlei Bedenken auf. Beim <u>Sterbezimmer</u> – Das bin ich mir jetzt bewußt; damals war mir das Bild noch zu neu – beim <u>Sterbezimmer</u> bin ich an vielen Stellen ganz entschieden <u>ausgeglitten</u>: ob diese Leinwand überhaupt noch <u>gezeigt</u> werden soll, ist die Frage. Ich bin gegen dieses Bild etwas mistrauisch geworden. Freilich bin ich nicht kompetent, so daß wenn Sie es doch behalten wollen, ich es Ihrer Verantwortung überlassen muß. – Das <u>Gelbe Bild</u>, sollte es einer zufällig kaufen wollen, darf erst nach einer durchgreifenden Bearbeitung übergeben werden. Hierüber bin ich mir völlig im Klaren. So wie es jetzt ist, kann es noch ruhig gezeigt werden: das Endgültige ist noch nicht daran getan. – Ich bitte Sie mit mir in diesen Sachen Geduld zu haben. –

Noch etwas: von den Aquarellen die ich bei Ihnen im Dezember 1915 hatte, wollte ich Ihnen längst eins dedizieren (vergass nur immer dieses Vorhaben zu erwähnen). Da fällt es mir plötzlich wieder ein. Wollen Sie mir bitte sagen welches von den Blätter [sic] Sie am liebsten haben möchten – wenn Sie sich irgend eines Blattes besonders erinnern – so sollen Sie's bekommen. Nur eins, die Skizze zu einem Klownbild, habe ich nicht mehr. –
Herzlichst an Sie beide,

Ihr Albert-Bloch

ALBERT BLOCH AN HERWARTH WALDEN

München, 4. Mai 1916

Lieber Herr Walden!

Es wird mich freuen Sie im Sommer hier zu begrüßen, falls ich nicht inzwischen als feindlicher Ausländer irgendwo in Deutschland interniert sitze, oder als Flüchtling in der Schweiz. Dann wollen Sie sich auch für Ihre Sammlung ein Aquarell aussuchen. Sie melden sich jedenfalls vorher an, damit ich ja nicht, wie das letzte mal, Ihren Besuch verpasse. Sie können sich denken daß es mich herzlich freuen würde, wenn, wie Sie mir in Aussicht stellen, »Das Bild ›Gebirgsdorf‹ in nächster Zeit ein Käufer« fände [sic]. Da eben ein zweites Kind bei uns angekommen ist und wir eben auch in eine neue Wohnung ziehen mußten, habe ich es jetzt umso notwendiger.
Mit den freundlichsten Grüßen an Sie Beide,

Ihr Bloch

ALBERT BLOCH AN HERWARTH WALDEN

München, 6. Februar 1917

Lieber Herr Walden: –

[…] Hiermit empfangen Sie auch die Bilderlisten (Katalog- und Nettopreisliste) für meine Maiausstellung. Der Sicherheit halber lasse ich sie Ihnen jetzt schon zugehen, da ich nicht wissen kann wie sich meine Verhältnisse in den nächsten Wochen gestalten werden. Es ist sehr wahrscheinlich, daß ich mit meinen Angehörigen in absehbarer Zeit Deutschland verlassen muß. Ich fahre dann voraussichtlich nach der Schweiz, von wo aus ich Sie über das nötige benachrichtigen werde. Allenfalls werden meine Interessen hier in den besten Händen sein, und der Maiausstellung wird nichts im Wege stehen. […] Eine Schülerin von mir übernimmt mein Atelier, und wird mich hier in Deutschland vertreten, so weit das nötig sein sollte. […]

Ich glaube daß <u>diese</u> 28 Bilder die zur <u>Ausstellung gelangen sollen, mitunter die stärksten + reifsten Sachen</u> enthalten die ich bisher gemacht habe. Ich hatte etwa 45 Bilder die noch nie ausgestellt waren, traf aber eine so peinliche Wahl, daß nur die 28 in Betracht kommen.

Meine Preise habe ich absichtlich in bescheidenem Masse gehalten, damit wenn irgend möglich Verkäufe zustande kommen. […]

Albert Bloch, Deathbed, 1915/16, destroyed by the artist, Photograph from artist's Record Book, vol. I, Courtesy of Mrs. Albert Bloch

Albert Bloch, Sterbezimmer, 1915/16, vom Künstler zerstört, Photo aus dem ›Recordbook‹ (Bd. I) des Künstlers, Mrs. Albert Bloch

ALBERT BLOCH AN HERWARTH WALDEN

München, 11. Juni 1917

Lieber Herr Walden:

Ich habe eine Bitte an Sie.- Eine Schülerin von mir legt großen Wert darauf, im Sturm auszustellen. Sie hätte selbst noch gerne gewartet, wiewohl sich ihre Bilder wahrhaftig sehen lassen können, aber ihrem Vater, der sich auch sonst sehr für die Sache interessiert, und schon einige sehr anständige Bilder gesammelt hat, würde es eine ganz besondere Freude machen. Wenn dies aber der einzige Grund wäre, würde ich nicht dafür zu haben sein. So, aber, kann ich mit gutem Gewissen für die Arbeiten der Dame eintreten und es vollauf verantworten. Es wären, glaube ich, höchstens <u>zehn</u> Sachen, die in Betracht kämen, keine über dem mittleren Format was Größe anlangt. Ich dachte, sie könnten sie leicht einmal während des Winters, mit anderen zusammen unterbringen. Was Qualität angeht, können Sie sich ruhig auf mich verlassen. Die Arbeiten sind stark und sehr selbstständig, und haben etwas ungemein <u>selbstverständliches</u>. Von Beeinflussung meinerseits werden Sie, glaube ich, sehr wenig entdecken – äusserlich jedenfalls nicht. –

Ich selbst hätte vielleicht noch etwa ein Jahr gewartet, ehe ich von Ihnen eine Ausstellung für meine Schülerin verlangt hätte; aber da sie jetzt plötzlich mit der Bitte an mich herantritt, ihr eine zu vermitteln, kann ich es gerne befürworten, und wäre Ihnen herzlich verbunden, wenn Sie ihr Gelegenheit geben wollten die Arbeiten zu zeigen.

Vielleicht wäre es Ihnen lieber der Dame selbst zu schreiben. In diesem Falle wäre die Adresse,

Frl. E. Klinker, Loherstr. 12, <u>Barmen</u>,

andernfalls, kann ich ja das notwendige besorgen.

Mit bestem Gruß

Ihr Bloch. –

– P.S. – Sie können auch bei Campendonk anfragen, der schon verschiedenes von Frl. Klinker gesehen hat. –

ALBERT BLOCH AN HERWARTH WALDEN

München, 26. Juli 1917

Lieber Herr Walden!

Danke für Ihren Brief vom 23 ten! Die Aufzeichnungen erhalten Sie dann sobald ich sie ausgewählt und abgeschrieben habe. Sind irgendwelche Aussichten daß Sie meine Bilder im kommenden Herbst oder Winter irgendwo unterbringen? Wie ich Ihnen unlängst schrieb, würde mir an <u>Dresden</u> sehr viel liegen. –

[…] Ob ich in München jetzt ausstellen werde, weiß ich nicht: mit Goltz möchte ich lieber nichts zu tun haben, und Caspari kann mir gestohlen werden (bietet, oder lässt mir eine Ausstellung anbieten, und dann kneift er aus). Bleibt nur Thannhauser – einige Leute haben sich erbötig gemacht, aber ich bettle ihn nicht an. Wenn er mir aus freien Stücken eine Ausstellung macht (im großen Saal) dann tue ich es; sonst nicht. –

Haben Sie Kandinsky in Stockholm gesehen? Oder ist er in Russland? Was wissen, oder hören Sie von ihm? Von der Münter ist über ihn sonderbarer Weise keinen Ton heraus zu kriegen. – […]

ALBERT BLOCH AN HERWARTH WALDEN

München, 8. August 1917

Lieber Herr Walden:

Ihren Brief vom 31. Juli hätte ich viel früher beantwortet, kam aber nicht eher dazu.

Ich werde Ihnen im Laufe der nächsten Monate, Gemälde, Zeichnungen, Aquarelle übersenden, die Sie dann gelegentlich oder Kollektiv ausstellen können. Aus Frankfurt lasse ich Ihnen auch was dort übrig geblieben ist zugehen: es sind darunter auch ältere Sachen sowie ganz neue. Allerdings bleiben die Bilder noch vorerst dort. Ich gebe Ihnen Nachricht wann sie zu erwarten sind.

In Frankfurt habe ich einen sehr befriedigenden Erfolg gehabt. Fünf der besten Bilder wurden dort verkauft. Wann ich das Geld bekomme ist freilich die große Frage, und es ist noch zu früh um darum zu mahnen. Hingegen ist das Benehmen des Zürcher Käufers ganz unerhört. Ich sitze hier mit meinen Angehörigen <u>fast mittellos</u> – nur ein ganz kleiner Rest von Geld ist mir übrig geblieben, und aus Amerika bekomme ich sehr unregelmäßig Zuwendungen. Der Käufer hat seit <u>April</u> doch reichlich Zeit gehabt für das Bild zu zahlen, und ich darf jetzt erwarten, daß Sie (oder die Zürcher Herren) das Geld mit äusserster Energie einfordern. Wenn das nichts nützt, dann auf gerichtlichem Wege. Auf Teil- oder Ratenzahlungen verzichte ich. Ich brauche das <u>ganze</u> Geld; und zwar <u>sofort</u>. Ich kann mit den meinen nicht noch mehr hungern, als wir es ohne hin tun.

Die »Aufzeichnungen« erhalten Sie in den nächsten Tagen.

Mit herzlichem Gruß

Ihr Bloch

ALBERT BLOCH AN HERWARTH WALDEN

München, 19. September 1917

Lieber Herr Walden! –

Ich wäre Ihnen ausserordentlich dankbar, wenn Sie mir auf meinen [sic] letzten Schreiben Antwort geben wollten, und ich hoffe, daß ich Ihnen mit meiner Bitte nicht lästig falle denn es ist mir wirklich viel daran gelegen zu erfahren, ob der Käufer des Zürcher Bildes nun richtig der Herr Falk in Mannheim ist (denn es kann sich <u>nur</u> um ihn handeln), oder nicht. […]

Im Laufe des nächsten Monates gehen Ihnen etwa zwanzig neue Bilder, nebst einige [sic] Zeichnungen zu; und von Frankfurt aus die einen 30 übriggebliebenen[?] Bilder.

Mit den freundlichsten Grüßen,

Ihr Bloch

III. ALBERT BLOCH – WALTER DEXEL 1917-21

ALBERT BLOCH AN WALTER DEXEL

München, 6. Januar 1917

Sehr geehrter Herr Doktor!

Dank für Ihren Brief vom 2<u>ten</u>. Die Mitteilung, daß sich Ihr Herr Schwiegervater entschlossen hat, eins meiner Bilder zu erwerben, hat mich natürlich sehr gefreut. Daß es gerade das »Tal Nachts« ist – ein Bild das in eine frühere Phase meiner Entwicklung zurückgreift – finde ich ja gar nicht unverständlich, wenn mir auch selbst die meisten der übrigen lieber sind. Ich verstehe vollkommen, daß das Stilleben X Ihre größere Liebe geniesst, und mache Ihnen darum den Vorschlag (falls es Ihnen angenehm wäre), dieses Bild für sich zu behalten, die 200 M., die Sie gegenwärtig bezahlen können, als Anzahlung zu leisten, und den Rest, wann und wie es Ihnen am besten passt, nachträglich abzuzahlen. – […]

Übrigens werde ich Ihnen zu gegebener Zeit die endgültige Entscheidung mitteilen, denn ob ich im März eine Ausstellung im »Reich«

werde machen können steht durchaus noch nicht fest: darüber muß ich noch mit Campendonk u. auch mit Bernus konferieren.

Ich sah heute im »Reich« zwei Ihrer Glasbilder. Das eine gefiel mir sehr gut; das andere (unverkäufliche), weniger.

Bitte lassen Sie in der Ausstellung das <u>andere</u> Stilleben (Nr. IX <u>Pflanzen</u>) als <u>unverkäuflich</u> bezeichnen. Hoffentlich wird es nicht inzwischen verkauft; denn plötzlich bin ich heute von einem Herrn darauf aufmerksam gemacht worden, daß er es schon im Sommer kaufen wollte, und daß ich zusagte. Das hatte ich irgendwie vergessen oder verbummelt. Geht es noch, das Bild vom Verkauf zurückzuziehen? Ich hoffe es! Es wäre mir sonst sehr peinlich.

Mit besten Grüßen, auch Ihrer Frau Gemahlin,

Ihr Albert-Bloch

P.S. – Wollen Sie bitte allen Käufern [sic] aufmerksam machen, daß die Reproduktionsrechte der Bilder nach wie vor <u>mir</u> gehören.

ALBERT BLOCH AN WALTER DEXEL

München, 15. November 1917

Sehr geehrter Herr Dexel! –
Dank für Ihren Brief.

Ich will jetzt gleichfalls an Schames schreiben, und gelingt es ihm, die Bilder abzusenden, so sollte in Jena eine ziemlich repräsentative Ausstellung meiner Arbeit der letzten Paar Jahren [sic] zustande kommen. Ich hoffe es – und daß auch die Sendungen rechtzeitig eintreffen.

Wegen Klee weiß ich nicht recht wie ich Sie verstehen soll. Jedenfalls bin ich mit Goltz nicht auf solchem Fuße, daß eine Überwachung der Auswahl durch mich irgendwie zu rechtfertigen wäre. Und Klee selbst ist beim Militär, und seine Adresse ist mir augenblicklich unbekannt. Nach München hat er sowie so seit einiger Zeit selten Urlaub, und neuerdings soll die Bahn für Urlauber ganz gesperrt sein. So wüßte ich nicht was in diesem Falle zu machen wäre. Übrigens, verstehe ich nicht, wie ich eben andeutete, was Sie in <u>dieser</u> Hinsicht zu einem Mistrauen Goltz gegenüber veranlaßen könnte. Es gibt ja keine schlechten Klees, und Goltz würde Ihnen jedenfalls solche aussuchen, die er entbehren kann – er hat sie alle ja selbst schon in seinen Räumen ausgestellt, sodaß es deswegen keine Schwierigkeit haben dürfte.

Was Preisfragen und das sonstige Geschäftliche anbelangt, könnte man sowieso nicht dreinreden. – Falls ich Sie misverstanden haben sollte, bitte klären Sie mich auf, und wenn ich Ihnen dann irgendwie dienlich sein kann, will ich es gern tun.
Mit freundlichstem Gruß,
auch Ihrer Frau Gemahlin,

Ihr Albert-Bloch

ALBERT BLOCH AN WALTER DEXEL

München, 1. Januar 1918

Sehr geehrter Herr Dexel!

Danke für Ihren Brief vom 27. Dezember, samt Einlagen. Was Sie mir über den Erfolg der Ausstellung berichten, erfreut mich sehr, so groß mein Bedauern auch sein mag, daß sie keine <u>praktischen</u> Folgen zuwege bringen konnte; denn daran ist mir (leider!) ganz besonders gelegen. Jedoch geht aus Ihrem Briefe hervor, daß es doch noch möglich wäre, das eine oder andere Bild zu verkaufen – und ich wills herzlich hoffen, da meine Lage im Moment eine solche ist, daß ich alles aufwenden muß, um einen Verkauf irgendwie zu ermöglichen. – So bin ich denn auch ohne weiteres gerne bereit dem erwähnten Herrn H. K., der so aufrichtig begeistert über die Ausstellung schreibt, beim Ankauf des größeren Brückenbildes entgegenzukommen. Ich würde mich also, wenn er durchaus nicht imstande ist mehr dafür zu geben, mit <u>400 Mk.</u> als äussersten Preis begnügen, d.h., wenn Zahlung sofort und im <u>Ganzen</u> geleistet wird. – [...] Was das Stilleben Nr. X anlangt, welches Sie so gern besitzen möchten (es <u>ist</u> auch mein bestes Stilleben), würde es mich freuen, Ihnen das Bild, vielleicht etwas billiger zu laßen, oder Sie können es behalten, und es in Raten von 50 Mark abzahlen. Im ersteren Fall, wollen Sie mir vielleicht angeben, wieviel Sie höchstens ausgeben können, und würde Ihnen dann nach Möglichkeit entgegenkommen. –

Das Schreiben der Dame, welches Sie Ihrem Briefe beifügten, hat mich aufrichtig gerührt. Ich lege eine Photographie bei, die Sie ihr gütigst übermitteln wollen. Da ihr das Bild so viel bedeutet, wollen Sie ihr bitte mitteilen, daß mich ihre so echte Ergriffenheit tief erfreut hat, und daß ich ihr deshalb das Bild wirklich gerne erheblich billiger laßen würde, wenn sie es kaufen könnte, weil ich wüßte, daß es sich dann in so guten Händen befände. Ich habe für das Bild den ziemlich niederen Preis von 600 Mark angesetzt: sie kann es für nur 400 Mark bekommen, und braucht diese Summe nicht einmal alles auf einmal zu zahlen, sondern es sich in Ratenzahlungen einrichten wie ihr am bequemsten ist. – Diese Preise verstehen sich natürlich alle <u>netto</u>. [...]

Wann wird die Ausstellung zu Ende sein? Die Bilder müßen nämlich baldmöglichst nach München zurück. Denn im <u>März</u> sollen Campendonk u. ich im »Reich« eine große gemeinsame Ausstellung haben. Wäre es garnicht möglich, trotz Sperre, eine Sondererlaubnis zu bekommen, die Bilder per <u>Eilgut</u> zurückzusenden, wie es mir seinerzeit von der hiesigen Eisenbahndirektion erlaubt wurde, die Bilder nach Jena zur Ausstellung zu schicken? Ich bitte Sie, sehen Sie, was sich tun läßt, – denn es ist wirklich <u>sehr</u> wichtig. Sobald Sie den Bescheid haben, werde ich Ihnen die Adresse des »Reich« und alles übrige Notwendige mitteilen. –

Mit den besten Wünschen für das Neue Jahr und freundlichen Grüßen an Sie wie auch an Ihre Frau Gemahlin

Ihr Albert-Bloch

[...]

Albert Bloch, Still Life X, 1916, Private collection
Albert Bloch, Stilleben X, 1916, Privatsammlung

ALBERT BLOCH AN WALTER DEXEL

München, 28. Januar 1918

Sehr geehrter Herr Dr.

Dank für Ihren Brief vom 24ten sowie für die Postanweisung. Es ist mir eine schöne Genugtuung, daß Sie an dem kleinen Bilde so viel aufrichtige Freude haben; und Sie müßen wirklich nicht fürchten, daß es mich gereuen wird, das Bild für eine so bescheidene Summe verkauft zu haben. Jedenfalls ist es mir lieber es in Ihren Händen zu wissen als in der prunkvollen und »Namen«-strotzenden Sammlung irgend eines reichen Protzes, der im Grunde nichts damit anzufangen wüßte: – ein Schicksal, dem meine armen Bilder meistens ausgesetzt sind. Sie wissen nicht wie mir vor dem ganzen »Kunst<u>betrieb</u>« ekelt, in der Seele ekelt: wenn ich nicht leider so sehr darauf angewiesen wäre, würde ich mich nie mals mehr der lästigen Arbeit einer Ausstellung unterziehen, nie mehr in der Öffentlichkeit erscheinen, niemals wieder ein Wort über mich schreiben laßen, nur für die paar Leute malen, denen meine Bilder etwas zu <u>sagen</u> haben. – Das [sic] Ihr Herr Schwiegervater soviel Spass an dem Thalbild findet, freut mich auch sehr. Hoffentlich ist seine Freude daran von Dauer! – [...]

ALBERT BLOCH AN WALTER DEXEL

München, 23. November 1918

Sehr geehrter Herr Dexel!-

Danke für Ihre Karte. – In der »freien Volksrepublik Bayern« geht es so ausgezeichnet, daß ich dabei bin, meine Siebensachen zusammenzupacken um baldmöglichst in die Schweiz zu fahren! Ob es mir gelingt, ist eine andere Frage; ich hoffe es aber. In der Schweiz bleibe ich mit meiner Familie ein paar Monate um mich etwas zu erholen, und dann fahre ich nach Amerika in persönlichen Angelegenheiten. Nach baldiger Erledigung derselben komme ich wieder nach Europa, laße mich entweder in

Catalogue for the solo exhibition "Albert Bloch," Kunsthaus "Das Reich," Munich, 1918, Courtesy of Mrs. Albert Bloch

Katalog der Einzelausstellung ›Albert Bloch‹, Kunsthaus ›Das Reich‹, München 1918, Mrs. Albert Bloch

der Schweiz oder in Holland nieder, und warte bis es in Deutschland wieder etwas ruhiger aussieht. In dieser losgelassenen Hysterie kann ich nicht arbeiten. –

Senden Sie mir bitte so bald es geht, die Photos zurück (da ich sie drüben brauchen werde), und reservieren Sie mir bitte ein Exemplar des Buches, wenn Sie es können, auf alle Fälle aber, ein Probedruck der Reproduktion. –

Für Sie und Ihre Frau Gemahlin alles Schöne und Gute! Ich werde Ihnen wohl Nachricht aus der Schweiz oder von drüben zukommen laßen. Mit herzlichsten Grüßen,

Ihr Bloch

ALBERT BLOCH AN WALTER DEXEL

Ascona, 22. April 1919

Lieber Dr. Dexel!

Seit Anfang März sitzen wir nun in der Schweiz, mitte Mai gehts dann weiter über Paris-Havre nach Amerika. In nicht allzuferner Zeit hoffe ich wieder in Deutschland zu sein, oder wenigstens in Europa, bis zum Herbst, denke ich, wenn alles gut geht, werde ich bereits zurückgekehrt

sein. – Ich will lieber nicht von Ascona und seiner Umgebung erzählen, schon nur um dem naheliegenden Verdacht zu entgehen, als möchte ich den Neid der Zurückgebliebenen erwecken. – Wir wollen indessen die Hoffnung nicht aufgeben, daß für das arme Deutschland wie auch für das übrige Europa, bessere und ruhigere Zeiten wiederkehren mögen, daß die Welt dann wieder für Alle offenstehen werde, und man nicht ins »neutrale Ausland« entfliehen muß um die ganze Trostlosigkeit der Zeit wenigstens auf einige Wochen oder Monate loszuwerden. Hier übrigens in der Schweiz ist es auch keineswegs so idyllisch als man anderwärts glauben mag: es gärt und knistert in allen Ecken und Enden, und mit einiger Bangigkeit harrt man dem vielberufenen 1. Mai entgegen. — [...] Mit Jawlensky und der Werefkin, die beide hier sind, und, besonders der erste, Wundervolle, und die zweite, immer sehr fesselnde und interessante Sachen machen, komme ich öfters zusammen. Sonst gibt es hier eine ungeheure Menge Zugereister – meistens Deutsche, natürlich! – und des Malens und Schriftstellerns ist in Ascona kein Ende! –

Ist die dritte Auflage von Cézanne u. Hodler noch immer nicht erschienen? Wäre es nicht möglich mir noch rechtzeitig ein Exemplar zukommen zu lassen?

Bitte schreiben Sie mir doch einmal, wie es Ihnen geht, und wie die Dinge bei Ihnen aussehen. –

Grüßen Sie mir bestens Ihre Gattin, und seien Sie selbst bestens gegrüßt, Ihrem

Albert-Bloch

ALBERT BLOCH AN WALTER DEXEL

Ascona, 6. November [1920]

Mein lieber Dr. Dexel: –

Nun halte ich mich wieder vorübergehend in Europa auf – bin schon seit August hier in Ascona; es dauerte aber von der Mitte September bis eben jetzt die Einreise- u. Aufenthaltsbewilligung in München zu erwirken! In einigen Tagen fahre ich dann nach München um mich dort umzusehen, meine Münchner Angelegenheiten abzuwickeln, Bilder, etc., verpacken zu laßen, u.s.w. – um nach einiger Zeit mich wieder in mein Heimatland zu begeben. Vielleicht sind Sie während meines Münchner Besuchs auch einmal dort: – es würde mich aufrichtig freuen, wieder mit Ihnen zusammenzukommen. [...]

Meine Münchner Adresse weiß ich noch nicht. Richten Sie bitte einstweilen Postsendungen per Adr. Fräulein Emmy Klinker, Schellingstraße 80 IV Atelier. [...]

ALBERT BLOCH AN WALTER DEXEL

München, Hotel Roter Hahn [Winter 1920]
(Postadresse noch immer Schellingstraße)

Lieber Herr Dexel: –

Ich kann Ihnen auf Ihren gestrigen Brief nur kurz antworten, da ich seit Sonntag abends hier krank liege; will mich aber beeilen Ihnen Empfang zu bestätigen, und für Ihre Mühe mich zu bedanken. [...]

Wie lange – jedenfalls aber nicht sehr lange – ich noch in München bleibe, hängt eigentlich von der Gnade der hiesigen kgl. republikanischen Regierung ab, mit der (nebst Polizeidirektion) ich mich schon seit drei Wochen raufe.

Es bleibt für mich hier noch allerhand Unerfreuliches und Lästiges zu erledigen – Haushalt aufzulösen, Mobiliar versteigern zu laßen, Bilder herbeizubekommen: Verbindungen zu lösen, u.s.w. ad infinitum ad nauseam. Ich dürfte kaum vor Mitte Januar ganz fertig werden, falls man mich nicht unverrichteter Dinge herausschmeißt!

Für Ihre freundliche Einladung haben Sie herzlichsten Dank. Ich glaube aber nicht daß ich da werde annehmen können. Sollte es mir aber unerwarteterweise doch möglich werden, so wird es mich riesig freuen, ein paar Tage nach Jena zu kommen. Kommen Sie denn nicht um die Weihnachtszeit nach München? –

Bitte grüßen Sie mir freundlichst Ihre Frau Gemahlin und auch die Kleinen, die ich sehr gern einmal sehen möchte, und seien auch Sie bestens gegrüßt von

Ihrem Bloch

ALBERT BLOCH AN WALTER DEXEL

Barmen, 12. Januar 1921

Lieber Dr. Dexel:

- Verzeihen Sie, daß ich erst heute dazukomme Ihre Karte zu beantworten. Auch, daß ich den Empfang Ihres »Cézanne u. Hodler« und der 500 Mk. zu bestätigen vergaß, wollen Sie bitte entschuldigen. Ich bin nämlich bisher so von allen Hunden und Teufeln gehetzt, daß ich garnicht weiß wo mir der Kopf steht. Erst jetzt, da ich hier auf kurzem Besuch bin, konnte ich ein wenig ausspannen; und als vor einigen Tagen Ihre Karte (aus München nachgesandt) ankam wurde mir erinnerlich, daß ich für das Buch noch nicht gedankt hatte. Hoffentlich ists noch nicht zu spät das heute aufs herzlichste nachzuholen? –

In einigen Tagen bin ich wieder in München, wo mich noch allerlei Scherereien erwarten. Sobald sich meine dortigen Angelegenheiten abgewickelt haben, muß ich wieder weg. Bis längstens Mitte Februar, hoffe ich alles in Ordnung zu haben. – Sieht man Sie vielleicht in München? Es würde mich freuen. Nach Jena kommen, wäre unmöglich. – Adresse wie bisher Schellingstraße. Beste Grüße, Ihnen und Ihrer Frau Gemahlin.

In Eile, Ihr Bloch

IV. ALBERT BLOCH – MARIA MARC 1935-38

MARIA MARC AN ALBERT BLOCH

Ascona, 11. August 1935

Lieber Herr Bloch –

heute will ich endlich einmal ausführen, was ich schon seit Jahren tun wollte – ich will Ihnen schreiben und Sie zu allererst herzlich grüssen und fragen – wie geht es Ihnen?

Wieviele Jahre haben wir uns nicht gesehen – und nichts von einander gehört. Zuletzt erzählte McCouch von Ihnen – er gab mir auch Ihre Adresse; aber auch dies ist über ein Jahr her! ich wohnte damals draussen in Porto Ronco bei M. C. [McCouch]. Nun bin ich aber schon wieder über ein Jahr in Ascona – und 5 $\frac{1}{2}$ Jahre sind vergangen, seitdem ich hierher übergesiedelt bin – mein Haus in Ried Kaminskis überlassend.

[…] Heut drängt mich noch etwas ganz Bestimmtes dazu, Ihnen zu schreiben; ich war im Frühjahr längere Zeit in Deutschland weil ich Geldschwierigkeiten habe, wie alle Deutschen, die im Ausland wohnen. Und da habe ich allerhand Einblick bekommen in die künstlerischen Verhältnisse, die natürlich überaus schwierig sind. Und doch spürt und weiss man, dass es ein geheimes Deutschland giebt. Jedenfalls ist es mir wie eine neue Verpflichtung klar geworden, dass ich den Nachlass von Franz nicht einfach still liegen lassen darf. Wenn auch heute nach aussen nichts geschehen kann, so muss es doch nach innen weitergehen. ich fühle die Verpflichtung, den Nachlass zusammenzuführen. Darum komme ich heute mit zwei Fragen und Bitten zu Ihnen.

Die eine ist die – haben Sie Briefe von Franz aufgehoben? sowohl aus dem Felde, wie aus anderer früherer Zeit? und würden Sie so lieb sein, sie mir zur Verfügung zu stellen – event. in Abschriften. ich denke jetzt noch nicht an die Möglichkeit oder den Zweck einer Veröffentlichung – ich möchte nur Alles, was mir zu erreichen ist, sammeln, zur Vervollständigung seines Lebensbildes, neben seinen Werken.

Und zweitens – würde es Ihnen möglich sein, irgend etwas aus der Erinnerung aufzuschreiben – etwas Persönliches aus Ihrem Verhältnis zu Franz Marc – od. irgend – irgend etwas, was Ihnen einfällt und was Sie freut od. bewegt. ich habe den Wunsch zum 4 März 1936 – ein kleines Gedenkbuch zusammenzustellen, mit Äusserungen nur von Freunden, die ihn persönlich kannten. Würden Sie mir dabei mithelfen? Sie täten mir damit einen wirklichen Freundschaftsdienst. Am 4. März 1936 sind 20 Jahre seit seinem Tode vergangen – lieber Bloch – mit welchen Schritten ist die Zeit vergangen?! – Und doch lebe ich heute in immer innigerer innerlicher Verbindung mit ihm, so sehr, als ob das Wesentliche unserer Beziehungen nur um so stärker geworden wäre. ich kann es nicht mit Worten aussprechen – und – schreiben kann ich noch viel weniger darüber. Aber diese innere Zusammengehörigkeit ist der Mittelpunkt meines Lebens geworden – und das äussere Leben hat eine sehr sekundäre Bedeutung bekommen. Das werden Sie verstehen.

Es ist nun so sehr mein Wunsch, dieses Gedenkbüchlein zu machen – wenn irgend möglich, nur für die Freunde drucken zu lassen, weil es für die Öffentlichkeit heute nicht geht. Bitte, lieber Bloch – helfen Sie mir dabei – und schicken Sie mir einen Beitrag. Und – geben Sie mir die Briefe, wenn sie welche aufgehoben haben.

Es besteht der Plan einer Neu-Auflage – resp. Herausgabe des Buches mit Briefen aus dem Feld. Ein Verleger ist da – aber – wir zweifeln an einer Herausgabe, weil die Entwicklung von Franz dem heutigen Lebensgefühl, wenn man dieses Wort dafür brauchen darf – ganz entgegengesetzt ist. ich möchte nun aber auf alle Fälle, ohne Rücksicht auf den Zeitpunkt der Veröffentlichung das Buch für die neue Herausgabe fertig stellen. Es soll eine etwas andere Form bekommen und durch Feldpostbriefe an Freunde ergänzt werden.

Das wären also meine beiden Fragen und Bitten!

ich bin in den vergangenen Jahren oftmals mit den Freunden von früher zusammengekommen – teils Berlin od. Weimar – od. Dessau. Das waren schöne Zeiten – die mir auch die sehr liebe Freundschaft mit Feiningers brachten. Klee's sah ich im Frühjahr – als ich zur einer grossen Klee-Ausstellung u. kl. Aquarell-Ausstellung von Franz in Bern war. Klee hat wunderbare Bilder gemalt – welch' eine Freude hätte Franz gehabt, die Reife jener heiss umstrittenen Anfänge zu erleben – nicht nur für sich selbst – auch bei den Freunden.

Es war eine grosse Bestätigung für alle unsere frühen Bestrebungen, dass in jenen Jahren zwischen 1920 u. 30 die 3 – Kandinsky, Klee u. Feininger in Dessau Haus an Haus als Meister lebten u. schafften.

Kandinsky sah ich dann auch immer, wenn ich in Norddeutschland war. Jetzt lebt er in Paris, und wir schreiben uns von Zeit zu Zeit.

Die Baronin Werefkin lebt hier in Ascona – und malt nach wie vor in erstaunlicher Frische.

Und wie geht es nun Ihnen, lieber Bloch u. Ihrer Familie? – Ihrer Frau und den – Kindern? – die jetzt in einigen Jahren in dem Alter sein werden, in dem wir uns damals kennen lernten?

Das Leben hat uns getrennt – ich habe aber immer mit der gleichen freundschaftlichen Anhänglichkeit an Sie gedacht. Sie gehören einfach mit hinein in diesen Erinnerungskreis – und ich denke auch oft an meine Besuche bei Ihnen in der Konradstr.

Inzwischen sind so viele Jahre vergangen – wir sind Alle so viel älter geworden und haben das Leben in der Hand gehabt. Es sieht im

Rückblick so kurz aus – und doch – was liegt dazwischen an Kämpfen und schweren Zeiten.

Das Haus in Ried existiert noch – und dadurch dass Kaminski [der Komponist Heinrich Kaminsky (1886-1946)] es mit seiner Familie bewohnt (er hat 5 Kinder!) – ist es auch mir eine Heimat geblieben. Allein hätte ich nicht dort leben können – und wenn ich es an Fremde hätte

Franz and Maria Marc in Wassily Kandinsky's and Gabriele Münter's apartment in Schwabing, Munich, 1911, Gabriele Münter- und Johannes Eichner-Stiftung, Munich

Franz und Maria Marc in der Wohnung Wassily Kandinskys und Gabriele Münters in Schwabing, 1911, Gabriele Münter- und Johannes Eichner-Stiftung, München

vermieten müssen, könnte ich doch nie in dem Sinne »nach Hause« kommen, wie es jetzt der Fall ist.

Erzählen Sie mir auch einmal ein wenig von Ihrem Leben u. Ergehen – lieber Bloch – ich würde mich so sehr freuen darüber.

Und lassen Sie sich mit Ihrer Frau von ganzem Herzen grüssen – mit meinen wärmsten Wünschen – in alter Freundschaft

von Ihrer Maria Marc

ALBERT BLOCH AN MARIA MARC

Lawrence, August/September 1935
(Entwurf, in der Abschrift vielfach abgeändert)

Meine liebe Maria Marc,

als Sie mir unlängst schrieben und von Ihrem Plan eines Gedenkbuches für Franz zu seinem 20. Todestag erzählten, war ich erfreut und dankbar, daß Sie auch mich, trotz meines langen Schweigens, zu jenen treuen Freunden noch immer zählen, an die Sie sich mit der Gewißheit wenden können, daß Ihre Bitte um einen Beitrag zu dem frommen Werke sofort gewährt werde. Ich muß Ihnen wohl nicht erst sagen, was mir Franz war – was er mir stets geblieben ist und bleiben wird. Vor mir, da ich eben schreibe, hängt, wo sie seit Jahren hängt, über meinem Schreibtisch zwischen zwei seiner Holzschnitte, sein Photoprofil – Sie wissen noch: die Vergrößerung, die Sie mir damals schenkten, nach der kleineren Aufnahme, en profile, im Wintermantel mit dem Pelzkragen. Und durch die Jahre sehe ich ihn so vor mir, freundlich sinnenden Blickes, sehe ihn täglich und traure ihm täglich nach. Sie wollen für das kleine Buch etwas Persönliches aus meinem Verhältnis zu Franz, schreiben Sie, oder irgend etwas, was mir einfällt und was mich freut oder bewegt. Nun, ich wüßte nicht, was ich zu solchem Anlaß sonst über ihn schreiben könnte. Und leider weiß ich auch nicht, ob ich überhaupt ein Recht habe, mich

bei dieser Gelegenheit vor deutschen Lesern blicken zu lassen. Denn wer im deutschen Sprachgebiet würde sich heute noch, nach so vielen Jahren – und solchen Jahren! –, der selbst damals kaum bemerkten Tatsache erinnern, daß ich dem Kreise um Franz angehörte, nein, ihm selbst nahestand? Aber glücklicherweise habe nicht ich über diese Taktfrage zu entscheiden, sondern Sie (ich wollte Ihnen nur »zu bedenken geben«), und an mir liegt nichts weiter, als Ihrer lieben Bitte, so gut ich dies kann, entgegenzukommen. Und so will ich Ihnen Folgendes zur Begutachtung und zum möglichen Gebrauch unterbreiten:

Vor etwa einem Jahr wurde ich von einem amerikanischen Kunstmuseum zu Gast geladen. Ich sollte dort drei Vorlesungen über die sogenannte moderne Kunst halten; man bat mich aber, auf den deutschen »Expressionismus« spezielles Gewicht zu legen, wozu ich mich, nachdem ich dies ursprünglich abgelehnt hatte, am Ende doch entschließen konnte, weil sich an eben diesem sagenhaften deutschen Expressionismus einige mir äußerst interessante und wichtig scheinende Ausführungen anknüpfen ließen. Natürlich mußte für mich der eigentliche Mittelpunkt eines solchen Vortrages der Mensch und das Werk Franz Marc sein, wenngleich, um dem Gegenstand historisch gerecht zu werden, die Malerei und der Einfluß Kandinskis die einleitende, sehr eingehende kritisch-theoretische Betrachtung bildeten. Es war die zweite, der Clou der drei Vorlesungen, und ich konnte sehr gerührt wahrnehmen, daß die Hörer meinen Ausführungen insbesondere über Franz Marc großes Verständnis und das tiefste Mitempfinden entgegenbrachten. Für Ihren Zweck wäre es nun garnicht von Belang, wenn ich alles aus dieser Vorlesung mitteilen wollte, was Franz betrifft. Aber an gewissen Stellen mußte ich, um die Person wie auch das Werk dem Laienverständnis näherzurücken, zu Persönlichem greifen, Erinnerungen aus meinem Verhältnis zu Franz hervorholen – wie Sie es eben für Ihre Gedenkschrift verlangen. Und so setze ich Ihnen ein paar Auszüge aus jener Vorlesung hirher, so richtig wie möglich aus dem Englischen verdeutscht, in der Hoffnung, daß etwas davon Ihnen geeignet erscheinen wird (die Striche deuten längere, die Punkte kürzere Weglassungen an):

» – auch diese stille und reine Seele wurde [wie Macke] hinausgeworfen, um aus dem Hinterhalt hingeschlachtet zu werden ... Er war mein Freund. Gerade an dem Tag, da er ermordet wurde, erhielt ich seinen letzten Gruß – eine Feldpostkarte aus Frankreich. – ... und war sechsunddreißig Jahre alt als ein zufälliges Schrapnellstück das glühend hingegebene Herz zum Stehen brachte – am 4. März 1916, genau ein Jahr bevor der seither in seinem Bett verstorbene Herr Wilson zum zweiten mal als Präsident in Washington feierlich eingeführt wurde, als Belohnung dafür, daß er unsere Nation dem Kriege ferngehalten hatte! ... «

» – Über seine Malerei ist erläuternd nicht viel zu sagen. Sie bedarf keiner Erläuterung, noch weniger einer Auslegung, welche auf jeden Fall unbescheiden wäre und außerdem ein Sakrileg. Der Betrachter, noch ehe er sich vergegenwärtigt, welch großes Fundament des Wissens, der anatomischen Gelehrsamkeit; welch feines, festgegründetes Handwerk nötig war, um diese Bilder zu malen; und ehe noch seine gebannte Phantasie sich Rechenschaft zu geben vermag des Zaubers, der ihn festhält – je, ehe er noch erkennen kann, daß das alles erkannt sein will, und ob er sogar dazu taugt oder nicht, es zu erkennen, findet sich in einer Marc-Komposition sofort zurecht, gleichsam heimgekehrt nach müden Wanderungen. Vielleicht nicht jeder Betrachter; er darf nicht allzu sehr Kind sein dieser Welt, denn das war auch Franz Marc nicht. Er muß sich dem verwandt fühlen, was Franz Marc liebte und verehrte, wie ihnen Franz selbst verwandt war – den kleinen Dingen, den hilflosen, aber auch den großen, den edlen, den gütig starken Dingen: einfache Dinge sie alle, tief und gut, wie Franz Marc ein einfacher, tiefer guter Mensch war. Er war der Maler des Unverdorbenen, der Maler unsrer verlorenen Unschuld. Und er hatte an sich nichts von einem Sentimentalisten, und mit nichten sind seine Bilder sentimental. Hier eine geringfügige Begebenheit, welche dartun soll, wie er unsentimental war: Ich hatte ein kleines Bild gemalt, welches ihm gefiel, und er erbat es sich für seine Sammlung von Gemälden aus Freundeshand. Später hing es auf der Wand des Treppenganges in seinem neuen Landhäuschen, und zwischen der Wand und dem Bilderrahmen hatten Schwalben im Frühling ihr Nest gebaut. »Hoffentlich stört Sie das Nest nicht«, sagte er als ich einmal draußen bei ihm war;

»ich mag's sehr gern hier im Hause, die Schwalben haben dem Bild nichts angetan … « Aber gewiß störte es mich nicht, und ich mochte es ebenfalls gern leiden. Einmal – es war im Winter und Marc war tot – war ich draußen zu Besuch bei seiner Witwe. Das Schwalbennest hing immer noch … Wer aber die Pointe der Anekdote nicht kapiert, dem sei bedeutet, daß dem Verfallenen unsrer heutigen Kunstlüge – eben dem Sentimentalisten – allemal wichtiger als Gottes Kreatur ein Werk aus Menschenhand, ein nichtiges Bild, erscheint …

»Was aber sind die Bilder von Franz Marc? Was war er selbst? Hochgewachsen, schlank, breitschultrig, mit großen Knochen, großen Muskeln, nur auf den ersten Blick etwas schwerfällig, denn er ging ein wenig vornübergebeugt, sich im Sprechen und Zuhören dem Begleiter entgegenneigend; doch war er rasch in seinen Bewegungen und geräuschlos wie die Katzen, die er liebte, abwechselnd täppisch in der Gangart wie sein Hund Russi oder graziös und von sicherm Schritt wie nur eines seiner zahmen Rehe; ein Mann von klaren Zügen, Kinn und Nase stark, leis-lächelndem Munde und dunkeln Augen, sanft, abwechselnd träumerisch und scharf. Das ist sein Porträt, und seine Gemälde sind alle in ihrer Art Ebenbilder dieser äußeren Erscheinung. Hirsch und Hindin [sic] liegen schwerfällig ruhend in einer Waldlichtung. Die beiden großen breitgemalten Tier<u>formen</u> (nicht individuelle Tiere) sind das Bild. Sonst ist wenig da – sie füllen fast die ganze Leinwand aus. Es ist gerade genug von ihrer Umgebung um sie und in ihnen angedeutet: in die kosend ineinandergeschlungenen Rhythmen, in dem spielerischen hin und her, dem gegenseitigen Anziehen und Abstoßen der zur Form schwellenden Farben, um den Betrachter die Waldtiefe ahnen zu lassen, weiter nichts. – Eine gelbe Kuh, lebensgroß, schlägt mit den Hinterbeinen in Brunftaufwallung aus. Die Farben des Frühlings spielen um sie herum, durch sie hindurch. – »Die Vögel schweigen im Walde«, sie fliegen durch das von der Sommersonne buntbesprenkelte Dickicht, ein Lichtstrahl bricht durch die Tiefe in das Dunkel der Waldeinsamkeit. – Katzen spielen ruhig in einer Zimmerecke. Es ist nur die Ecke da des Zimmers; nur die Katzen – Katzenformen, niemals eine individuelle Katze, niemals ein Porträt, immer ein Symbol. –

»Und doch war es während dieser Periode, daß er manche seiner wichtigsten Werke schuf. Und das vielleicht allerwichtigste mußte – ein Jahr nach seinem Tode – seine Tragödie teilen. Tierschicksale! Da kauern sie, dicht aneinander gedrängt, hilfloser Mittelpunkt einer stürzenden Welt, die Köpfe emporgerichtet auf straffgespannten Hälsen dem drohenden Entsetzen entgegen. Die suchende Kreatur, in einer Welt der Wunder und Fremdheit und lauernden Gefahren verrannt, tastet zurück in das Dunkel durch die eigene Dunkelheit … Ein gellender Farbenschrei, widerhallendes Gebrüll, ein Tumult der Töne; es läßt nach – ein Stöhnen und Flüstern, dann Stille. Die Schöpfung hinuntergeschleudert in die Nacht allen Ursprungs; und dies ist das Ende … Doch stand bereits das große Bild ein volles Jahr fertig, ehe das Débacle da war, und als dies seinem vermeintlichen Ende sich näherte, folgte das Werk seinem Schöpfer durchs Feuer.

Tierschicksale! Fatum der Kreatur! Nur darf nicht etwa angenommen werden, daß Franz Marc, als er dieses mächtige Bild schuf, irgendeine romantisch-philosophisch-literarische Idee im Sinne hatte. Ich habe gesagt, daß er kein Sentimentalist war und ich habe es bewiesen; entschieden noch weniger war er Marktschreier, und in dem besondern Falle weiß ich genau wovon ich rede; denn wiewohl ich bei der Taufe des Bildes nicht mitgeholfen habe, wurde ich um meine Meinung über den Namen gefragt … Wieder nur eine Anekdote und wieder waren die Partner Franz Marc und ich. Es war draußen in Sindelsdorf, wo ich ein paar Tage bei ihm zu Besuch war; und dieses Bild … stand soeben fertiggemalt in seinem Atelier. Marc hörte immer gern die Kritik seiner Freunde, aber wie sollte <u>ich</u> mich über dieses Werk kritisch äußern? Plötzlich wandte er sich mir zu: Sagen Sie, wie in aller Welt soll ich das Ding betiteln? – »Ja mein Gott; ich bin der letzte, der's sagen könnte! Das liegt ja an Ihnen.« – Gewiß, aber ich kann mich nicht entscheiden. – »Nun, Sie werden doch wissen, was Sie im Sinn hatten, als Sie's malten?« – Sehn Sie; das ist's eben. So genau weiß ichs g'rad nicht. Ich hab's schon die längste Zeit malen wollen. Es war nur so ein unbestimmtes Gefühl – ganz undefinierbar. Bevor ich anfing, machte ich allerhand

Albert Bloch in his study in Lawrence, Kansas, c. 1924; with a photograph of Franz Marc in profile, dated 1911, above the desk, Courtesy of Mrs. Albert Bloch

Albert Bloch in seinem Arbeitszimmer in Lawrence, Kansas, um 1924; über dem Schreibtisch ein Profilphoto von Franz Marc von 1911, Mrs. Albert Bloch

Zeichnungen, Skizzen, Notizen, und hab's unausgesetzt im Kopf gehabt. Aber jetzt, da es fertiggemalt ist, hab' ich keine Ahnung wie ich's eigentlich nennen sollte. – »Nun«, sagte ich, »vielleicht ist das nicht so wichtig, außer für Ausstellungszwecke. Wissen Sie was – wenn Sie um einen Titel verlegen sind, warum nehmen Sie nicht an K. einen [sic] Beispiel und kleben einfach eine Nummer drauf?« Dazu lachte er bloß. – Klee, sagte er dann, war einige Tage vor Ihnen heraußen, und er schlägt »Tierschicksale« vor. Was meinen Sie? – Aber ich meinte: lieber nicht, und sagte es. »Ich fürchte, das würde etwas anspruchsvoll klingen; auch schiene mir so ein Titel eher zu literarisch – doch irre ich mich wahrscheinlich.« – Es wurde darüber nicht weiter gesprochen; aber daß ich mich geirrt habe, steht fest, und ich kann mich nur freuen, angesichts der nachfolgenden Ereignisse, daß ich im Irrtum war … Gegen das Ende – einige Monate vor Einbruch der Sündflut – schien es, als ob Franz Marc in seiner Malerei einen neuen Weg suchen wollte. Diese letzten Bilder wurden erst in der großen Gedächtnisausstellung nach seinem Tode gezeigt; als ich aber das letzte mal vor dem Krieg, im Frühsommer 1914, bei ihm zu Besuch war, sah ich sie alle, einige davon bereits fertiggemalt, einige erst begonnen. Es waren die reinsten Abstractionen! Aber Abstractionen, wie nur Franz Marc sie hätte malen können. Dieselbe Farbe, dasselbe Empfinden, dieselbe Atmosphäre – selbst Form und Rhythmus waren sich gleich geblieben, wenn auch sehr gesteigert, wiewohl man nur wenige der Formen objektiv gegenständlich erkennen konnte. Es war der klarste Farbensang. Doch war sich Marc wohl bewußt, während er an diesen Bildern malte, daß eine solche Entwicklung bei ihm nur eine vorübergehende sein konnte; es war gleichsam ein ziemlich selbstvertrauliches Tasten auf unbekanntem, längst geahntem neuen Pfade, welches ihn führen sollte er wußte noch nicht wohin. Er war arglos willig ja willens, sich eben leiten zu lassen. Denn schon damals hatte er zu zweifeln begonnen, daß K.[andinsky], dessen Anregung er so viel verdankte, selbst auf dem rechten Weg war. Und in der karg bemessenen Mußezeit, welche er in Gräben und anderswo an der Front genießen durfte während der anderthalb Jahren seiner klagelos getragenen Knechtschaft, konnte er sich von allem früheren Einfluß los- und in die vollkommenste Emanzipation freidenken. Das ist aus vielen Stellen seiner veröffentlichten Briefen [sic] aus dem Felde klar ersichtlich.

Wohin ihn dieses tiefe Selbsterforschen schließlich geführt hätte, wäre es uns gegönnt worden, ihn wieder unter uns zu sehen, muß keiner zu erraten suchen. Aber ich verweigere mir den traurigen Trost eines Glaubens, daß Franz Marc uns bereits alles geschenkt hatte, was zu schenken ihm gegeben ward; denn es ward ihm zuviel gegeben, und wie dankbar war er stets, aus seinem Überfluß spenden zu dürfen! … –«

Und so, verehrte liebe Freundin, haben Sie das leider nicht sehr Wertvolle als Beitrag für Ihr Gedenkbuch, was sich in Bezug auf Franz jenem Vortrag exzerpieren läßt. Ich habe es eben wieder durchgelesen, und muß sagen, wenn sie darin für Ihren Zweck nichts taugliches finden, würde es mich nicht wundern. Aber besseres zu bieten bin ich anscheinend nicht imstande. Die kleinen persönlichen Züge und Begebenheiten, an die ich mich mit solcher Freude und Wehmut erinnere, würden hierher kaum passen – etwa der liebliche Anblick, wie Sie und Franz in Bauerntracht – es war in München, ich glaube während des letzten Karnivals vor dem Kriege – einen unvergleichlich graziösen Bauerntanz vorführten.

Photograph of Franz Marc in profile, 1911, photo given by Maria Marc to Albert Bloch as a present following Marc's death in the war. Remained in Bloch's personal ownership until his death. Original Franz Marc Bequest, Germanisches Nationalmuseum, Nuremberg

Profilphoto von Franz Marc, 1911, Geschenk von Maria Marc an Albert Bloch nach dem Kriegstod ihres Mannes, befand sich lebenslang im Besitz von Albert Bloch. Originalphoto Nachlaß Franz Marc, Germanisches Nationalmuseum Nürnberg

Es war auch eher eine Pastorale als ein Bauerntanz; die erstaunte Runde konnte es nicht begreifen, konnte sich vor Entzücken kaum fassen – nie vergesse ich es! – Oder Franz bei Tisch – seine Sprechstimme und sein seltenes Lachen sind mir noch so lebendig gegenwärtig; seine unschuldige Freude an einem schmackhaften Gericht; wie er vergnügt saß bei einer Zigarre über einer Flasche Wein (»Sie, das trinken Sie mit Andacht! Das hat Köhler geschickt!«); wie er mit Ihnen während des ersten Urlaubs aus dem Feld zu uns zum Thee kam und – die große Not war noch nicht eingebrochen – sich an Theegebäck und amerikanischen [sic] Tabak, den ich damals noch hereinbekommen konnte, ergötzte! […] Auf meinem Schreibtisch liegt sein altes Taschenmesser. Er hatte es bei mir im Atelier vergessen – zu welchem Zweck er es damals gerade gebraucht hatte, weiß

ich leider nicht mehr. Später fand ich es auf einem Tische liegen, wollte es immer zurückgeben, verbummelte es aber jedesmal. Einmal, lange nachher, als Sie bei mir waren, bot ich es Ihnen an; Sie baten mich aber freundlich, es für mich zu behalten. […] Eben fällt mir ein – und warum es mir plötzlich erst jetzt einfallen soll, ist mir ein Rätsel, da ich in all diesen 22 Jahren immer wieder daran denke und es doch sicherlich hirher gehört und vielleicht sogar eher als alles andere – aber dennoch fällt mir nun erst ein, wie ich mich einmal an Franz wandte, mit der Frage, wie man eigentlich ein springendes Pferd zeichne. Ich hatte gerade ein Bildexperiment in Arbeit, da schien mir aus irgendeinem Grund als kompositionelles Nebenelement im Hintergrund ein springendes Pferd notwendig. Er antwortete sofort – den Brief finden Sie unter der Korrespondenz, welche mittlerweile an Sie abgegangen ist – und schrieb sehr erheitert über meine Anfrage, daß ein Pferd im Grunde genau wie ein Mensch gebaut sei – was ich sehr wohl wußte, nur daß trotz analogem Knochenbau sich die Ähnlichkeit funktionell nicht <u>äußert</u>, denn der Mensch <u>springt</u> zum Beispiel doch ganz anders als das Pferd, und dies eben hat Franz übersehen –, daß ich, nebenbei bemerkt, gerade so gut zeichne wie er – was nebenbei bemerkt, <u>nicht</u> stimmte – und daß es vollends unnötig sei, mich in solcher Angelegenheit an andere zu wenden. […]; und zum Überfluß – ich dank's ihm noch heute, wenngleich ich schließlich von seiner Hilfe keinen Gebrauch machte – zeichnete er mir auf dem Briefpapier, sorgfältig und schön, mit der Feder ein springendes Pferd hin, mit Knochengerüst und Muskelgliederung sauber angedeutet. damit ich nur ja einsehe, daß zwischen Mensch und Tier eigentlich kein so großer Unterschied bestehe, wie ich anscheinend meinte. Daß aus dem Bild nichts wurde, ist gleichgültig – am springenden Pferde scheiterte es nicht! Was aber keineswegs gleichgültig ist, das ist die kleine Begebenheit selbst. <u>Denn so war Franz:</u> immer bereit in welcher Angelegenheit immer dem Freunde und selbst dem Fernerstehenden mit seiner Hilfe beizuspringen; immer erfreut, wenn er sogar mehr geben konnte, als von ihm erbeten wurde.

Sie sehen also, liebe Freundin, wie wenig ich eigentlich über Persönliches zu sagen finde. Wir sahen uns ja nicht allzuoft, Franz und ich; Sie wohnten immer draußen, kamen dann und wann auf einen Sprung in die Stadt und waren immer sehr in Anspruch genommen. Leicht war es Ihnen nicht sich die wenigen Stunden oder paar Tage einzuteilen; und so sahen wir uns nicht einmal jedesmal, wenn Sie in der Stadt waren. Und ich saß dort in meinem Atelier, konnte mich immer nur schwer zu einem Ausflug entschließen, und so kam ich nur selten zu Ihnen – umso freudiger aber, wenn ich die Arbeit hinwerfen und mich freimachen konnte! Und – das verzeihe ich mir niemals – den letzten Besuch den mir Franz machen wollte, (es war der letzte Urlaub!), versäumte ich! Überall hatte er mich gesucht, schrieb er in einer Feldpostkarte kurz darauf: in der Wohnung, im Atelier, sogar im Kaffeehaus; ich war nirgends zu finden. Ich war bei einer Schülerin zum Tee, und ahnte nicht einmal, daß Franz einen Urlaub hatte! – Nach dem Begräbnis in Kochel – ich lief während der Salbaderei davon – sagte Campendonk, Franz sei ihm wie ein Vater gewesen. »Mir war er mehr«, kann ich mit Claudius stolz sagen: <u>ein älterer Bruder!</u> Wiewohl er kaum älter war als ich, waren ihm eigen alle Tiefe und Weisheit, die mir mangelten; und er hielt mich würdig seiner Freundschaft.

In alter Treue,

Ihr Bloch

MARIA MARC AN ALBERT BLOCH

Ascona, 20. November 1935

Mein lieber Bloch –

ich habe ein sehr schlechtes Gewissen, weil ich Ihnen auf nichts geantwortet habe und alle Ihre lieben Sendungen noch ohne Dank geblieben sind. Es war viel los um mich – vor Allem hat mich eine Arbeit sehr stark in Anspruch genommen – sodass Alles liegen blieb, was mir sonst an Pflichten hier bleibt.

Und nachdem die Arbeit beendet war, lag zu vielerlei vor mir zur Erledigung. Es giebt jetzt auch mehr Korrespondenz für den Nachlass. »Man« will (nicht eigentlich ich) im Frühjahr eine grosse Ausstellung von Franz in Deutschland machen – das bringt allerhand Schreiberei mit sich.

Aber heute sollen Sie meinen herzlichsten Dank für Alles haben – die Briefe von Franz, die gut ankamen – für das, was Sie geschrieben haben, das mich sehr erfreute und bestimmt seinen Platz in dem Buche bekommen wird – und dann auch Dank für Ihre lieben Briefe an mich.

[…] Heute möchte ich Ihnen ganz kurz noch etwas von den Schicksalen der Freunde erzählen, nach denen Sie fragen. Es ist nicht viel Erfreuliches zu berichten – Jeder hat ein schweres Schicksal auf sich nehmen müssen.

Der arme Niestlé ist wohl am schwersten daran – er hatte vor vielen Jahren die Schlafgrippe und ist seitdem nie mehr gesund geworden. Es kamen schwere Lähmungserscheinungen, die immer schlimmer werden. Er kann ohne das starke (natürlich Giftmittel) Skopolamin überhaupt nicht existieren. Die Dosis muss immer verstärkt werden – bis – ja – bis es eben nicht mehr geht. Seine Frau ist in ihre schwere Aufgabe hineingewachsen – sie ist bewunderungswürdig. Die beiden sehr reizenden Zwillingstöchter sind sehr musikalisch u. werden Geigerinnen. Niestlé der [Wort unleserlich] noch sehr auf der Höhe war – hat bis vor zwei Jahren noch manchmal gemalt – mit seinen zitternden Händen – ganz fein durchgeführte Wiesenblumen mit irgend einem Vogel – nicht ganz so naturalistisch wie früher – u. sehr schön. Sie wohnen schon lange in Seeshaupt am Starnberger See – u. wir sind immer in freundschaftlicher Verbindung geblieben.

Campendonks zogen vor Jahren an den Rhein – wo ihnen von einem Sammler ein Haus gebaut wurde. Später berief ihn Käsbach, der Akademie Direktor in Düsseldorf war – an die Akademie als Professor. Mit dem Umschwung musste er fort – ging nach Belgien u. soll dort eine Lehrstelle haben. Seine Ehe mit Adda ist geschieden – es sind 2 Kinder da – u. selbst soll er in Brüssel verheiratet sein.

Jawlensky lebt in Wiesbaden – er hat die Helene geheiratet – die Verbindung mit der Baronin ist gänzlich zerrissen. Jawl. ist auch sehr krank – fast gelähmt vom Gelenkrheumatismus u. hat garkein Geld. André sah ich vor Jahren bei Kandinsky in Dessau – er kam mit seiner Frau – u. war ein bärtiger Mann geworden – er hatte einen ganz dicken Vollbart. Vom Malen keine Spur – er ist Reisender für ich weiss nicht was – Zigarren od. Kaffee. Die Frau ist ihm gestorben.

Walden soll in Russland sein – seine blonde Frau Nell ist in Ascona, hat 2 Häuser u. eine fabelhafte Sammlung von Exoten – ausser der Bildersammlung. Ich sehe sie hie u. da – halte mich aber sehr zurück. […]

Heute nur in groben Zügen ein wenig von Jedem – ich erzähle Ihnen gelegentlich mehr davon.

ich muss noch allerhand schreiben – an Kandinsky, der in Paris mit einer jungen Frau lebt. Es soll in den Cahiers d'art etwas von Franz publiziert werden – da muss ich heute an ihn schreiben. Auch wegen der Ausstellung nach Deutschland!

So höre ich heute auf –! ich freue mich wenn Sie mir einmal einen kl. Lebensbericht geben – wenn Sie gelegentlich Zeit haben. Auch über Ihre Tätigkeit und die Malerei.

Ist Ihre Frau wieder daheim? grüssen Sie sie vielmals von mir. Und Ihnen – mit nochmaligem Dank meine herzlichsten freundschaftlichsten Grüsse!

Ihre Maria Marc

ALBERT BLOCH AN MARIA MARC

Lawrence, Januar 1936 (Entwurf)

Meine liebe Maria Marc –
haben Sie vielen Dank für den lieben Brief vom 20. November mit den Mitteilungen über die alten Freunde und Bekannten. Auch was Sie über sich selbst mitunter berichten – von Ihren Gobelinsarbeiten – interessiert mich lebhaft, und ich würde mich freuen, mehr davon zu erfahren. Ver-

wenden Sie auch manchmal alte Entwürfe von Franz dazu? Ich weiß noch, daß er Ihnen einen ganzen Haufen solcher skizziert hatte. – Und Klees? Von allen erzählen Sie etwas, außer von den Klees! Einmal nur hatten Sie eine große und schöne Ausstellung von seinen Arbeiten in Bern erwähnt; aber wo die drei jetzt wohnen, wie es ihnen geht, davon zu erzählen, scheinen Sie wohl vergessen zu haben. Es würde mich sehr interessieren. (Ach ja – und der Wolfskehl! was ist aus dem geworden? In dem heutigen Deutschland kann es ihm kaum behagen? – Von der Lasker-Schüler hörte ich, daß sie etwa vor Jahresfrist in Palästina war, seitdem sei sie aber nach Europa zurück – wohin aber? Holland? Schweiz? Die arme Münter schmollt wohl andauernd in Murnau?) Daß Ihnen mein Beitrag zu dem Gedächtnisbuch so gut gefallen habe, wie Sie sagen, will ich hoffen; ich würde es mit Freude glauben, wenn er mir selbst gefiele!

Ich versprach Ihnen vor einiger Zeit, einen kurzen Bericht von meinem Lebenslauf seit meiner Rückkunft zu senden. Was das Äußerliche angeht, ist ja auch nicht viel zu sagen … Ich kam also im Juni 1921 das letzte mal zurück, und habe seitdem das Land nicht wieder verlassen, einerseits weil ich mich nie für sehr lange Zeit freimachen konnte, andrerseits weil mir die Lust fehlte. – Als ich nachhause kam, war ich fast vollständig mittellos. Im Herbst 1921 machte ich in New York eine Kollektivausstellung, deren Resultat mich und meine Familie durch den Winter und bis zum Anfang des folgenden Sommers über Wasser hielt. Mitunter wurden nebstbei einige Zeichnungen verkauft, und eine New Yorker Monatsschrift erwarb eine Kunstbetrachtung, welche ich in Europa geschrieben hatte und die, als sie gedruckt erschien, einige Aufmerksamkeit erregte. – Als nun wieder meine Mittel erschöpft waren, regten ein paar bekannter [sic] Schriftsteller aus Chicago bei der dortigen Akademie an, daß man mich als Lehrer berufe, was auch geschah, und so waren wir wieder eben gerade vor dem Nichts gerettet.

Das Gehalt war aber minimal, ich mußte allein in Chicago das Jahr verbringen (was keinem von uns geschadet hat) und meine Frau und zwei Kinder mußten in St. Louis in der Nähe von meinen Verwandten Unterkunft finden. Diese ersten zwei Jahre in der Heimat waren wirtschaftlich – aber auch anders – unbeschreiblich schwere. In Chicago habe ich mich kümmerlich durchgeschlagen mit erborgtem Gelde (denn den kleinen [sic] Gehalt, der für mich allein ausgereicht hätte, sandte ich regelmäßig nach St. Louis), ein paar Verkäufen und einigen öffentlichen Vorlesungen aus eigenen Arbeiten. Nach Ende des Schuljahres erhielt ich den Ruf hierher, welcher mir ein immerhin auskömmliches Jahresgehalt einbringt, und wurde Professor und Leiter der Abteilung für Malerei in der Kunstschule, welche der Staatsuniversität angegliedert ist. Seitdem geht es einigermaßen, wiewohl ich, mit allen anderen Lehrkräften, infolge des katastrophalen wirtschaftlichen Kraches seit drei Jahren unter einem sehr empfindlichen Gehälterabbau zu leiden habe; aber trotzdem brauche ich mich Gott sei Dank nicht mehr um Bilderverkäufe zu kümmern, und stelle höchst selten mehr aus, und dann nur wenn's mir gerade paßt, auf direkte und persönliche Einladung hin. Freilich ist, ohne daß ich mich darum bemüht hätte, in der Zwischenzeit einiges verkauft worden, und hie und da hängt etwas von mir in einer öffentlichen Sammlung – altes Zeug aus der Münchner Zeit, welches ich gar zu gern vernichten wollte, wenn ich's nur dürfte. Das obere Stockwerk meines kleinen Hauses habe ich in ein ganz brauchbares Atelier, mit Nord- und Oberlicht, verwandeln lassen, und dort in meiner freien Zeit, welche mir reichlich, doch nicht reichlich genug bemessen ist, und nachts hier am Schreibtisch in meinem Studier- und Schlafzimmer, verbringe ich meine glücklichsten, sehr fleißigen Stunden. Ich gehe unbekümmert meinen Weg, weiß kaum, was die Maler in Paris oder New York treiben, male wie mir halt der Pinsel aus der Hand wächst, schere mich den Teufel um neue Bewegungen und »moderne« Strömungen, halte aber Franz Marc nach wie vor für einen großen Künstler, der vielleicht doch mit meinem heutigen Entwicklungsstadium einverstanden wäre und die Logik des Fortschrittes – der auch als bewußter »Rückschritt« angesehen werden könnte – wohl erkennen würde. Vor 25 Jahren aber hätte er ebenso heftig wie ich, den Kopf darüber geschüttelt, und ich wäre wahrscheinlich jedem an die Kehle gefahren, der mir prophezeit hätte, ich würde heute alles, was ich damals in München und Paris gelernt hatte, so verwerten, daß man mir zwar noch immer die »Schule« ansehen kann, mir aber nimmer zutrauen würde, solche Bilder gemalt zu haben, die ich in den Blauen Reiter Ausstellungen gezeigt habe. Indes glaube ich mit größter Zuversicht, daß ich endlich meinen ureigenen Weg gefunden habe, wovon ich umso überzeugter bin, als ich deutlich merke, daß er mich zu dem Ausgangspunkt meines künstlerischen Werdens in einem großen Bogen zurückgeführt hat. Wenn auch immer noch die Masken und Karnivalgestalten durch manche Arabeske und manches Impromptu ihr farbenseeliges Unwesen treiben und die verhüllten Figuren der Trauernden und Elenden sich in meinen bescheidenen Formaten zu einer düsteren Monumentalität erheben, so geschieht das heute vermöge einer Verinnerlichung, zu der ich damals bei weitem noch nicht reif war, und unterstützt durch ein so eingehendes Naturstudium und Durchempfinden des jeweiligen Motivs, daß, wie ich hoffe und glaube, Franz selbst eine helle Freude daran gehabt hätte. Und ich bin noch lange nicht fertig; – ich entwickle mich erst. Ich habe einsehn gelernt – und Sie ahnen nicht, wie unendlich viel man von Schülern und Anhängern lernen kann, lernen <u>muß</u>, wenn man als Lehrer etwas taugen will –, wie <u>wenig</u> ich eigentlich kann und weiß! Und habe nie so gut gemalt wie heute, da ich andächtig und demütig vor dem unscheinbarsten Gestrüpp auf dem Wegrande stehe. Hier, in diesem Nestchen – einer entzückend gelegenen von Thal- und Wellengelände umgebenen, von mächtigen Ulmen beschatteten Kleinstadt – habe ich erst, als bestallter Professor der Malerei, eigentlich mich angeschickt, in die Schule zu gehen. – Nun, ich weiß nicht, ob Sie das alles sehr interessiert, und ich will nicht riskieren, daß ich Sie langweile … Vielleicht wäre es Ihnen lieber, wenn ich zum Schluße ein paar Worte über meine Familie mitteile. Meine Frau ist die alte geblieben. Darin ist viel Lob enthalten. Das Verhältnis zwischen uns ist ein freundliches und inniges geblieben, aber wir hatten einander eigentlich nie viel zu sagen, und wir sehen uns hauptsächlich bei den Mahlzeiten; für meine Interessen kann sie kein richtiges aufbringen, ich für ihre, die ja nur häusliche und gesellschaftliche sind, nicht das geringste. Bernard, der ältere Sohn, Doktor der Philosophie, hochgewachsen und bebrillt, ist mit einer lieben und schönen, sehr gescheiten, seine Interessen völlig teilenden Frau verheiratet. Sie ist eine rotköpfige Amerikanerin, irländischer Abkunft und Katholikin, während ihr Mann unverbesserlicher Skeptiker bleibt. Bernard wird allmählich als Philologe, d. h. nicht als Literaturhistoriker, sondern als Sprachforscher bekannt, und bekleidet gegenwärtig eine verantwortliche Stellung an einem rein wissenschaftlichen Unternehmen, welches sein [sic] Sitz im Osten des Landes an einer großen Universität hat. – Der jüngere Sohn, Walter, jetzt bald 20jährig, ist ein lieber fauler Schlingel, Universitätsstudent sozusagen (ich gäb' was drum, wenn ich nur wüßt', womit der Bengel beschäftigt ist!), ein Hüne, steht fast 190 cm lang vor einem da und versichert, er sei ein geborener Schauspieler und wolle es auch werden. Ich habe ihn auch ein paar mal in Amateuraufführungen spielen sehen, und muß zugeben, daß ich schon schlechteren Schauspielern begegnet bin – was aber vorläufig nichts besagen will …

Und so, für dieses Mal will ich mich von Ihnen verabschieden, in der Hoffnung, daß Sie mich gelegentlich wieder mit einer Nachricht erfreuen werden. Sie haben viel zu tun – ich auch –, und wenn Sie hie und da für mich etwas freie Zeit finden können (und Lust haben), würde ich es sehr zu schätzen wissen.
Leben Sie wohl, und seien Sie, mit allen guten Wünschen zum neuen Jahr, vielmals gegrüßt von Ihrem alten

Bloch

Grüßen Sie mir bitte die Baronin, wenn Sie sie sehen; auch Klees. Von McCouch höre ich regelmäßig. Er mit seiner Familie sollen im Frühjahr nach Amerika zum Besuch bei seiner Mutter; da gibt es auch für mich hoffentlich ein Wiedersehen mit ihm!

ALBERT BLOCH AN MARIA MARC

Lawrence, 18. April 1936 (Entwurf)

Liebe Maria Marc,
ich will nun doch versuchen, jenen Vortrag, der sich so innig mit dem Interesse und der Persönlichkeit Franz' beschäftigt, umzuarbeiten und

veröffentlichen zu lassen, sei es in einem Buche oder in einer Zeitschrift. Zu diesem Behufe möchte ich aber vorerst Ihre Erlaubnis der photographischen Reproduktion und Abdruck der zwei Aquarelle »Kühe« (1911) und »Füchse« (auf der Rückseite einer Postkarte), die ich besitze, einholen, sowie der Porträtphotographie, die über meinem Schreibtisch hängt. Die sollen als Illustrationen gebracht werden. Auch wäre ich ihnen für die Überlassung eines <u>guten glatten</u> photographischen Abzuges der <u>Tierschicksale</u> und die Übersendung des <u>Briefblattes</u> mit den Pferdezeichnungen für denselben Zweck dankbar.

Wenn Sie mir die Adressen Klees und Kandinskys freundlich zukommen lassen wollen, werde ich mich auch an diese wenden, um die Erlaubnis der Reproduktionen von den Bildern ihrer Hand, die sich in meinem Besitz finden, ebenfalls zu erlangen.
Mit dem besten Dank im Voraus,
und den herzlichsten Grüßen,

Ihr Bloch

MARIA MARC AN ALBERT BLOCH

Berlin (bei E. Erdmann-Macke), 9. Mai 1936

Lieber Bloch –
herzlichen Dank für Ihre lieben Zeilen vom 10. April!

Es freut mich sehr, dass Sie etwas Geschriebenes herausgeben werden – u. gerne dürfen Sie alles reproduzieren, was Sie freut. Eine gute Aufnahme der Tierschicksale habe ich selber nicht – aber Prof. Schardt freut sich, Ihnen eine zugehen zu lassen. Das Buch ist jetzt erschienen – ich werde Ihnen ein Exemplar schicken und ich hoffe von ganzem Herzen, dass Sie die Liebe u. Herzlichkeit und das Verständnis für Franz darin spüren u. Freude haben werden.

Die Briefe sind noch in Ascona – sobald ich zurückkomme – erste Hälfte Juni – werde ich sie sofort schicken.
Die Adressen sind folgende:

> <u>Kandinsky</u> – Paris – Neuilly ^S/Seine
> 135 Bd de la Seine (Seine)
> <u>Klee</u> – Bern (Schweiz)
> Kistlerweg 6

Klee war sehr schwer krank – er erholt sich aber langsam!
Die Aufnahme der Ausstellung u. des Buches ist sehr gut – Presse positiv – ein andermal mehr davon!

Die Ausstellung wurde mit einem wunderbaren Vortrag von Schardt eröffnet – es ist Alles so schön für mich. das ganze Erleben der Vergangenheit ersteht neu und lebendig in mir – und mit viel mehr künstlerischem Verständnis.
Heut nur dies – mit den herzlichsten Grüssen u. Wünschen –

Ihre Maria Marc

ALBERT BLOCH AN MARIA MARC

Lawrence, 25. Mai 1936 (Entwurf)

Liebe Freundin –
Herzlichen Dank für Brief, Adressen und freundliche Erlaubnis. An Kandinsky und Klee bereits geschrieben. Erwarte täglich die versprochene Photographie d. Tierschicksale von Dr. Schardt und hoffe, bewußtes Briefblatt von Ihnen bald nach Ihrer Ankunft in Ascona zu erhalten.

Wurde heute mit letzter Arbeit am Buche fertig, das mit den Illustrationen ein ganz hübsches Bändchen ergeben dürfte; die Abhandlung über die deutschen »Expresionisten« [sic] bildet den Mittelpunkt. Meine Sekretärin ist jetzt mit der Maschinschrift [sic] des Manuskriptes beschäftigt. Dann muß ich den geeigneten Verleger suchen – ließe er sich nur gleich finden, denn ich lasse mich sehr ungern in derlei Scherereien ein.

Daß Klee so schwer erkrankt war tut mir natürlich sehr leid; doch freue ich mich umso mehr, daß zu ernster Besorgnis der Grund bereits verschwunden ist.

Mit wiederholtem schönen Dank und
den herzlichsten Grüßen und Wünschen
von uns beiden, in größter Eile,

Ihr Bloch

ALBERT BLOCH AN MARIA MARC

Lawrence, 23. August 1936 (Entwurf)

Liebe Maria Marc –

die Briefe von Franz sind vor einigen Tagen gut wieder angekommen. Vielen Dank! Auch für die liebenswürdige Erkundigung um den Gesundheitszustand. Es geht! Anfänglich war der Arzt, der meistens dazu neigt, die Sachen »nicht so schlimm« zu finden, eher pessimistisch; nach weiterer Behandlung mit Diät verbunden, ergab eine spätere Untersuchung eine günstigere Aussicht, sodaß die erwartete Operation vorerst nicht stattfinden muß – vielleicht, wenn's so weiter gut geht, überhaupt nicht! Inzwischen, trotz der geradezu tollen Hitze (Temperaturen bis zu 45 Grad!), habe ich sehr fleißig gearbeitet, und werde es hoffentlich ununterbrochen fortsetzen können bis mitte September, da ichs wieder mit dummen Studenten zu tun haben werde, die meine Zeit verflucht in Anspruch nehmen. Trotzdem kann ich immer zwischen Herbst und Sommer allerhand für mich arbeiten, und darf mit meinem Los eigentlich zufrieden sein. […] Mein kleines Buch kann vorläufig nicht erscheinen. Der geeignete Verleger für derlei läßt sich hierzulande nicht so leicht finden, wo offene Sprache und schonungslose Kritik der herrschenden Richtungen nicht begehrt sind ….. Über Ihre Arbeit, von der Sie nur andeutend sprechen, hätte ich gerne näheres erfahren …. Was ist aus Feininger geworden? Den habe ich seit dem Berliner »Herbstsalon« 1913 nicht mehr gesehen. – Nun Schluß! Die paar Zeilen sind bloß eine willkommene Unterbrechung der Arbeit, an die ich jetzt wieder zurück muß. […]

MARIA MARC AN ALBERT BLOCH

Ascona, 6. Dezember 1936

Lieber Bloch –

wie geht es bei Ihnen – was macht Ihre Gesundheit? –

ich möchte Ihnen heute noch von hier aus einen Gruss senden. ich fahre in ein paar Tagen nach Deutschland – über Weihnachten nach Ried und Anfang Januar nach Berlin, wo wir weiter an dem Nachlass – diesmal vor Allem am schriftlichen – arbeiten wollen. Dies – trotz Allem –; denn alle Ausstellungen, Vorträge, – Buch – alles ist verboten worden.

Wenigstens ist Klarheit der Situation geschaffen – die Sache selbst ist unantastbar – und bliebe besser in der Stille – bis die Menschen dafür da sind – und die Zeit die geeignete Athmosphäre schaffen kann. – Die heutige traurige Wirklichkeit ist nicht mehr zu begreifen.

Wenn Sie mir einmal schreiben – was ich sehr wünsche u. hoffe – auch von Ihren Plänen – dann bitte mit Vorsicht. Die Briefe nach Ascona werden mir nachgeschickt nach Deutschland. […]

Noch ein Nachwort:

Sie fragten einmal nach Feininger – u. ich gab, glaube ich, noch keine Antwort darauf.

Er hat sich wunderbar entwickelt – ist einer der Grössten geworden – auch menschlich.

ich stehe mit ihm u. seiner Familie in engsten freundschaftlichen Beziehungen – weiss aber im Augenblick nichts Näheres. Er war mit seiner Frau in Amerika. Wenn ich nun nach Berlin komme, werde ich ihn sehen – dann schreibe ich Ihnen gern noch von ihm.

ich liebe seine Bilder sehr – und seine Zeichnungen u. Aquarelle.

Heut nur noch diesen Nachsatz – damit Sie sehen, dass ich es nicht ganz vergessen habe.

Herzlichst

Ihre M. M.

ALBERT BLOCH AN MARIA MARC

Lawrence, Mitte Januar 1937 (Entwurf)

Liebe Maria Marc –

Erst jetzt komme ich dazu, den Empfang Ihrer so willkommenen Zeilen vom 6. Dezember zu bestätigen und Ihnen die gewünschte Nachricht zu geben.

Gesundheitlich geht's eben – immer wieder Unpässlichkeiten, immer wieder wohlauf, bis es endlich eines Tages nicht weitergehen wird. Nicht, als ob ich »leidend« wäre. Bewahre! Aber man ist halt nicht mehr so jung wie einst; die kleinen Alterserscheinungen melden sich nach und nach – ich stehe jetzt im 55. Jahr! – scheinbar längst überwundene Übel tauchen wieder auf (oder deren Folgen); kurzum, man ist nicht mehr jung. Das heißt körperlich. Geistig bin ich jünger als jemals ich gewesen – oder vielleicht schmeichle ich mir nur; denn so manches, wofür die eigentlich jüngeren sich heute begeistern, ist mir ein Greuel, wie ich z.B. vieles in der neuen »Kunst« für Dreck oder Schwindel oder beides zugleich halten muß. Die eigene Arbeit geht weiter – unentwegt, unausgesetzt; und ich glaube zuversichtlich, daß ich die mir angemessene Klarheit gewonnen habe, welche aber jetzt die ihr angemessene Reinheit des Ausdrucks verlangt. Das ist jetzt mein Streben … Von Kandinsky, der mir hin und wieder sehr liebenswürdig und anregend schreibt, und von der Lili Klee hörte ich vor Monaten von dem Schicksal der Ausstellungen und des Buches. Mir unergründlich. Aber die Zeit wird kommen, da man endlich einsieht, daß man gerade in dieser Kunst, wie nur sonst vereinzelt bei Cranach oder Altdorfer, nicht vor etwas »enorm« revolutionärem, sondern mitten in der tiefsten deutschen Tradition steht: in dem Urwalde der deutschen Märchenwelt. Was Sie über Feininger schreiben ist erfreulich und interessant. Ich habe ihn nur flüchtig kennengelernt, einmal durch Walden, damals im »Herbstsalon« mit ihm zusammengetroffen. Ich hätte ihn gern besser gekannt; eine durchaus sympathische Erscheinung. Vieles in seiner Malerei hat mich früher sehr angeregt. Später glaubte ich etwas erstarrendes, allzu doktrinäres darin zu entdecken, sodaß mir seine Bilder mit der Zeit immer fremder geworden sind. Das hätte mir bei Franz nie passieren können, eher bei Klee, dessen neuere und neueste Arbeit, soweit ich sie kenne, für mich nicht nur das wundervoll Anregende im Handwerklichen verloren haben, sondern auch bild-architektonisch mich lange nicht mehr so anziehen wie vor 15 – 20 Jahren. Der merkwürdigste von allen aber ist Kandinsky, der mir unlängst einige Photos zugeschickt hat, dem ich heute theoretisch nicht mehr wie früher zustimmen kann, der aber in seinen Arbeiten so jugendfrisch und frei geblieben ist, daß man glauben könnte, man habe es, trotz aller Reife, mit der Malerei eines ganz jungen zu tun. – Nun wäre ich aber neugierig zu hören, wie sich Campendonk entwickelt hat. Vor ein paar Jahren sah ich irgendwo eine schwarz-weiß Reproduktion eines seiner neueren Bilder. Soweit ich da urteilen konnte, schien er nicht viel weiter gekommen zu sein als damals: kompositionell waren dieselben Unstimmigkeiten und Willkürlichkeiten auffallend, es waltete dieselbe störende »Unmusikalität« des architektonischen Aufbaus vor wie ehedem, wenn auch immerhin die Bildidee anregend und wertvoll geblieben war …

Von meinen Plänen kann ich Ihnen nichts sagen, weil ich gelernt habe, keine zu machen. Das Geld ist knapp, die Preise steigen. Verflossenen Sommers konnte ich mir keine Ferienreise leisten; mußte zuhause bleiben und in dieser Höllenhitze braten. Konnte aber viel arbeiten und denken, denn Gott sei Dank war's noch immer nicht so schlimm, daß die Anderen auch zuhause bleiben mußten. So hatte ich Stille um mich und Ruhe in mir.

Es ist mir immer eine Freude, Nachricht – auch wenn sie knapp sein muß – von Ihnen zu bekommen. So schreiben Sie mir denn auch gelegentlich wieder. Hoffentlich kann's recht bald sein.

Meine Frau läßt grüßen.

In alter, treuer Freundschaft,

Ihr Bloch

ALBERT BLOCH AN MARIA MARC

Lawrence, 19. Januar 1938 (Entwurf)

Liebe Maria Marc,

[…] Bitte seien Sie mir nicht böse, daß ich so saumselig scheine. Momentan geht es mir immerhin leidlich, aber ich war seit fast einem Jahre krank gewesen, mußte zweimal ins Krankenhaus, bin eben vor etwa 10 Tagen aus unsrer Universitätsklinik entlassen worden, und hoffe nun das Beste. Meine Frau erlitt im Juni hier im Hause einen sehr schweren, wenn auch nicht lebensgefährlichen Unfall, durch welchen sie sich mehrere Knochenbrüche, darunter ein zertrümmertes Nasenbein, und eine Rückenverrenkung zuzog. Noch heute leidet sie zwischendurch an den Folgen; im Augenblick ist sie mit einer leichten Grippe bettlegerig. Daß man nun bei alledem zum Briefeschreiben nicht sehr aufgelegt ist, zumal da es in den Zwischenzeiten, wo man selbst nicht gerade so leidend war, daß man zur gänzlichen Untätigkeit sich verurteilt sah, der beruflichen Arbeit in Überfülle gab, ist wohl einleuchtend. (Und daß die Malerei unter solchen Umständen leiden muß, ist selbstverständlich. Seit dem Frühjahr sind genau <u>vier</u> Bilder zustande gekommen, darunter allerdings ein größeres: das stärkste, das ich bisher von mir kenne; doch wie das leider so zu gehen pflegt, werde ich es wahrscheinlich übermorgen nicht mehr ansehen können!)

Ihr Lebenszeichen aus Ascona hat mir Freude gemacht – als <u>Lebenszeichen</u>; der Inhalt des Schreibens weniger, wiewohl mir die jüngsten Kunstereignisse unter der machtbesoffenen Verbrecherbande schon zu Ohren gekommen waren. Darüber ist doch wohl kein Wort zu verlieren; und ich denke auch, daß angesichts der Lebensgefahr in der sich heute eine bangende Erde befindet, diese Angelegenheit, so sehr man durch sie selbst in Mitleidenschaft gezogen ist, kaum einmal zu den beträchtlicheren Symptomen der Zeit gerechnet werden darf, sondern höchstens als die Privatsorge derer anzusehn ist, die einerseits sich als Vaterlandsretter aufspielen, oder die, wie unsereins von ihr zufällig betroffen werden. Ich selbst sehe mich leider gezwungen, alles öffentliche Kunstgetue in solcher Stunde als Blasphemie an der leidenden Menschheit anzusehen, und weigere mich seit langem, anders als im Stillen tätig zu sein. Ein Hervortreten irgendwelcher propagandischer Art auf diesem Gebiet ist von Übel, und im positiven Sinn bleibt es mit Recht unwirksam. Warten wir ab! Wenn einmal sich Himmel und Erde nicht mehr bespeien lassen wollen und der getretene Menschengeist sich wieder aufrichtet, wird der ganze Fanatikerschwarm, wo immer er sich befinde, weggefegt, und die Namen der emporgeklommenen Kanaillen aller Terrorländer werden nur den zurückbleibenden Rest eines überstandenen Alpdrucks der Erinnerung noch bedeuten. Wir selbst dürften es kaum noch erleben; doch wollen wir es für die Nachwelt erhoffen. Warten wir ab! […]

Für die Grüße von <u>Davringhausen</u> meinen besten Dank. Falls er noch in Ascona ist, grüßen Sie ihn bitte von mir. Wo ist <u>Wolfskehl</u>? Ich weiß, daß die Lasker-Schüler in Zürich ist. Und die <u>Baronin</u>? Ich hörte, sie sei jetzt sehr leidend.
Ihnen zum neuen Jahr allen Segen holder Erinnerung!

Ihr Bloch

MARIA MARC AN ALBERT BLOCH

Bern (bei Dr. Klipstein), 10. April 1938

Mein lieber Bloch,

auch ich habe Sie diesmal lange auf eine Antwort und auf meinen Dank für Ihren lieben Brief warten lassen,- und komme erst einen Tag vor meiner Osterreise nach Deutschland dazu Ihnen noch ein Wort zu schreiben. Der Grund meines Schweigens war diesmal meine Arbeit, ich bin in einer förmlichen Arbeitsraserei gewesen und habe auch meinen Teppich fertig bekommen. Zum erstenmal seit 8 Jahren, seit ich in Ascona lebe, will ich versuchen zwei Arbeiten mit nach Deutschland zu nehmen, mit Freipass, – den ich von der Schweiz bekommen habe. Hoffentlich lässt man mich nach Deutschland hinein. […]

Nun will ich aber nicht aus der freien Schweiz fortfahren, ohne Ihnen einen Gruss zu schicken. Bei meinem Besuch bei Klee ist auch alles wieder so besonders lebendig geworden und wir haben auch viel von Ihnen gesprochen. Wie traurig, dass auch bei Ihnen so viel Krankheit gewesen ist, – ich hoffe von Herzen, dass Sie Beide jetzt wieder ganz wohl sind. Klee ist wohl immer noch krank, – allerdings kann ja einer, der aussensteht, nicht beurteilen, wie es eigentlich bestellt ist, und, nach allem, was man hört, hat sich Klee doch schon sehr erholt.

Es war ein sehr schöner Nachmittag und Abend, den ich bei Klee's erlebte, ich sah auch viele sehr starke ausdrucksvolle Arbeiten, denn die Arbeitskraft ist bei Klee nicht beeinträchtigt, – sicher ein gutes Zeichen!

Und es scheint, als ob Klee in Paris viel Liebe mit seinen Sachen erweckt hat und erfreulichen Kontakt bekam. Das ist doch schön! Über Deutschland will ich schweigen, was soll man sagen? – es ist Schicksal und, wie Sie es auch in Ihrem Brief andeuten, alles Reden nach aussen nur von Übel, – man darf nicht zur Unzeit reden, sonst wird alles nur viel schlimmer. Nur warten können und das Vertrauen nicht verlieren, dass es alles wieder anders kommen muss. Nur manchmal bangt einem vor dem Gedanken, dass alle die Bilder vernichtet werden könnten, wie es schon ausgesprochen worden ist. Aber, – auch das wäre irgendwie Schicksal! wenn ich es mir auch nicht vorstellen kann, wie man eigentlich darauf reagieren würde und müsste. Aber auch das wird sich ergeben und ich habe es mir auch abgewöhnt, über Dinge, die einmal kommen könnten, den Kopf zu zerbrechen. Von Kandinsky hörte ich vor einiger Zeit Gutes, er soll erstaunlich frisch und arbeitsfähig sein. Gern würde ich einmal nach Paris fahren, habe aber kein Geld […]. Mit Amerika ist die Sache ja ziemlich hoffnungslos, wie sollte ich je dort hinkommen? und doch sind jetzt mehrere liebe Menschen dorthin ausgewandert. Übrigens ist auch Feininger in New York, – es wäre doch schön, wenn Sie sich einmal begegnen würden. Er hat es sehr schwer, wohnt momentan mit seiner Frau in zwei Zimmern in einem Hause der City, im 5. Stock oder gar noch höher, – sehr gestört und bedrängt von all der vielen Menschennähe und dem Lärm und den vielen Lifts des Hauses. Wenn ich die genaue Adresse einmal habe, will ich sie Ihnen schreiben, vielleicht ergiebt es sich doch einmal, dass Sie sich kennen lernen.

Haben Sie es eigentlich erfahren, dass die Baronin Werefkin gestorben ist? sie hat sehr leiden müssen in den letzten zwei Jahren und ganz zuletzt war es für uns, die es mit erlebten sehr schmerzlich, mit anzusehen, wie hilflos dieser stolze Mensch geworden war, die das Leben gemeistert hatte wie selten einer. Für mich ist es ein schmerzlicher Abschied gewesen, ich vermisse sie sehr, denn wir waren in den letzten Jahren auch persönlich befreundet, abgesehen von den Beziehungen der früheren Jahre.

Sie fehlt mir sehr in Ascona, denn auch dort hat sich das Leben und der Zusammenhang der Menschen und Freunde ganz verändert gegen früher, sodass ich recht einsam geworden bin. […]

ALBERT BLOCH AN MARIA MARC

Lawrence, 20. Juni 1938 (Entwurf)

Meine liebe und verehrte gute Freundin –

Daß ich Sie wieder so lange auf einen Dank für einen Brief warten lassen mußte, werden Sie mir einsichtsvoll verzeihen. Arbeitsüberlastung! […]

Daß sich Klee erholt und seine Arbeitskraft sich nicht vermindert hat ist ein tröstliches Zeichen; auch ist es erfreulich, daß er in Paris so schöne Erfolge erntet. Von dem Tode der Baronin gibt mir Ihr Brief die erste Kunde; McCouch, von dem ich seit einiger Zeit nichts höre, hatte in seinem letzten Schreiben kein Wort darüber gesagt – vielleicht auch, daß der Tod damals noch nicht eingetreten war. Ich erinnere mich der geistreichen, gastfreien Frau und der anregenden Unterhaltungen, die ich so oft in Ascona mit ihr hatte, immer wieder und stets mit den angenehmsten Empfindungen. Daß ihr Hingang Ihnen ein schmerzlicher Verlust bedeutet, ist nur zu verstehen; und ich bitte Sie, von meiner aufrichtigen Teilnahme überzeugt zu sein. Um uns alle wird es immer stiller; mit jedem Tag werden wir nur noch einsamer.

Es würde mich freuen, die Adresse Feiningers zu erhalten. In einer Kunstzeitschrift erschien unlängst eine lange Würdigung seiner Arbeit, deren Lektüre ich mir leichten Herzens erspart habe, da ich den Inhalt des Geschwätzes unsrer ästhetischen Flachköpfe lange schon unbesehen vorwegnehmen kann; aber die Reproduktionen waren recht gut und mir sehr interessant, und es ist immerhin erfreulich, daß man hier auf diesen feinen und ernsten Künstler aufmerksam wird.

In letzter Zeit geht es mir wieder viel besser – meine Frau hat sich von ihrem schweren Unfall längst gründlich erholt –, nur daß meine Nerven so erschöpft sind und ich geistig und körperlich sehr ermüdet bin. Den Winter über war die Arbeitskraft infolge andauernder Unpäßlichkeit sehr beeinträchtigt; immerhin konnte ich zehn Bilder (darunter ein größeres) und einige Aquarelle malen und auch manches schreiben. Ich muß jetzt trachten, irgendwohin zu kommen, wo ich mich den Sommer über im Freien ausruhen kann; aus mancherlei Grund ist das aber nicht so einfach.

Von Kandinsky die längste Zeit kein Lebenszeichen … Was wollen denn Sie in Amerika? Ich, freilich, würde es begrüßen, wenn Sie herüberkämen – aber Sie selbst? Bleiben Sie lieber in der Schweiz solange es geht, auch wenn dort das Geld knapp ist; denn hier würde es Ihnen wohl viel knapper sein!

Von Herzen alle guten Wünsche und die liebsten Grüße,

Ihr alter Bloch

MARIA MARC AN ALBERT BLOCH

Ascona, 15. Oktober 1938

Lieber Bloch,

wie geht es Ihnen? ich habe lange nichts gehört und Sie haben mir auch meinen Brief mit den eingelegten Photos nicht beantwortet. Hoffentlich hat das keine besonderen Gründe, als nur solche, die einen manchmal nicht zum schreiben kommen lassen.

Heut kann ich Ihnen nun die Adresse von Feiningers in New York geben,

– 235 East – 22 Street N.Y. City

Es wäre doch sicher schön, wenn Sie einmal in eine Verbindung miteinander kämen. ich hatte in diesen Tagen endlich persönliche Nachricht und gute dazu, was mich sehr freute! Es ist ja allerhand, dass sich Feininger in seinem Alter noch einmal so umstellen musste, – aber, – nach den neuesten Ereignissen in Europa werden F's nur froh sein, draussen zu sein. Es waren sehr aufregende schwere Tage hier, ich bin mit den Nerven ganz herunter gekommen. Trotzdem arbeite ich, so viel es geht, – es ist das Einzige, was einem etwas Erleichterung bringt. Sie können es verstehen, dass meine Gedanken weit zurückgingen zu dem Erlebnis vor 24 Jahren, – ja, – man kann, wenn es einem Ernst ist, auch aus dieser letzten Krise nicht mehr im gleichen Sinne weiterleben, man geht als ein andrer Mensch daraus hervor! […]

(ab hier handschriftlich weiter)

V. ALBERT BLOCH – WASSILY KANDINSKY 1936-37

ALBERT BLOCH AN WASSILY KANDINSKY

Lawrence, 21. Mai 1936

Lieber Herr Kandinsky,

von Maria Marc erfuhr ich soeben Ihre Adresse, und will hoffen, daß dieses plötzliche Lebenszeichen Sie nicht allzusehr überraschen oder gar stören wird. Ich belästige Freunde und Bekannten [sic] ohne zwingenden Grund ungern mit Briefen, und wenn ich jetzt unerwartet schreibe, können Sie sicher sein, daß ich etwas von Ihnen will und auf Ihre altgewohnte Liebenswürdigkeit rechne.

Ich beabsichtige nämlich, wenn sich der geeignete Verleger finden läßt, unter anderem den revidierten Text einer Ende 1934 geschriebenen Abhandlung mit dem Titel »Kandinsky, Marc, Klee – Reminiszenz und Kritik« erscheinen zu lassen. Maria Marc hat bereits meinem Wunsch zugestimmt, die paar Aquarelle, die ich von Franz besitze, reproduzieren zu lassen, und gleichzeitig werde ich mich auch an Klee wenden, um die gleiche Erlaubnis für seine Bilder zu erlangen. Ihnen wäre ich nun ebenfalls sehr dankbar, wenn sie gestatten wollten, daß ich die schöne Aquarelldetailstudie zu Ihrer Komposition VII – leider das Einzige, was ich von Ihnen besitze – reproduzieren lasse, und vielleicht wollten Sie so freundlich sein, mir zu demselben Zweck ein paar gute Photos Ihrer neueren und neuesten Arbeiten zur Verfügung zu stellen.

Mit Persönlichem will ich Sie lieber nicht behelligen. Es geht mir leidlich, ich arbeite sehr fleißig, darf mich nicht beklagen; wäre aber dankbar, wenn diese leidige Professur mir mehr eigene Zeit ließe. Vor $1^1/_2$ Jahren kam ich mit dem Plastiker Rönnebeck in Denver zusammen, wo er Professor ist und wo ich im dortigen Museum eine Reihe von Vorträgen zu halten hatte. Wir sprachen viel von Ihnen und wie er ihn damals vor bald einem Vierteljahrhundert mit dem Maler Hartley zu mir auf die Bude schickten. Auch den Hartley habe ich bisher nur ein einziges mal gesehen, als ich vor 15 Jahren in New York eine Kollektivausstellung machte, sechs Monaten [sic] nach meiner letzten Heimkehr aus Europa.

Ich hoffe sehr, daß es Ihnen seit dem Einbruch des Grauens in Deutschland doch passabel geht und daß sie sich in bester Gesundheit befinden.

Mit den herzlichsten Grüßen, in alter Dankbarkeit,

Ihr Albert Bloch

WASSILY KANDINSKY AN ALBERT BLOCH

Neuilly ^{S}/Seine (Seine), 2. Juni 1936

Lieber Herr Bloch,

Sie haben mich mit Ihrem Brief erfreut. Ich habe doch 7. [sic] Jahre in Russland verbracht, den Krieg (nicht als Teilnehmer, sondern nur Beobachter), die Revolution (als Beobachter, aber auch gewissermaßen Teilnehmer) erlebt, was alles manche gründliche Veränderungen in die Psyche mitbrachte, manche »Löcher« in die Vergangenheit hineinriss. Manche Erinnerungen an die Vorkriegszeit, die wir zusammen in unsrem lieben München erlebten, haben stark gelitten und bekamen die erwähnten Löcher.

Trotz dem, als ich Ende 1921 wieder nach Berlin kam, habe ich mich sofort erkundigt, wo meine ehemaligen Kollegen, Freunde, Mitarbeiter sich befinden und wie es ihnen geht. Darunter hörte ich, dass Sie in Amerika sind und dass es Ihnen gut geht. Keine Einzelheiten aber. Später hörte ich, Sie wären Irgendwo in Amerika Professor und unterrichten also in einer Kunstschule.

Jetzt höre ich direkt von Ihnen Einzelheiten, die mich sehr interessierten und für Sie freuten.

Mein Leben bleibt bewegt. Vor ca. 3. Jahren habe ich Deutschland wieder verlassen, was ich bis jetzt nicht bedaure. Es wäre für mich unmöglich, dort zu bleiben, d. h. mit Ruhe weiter arbeiten zu können. Ruhig ist es ja hier auch nicht. Wenigstens wird man bis jetzt nicht in der Arbeit gestört. Ich weiss selber, was ich zu machen, wie ich zu arbeiten habe.

Wassily Kandinsky, Study for Composition No. VII, 1913, formerly in Albert
Bloch's possession, Private collection

*Wassily Kandinsky, Entwurf für ›Komposition VII‹, 1913, ehemals im Besitz Albert
Blochs, Privatsammlung*

und brauche keine staatlichen Anweisungen dafür.

Dass Sie ein Buch über Marc, Klee und mich schreiben, ist ein
Beweis dafür, dass Sie die alten, tatsächlich klugbewegten Zeiten noch
frisch in Erinnerung haben und ein lebendiges Beziehen dazu erhielten.
Das freut mich, und ich bin sehr für Ihr Buch interessiert. [...]

Mit Vergnügen gebe ich Ihnen die Erlaubnis, das Aquarell, das Sie
von mir besitzen (Studie zu Komposition 7) zu reproduzieren.

An Hartley kann ich mich noch gut erinnern. Er gefiel mir damals
sehr, weshalb ich ihn Ihnen damals »auf die Bude schickte«. [...] Dass
Sie mich mit »Persönlichem« nicht »behelligen« wollten, ist schade, da
es mich bestimmt interessieren würde, Näheres über Ihre persönliche
[sic] Dinge zu hören. Vielleicht holen Sie es einmal nach?

Ja, ich kenne, was an Zeit und Kraft es kostet, Professor zu sein.
Ich habe in Moskau während der Revolution 2-3 Jahre unterrichtet, und
später in Deutschland 10 Jahre. Ich habe gern die Jugend und es machte
mir Freude, mit jungen Menschen zu verkehren und ihnen behilflich zu
sein. Aber trotz dem freue ich mich, jetzt frei von solchen Pflichten zu
sein. Die Kunst ist eifersüchtig und will »den ganzen Mann«. Ich hatte
immer nur 2. Tage in der Woche zu unterrichten. Die Vorbereitungen
aber und die grosse innere Spannung, die zum Unterricht nötig ist,
brachten mich aus dem Konzept und schadeten meiner persönlichen
Arbeit. Hoffentlich ist die Krise bald vorbei, und damit finden auch Sie
die Möglichkeit, Ihren Unterricht wenigstens sehr zu reduzieren, aber
noch besser, ihn ganz fallen zu lassen. Das wünsche ich Ihnen sehr und
begrüsse Sie sehr herzlich.

Ich war erstaunt, wie schön Sie deutsch schreiben, obwohl Sie wahrscheinlich nicht viel Gelegenheit haben, Ihre Kenntnisse immer zu er-
frischen.

Ihr Kandinsky

ALBERT BLOCH AN WASSILY KANDINSKY

Lawrence, 22. Juni 36

Lieber Herr Kandinsky,

Herzlichen Dank ! – nicht nur für die Photos, sondern – hauptsächlich –
für den schönen liebenswürdigen Brief. – Ich schreibe hier bei <u>40 Grad
Hitze</u> – Gott sei Dank haben wir jetzt bis Ende September Ferien – und

da voraussichtlich auf einen Rückgang der hohen Temperaturen nicht gerechnet werden kann, will ich meine Antwort nicht auf unbestimmte Zeit
aufschieben und nur hoffen, daß ich unter so großem Hindernis einen
Brief zustande bringen kann, der nicht unwürdig sein wird Ihres interessanten und gütigen Schreibens.

Zunächst aber muß ich Sie über ein Mißverständnis aufklären. Das
kleine Buch, welches ich herauszugeben hoffe, ist keines »über« Sie und
Marc und Klee, sondern eine Sammlung von fünf meiner öffentlichen
Vorträge nebst zwei Essays, deren <u>Mittelpunkt</u> allerdings jene kritisch
rückblickende Betrachtung bilden soll. Ich weiß noch nicht einmal, ob
sich ein Verleger, d.h. ein geeigneter dafür finden lassen wird, und darum
auch nicht, ob, im Falle des Erscheinens, Photographien überhaupt ver-
wendet werden können. Ich wollte nur, für alle Fälle, die Reproduktionserlaubnis von Ihnen und den anderen erhalten, nebst dem Illustrations-
material, um welches ich Sie gebeten hatte. [...]

Über die Photos selbst, als schwarz-weiße Wiedergaben Ihrer Bilder, ließe sich nur wenig sagen, auch wenn Sie ein Urteil über sie von
mir hören wollten. Aber daß selbst die kleinen Reproduktionen mich
furchtbar an – und aufregen – ich weiß nicht, ob mehr an oder auf –, das
können Sie mir glauben! Sie sind der alte geblieben und der junge geworden! Das muß selbst der Totfeind [sic] Ihrer Malerei zugeben, und
ich war immer ihr Freund, wiewohl ich nicht verhehlen darf, daß ich ihr
– als Richtung – heute nicht mehr so kritiklos begeistert gegenüberstehe
wie vor 25 Jahren, da ich noch nicht imstande war ihr etwas anderes als
intuitives Erfassen und jugendlichen Enthusiasmus entgegenzubringen.
Ach wie war das damals schön! Aber ich könnte nicht sagen, daß der
seitherige Gewinn an Einsicht und Urteil den doch schmerzlichen Verlust an leidenschaftlicher Begeisterung nicht schließlich aufwögen. Heute
kann ich mir Rechenschaft geben, wodurch der bloß instinktive Genuß
so sehr verinnerlicht wird; damals konnte ich es noch nicht – wollte es
auch nicht. Ich vermag es jetzt, nachdem ich ein Kunstwerk unmittelbar
<u>erfühlt</u> habe, mich zu einem Urteil <u>durchzudenken</u>; und das steigert so
ungeheuer mein Erlebnis.

Von der eigenen Malerei kann ich und will ich nicht viel mitteilen,
weiß auch nicht, ob es Sie interessieren würde. Gute Photos habe ich nur
wenige; doch will ich einige auf's Geratewohl beilegen, auf die Gefahr
hin, daß sie Sie langweilen und Sie mich endgültig »aufgeben«. Denn ich
male noch immer »gegenständlich«, wie Sie sagen; gegenständlicher als
jemals. Aber ich stelle mich hier ganz auf der Seite [sic] <u>Schardts</u>, wenn
er in seinem Buch über Marc so schön sagt: »In der Zukunft hat nur
<u>diejenige</u> <u>Gegenstandsmalerei</u> ein Recht auf Symbol und Glaubfähigkeit,
<u>die durchleuchtet ist von der neuen Gewißheit eines sich gegenseitig
durchdringenden ewigen Lebens«!</u> Diese Gewißheit glaube ich zu besitzen, und Sie werden diesen Bildern, trotz allen offenbaren Schwächen
und Mängeln und soweit sie sich nach schlechten Photographien beurteilen lassen, jenes »Recht auf Symbol und Glaubfähigkeit« vielleicht
nicht ganz absprechen. Sie haben sich dabei die Palette sehr abgekühlt
und zurückhaltend zu denken. Die Cadmiums, Zinnober, Krapplack u.
dgl. fehlen jetzt. Weiß und Blau spielen eine ungeheuer wichtige Rolle
in der Entstehung von fast jedem Farbklang: die <u>Erdfarben</u> sind mir
<u>wesentlich</u> [dreifach unterstrichen] geworden – früher hatte ich höchstens
Lichtocker auf der Palette –; durch das Weiß und das Blau lassen sie sich
so <u>entrücken</u> und vergeistigen, so vertiefen und entkörpern, daß sich z. B.
das rohe und herbe Indischrot geradezu als Engelssang warnehmen [sic]
läßt. Die Farbenorgien eines <u>Matisse</u> sind ein Greuel vor Gott: es ist bei
ihm zum Orgasmus der banalsten Buntheit geworden, die jede Form ver-
wüstet und allen Geist zerstört. Und ich liebte ihn einmal! (Aber das
brauche <u>ich</u> alles zu allerletzt <u>Ihnen</u> zu sagen – entschuldigen Sie!).

Nicht allzusehr »berühmt« bin ich geworden, ich gehöre zu den
Malern, die man halt so »kennt«, doch Gott sei dank nicht zu den Tagesgrößen; denn nach meiner ersten (und einzigen) großen Ausstellung in
New York, die einen ganz guten Erfolg hatte, habe ich mich geflissent-
lich von dem öffentlichen Kunsttreiben zurückgezogen. Ein paar Sachen
sind hie und da in Museen gekommen, ich habe einige Anhänger und
Imitatoren nicht gesucht, aber leider gefunden, doch hört man von mir
nur sehr selten, Bitten um Reproduktionserlaubnis in Zeitungen oder
Zeitschriften schlage ich meistens ab und auf den großen Ausstellungen

bin ich fast nie zu sehen, denn ich stelle immer sehr ungern aus und immer nur auf direkte persönliche Einladung, die ich aber lieber ablehne als annehme. Ich will nichts als meine Ruhe, und hier in diesem lieblichen Universitätsnestchen, wo die staatliche Kunstschule der Universität angegliedert ist und ich Leiter der Abteilung für Malerei bin, habe ich sie endlich gefunden.

In diesem Sommer werde ich 54 Jahre alt. Nerven und Gesundheit haben in den letzten 20 Jahren vielfach gelitten, und die Professur ist eine verfluchte Last – dem großen Glücke zu trotz, daß ich sie habe und wenigstens von allen dringenden wirtschaftlichen Sorgen bis auf weiteres befreit bin. So läßt man mich jetzt in Ruhe, nachdem ich allen »irdischen« Allüren abgesagt habe, und allmählich komme ich durch meine Arbeit vorwärts und zu mir selbst. Ich habe eine unermesslich große Dankesschuld abzuarbeiten ehe ich von hinnen muß – drum will ich lange leben!

Wundern Sie sich bitte nicht allzusehr über mein »schönes deutsch«, welches sich vielleicht von einem Negativen herleiten läßt: indem ich nämlich in der Literatur der eigenen Sprache seit einem Jahrhundert leider so verschwindend wenig finde, daß [sic] meinen Bedürfnissen adäquat wäre, und in der deutschen des 18. und 19. so viel – um von <u>Karl Kraus</u>, dem ich ja schließlich <u>alles</u> verdanke, überhaupt zu schweigen (aber nicht, wie die Welt über ihn schweigt!). Außerdem habe ich noch einige deutsche Korrespondenten, mit denen ich zeitweise in ziemlich regem Briefverkehr stehe.

Und so, lieber und altverehrter Freund, haben Sie auch noch einiges »Persönliche« von mir, wie Sie es sich erbeten haben. Wenn Sie sich dann und wann Zeit nehmen könnten, mir kurze Nachricht von Ihnen zu geben –, denn da ich Sie nun wiedergefunden habe, möchte ich Sie nicht aus den Augen verlieren! –, würde mir das sehr große Freude machen. Es grüßt Sie sehr herzlich nochmals dankend

Ihr Bloch

WASSILY KANDINSKY AN ALBERT BLOCH

Neuilly ˢ/Seine, 20. Oktober 1936

Lieber Herr Bloch,

Ihr letzter Brief war vom 22. Juni. Damals litten Sie an Hitze und freuten sich über die Ferien »bis Ende September«. Nun haben wir jetzt bereits Ende Oktober. Die Zeit nimmt immer an Tempo zu.

Ihr Brief hat mir eine spezielle Freude gemacht, weil er ein Brief eines echten Malers ist. Sie schreiben sehr schön und lebendig von Farben, und speziell von Erdfarben. Was mich anlangt, habe ich manchmal keine Angst vor »Buntheit«. Auch die grellsten Zusammenstellungen können »vergeistigt« werden. Nicht wahr? Schlimm ist es, wenn solche Zusammenstellungen »brüllen«! Oder überhaupt »banal« werden, was ja leicht der Fall werden kann. Und gerade reizt es mich manchmal, Ruhe durch »Lautes« zu erreichen. Meine eignen Bestrebungen machen mich aber nicht blind für Bestrebungen Andrer. […]

Ich danke Ihnen für den ausführlichen Bericht über Ihr Leben, Schaffen und Verhalten. Alles hat mich sehr interessiert, und ich habe den Eindruck gewonnen, ich hätte selbst und mit eignen Augen Ihr Leben in der Nähe gesehen. Ich freue mich speziell für Sie, weil Sie die gesuchte Ruhe im kleinen »Nestchen« gefunden haben. Es gehört heute zu grossen Wundern, sich das Leben so gestalten zu können, wie man es haben möchte. Natürlich gibt es überall »Minusse«, die aber m. M. nach notwendig sind – Gesetz des Gegensatzes.

Ich weiss nicht vom welchen [sic] Buch von Schardt über Franz Marc Sie schreiben. Ich habe früher keins gekannt, und das neue ist ja eben erschienen. Es ist sehr schön gemacht, mit reichem Bildmaterial und schönen Texten von Schardt. Frau Marc hat Ihnen wohl über die Ausstellung von Marc in Berlin berichtet. Nun sind aber leider diese Ausstellungen in Hamburg und in Köln verboten, da sie dem reinen deutschen Geist nicht entsprechen. Gleichzeitig hing aber ein Portrait von Marc (von August Macke gemalt) in Berlin unter den Bildnissen der »Grossen Deutschen«. Es gehört zu den heutigen »Lebenswitzen«, solche »qui pro quo« zu schaffen. Die Menschheit wird immer witziger

Albert Bloch, Harlequin, 1931, Private collection, from a photograph taken in the 1930s and enclosed in a letter to Kandinsky dated 22 June 1936, Courtesy of Mrs. Albert Bloch

Albert Bloch, Harlekin, 1931, Privatsammlung, Abzug eines Photos aus den 30er Jahren, im Brief an Kandinsky vom 22. Juni 1936 beigelegt, Mrs. Albert Bloch

– womit soll es nur enden? Am wenigsten weiss man es, glaube ich, in Frankreich. Hier weiss man nicht mal, wie »Morgen« aussehen wird, weil auch das »Heute« keinem Menschen klar ist – vielleicht am wenigsten dem Politiker. Sie haben es besser in Amerika, wie es jedenfalls uns hier erscheint. Und Sie persönlich haben es vielleicht am Allerbesten – in Ihrem Nestchen.

Ich könnte fast neidisch werden! Schon deshalb, weil es für mich unmöglich wäre, mich so zurückzuziehen, wie Sie es gemacht haben. Ich lebe von Bilderverkäufen, weil ich sonst <u>nichts</u> habe. Es muss also an mich ständig erinnert werden, wofür Ausstellungen, Publikationen, Reproduktionen sorgen. […]

Ich würde mich sehr freuen, von Ihnen wieder mal bald zu hören und im Briefwechsel mit Ihnen zu bleiben. Sieht man sich noch irgend einmal? Wir leben weit von einander – so weit, wie es auf dem Erdball nur geht – d. h. als Antipoden. Das ehemalige München verbindet uns aber – der Entfernung und der Zeit zum Trotz.

Viele herzliche Grüsse, lieber Herr Bloch, und lassen Sie es Ihnen [sic] recht schön und befriedigend ergehen.

Ihr Kandinsky

ALBERT BLOCH AN WASSILY KANDINSKY

Lawrence, 20. November 1936

Lieber Herr Kandinsky:

Ihren Brief vom 20. Oktober, der mich sehr freute, erhielt ich vor ein paar Wochen; ich hätte ihn früher beantwortet, aber ich hatte nicht nur sehr viel zu tun, sondern war auch leidend. Zu tun habe ich freilich noch immer sehr viel, doch gesundheitlich geht's jetzt etwas besser (ich bin mit einem Hüftbandbruch behaftet und trage noch die Gürtelbinde, die aber hoffentlich bald wegkommt), und so ergreife ich die erste Gelegenheit, Ihnen zu schreiben. Die Photos konnte ich glücklicher Weise fast sofort abgehen lassen, eingeschrieben und gut verpackt, und ich hoffe, dass sie Sie unversehrt rechtzeitig erreichen werden.

Mein kleines Buch hat bis jetzt kein Glück gehabt; soll heissen, dass ich es vorläufig, im Juni war's, einem einzigen Verleger unterbreitet habe, der es unter allerhand Verbeugungen bedauernd refusierte. Im weiteren Verlauf des Sommers war's mir zu heiss, mich darum zu bemühen, und seitdem fehlt's mir an Zeit und, ehrlich gestanden, an Interesse. So geht's mir immer: für die Arbeit selbst bin ich Feuer und Flamme; gilt's aber nach vollendetem Werke, mich um dessen Schicksal zu kümmern, so flaut das Interesse ab, denn da stecke ich schon mitten in der nächsten Arbeit und will mich nicht stören lassen. Auch meinen Bildern geht es so; wenn

Albert Bloch, Autumn Night, 1934, Bernard O. Stone, from a photograph taken in the 1930s and enclosed in a letter to Kandinsky dated 22 June 1936, Courtesy of Mrs. Albert Bloch

Albert Bloch, Herbstnacht, 1934, Bernard O. Stone, Abzug eines Photos aus den 30er Jahren, im Brief an Kandinsky vom 22. Juni 1936 beigelegt, Mrs. Albert Bloch

ich manchmal eine mir passende Ausstellungsgelegenheit willkommen heisse – d. h. wenn sie sich von selbst bietet und ich sie nicht erst suchen muss –, so ist das nur, weil ich mich dann eine Zeit lang in meinem immer enger werdenden Arbeitsraum etwas freier bewegen kann; denn die eigenen Bilder hänge ich im Hause nie auf, weil sie mir, wo immer sie mir vor Augen kommen, Vorwürfe machen! […]

Dass Ihnen meine Briefe Spass machen, freut mich sehr, und ich bin dankbar, dass Sie mit mir im Briefwechsel zu bleiben wünschen. Dass ich es selbst so wünsche, ist nur natürlich, denn ich weiss, dass ich von diesem Verkehr mehr profitieren werde als Sie, und ausgelernt habe ich noch lange nicht. Es ist übrigens merkwürdig, wie viel man mit zunehmendem Alter lernt, und oft gerade von solchen, von denen man es am wenigsten erwartet hätte. Wie zum Beispiel von seinen Schülern! Was habe ich da alles von den meinen gelernt, und selbst von den geringer begabten, seit ich diese 15 Jahren zu ihnen in die Schule gehe – wenn bloss die armen jungen Menschen ahnten, was ich ihnen alles abgucke, was ich ihnen verdanke, wie mich ihre jede Entgleisung anregt, welchen Anreiz jeder falsche Pinselstrich mir bietet! Ein berühmter Musiklehrer äusserte sich einmal, dass es keine guten Lehrer gibt; es gebe nur gute Schüler. Das ist witziger als wahr, denn ich habe gefunden, dass die guten Lehrer jene sind, die von den schlechtesten Schülern lernen können; und ich weiss, dass wenn sie mir nicht unbewußt hülfen, ich ihnen mein Lebtag nicht helfen könnte … Sie hatten es bei Ihrer deutschen Professur wöchentlich um einen halben Tag besser als ich es hier habe: ich muß 2$^{1}/_{2}$ Tage in der Woche in den Ateliers herumspuken. Am meisten Spass macht mir dabei mein allwöchentliches »Kompositionseminar«; da sitze ich ein paar Stunden lang unter 15-20 jungen Leuten, die einer nach dem anderen ein paar kleine Kompositionsskizzen oder -studien vorzeigen. Diese werden zuerst von dem Verfasser selbst besprochen und kritisiert, dann der Reihe nach von allen Mitschülern, zuletzt, zusammenfassend, von mir. Sie machen sich kaum einen Begriff, wie das für mich oft belehrend ist, und wenn die Schüler nur argwöhnten, wie sie dabei

vom Herrn Professor förmlich ausgebeutet werden und was er ihnen alles verdankt, würden sie mit recht eine Entgeltung von ihm fordern … Dann lese ich an zwei Vormittagen Kunstgeschichte vor, aber keine, wie sie im Buche steht, sondern das gerade Gegenteil. Denn für das Unwesentliche, das eigentlich Kunsthistorische, finden die Hörer in unserer Bibliothek Bücher im Überfluss; und ich habe es mir zur Aufgabe gemacht, ihnen, so gut ich es kann, klarzumachen, wie Bilder betrachtet werden wollen, aus welchem Geiste das echte Bild geboren wird – alles übrige ist Mumpitz. Auch dieser Kursus, wozu mir die alten Meister aller Schulen am besten zu taugen scheinen, ist für mich ungeheuer wertvoll, denn dabei finde ich immer von neuem Gelegenheit, mir Rechenschaft zu geben über das, was ich denke, und in manchem Punkte sogar zu entdecken, wie ich überhaupt denke … Mit Routine wie Aktmalerei, Aktzeichnen u. dgl. gebe ich mich nicht ab – das überlasse ich den anderen Herren; aber zuweilen finde ich in den Stilleben und Porträtateliers wundervolle Gelegenheit für Form- und Farbenforschung und –analyse … Sie sehen also, dass ich mich hier im Allgemeinen nicht unglücklich fühle. Aber geistigen Verkehr unter den Menschen hier habe ich sonst so gut wie gar keinen. Merkwürdiger Weise geht er mir auch nicht ab. Seit mein älterer Sohn aus dem Hause weg ist und mit seiner Frau im Osten des Landes lebt, habe ich kaum einen Menschen um mich, mit dem ich mich manchmal aussprechen könnte. Der jüngere Sohn, der Schauspieler werden will (er ist, in München während des Krieges geboren, jetzt bald 21 Jahre alt), interessiert sich wenig für das, was mich im Innersten angeht, und seine Mutter noch weniger; und die einzige Oase in dieser Geisteswüste, ausser meiner Arbeit, ist meine kleine Sekretärin, die mir von der Universität beigestellt wird und seit Jahren mir und den Meinen herzlich zugetan ist, und die unglaublich viel von Malerei, Literatur und Musik ganz instinktiv begreift. Eine Stockamerikanerin, d. h. von englisch-französischer Abkunft, ist ihre Lieblingslektüre Deutsch; und um Ihnen das Lesen zu erleichtern, wird sie diesen Brief mit der Maschine abschreiben.

Der Inhalt Ihres Briefes interessiert mich sehr. Was Sie über die »grellsten Zusammenstellungen« schreiben, stimmt ja vollkommen, und es ist gar nicht ausgeschlossen, dass ich zwischendurch wieder zu ihnen zurückkehre. Und Ihre Angstlosigkeit vor »Buntheit« teile ich auch; aber das Malkauderwelsch eines Matisse, das überhaupt mit Farbe nichts mehr zu tun hat, ist auch nicht bloss bunt. Gerade das aber nimmt mich immer wunder: <u>wie</u> bunt sich die Erdfarben malen lassen, wenn man ihnen auf den Grund gekommen ist! Früher hätte ich das gar nicht geglaubt. Aber dem verführerischen Reiz der Cadmiums usw. will ich nicht bloss ausweichen; sie widerstehen mir keineswegs, ich widerstehe <u>ihnen</u>. Und ich wollte nur andeuten, dass in [sic] diesem Zeitpunkt, der jetzt einige Jahre zurückreicht, die geistigen Möglichkeiten der »nüchternen« Erdfarben meiner inneren Notwendigkeit adäquater sind als die der verlockenderen Palette … In Italien war ich noch nicht, und werde es wohl, da nun der entsetzliche Mussolini und sein Geist herrschen, nicht mehr sehen. Auch Deutschland nie wieder! […]

Das Buch von Schardt, aus welchem ich den Satz zitierte, ist dasselbe über Franz Marc, das Sie anscheinend erst kürzlich gesehen haben. Ich erhielt im Spätfrühjahr ein Exemplar von Maria Marc geschenkt; ich nahm an, das Buch sei schon damals im Handel erschienen. Frau Marc hatte mir seinerzeit über die Ausstellungen in Hannover und Berlin geschrieben und gleichzeitig einen Schock Zeitungsausschnitte gesendet, angefüllt mit einem guten Teil des banalsten Kritikerenthusiasmus, der aber wohl sehr bald darauf verstummen musste. Nette Zustände sind das jetzt in unserm geliebten Deutschland! Etwas andere sind es, die in den übrigen Ländern herrschen, aber doch kaum bessere. Doch über das Politische (Verschönerungswort für »Gaunerisch-mörderische«) kann ich nichts schreiben und einen klaren Kopf bewahren. Ich muss mich damit begnügen, mir meinen Teil zu denken und, wenn möglich, nicht zu verzweifeln. Ihnen aber, wenn ich mir einen Rat erlauben darf, würde ich vorschlagen, sich aus dem Staube rechtzeitig zu machen, nach Skandinavien wieder zu entfliehen, oder besser, wenn Sie es irgend können, hierher zu übersiedeln. Da Sie auf den Verkauf Ihrer Bilder angewiesen sind, werden Sie jetzt in Amerika doch sicherlich mehr Chancen finden als in Europa?[1] Selbst ich verkaufe hie und da unversehens etwas; und wenn Sie sich mit einem gewandten Bilderhändler in New York liieren könnten, wäre es ja möglich, dass es ginge. Wenn ich nur selbst eingreifen könnte, um Ihnen tätig beizustehen, anstatt bloss darüber zu faseln, wäre es mir eine Ehre und eine grosse Freude. Ich werde es Ihnen niemals vergessen, wie Sie sich für mich und meine Arbeit, wo Sie nur konnten, einsetzten. Eddy war als Sammler zwar ein schäbiger Ausbeuter (und als Kunstschriftsteller ein noch schäbigerer Analphabet), aber wie froh war ich damals, mich von ihm ausbeuten zu lassen: er hielt mich ein paar Jahre lang über Wasser! [...] Während der Münchner Jahre war ich von solchen Sorgen kaum jemals eine ganze Woche lang frei. Ich war ja nicht von Haus aus vermögend (nicht, als ob ich jetzt vermögend wäre; ich bin von meinem Universitätsgehalt, das in den letzten Jahren auch noch stark »abgebaut« wurde, ganz und gar abhängig); und zwischen meinem 26. und meinem 41. Jahr hatte ich buchstäblich nichts, das ich mein eigen nennen konnte. Wie ich damals manchmal lebte, weiss ich heute kaum; dass es mir zuweilen zum Verzweifeln schlecht ging, können Sie mir glauben. Doch war ich in jener Zeit noch jung, und ich wusste, was immer mit mir geschähe, wenigstens für meine Angehörigen würde gesorgt werden. Das [sic] es Ihnen aber jetzt so gehen soll wie damals mir, oder dass Sie solcher Gefahr ausgesetzt sind, ist herzbrechend – umso mehr, als ich mich dabei so beschämend hilflos, d.h. zur Hilfe unfähig weiss. Ich will nur hoffen, dass meine Bangigkeit um Sie grundlos sei.

Es ist, fürchte ich, ein langer Brief geworden, viel länger als ich anfangs beabsichtigte. Aber wie gesagt, ich habe hier so gar keinen geistigen Verkehr, und so habe ich die unverhoffte Gelegenheit ergriffen, mich einmal etwas aufzuknöpfen, leider ohne zu bedenken, dass ich Sie dabei vielleicht langweilen könnte … Und es fällt mir eben ein: Im Frühsommer legte ich einige Photos einem Briefe bei; da Sie sich zu ihnen nicht äussern, muss ich annehmen, dass Sie die abgebildeten Kompositionen nicht interessieren. Ist das der Fall, dann bitte ich Sie, es nur geradheraus zu sagen, tout-à-fait sans gêne. Ich würde Ihnen nichts dergleichen übelnehmen, und Ihre schärfste Kritik würde ich wenigstens zu würdigen wissen. Ich lege jetzt wieder ein Photo bei, das Sie aber nicht in Verlegenheit bringen kann: eine Momentaufnahme ca. 10 Jahre alt. Ich soll mich seitdem nicht sehr geändert haben, auch nicht sehr gealtert sein. Der liebe Bulldog ist aber tot. [...] (Wenn Sie eine kleine Selbstphotographie haben, die Sie entbehren können, möchte ich sie gern haben. Ich habe Sie seit mehr als 22 Jahren nicht gesehen!) [...] (Sie könnten mir aber doch noch ein [sic] Gefallen tun! Jetzt, da ich Sie wiedergefunden habe, bitte ich Sie recht herzlich, von nun an das Wort »Herr« in der Anrede an mich fallen zu lassen.)

Und nun endlich Schluss! Ich erinnere mich plötzlich, dass Sie im nächsten Monat Geburtstag haben, und zwar jenen, zu dem man nur ehrerbietig gratulieren darf. Das tue ich in aller Aufrichtigkeit, mit allen guten Wünschen für die nächsten zehn Jahre und darüber hinaus, und grüsse Sie herzlich.

Ihr Bloch

Hören Sie manchmal etwas von Klee? Wie geht es ihm jetzt? Vor Monaten schrieb seine Frau, er sei so weit wieder hergestellt, daß er zur Erholung nach dem Engadin fahren konnte. Seitdem höre ich nichts.

1   Sonst würde ich weiß Gott keinem Menschen, keinem Europäer, raten, sich in dieser Barbarei niederzulassen!

WASSILY KANDINSKY AN ALBERT BLOCH

Neuilly S/Seine, 2. April 1937

Lieber Bloch,

ich streiche gern den »Herr«. Ihr letzter Brief war v. 20. 11. 36. Die Zeit rast unglaublich.

Es hat mich sehr interessiert, was Sie über Unterricht sagen. Nach meiner Erfahrung, kann man die Kunst nicht direkt »lehren«, aber so zu sagen indirekt – durch Winke, Stösse, zeitliches Bremsen, hier und da durch einen direkten Rat und dgl. Das [sic] man aber bei eignen Schülern

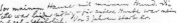

Ca 1927   DD für Kandinsky

Albert Bloch with his dog in Lawrence, c. 1927, Original photograph enclosed in a letter to Kandinsky dated 20 November 1936, Musée National d'Art moderne de Paris, Centre Georges Pompidou, Donated by Nina Kandinsky

Albert Bloch mit seinem Hund, Lawrence, um 1927, Originalphoto im Brief an Kandinsky vom 20. November 1936 beigelegt, Musée National d'Art moderne de Paris, Centre Georges Pompidou, Donation Nina Kandinsky

selbst lernt, ist unbestreitbar. Ich denke sogar: wenn ein Lehrer bei seinen Schülern nicht lernen kann, ist er nicht nur kein Lehrer, sondern auch kein Künstler. Können Sie sich noch an die Entdeckung erinnern, die in München gemacht wurde? Alte italienische Rezepte – Farbenreiben, Grundieren usw., aber auch »Wenn Du einen Fisch im Wasser malen willst … «, oder »Wenn Du einen Greis im Schatten malen willst … « Uns hat man aber nie was von Farbe oder Grund gesagt, das mussten wir allein erfahren, oder »Quellen« lesen. Es ist tatsächlich erstaunlich, wie wenig hier in Paris die grossen Künstler von der notwendigsten »Technik« verstehen. Schon nach 2-3 Monaten blättern die Farben ab (manchmal natürlich, aber ziemlich oft bei manchen), oder springen sie, oder verändern sie sich. Auch ich habe s. Z. allerhand Unsinn mit Grundierungen, Farbmischungen usw. gemacht, aber doch etwas dabei gelernt. [...]

Zu viel darf dem Schüler nicht gesagt werden, damit er am eignen Leibe die Schwierigkeiten kennen lernt, aber manche ganz schlimme »Seitensprünge« kann man ihm ersparen. Es gibt auch hier keine festen Regeln – wie ja auf sämtlichen Lebensgebieten. Wichtiger als Regel ist der Takt. Und der Takt kommt vom inneren Diktat. Wir haben alle eine klare innere Stimme, die deutlich spricht »Ja, so ist richtig« oder »Lass' es doch! Falsch«.

Von diesem Standpunkt gibt es keinen Unterschied zwischen Kunst, Küche, Eheleben, Wissenschaft, Autolenken, Kindererziehen, Garten- und Feldbauen und … der Politik. Ich freute mich zu hören, dass Sie »das Politische« durch »Gaunerisch-mörderisches« ersetzen. Vollkommen auch meine Meinung. Sie sagen weiter, Sie würden nie einem Europäer raten, nach Amerika, ins Land der Barbarei zu ziehen. Glauben Sie wirklich, dass wir hier nicht auf barbarische Weise leben? Warum ist aber die Politik so scheusslich? Warum kehrte die Barbarei zurück? Warum nimmt das Barbarische ständig zu und auf Kosten des Menschlichen? Warum ist es für den Menschen die höchste Schande geworden, »sentimental«, »liberal«, »menschlich« zu sein? Ich meine: weil das innere Leben immer mehr verschwindet und durch die »Realität«, d. h. durch die unendliche Äusserlichkeit ersetzt wird. Die erste Folge ist der Verlust am Taktgefühl und endlich sein komplettes Verschwinden. Es gibt heute sogar Künstler (die ich lieben [=r] »Künstler« nennen möchte), die sich einbilden, ohne »Gefühl« (d. h. ohne Taktgefühl) arbeiten zu können und zu … müssen. Sie meinen, dadurch »objektive Kunst« herstellen zu können. So macht einer ein »Werk« ohne Gefühl, und ein andrer stellt sich davor ohne Gefühl. »Objektives Idyll«. Wie ein Münchner Professor zu seinen Studenten sagte: »Meine Herren, merken Sie sich das bitte: alles in der Welt ist begrenzt, nur die menschliche Dummheit nicht«. Manchmal bin ich wirklich überzeugt, dass die heutige Welt vom Teufel gelenkt wird, und nicht von einem kleinen schäbigen, sondern von einem alten, klugen, erfahrenen.

Genug des Pessimismus. Ich weiss, dass trotz allem die Zeit des Geistes bereits heute dämmert. Wie lange dieses Morgendämmern dauern wird, wann der erste Strahl herausplatzt, weiss ich natürlich nicht.

Sie schreiben, es wäre Zeit für mich, mich aus Frankreich zu retten. Vielleicht haben Sie recht, weil es hier ziemlich blöd aussieht. Aber wohin? Skandinavien? Bedenken Sie, dass ich fast 12 Jahre in schlimmsten Provinzstädten gelebt habe. Von Paris als »Weltgrosstadt« profitiere ich wenig, aber ein »Etwas« tut mir hier wohl, d. h. ich arbeite hier ganz besonders gut, was mir wiederholt gesagt wurde und – wichtiger! – was ich auch selbst weiss. Die Umgebung wirkt auf mich immer. Worin dieses »Etwas« besteht, habe ich keine Ahnung. Es ist wohl die Pariser »Luft«. Was ist aber »Luft«? Mit einem Wort, würde es mir sehr leid tun, Paris verlassen zu müssen. So warte ich – vielleicht leichtsinnig. Nach Amerika zu ziehen, habe ich noch keine Lust – vielleicht bin ich zu sehr von der europäischen Barbarei durchdrungen. Besuchen würde ich sehr gern Amerika, was <u>vielleicht</u> im nächsten Jahr kommt. Leider kann ich nicht englisch, was aber, wie Amerikaner sagen, nicht so schlimm ist. Wir wollen also sehen.

Dass Sie mir so gern helfen würden, hat mich direkt gerührt – weil »Helfenwollen« zu einem deluvialen Ding geworden ist. Es gab tatsächlich nicht schlechte vorsintflutliche Dinge. Was weiter wird und kommt, kann ich nicht erraten, heute geht es mir aber ganz gut. Als Beispiel lege ich Ihnen den kleinen Katalog meiner Pariser Ausstellung bei, die zum Zweck hatte, meine graphische »Entwicklung« zu zeigen – die paar Bilder und Aquarelle waren nur kleine Beispiele meiner Malerei der letzten zwei Jahre. Diese kleine Ausstellung verlief <u>sehr</u> gut – als Resonanz, Anerkennung, und pekuniärer Erfolg (ich habe auch an das Pariser Museum »Jeu de Paume« verkauft). Vom 21.2. bis 29.3. hatte ich eine grosse Ausstellung in Bern – Werke von 1902 bis 1936, 71 Bilder und 15 Aquarelle (darunter eine Anzahl ganz grosser Gemälde). Der Erfolg war ausgezeichnet – in jeder Beziehung. Ich möchte Ihnen mit diesen Beispielen nur sagen, dass es mit mir nicht schlecht bestellt ist. Auch Amerikaner kaufen genügend bei mir, wenn sie nach Paris kommen. Wenn es so weiter bleibt, bin ich ganz befriedigt. Reichtum hat mich nie gelockt.

Es hat mich sehr erfreut, Ihr kleines Bild zu bekommen. M. M. nach haben Sie sich sogar seit München kaum verändert. Als »Revanche« lege ich mein kleines Bild bei, das 1931 in Berlin aufgenommen wurde. Ich wurde im Musikraum aufgenommen, der ein Teil der Internat. Architektur-Ausstellung in Berlin war und der nach meinen Entwürfen als Wandmalereien ausgestaltet wurde (in Keramik). Sie können eine Spitze auf dem Bildchen sehen. Neben mir stand die Besitzer[in] einer keramischen Anstalt in Berlin (teils wurden die Arbeiten von ihr, teils von der Meissner Manufaktur ausgeführt), die ich abgeschnitten habe, da sie Sie wohl nicht besonders interessieren würde. (Die Besitzerin nämlich). Sie nehmen mit Unrecht an, dass mich Ihre Bilder nicht interessierten, weil ich nichts über die zugesandten Photos geschrieben habe. Allerdings kann man sich auch keine genauere Vorstellung von Malreien [sic] machen, wenn man nur schwarz-weisse Reproduktionen vor Augen hat. Besonders, wenn man keine Bilder von einem Künstler seit Jahren gesehen hat – wie es mit mir und Ihnen der Fall ist. Es bleiben also: das »Thema«, Kompositionsart, Ausdruckskraft und Zeichnung, die man auf Photos zu sehen bekommt. Das Wort »Thema« habe ich eigens in »« gebracht, weil unter dieser Bezeichnung gewöhnlich (und mit Unrecht) der literarische »Inhalt« allein verstanden wird. Das Hauptthema jedes Bildes ist und bleibt das malerische – Kompositionsart, Farbe, Zeichnung mit damit verbundener Ausdruckskraft. Sie wissen, dass ich schon seit vielen Jahren mit

diesem »Material« auskomme. D. h. das 2-te, oder das »Nebenthema«= literarisches Thema lehne ich nur für mich und Meinesgleichen ab, die andren Künstler aber, die ein »Nebenthema« brauchen, lehne ich deshalb nicht ab. D. h. ich gehe auch hier nicht »prinzipell« [sic] vor, weil auch hier einzig und allein das »WIE« wesentlich ist.

Aus eigner Haut kann man aber nicht heraus: ich ziehe auch bei nebenthematischen Malereien den kühleren Ausdruck vor.

Und das Einzige, was mich bei Ihren Bildern befremdet, ist der zu »unterstriche« [sic], oder zu »dramatischer« [sic] Ausdruck. Sie sehen, ich sage Ihnen meinen Eindruck vollkommen ehrlich. Das Übrige, d. h. die Kompositionsart, die Zeichnung habe ich in Ihren Bildern sehr gern. (Allerdings könnte die Zeichnung ev. etwas trockener sein – m. M. nach). Sehr gefällt mir auch die Zusammenstellung des Menschen zur Landschaft – sehr feinfühlend und im besten Sinne »poetisch«.

Wenn einer eine Tenorstimme hat, kann man ihm doch nicht sagen: Ach, warum haben Sie keine Basstimme! Und umgekehrt. Aber trotz dem manche ziehen Tenoristen vor (Caruso!), andre wieder Bassisten (Schaljapin!). Das russische Sprichwort erklärt: »Der eine hat Melonen gern, der andre Schweinsknörpel – und keiner soll den andern belehren«. Habe ich mich klar genug ausgedrückt?[…]

Waren Sie schon, als wir uns in München trafen, verheiratet? Sie haben schon so erwachsene Kinder. Allerdings sahen wir uns zum letzten Mal 1914, also vor 22 Jahren. Eine Generation kam seit dem auf die Welt. […]

Sie fragen, wie es Klee geht. Wir haben ihn jetzt in Bern gesehen. Er hatte kürzlich Grippe, dann Magengeschwür. Er war noch bettlegerich [sic], als wir in Bern waren. Seine Frau schrieb uns aber, dass er jetzt glücklicherweise wieder arbeitet, es geht langsam bergauf.

Von Frau Marc hörte ich seit Monaten nichts. Sie hatte damals die Absicht, für ein paar Monate nach Deutschland zu fahren. Ich erwarte Nachrichten von ihr, wenn sie wieder in Ascona ist.

Das Buch von Schardt über Franz Marc wurde ja, wie Sie wahrscheinlich wissen, von den Behörden verboten. Auch weitere Ausstellungen von Marc. Das seinem Held dankbare Vaterland.

ALBERT BLOCH AN WASSILY KANDINSKY

Lawrence, 10. Juni 1937 (Entwurf)

Lieber Herr Kandinsky –

Es sind jetzt 2 Monate verstrichen, seit ich Ihren letzten Brief erhielt. Es gab so viel zu tun und ich konnte nur die notwendigsten Korrespondenzen erledigen. – Ich danke Ihnen sehr für den Katalog Ihrer Ausstellung (der Holzschnitt aus »Klänge«, selbst in klischierter und verkleinerter Reproduktion, wirkt noch immer sehr lebendig); ganz besonders aber danke ich für das kleine Photo von Ihnen, das Sie nach all den Jahren doch kaum gealtert, aber ein klein wenig »stärker« zeigt.

Ihr Brief hat mich über Ihre persönliche Lage sehr beruhigt, und es freut mich aufrichtig, daß es Ihnen jetzt wieder (oder noch immer) verhältnismäßig gut geht. Sollte der angedeutete Plan, nach Amerika auf Besuch zu kommen, in Erfüllung gehen, so rechne ich mit Bestimmtheit darauf, daß Sie mich hier in Lawrence aufsuchen und mir ein paar Tage schenken. […] Aber sollte es mit dem Vorhaben, nach Amerika zu kommen, »Pappe« werden, so ist es doch nicht ganz ausgeschlossen, daß ich Sie in Europa sehe! Ich trage mich nämlich mit dem Gedanken, wenn es irgend zu machen ist, mich ein Jahrlang beurlauben zu lassen, und sollte inzwischen die Hölle in Europa <u>nicht</u> ausgebrochen sein, so gedenke ich wenigstens einen Teil meiner Freiheit in Europa zu verbringen: England, Frankreich, Schweiz, Österreich – nur um eine Runde Visiten zu machen, jene alten Freunde und Bekannte aufzusuchen, die das Glück haben, jetzt nicht in Deutschland zu leben, und ein letztesmal zu sehen, was sie machen und wie es ihnen geht. Das ist aber noch kein Plan; vorläufig nur ein Wunschtraum!

Ja, über das Kapitel »Maltechnik«: Betreffend der Farben, erlaubte und unerlaubte Mischungen, Grundierungen, Malmittel u. dgl., gäbe es unendlich viel noch zu sagen; aber ich teile Ihre Ansicht ganz und gar, daß die heutige Malerei, insbesondere die heutige Mal_weise_ auf den Hund gekommen ist – nicht nur, daß die gegenwärtigen Maler, und vornehmlich die »modernen«, von der Technologie ihres Handwerkes keinen Schimmer haben (das kann man ihnen vielleicht nachsehen, weil eben das Handwerkliche – das einzige, was man ihnen beibringen könnte – halt nicht mehr gelehrt wird –, sondern weil sie sich eines so schäbigen, schlampigen, halunkenhaft-légeren Auftrags geradezu zu befleißigen scheinen. Sehen Sie sich nur um; was sich die meisten (und »berühmtesten«) dieser Rapins mit dem Pinsel herausnehmen: Lurcat, Chirico, oder wie sie alle heißen. Da bekommt man vor einem Münchner Schinken aus dem alten Glaspalast ordentlich Respekt! (Und könnte vor dem Kitsch der Bougereau und Gérome kniefällig werden.)

Wissen Sie was mich in Ihrer letzten großen Ausstellung bei Thannhauser in Erstaunen gesetzt hat? Sie werden's nicht erraten. Von den Bildern selbst will ich nicht sprechen: sie waren schön, gaben mir das, was ich von Ihnen zu erwarten längst gewohnt war. Aber zum ersten mal ward ich inne, daß Ihre Bilder gemalt seien! Das rein Handwerkliche bei Ihnen war mir bis dahin noch niemals aufgefallen. Oder vielmehr schien es mir offengestanden bei manchen etwas früheren Arbeiten – etwa bei dem Moskauerbild in der ersten »blauen Reiter« Ausstellung – zu fehlen. Aber jetzt war ich ganz Bewunderung vor der souveränen Beherrschung der Mittel oder eigentlich: vor Ihrer Beherrschtheit von den Mitteln, Ihrer seligen Ergebung an sie. Ich sagte damals: daß die Kritik mit den Bildern als solchen noch nichts anzufangen weiß, sei weiter nicht erstaunlich; zugeben müsse sie aber doch, daß Kandinsky ein ausgezeichneter Maler geworden sei! ... Und eben dieses Handwerkliche (in jeder Hinsicht), ist der heutigen Malerei abhanden gekommen. Ist das nicht ein erschütterndes Paradoxon? Die Malerei – das Handwerkliche! Ohne dieses gibt's jenes gar nicht: Malerei ist Handwerk. Ergo haben wir heute keine Malerei mehr! (Das »Was« ist mir wurst. Ich habe viele Klees und Feiningers gesehen, die mich »thematisch« kaltließen, aber wie gepflegt ist das Handwerk! Sie malen mit Liebe. Das ist es! Die Nonchalanten, die Malflegels, sind ohne Liebe.)

Was Sie mir über Ihren Eindruck nach den kleinen Photographien meiner Bilder schreiben, glaube ich sehr gut zu verstehen. Es dürfte Sie überraschen, daß ich damit vollkommen einverstanden bin; und ich danke Ihnen herzlich für Ihre schonende aber offene Kritik, die mir als Kritik nur darum so wertvoll ist, weil sie mir die Bestätigung meiner schonungslosen Selbstkritik bringt. Meine große Schwäche in der Malerei ist die Sucht nach Deutlichkeit, vielleicht entstanden aus dem immer lebendigen Mißtrauen gegen das Fassungsvermögen des Beschauers. Die Folge ist, daß ich meiner Fantasie zu wenig Spielraum lasse. Andere Hemmungen sind meine oft übergewissenhafte Zeichnung (ich zeichne zu »gut«) und die Last eines vielleicht zu großen, d. h. unvollkommen verdauten und assimilierten Wissens um das Tatsächliche der Naturerscheinungen. Ich kenne zu viel und kann noch zu wenig; will sagen: ich kann nicht immer im richtigen Augenblick vergessen, was ich alles kann. Dazu kommt meine stets wache Reaktion gegen den schweinischen Unfug der Schmierage, die momentan Malmode ist; das verführt mich wohl manchmal ganz unbewußt in eine anscheinend gequälte Genauigkeit, zu einer Betonung des Nebensächlichen (des »Thematischen [«], nach Ihrem Ausspruch),

Wassily Kandinsky in Berlin, 1931, Original photograph enclosed in a letter to Bloch dated 2 April 1937, Courtesy of Mrs. Albert Bloch

Wassily Kandinsky in Berlin, 1931, Originalphoto im Brief an Bloch vom 2. April 1937 beigelegt, Mrs. Albert Bloch

nur weil die Pfuscher das Wesentliche vernachlässigen. Sie könnten da freilich einwenden, daß meine allergrößte, meine unverzeihliche Schwäche wäre: daß ich mich so sehr von meinem Ekel beherrschen lasse! Und wenn es sich so verhält, hätten Sie natürlich recht. Nur daß ich nicht weiß, ob es sich wirklich so verhält. Ich weiß bloß, daß ich, wie und wo ich nur kann, mich abschließe, und das meiste, was ich von heutiger Malerei in den letzten Jahren gesehen habe, aus kleinen schwarz-weißen Wiedergaben in Büchern, Zeitschriften und Katalogen kenne. Daß ich da vielleicht den Leuten gar Unrecht tue und selbst überhaupt kein Recht habe, mitzureden. Ich bin's zufrieden, will's dabei bewenden lassen! So tolerant wie Sie es sein dürfen, darf ich leider nicht sein, sonst liefe ich Gefahr, mir selbst zuviel nachzusehn!

Es ist ein Glück, daß ich Sie wiedergefunden habe. Bitte, lassen Sie mich nicht mehr ganz ohne Nachricht bleiben!
Es grüßt Sie herzlichst, mit allen guten Wünschen

Ihr Bloch

Ich bin bald 32 Jahre verheiratet. Der ältere Sohn, in New York geboren, war 7 Jahre alt als der Krieg ausbrach. Der jüngere überraschte uns 1916 in München.

VI. ALBERT BLOCH – LILY UND PAUL KLEE 1936-39

ALBERT BLOCH AN PAUL KLEE

Lawrence, 21. Mai 1936

Lieber Herr Klee –
Maria Marc schreibt mir, Sie seien vor kurzem ernstlich krank gewesen, daß Sie aber nunmehr gottlob sich wieder langsam erholen. Das ermutigt mich, an Sie die paar Zeilen zu richten, die ich Ihnen schon längst schreiben wollte.

Ich beabsichtige nämlich, wenn sich der geeignete Verleger finden läßt, unter anderem den revidierten Text einer Ende 1934 geschriebenen Abhandlung mit dem Titel »Kandinsky, Marc, Klee – Reminiszenz und Kritik« erscheinen zu lassen, und möchte sie sehr gern von einigen Illustrationen begleiten lassen.

Maria Marc hat bereits meinem Wunsche zugestimmt, die paar Aquarelle, die ich von Franz besitze, zu reproduzieren; auch Kandinsky will ich gleichzeitig um seine Erlaubnis schreiben, und Ihnen wäre ich nun ebenfalls sehr dankbar, wenn sie mir gestatten wollten, ein oder zwei, vielleicht mehr, von den Bildern reproduzieren zu lassen, die ich von Ihnen habe und die übrigens bisher noch nicht im Druck erschienen sind.

Von mir selbst ist nicht viel zu sagen. Abgesehen von der Brotarbeit, die mich allzusehr in Anspruch nimmt, bin ich sehr fleißig, stelle augenblicklich ein paar Bilder auf Einladung in New York wieder aus, außerdem eine eigene Kollektion neuerer Arbeiten von 35 Aquarellen, verkaufe sogar hie und da a wengerl und klage über nichts, außer den irrsinnigen Lauf der Welt, und da nützt kein Klagen. Nerven und Gesundheit in den letzten Jahren, jene sehr, diese weniger angegriffen, doch wird's wohl wieder auch so gehn. – Bernard, der ältere Sohn […]; der jüngere Sohn Walter […]; ihre Mutter, die Sie beide grüßen läßt, ist verflucht stolz auf die Söhne, vielmehr als auf deren Vater und kein Wunder: der malt halt so Bilder, denkt sich sein Teil und schön is er aa nimmer!

Aber was macht denn der Felix? Der sollte meines Erinnerns Kunstgewerbler oder Kunsttischler werden. Und geht es Ihnen und der Frau Lili seit dem Höllensturz in meinem armen Deutschland halbwegs passabel? Hie und da sehe ich etwas von Ihnen reproduziert, überall in Kunstzeitschriften und -büchern wurden Sie erwähnt und vor einigen Jahren sah ich in New York neue Arbeiten von Ihnen. Ja, wir sind alle mit der elenden Zeit »berühmt« geworden – sogar ich ein wenig hier zuhause, doch lasse ich mich selten blicken und halte mich dem Kunstrummel möglichst fern. Ich wollte gern wieder einen Sprung nach Europa machen, sehe aber vor Ausbruch des kommenden Krieges kaum die Möglichkeit.

Und nachher? …

Mit den allerbesten Wünschen für Ihre rasche und völlige Genesung wie für die Zukunft, und den herzlichsten Grüßen an Sie beide und für Felix,
in alter Freundschaft

Ihr Bloch

LILY KLEE AN ALBERT BLOCH

Bern, 16. Juni 1936

Lieber Herr Bloch,

Das war aber eine freudige Überraschung als Ihr lieber Brief vom 21. Mai bei uns ankam, nachdem wir so lange Jahre nichts von Ihnen u. Ihrer familie gehört hatten. Sie müßen entschuldigen, daß ich für meinen Mann antworte u. Ihnen für Ihren brief herzlichst danke. für ihn ist briefschreiben noch immer etwas anstrengend. Außerdem ist er vor kurzem zu weiterer Erholung ins Unterengadin gefahren mit freunden. Da eine Luftveränderung dringend nötig war. Sie haben durch Maria Marc von der schweren Erkrankung meines Mannes gehört. Es war eine furchtbare Zeit u. es ist ein Wunder, daß er noch lebt u. davon gekommen ist. Da ich ihn ³/₄ Jahre alleine gepflegt habe bin ich auch ziemlich fertig mit d. Nerven u. ist die momentane Ruhepause eine Erholung für mich. Klees Krankheit fing im Juli 1935 (!) mit einer versteckten bösartigen Bronchitis an. Er kränkelte so herum, da er vorher nie krank war wollte er keinen Arzt – u. mußte sich dann im Oktober definitiv legen. Der Arzt konstatierte chronische Lungenentzündung, dazu Herzkomplikation. Im November bekam er plötzlich noch die Masern in schwerer form u. dazu die Lungen u. Herzkomplikation. Es war furchtbar u. er war in größter Lebensgefahr. 2 Monate bin ich aus d. schweren Sorge nicht heraus gekommen. Dann nahm es eine Wendung zur Besserung – aber wie langsam: Januar, februar, März u. April. Im April konnten wir endlich zu einer Roentgenaufnahme fahren u. Mitte Mai machte er s. 1. kl. Spaziergang um's Haus herum. So ist es schrittweise aufwärtsgegangen u. noch als Reconvalescent ist er hier abgereist – aber doch schon kräftiger geworden. […]

Mein Mann läßt Ihnen sagen, daß er seine Erlaubnis gibt, soviel Werke von ihm als Sie für Ihr Buch brauchen, zu reproduzieren.

[An den Rand geschrieben: Wenn Ihr Sohn Bernard in d. Schweiz kommt, würden wir uns sehr freuen, ihn zu sehen. bitte um vorherige Anmeldung.]

Daß es Ihnen gut geht, Sie erfolgreich arbeiten u. thätig sind, hat uns sehr gefreut. Auch die guten Nachrichten über Ihre lieben Söhne. Bernard als Wissenschaftler, verheiratet. Walter als Student. Ich sehe Bernard noch vor mir, den bildschönen buben mit felix spielen. Und Walter als baby, wie er zu uns kommt, unsere Katze zu besuchen u. herein kommt »where is the cat? [An die Seite geschrieben: Wir haben wieder eine wunderschöne Katze. Weiße Angora namens »bimbo«, die wir zärtlich lieben] Ja das wächst heran unheimlich rasch geht so ein Leben dahin. felix hat seinerzeit in Weimar das Bauhaus besucht u. das Tischlerhandwerk erlernt. Daneben Sprachen u. Musik u. viel gemalt. Mit 18 Jahren ging er zum Theater u. lernte d. beruf d. Opernregisseurs von d. Pike an zuerst immer als Volontär u. seit 5 Jahren in Engagements an zunächst

Christmas card from Albert Bloch to Paul Klee, with motif from Bloch's painting Sleigh Ride, (1936), based on the poem "Fahrt ins Fextal" by Karl Kraus, 1939, Kunstmuseum Bern, Paul-Klee-Stiftung

Weihnachtskarte von Albert Bloch an Paul Klee, 1939, mit dem Motiv seines Gemäldes ›Sleighride‹, 1936, nach dem Gedicht von Karl Kraus ›Fahrt ins Fextal‹, 1939, Kunstmuseum Bern, Paul Klee-Stiftung

kleinen Bühnen. Er ist sehr begabt für diesen Beruf, hochmusikalisch, auch für die Scene enorm fleißig, ausdauernd u. strebsam. Er hat viel Erfolge u. immer gute Kritiken. Vor 4 Jahren hat er in Basel eine Bulgarin geheiratet. […] fantastisch – nicht? Aber die Jugend macht was sie will u. setzt sich durch.

Uns geht es gut u. wir sind froh hier zu sein. Ja das war wirklich ein Höllensturz in D[eutschland]. Im Dezember 1933 sind wir hier angekommen. Zuletzt war m. Mann 2¹/₂ Jahre Professor an d. Akademie in Düsseldorf. Man hat ihn dort, trotz des laufenden vertrags einfach raus gesetzt mit vielen Anderen./ Auch Campendonk, der jetzt Professor an d. Rijksacademie in Amsterdam ist. Grund – die moderne Kunstrichtung. Da es kein Recht mehr gibt in D. konnte man auch nichts machen u. da kehrten wir in Klees alte Heimat zurück. Wir haben es nicht bereut. Haben uns in jeder beziehung gut eingelebt u. einen angenehmen Kreis von freunden u.s.w. um uns. Bis zum Ausbruch seiner Krankheit, hat er rastlos gearbeitet. Viele z. Zeit große umfassende Ausstellungen in der Schweiz.

Auch in Paris, London, New York, Los Angeles u.s.w. Vor 1¹/₂ Jahren ist in Deutschland noch ein band mit Handzeichnungen von ihm erschienen. (Text von Dr. W. Grohmann.) Dieser band wurde ¹/₂ Jahr nach d. Erscheinen in D. verboten, nachdem sie schlau das Geschäft mit der Luxusausgabe gemacht hatten. Alles das macht uns keinen Eindruck mehr. – Auch die Musik haben wir weiter gepflegt. Ich sehr intensiv, da sie mein Leben bedeutet. Stunden gebe ich seit Jahren nicht mehr – aber ich arbeite noch mit jungen Talenten um sie zu fördern. – Schön wäre es, wenn man sich einmal wiedersehen könnte! Aber in solchen Zeiten kann man keine Pläne machen. Man lebt wie im Krieg nur dem Heute. Leben Sie wol [sic]. Die herzlichsten Wünsche u. alles Gute für die Zukunft. Mit herzlichsten Grüßen für Sie, Ihre liebe frau u. Ihren beiden Söhnen in alter freundschaft

Ihre Paul u. Lily Klee.

ALBERT BLOCH AN LILY UND PAUL KLEE

Lawrence, 26. Juli 1936

Liebe Klees!

Die entsetzliche Hitze, viel Arbeit und zeitweise Unpäßlichkeit haben meinen herzlichen Dank für den langen, schönen und interessanten Brief der Frau Lili unentschuldbar verzögert. [...] – aber da ich gerade heute etwas freie Zeit habe, will ich sie gleich ausnützen, um zunächst wenigstens meine große Freude darüber, daß Klees Gesundheit sich endlich definitiv zu bessern scheint und meine Hoffnung für seine vollständige Wiederherstellung auszudrücken. Sie haben beide fürchterliche Monate durchgemacht, und der Patient war wohl kaum schlimmer daran als seine aufopfernde Pflegerin, der nicht minder eine gute und friedvolle Erholung zu gönnen und zu wünschen ist. – Was Sie in dem lieben Brief alles erzählen, hat mir ein rechtes Heimweh nach Ihnen beiden eingeflößt, und es wäre mir im Augenblick nichts lieber als mit Ihnen allen wieder eine schöne, vertrauliche Teestunde zu verbringen – unter Aufsicht des Bimbo (wie kommen sie nur auf diesen amerikanischen Scherznamen?). Allein, es muß inzwischen bei dem Wunsch sein Bewenden haben, und bei der täglich schmäler werdenden Hoffnung, daß es mir doch noch einmal vergönnt sei, die alten Freunde wiederzusehen. –

Auch von Kandinsky habe ich neulich einen so herzlichen und ausführlichen Brief erhalten; und Maria Marcs Briefe sind immer so liebenswürdig und voll Freundschaft, daß es mir hier in meiner großen Isolierung manchmal vor Sehnsucht schwer ums Herz wird. Einen einzigen, leider viel jüngeren Menschen habe ich um mich hier, mit dem ich mich zuweilen wirklich frei aussprechen kann. Ein amerikanisches Geistesleben in einem fruchtbaren Sinne gibt es überhaupt nicht; und da ich darum nirgends die Möglichkeit fände, auch wenn ich sie suchen wollte, meinen unpopulären Ideen, künstlerisch wie menschlich, außer sehr indirekt in den Werken selbst einen Ausfluß zu verschaffen, so muß ich immer mehr und mehr zurück in mich hineinkriechen – was allerdings seine Gefahr hätte, wenn ich eine vergrübelte Natur wäre. Das bisserl Anerkennung, das mir hie und da zuteil wird, beruht eigentlich nie auf richtiges [sic] Verständnis, sondern durchwegs auf irgendwelchen ganz nebensächlichen, zufälligen Faktoren, und wenn nur nicht die Arbeit an sich schon genügend Glück und Lohn wäre, könnte ich sie endgültig an den Nagel hängen. Klee kann noch immer von Glück sagen, selbst wenn's ihm schlecht ginge!

Daß es mit Felix so schön vorwärts geht, ist sehr erfreulich. Ich gratuliere ihm und Ihnen! [...] Alle lassen herzlichst grüßen – selbst Walter, der von Ihrer Anekdote von seinem Besuch an die Katze [sic] entzückt war. Diesen Grüßen will ich nur noch die meinen anschließen – auch für Felix und seine Frau! – mit allen guten Wünschen und zuversichtlicher Hoffnung für Sie beide, insbesondere aber für Klees fernere vollkommene Genesung.

Ihr Albert Bloch

LILY KLEE AN ALBERT BLOCH

Ascona, 29. 9. 1937

Lieber Herr Bloch,

[...] – Ich bin sehr in Ihrer Schuld und bitte Sie, zu verzeihen, daß ich Ihre lieben Zeilen vom Ende vorigen Jahres noch nicht beantwortet habe. Mein Mann hatte wieder keinen guten Winter und war viel krank. In solchen Zeiten hat man auch wenig Lust zum Schreiben. Im frühling ging es dann wieder aufwärts.

Und das Beste war, daß Klee wieder sehr viel u. gut gearbeitet hat u. viel neue dinge entstanden sind. Wenn er auch noch immer nicht ganz gesund ist u. noch mancherlei beschwerden hat, so hoffen wir von dieser Luftveränderung eine gute Erholung für ihn. Der Herbst ist hier so mild u. sonnig. Sie kennen ja auch von früher diese schöne Landschaft der südlichen Schweiz. Hoffentlich haben Sie ein gutes Jahr verbracht und geht es Ihnen und Ihrer lieben Familie gut.

Von der Ausstellung für »entartete Kunst« in München werden Sie gehört haben. Man hat die besten Sachen a. Kronprinzenpalais u. Museen v. moderner Kunst dafür ausgestellt. Dazu auch in 1. Linie franz Marc, der fürs »Vaterland« gefallen.

Es ist besser zu schweigen über diese Dinge. Es ist zu traurig! Ascona hat sich sehr verändert. Es ist sehr viel gebaut worden, aber man kann sehr gut abseits leben hier. Werefkin (sehr alt u. leidend) lebt noch hier. Ich werde sie demnächst aufsuchen. Laßen Sie, trotz meines langen Schweigens wieder einmal von sich etw. hören. Ab November wieder Bern. Mit vielen herzlichen Grüßen auch für Ihre familie

Ihre Paul u. L. Klee

ALBERT BLOCH AN LILY UND PAUL KLEE

Lawrence, 9. März 1939

Meine lieben Klees,

es hat mich herzlich gefreut, wieder ein Lebenszeichen von Ihnen zu erhalten, umso mehr als damit die Nachricht verbunden war, daß es Klee seit Monaten nun entschieden besser gehe. Was ich kurz zuvor von Maria Marc und Feininger gehört hatte, hätte mir kaum den Mut eingeflößt, so sehr zu hoffen. Möge es von nun an mit ihm endgültig aufwärts gehen! Was sollen wir uns denn sonst für unsern Lebensabend wünschen, als daß, wenn es uns schon »vergönnt« ist, noch weitere Jahre in dieser besten aller möglichen Pesthöhlen zu verbringen, wir die Wartezeit bei gesundem Leib und Nervensystem durchhalten, damit wenigstens der kleine Rest von Arbeitsfreude, der unsereinem vielleicht noch geblieben ist, nicht ganz vom Teufel durch seine in Deutschland und sonstwo hausenden Stellvertreter geholt sei! Also Prost, lieber Klee und liebe Frau Lili!

Mit Feininger stehe ich seit einiger Zeit in ziemlich regem Briefverkehr, und ich glaube, den kommenden Sommer mit ihm im Osten des Landes zu verbringen. Ich freue mich schon sehr darauf; hoffe nur, daß unser Vorhaben durch kein dazwischentretendes Hindernis zu nichts werde. Feininger habe ich in Berlin vor vielen Jahren im Herbst 1913 – ganz flüchtig kennengelernt, aber der überaus freundliche Eindruck dieser einen Begegnung ist mir stets frisch im Gedächtnis geblieben. Jetzt, wie sich mir der Mensch Feininger nunmehr aus seinen Briefen offenbart, ist er mir so sympathisch, daß ich fast schon sagen könnte, ich habe ihn liebgewonnen! Für seine Malerei hatte ich von jeher viel übrig, und heute gehört Feininger zu den ganz wenigen <u>Malern</u>, die ich noch achten kann.

Maria Marc schrieb mir um Weihnachten von ihrer schweren Krankheit; sie war noch bettlägerig, aber der Zustand schien sich allmählich zu bessern. [...]

Ich muß abbrechen. Für jeden Brief, den ich den letzten paar Jahren schreibe, muß ich mir die Zeit geradezu stehlen. Aber für jedes fernere Lebenszeichen von Ihnen wäre ich sehr dankbar.
Mit allen guten Wünschen und den herzlichsten Grüßen,

Ihr alter Bloch

VII. ALBERT BLOCH – LYONEL FEININGER

LYONEL FEININGER TO ALBERT BLOCH

[New York] December 14th 1938

Dear Mr. Bloch:

Indeed I do remember the occasion of our meeting and introduction to each other at the Herbst-Salon in Berlin through Walden, and I have often, and even quite recently, thought of you and wondered where you might be. I was therefore delighted to receive your letter, and it is the pleasantest kind of a surprise, after all these intervening years, to renew our old acquaintance.

I am very willing to let you see some of my work. Please let me know what period of the year would best suit you, and how much space you should have at your disposal; also whether in one large gallery, or in two or more smaller rooms. It is true, as you surmise, that the demand for my paintings is considerable and my reserves of recent works small; but I think that it will be quite possible to give you a rounded out exhibit of paintings and water colors, especially as they are not liable to be sold, as you say. So I could give works from our private collection. And transporting expenses would be paid by the University Gallery? — There is so much to talk of, so many thoughts come teeming into my head, that it is difficult to refrain right now from writing a long letter about old pre-war times and the "Erster Berliner Herbst-Salon"; but perhaps it might lure me on to writing of present-day Germany, and that is no good subject.
So, with most cordial greetings,
(and a longer letter to follow soon!)

Yours sincerely,
Lyonel Feininger

LYONEL FEININGER TO ALBERT BLOCH

[New York] Jan. 7th 1939

Dear Mr. Bloch:

[...] The date for the exhibition stands fast, and during the Summer I shall group together the material so as to give a harmonious collection.

This Summer I fully expect to be in Connecticut, at Falls Village, on the Housatonic River in the Northwestern part of the State. The country is charming, not very densely inhabited, hilly, mountainous, occasionally quite primaeval in its character; the Housatonic, winding and ever-varying in aspect. Beautiful villages, great old trees, farms and old homesteads scattered here and there. We lived last Summer, from the 1st of July till the 11th of October, in a wooden camphouse situated on a slope overlooking the River. We had living-room, three bedrooms, kitchen with oil-buring range, bathroom, a big wood-burning stove in the living-room, and electric refrigerator in the kitchen, as well as electric light throughout the bungalow, and a closed-in-with-fliegendraht porch the entire length of the one-storey house, — all for $150 for as long as we wanted to stay. We might have taken the place in May for the same price, if we had known of it before. And — very important! — our host is a fine man, a former marine officer, of Norwegian descent, (good stock, that) now running a big chicken-farm.

This by the way of introduction to the theme of your possibly caring to spend your Summer in New England. Perhaps you prefer (as we ourselves should) the Coast of Maine or Massachusetts. But for care-free, happy and not over-crowded Summer-existence, and with a host who is liberal and attentive to all your needs, "Three Knolls" is a good place to be in. There lies a sucession of gentle upward slopes in back of our camp, and about 150 yards above our place, there is a second camp, with an equal amount of rooms and the same conveniences, with a south porch facing a lovely distance of blue hills and Connecticut mountains, to be had on the same terms as our bungalow. If you are interested, let me know, and I can add details of information. [...]

What you say about your work seems to me to be very much what I myself should have to say concerning my own. And if I were by any chance to talk with Kandinsky about — Painting — which I have never thought of doing all the years of our intimacy! — I am positive that his dictum would be similar to his comments on your work, as you write. — I fully understand the immense task that lies in creating pictorial values anew, in non-representative Art, and I admire very much the really great examples of such creations; but I cannot bring myself to concede that they represent the <u>entire</u> values in Painting, nor that there be any more purity of abstraction in ornamental or decorative formulae than can be attained to in a formally clear representation of visualised nature, or of "objects". After all, a geometrical figure, or a curve, or an ornament, (however "shapeless"), remain still "Representation", and ulterior high-class show-window decoration can attain exactly the same values. I find much modern Art perilously close to Aestheticism. I find much of it exceedingly poorly painted, and there are lapses of continuity in works of Bracque [sic], Dérain and Picasso, which in my own creative work would shock me to leave unattended to. I should like to sum it up as being thoroughly characteristic of our present time, with every man doing his damndest to outbid his rivals, and they certainly are having a glorious time and "a swell run for their money". Which summing up may very well go to prove my incapacity. — But have you ever compared modern Expressionism (z.B.) with works of the 12th to 15th Centuries? what weak stuff do efforts of our own extremist time appear, as against the intensity and depth, the creative vitality, of long–forgotten primitive artists of the early Middle-Age?
— Why? — can we no longer invent form? surely yes! — but how <u>deep</u> does the invention, the <u>inner</u>, <u>soulish need</u>, reach down? I find it often "amusing" (a word I detest in connection with Art), or fantastic, or simply ingenious; but it has no deep-rooted message. — Art is our solace and our Despair. —

I do appreciate your generous words concerning my painting, but Despair is no stranger to me.

Now I've spent more time at these few lines than youd [sic] believe possible, so I must now stop for this time, and get to work. I'm just beginning to paint once more, after a pause of more than 18 months. Schreiben Sie bald wieder!
Herzlichst ...

Ihr
Lyonel Feininger

LYONEL FEININGER TO ALBERT BLOCH

New York, Feb. 5th, '39

Dear Mr. Bloch:

Thank you very much for your most kind letters which I should have answered long ago. Please forgive the delay, which certainly was not intentional, for I have had you often in mind; and I want to thank you most especially for the trouble you have taken about an exhibition in Kansas City, in connection with the one we have planned to have in your gallery. However, the date, March, 1940, which you suggest as a possibility, is very distant, and I am very well content to give you the show for yourself, next October.

There is also another thing to be considered, and that is, that if the exhibition of modern German Art which the museum in Kansas City intends to hold in November, I must positively be let out of having paintings of mine included. The same exhibition was held last year in

April 18th, 1940

Dear Bloch:

It was so good of you to write! — No, there is nothing especial the matter; just an almost unsurmountable disinclination against writing, and airing purely imaginary troubles. In fact, the Winter has been kind to us all. We have kept well, free from illness and colds. And with two of our three boys with us, right within reach; that is a happiness we scarce dared to figure out, a year ago. — — Still, you'll admit, the world is in a bad way; das schlägt aufs gemüt! — We were very sorry to learn that Anna's father is critically ill; we do hope that his condition will continue now to improve; we feel keenly the state you all must be in, between hope and fear. Give her our love and best wishes. We have not yet definitely settled the question of our abode, in Falls Village this Summer, for there are possibilities open for our renting a place sufficiently roomy to accomodate the children also — but it is even not yet certain that they can join us in the Country. We, Julia and I, are coming by all means, and in case we are alone, as last year, we wish very decidedly to live in our old place at

Letter from Lyonel Feininger to Alfred Bloch, 18 April 1940, Munson-Williams-Proctor Institute, Museum of Art, Utica, New York

Brief von Lyonel Feininger an Albert Bloch, 18. April 1940, Munson-Williams-Proctor Institute, Museum of Art, Utica, New York

London, and there were a number of my works loaned by private collectors, none of whom had notified me of their intention to include me amongst the Germans. Still, it was different for them to be shown in England, where I am unknown, and there was no great harm done, so far as I can judge. But here, in my native land, I am having a difficult struggle to overcome the idea many critics and friends of my works have, that I am a German artist! I make a point of exhibiting as an <u>American</u>, and cannot under the circumstances exhibit with the Germans. You have known me, or at least my work, in Germany, and know as well as any one could, how impossible it always has been, to classify my work under German art. I have always been "der Amerikaner Feininger" and no one in Germany thought of calling me a German artist.

The mere fact of a native born American living for a long period in a foreign country does not make him a foreigner, and there are many American artists living habitually in France and Italy, whom no one here dreams of calling French or Italian artists. No one could be more proud of the close friendship which binds me to the modern German artists, but that does not make me a German, any more than my French and Italian ancestral strain makes me French or Italian.

When you come into contact with the Director of the Kansas City museum, would you explain to him the reasons I have for not permitting my work to be shown as "modern German art"? And could you give me his name, so that I can write to him personally on the subject?

And now, the difficult part of my letter being achieved, I want to tell you how very much I anticipate seeing you, and seeing your paintings, both the old and the new. For, believe me: "Albert Bloch" ist meiner Frau und mir seit vielen Jahren ein Begriff, — and we missed seeing anything of your work during the last 15 years or so. I recall very distinctly the impression which your "Pierrot", at the Erster Deutsche Herbstsalon 1913 made on us, of echter Malkultur und Farbigkeit, Tiefe; qualities of which, at that time, my wife understood far more than I, for I was very much of a beginner at the oils! It was a great time, for Berlin, beginning in 1910 with the advent of the "Blauer Reiter" and the

"Brücke" and the "Neue Secession", Herwarth Walden, die Wittwe Macht, "Der Sturm", und die "Aktion"! — and actually culminating in the Erste Deutsche Herbstsalon, — for the War came next year. I wonder how you have made out, in American surroundings? Marsden Hartley, whom I came to know in 1915, in Berlin, claimed that Germany was the only country he could paint in. I've never seen him since, and have wondered how he would express himself now. Judging only by a few inadequate reproductions of later paintings of his, I should imagine that he would, today, find that we had certain things in common, which he denied at the time. He certainly has turned towards Nature, (which he interpretates [sic] somewhat heavily, I find; but heavy color and forms were always in his early works, which avoided Nature strenuously). I hope to meet him some time. Another painter whom I have not seen since '15 or '16, is Max Oppenheimer (Mopp), from whom I've just had a note, indicating that he lives right here in N.Y. Our old German Kulturkreis is filling up rapidly around us here, almost all our old collegues and friends have been forced to get away from Naziland. Of Germany itself there remains nothing whatever that is not infested by the poison-virus of Nazidom. So that, so far as we are concerned, there is no Cultural Atmosphere any longer in the "Vaterland". You'll find its remaining exponents all gathered right here in the free air of America and doing their utmost to adapt themselves to the new breathing facilities.

[...] The Address of our landlord in the Summer is: Mr. Cornelius Petersen, Falls Village, Connecticut. And you certainly may use our name as "reference"!

Hoping to hear from you soon, and with cordial greetings

Yours faithfully
Lyonel Feininger

LYONEL FEININGER TO ALBERT BLOCH

[New York] 26th Feb. 1939

Dear Bloch:

Thank you for your long and interesting letter. It was a surprise to me that you seem to find it necessary to warn me against stressing my American nationality. I assure you that nothing is further from my wish than to claim consideratiom [sic] from that fact. In regard to the exhibition of German modern art which is to be held in Kansas City some time in the late Fall, I should say that since the show will very likely be going the rounds through other cities in the U.S. I would have great difficulty in explaining everywhere that I am an American painter whose works, created in Germany, have been routed out of museums and private collections there, together with works of modern German painters, by the Nazi Government. But since you are acquainted with the Kansas City art director, I beg you will tell him how it happens that my works are included amongst the Germans by a group of people interested. In Germany I never exhibited as a German artist. I was always the "Amerikaner Feininger" and as such, occasionally a thorn in the eyes of critics and public. No Kunsthistoriker or Kritiker in Germany has ever been able to classify my work amongst modern painters. Equally in my own native country America, I am artistically speaking hard, if not impossible, to classify. You will know that.

You express some astonishment that I never exhibited in America. Well, I did send forth a few ventures, but my work simply could not be cared for, here, and critics, who should perhaps have known better than to write such nonsense, when the Modern Museum exhibited a few of my works in the show "19 Living Americans", very indignantly asked: "Who is this man? We don't know him!" Here and there an etching, or a wood block print, was sold; not half a dozen in ten years. In Germany I at least earned my living, and as I am a slow and sometimes a painful worker, I never had a surplus of works to send over the Water. Since 1924, Mrs. Galka E. Scheyer, herself an artist and an unusually cultivated connoisseur, has been showing works by "The Blue Four" (Klee, Kandinsky,

Jawlensky and myself) on the West Coast. In those 15 years I sold two paintings and coupla wood-blocks! So much for my attempts here during my residence in Germany. As for coming over on a visit, I never was in a position to afford the expense. I have lived up to my ears in Verpflichtungen. If Mills College had not invited me to direct the art class in the 36 and 37 Summer Session and payed me decently, I should now be perhaps rotting in Naziland. As it was, my wife and I entered the U.S. with two dollars. I have no relatives living. But we have three sons, (and I have two daughters living in Germany, aus erster, geschiedener Ehe).

Now it looks as though I had to say that, in speaking in my last letter of having almost our entire Kultur-Kreis versammelt auf dieser Seite, I did certainly not dream of including Mopp [Max Oppenheimer], but his name cropped up, because I had heard, a day or two before, that he had come to N.Y. I hadn't seen him since 1915, when he was at the Zenith of his Berlin success, and we had certainly no points whatever in common. I did not interest him (how could I as a beginner and a painter of strenger Architektur?) and our meeting was by chance, im Kaffee Grössenwahn. Since then we never met, and for many years I had forgotten his existence, until I saw him at the Nierendorf Gallery and he recognised me. I will say that he has suffered cruelly, the Nazis treated him damnably, demolished his studio, cut his paintings into shreds, destroyed his valuable graphic collections, and he himself just barely escaped being beaten to death. He just got away over the border, with only his beloved Amati violin under his arm. — Impossible to refuse him sympathy and comfort, such as we can give one in deep misfortune. But we feel sure that he will soon succeed here, he is, as you say, very talented. There is something of a terrified child in his expression. We have seen him but twice. I hear that he has done a portrait and is getting acquainted with the right people for such painting orders.

I should like very much to have you tell me what you are doing. Remember that we have seen none of your paintings for about 20 years. Do you have sufficient time for yourself and can you work outside of your directorship?

I am glad that you understood my "Lieber Albert Bloch" to apply to the artist. I also gladly meet you half-way in dropping the "Mr.", but never fear familiarity from one who dislikes it. I knew many painters in Germany, but my two only Duz-Freunde sind der Bildhauer Gerhard Marcks and the painter Karl Schmidt-Rottluff.
Mit sehr herzlichem Gruss!

Ihr
Lyonel Feininger

LYONEL FEININGER TO ALBERT BLOCH

N.Y., March 7th, '39

Dear Bloch,

I was perfectly certain that we thought alike on the subject in question; I am sure that I understood the kindness underlying your words of caution; believe me, I read no other meaning than the one so kindly intended, into your sentences. But it seemed at the time I answered, that first I should clear away any doubts you may have had, as to my being sufficiently aware of our good countrymen's attitude towards so-called expatriates.—And then, I wanted to reassure you on another point: that I, like yourself, had no inclination towards easy familiarity of intercourse. Well, I explained that, and after I had sent off my letter, I felt that the way was cleared and that a very interesting and "anregender" exchange of ideas and views might be entered on. And now your good letter and the accompanying photographs of some of your recent paintings have given me much pleasure. It may seem strange to you, but actually I have hardly anyone here with whom I correspond on subjects in connection with my work. My wife, who is my most understanding critic, and my youngest son Lux, who is a painter heart and soul, are

Albert Bloch, Boats at Night, 1939/40, Private collection
Albert Bloch, Boote bei Nacht, 1939/40, Privatsammlung

almost the sole beings I have any intercourse with, when it comes to talking about painting. But once you and I get started, I think we will have a lot to talk over. Less, perhaps (on my part), about my work than about visual phenomenae observed in Nature. There are also rules of composition which I always attempt to fathom. It is most interesting to talk about these things and to compare experiences. I feel sure that I could learn a good deal from your treatment of earth colors z.B.! and we both have the tendency to simplify form and composition. I believe simplicity of form and composition to be important, but it would often seem to be very difficult of achievement. — Dont [sic] I talk as though we were both still young men, as at the time of our meeting, 25 years ago? In truth, I am scarcely further advanced than at that time. Like yourself, bin ich ein "Spät-Entwickler". ++++++ I have your photographs spread out beside me as I write, and feel my way slowly and cautiously into the new world they suggest. I see that they are lonely places, very far away from everyday. Now, when you see the pictures I shall send you, you will tell me the same thing about them. They too, are lonely. I first became conscious of escaping into my own paintings, in 1915, when the actual world of men and warfare became unbearable to me. And I have never since painted a picture into which I did not escape, driven by sometimes desperate longing nostalgia. Painting was a pleasure, a delightful new adventure only in the first few years. When the War began, in '14, I lost all delight in my art, and have never regained it; it has become a fateful responsibility, and often a torment. It is only after years, that I begin to care for a work; very seldom indeed, that I am happy at the time of laying aside the finished painting. In my drawings, thank Goodness, I have an immediate pleasure; they make it all the harder for me to paint. There come times when I hate painting, it causes me much suffering. But to return to your photographs: it is of course quite impossible to render their color, being as they are conceived as orchestrations in their medium. But even although the photos, as you say, are poor, they give very well the suggestion of depth and richness. It impresses me that you use a very restrained palette:: [sic] myself, I use entirely too many colors, and have endeavoured to confine myself to earth colors, at times with sucess; but I have never been happy altogether without prussian blue, cobalt and occasionally, ultramarine; and as to chromoxyde green, and cobalt green — well, there you have it! even in very simplified color-ensemble. It will be very interesting and certainly useful, to have a few talks with you on the subject. Nine-tenths of the colors one uses are used to no real purpose, and for building up a foundation there are no colors so good as the earth-tones. — The intenseness of your paintings is amazing, as is likewise their tonal quality. And you have the love of dead trees and bare hill forms that obsess me, and which express the inner lonesomeness of life on this planet, better than almost any other object. I experience this sense of loneliness far more here than evr [sic] in Germany. March 10 th[…]

We had a long letter from Frau Maria Marc yesterday. She is now on the way to recovery, but has still to take very great care of herself. She is still under treatment, at a home. She is a brave soul. Don't let me get talking about her now, nor about any of our old friends in Germany. I've been since days thinking a dozen long letters to you, we've got a lot to talk about when we meet. You are the only one here of the Alte Garde, to whom I could talk. Next time I'll write about Falls Village and our plans for the Summer there. — How large is your family? How many heads shall you be, to spend the Summer in Connecticut? I'll tell you about bedding and whatever details may be of use to you if you decide to come. The beds are A No[.] I! and at a pinch, I dare say Petersen's could lend you blankets. They offered to lend us some, but we were provided for. We do hope you'll decide to come.
Mit herzlichem Gruss
Ihr getreuer

L. Feininger

P. S. and forgive the type-writing! My pens are impossible!

LYONEL FEININGER TO ALBERT BLOCH

[New York] Apl. 17th 1939

Dear Bloch:

The last 4 weeks were not easy, and I just couldn't write as I wanted to, in reply to your good, long letter of March 29th. I do want to tell you how glad I am, that you are coming to Falls Village! I expect, or rather,

I can only hope, to get there myself about May 15th, on the completion of my Murals for the "Masterpieces of Art"- Gallery, at the World's Fair. They are completed in the design, but the building has been so retarded that the show will only be opened on May 15th, if then! — […]

I was very pleased with your manuscript; vieles ist mir "aus der Seele gesprochen", right from the beginning. I am returning it and your photos soon. + + + +

Dear Bloch, you write that you are tired and much in need of rest; I do understand that, and I believe you will regain vitality + strength in Petersen's Cottage. How well I know what you feel, when you write of not being "acclimatized even yet." You, I, we, my wife, none of us, will ever become so, for that, indeed, would mean "capitulation." As long as we live, we must fight the mediocre, and we shall always feel Nostalgia. […]

I expect to work quite assiduously this summer, at Falls Village, at Water-color drawings, chiefly. I should like to paint, but fear the added encumberance of toting easel + material into the country.

I shall bring along my violin + practice; I had given up playing for many years, but find taking up the practice wonderfully interesting and conducive to concentration. Repeating a musical exercise, a passage, a bar, correcting a fault in intonation, drawing forth a clear tone — all these practised in my early youth, have been duplicated in my methods of correcting and disciplining in my painting.

I destroy + rebuild time and again, a picture, until it satisfies me as a unity — it is the same in violin-practice until I have mastered the difficulties of a composition.

Speaking of your not being yet 60, why, you are young! I shall be 68 in July. Well, I guess I am young too, for I sometimes look upon this process of getting to be (outwardly) an "old man," as a surprising game, out of which I still could very well step, if so inclined. Ich kann's immer noch nicht fur Ernst halten (Only, I mustn't look at myself in a mirror.)

I like your yellow writing-paper! forgive this distracted letter!
Herzlichste grüsse Ihres getreuen

Feininger

VIII. ALBERT BLOCH – HAROLD BUTLER 1923

In 1923 Albert Bloch applied for the position of professor of painting and drawing at the University of Kansas, Lawrence. As part of that process, he sent this auto-biographical letter detailing his professional experience to Harold Butler, dean of the School of Fine Arts at the University. This letter is one of the few documents which sheds light on Bloch's artistic training and his activities after returning to the United States in 1921.

Den autobiographischen Brief mit Angaben zu seinem beruflichen Werdegang schickte Albert Bloch 1923 als Bewerbungsschreiben für die Stelle eines Profes-sors am ›Department of Painting and Drawing‹ der University of Kansas, Lawrence, an den damaligen Dean der ›School of Fine Arts‹ der Universität, Harold Butler. Dieser Brief ist eines der wenigen Dokumente, die Aufschluß über Blochs künstlerische Ausbildung in den frühen Jahren bis 1909 sowie seine Tätigkeit unmittelbar nach Rückkehr in die USA 1921 geben.

60 East Chicago Avenue,
Apartment 7
Chicago, Illinois   23 June, 1923

My Dear Mr. Butler:—
Thank you for your letter of the 21st of June.

The detailed statement of my academic and artistic training for which you ask, will perhaps seem to you unimpressive, since it consists of so few actual details. However, if I may speak of the various phases of my career (such as it is) as they come to me, the recital might possibly serve to give you some clearer idea of my character and ablility. But I fear you are in for a very long letter!

To begin with:— I am forty fears [sic] old — nearly forty-one in fact. I was born in St. Louis and grew up there; but since 1903 have not resided there excepting during one or two short intervals. I attended the Public Schools and the Central High School in St. Louis, but left

the latter before graduation, because by the time I was sixteen the thought of an artistic career had so taken possession of me that an en-forced occupation with anything else amounted to mere drudgery.

Even before leaving High School I had a season of extra-time study in drawing at a local private school; and afterwards entered the St. Louis School of Fine Arts, where I remained for two years. Then I did newspaper illustrating in St. Louis for three years, and in 1903, when I was 21 years old, went to New York, where I worked as a free-lance illustrator, drawing continuously from the model, and keeping up my art studies and my reading, privately but without interruption. In the year 1905 I married, going to St. Louis for a short time, but returning to the East in the Summer of 1906. In the interval I had been "discovered" by the late William Marion Reedy, Editor of the Mirror, and became con-nected with his paper, both in a critical and an artistic capacity. With Reedy I remained in close association for years, and in more or less permanent contact until the day of his death three years ago. At about this time (1905-6) I made my first faltering attempts at painting under the friendly guidance of Dawson Dawson-Watson, an Englishman and an instructor at the St. Louis School of Fine Arts. The preliminary training I received with Watson has proved extremely valuable to me; it was the only actual instruction in painting I have ever had, but it gave me a foundation that enabled me to carry on my studies alone from that point. Toward the end of 1908, at the earnest urging of Reedy, I went abroad, remaining there, with one interruption of four months in the Summer of 1912, until the Summer of 1919. In 1920 I returned to Europe, but the conditions prevailing on the Continent did not encourage me to remain, so in the Summer of 1921 I came back to this country, where I have been ever since, and where, if possible, I hope to remain.

While in Europe I have several times visited Paris and Vienna, also London, Berlin and other centers; but my pied-à-terre on the continent was Munich. It was there chiefly that I lived and studied and worked during a sojourn of twelve years. My studies were not academic, however. It had been my intention to enter the Royal Academy at Munich; but the men with whom I wished particularly to study (Samberger the portraitist and Volkert the etcher) were no longer officially connected with the Academy. In fact, when they saw my work, they definitely discouraged the idea of further academic study, each of them being of the opinion that I had gone so far toward the development of a personal style, that direct academic instruction would rather harm than help me; and that furthermore I had already advanced to a point in my painting where my technique could safely be left to take care of itself. Samberger however consented willingly enough to give me the benefit of his criticism in painting; and Volkert taught me all I was capable of learning from him technically of the dry-point etching method — and neither of these two gentlemen would accept a tuition fee. During all this time I kept up my work from the model, of course, drawing either in my own studio, or in the evenings in any one of the private life classes with which Munich abounded. But my chief source of study, aside from all this, have been the various European museums.

And throughout all these years I have been a pretty incessant reader and student. Such education as I have is self-acquired, of course; but it naturally happens that the history of art is one of the topics that have claimed my strongest interest; so that, though not in any sense equipped from the "scholarly" standpoint, I am well enough grounded in the history of art., [sic] to have developed from its study a kind of philosophy of art. Until now I have never given university lectures. But I was engaged in the early Spring of this year to address a group of students of the University of Chicago on my subject (let me refer you to the director of this group: R. D. Jameson, Department of English, U. of C.);— and R. M. Lovett, former Dean of the Department of English there, suggested last Winter that I prepare a course of lectures to be delivered at the Univer-sity. This invitation, for various reasons, I was forced to decline. Also, an invitation earlier in the season, to address one of the university societies. I have, however, spoken at various other times before public audiences or societies, and have always been fortunate in receiving most appreciative attention. Last month I spoke (or rather, read) before a crowded auditorium at the Artists' Guild in St. Louis for two hours and a half, and was able to hold the interest of the audience throughout. I may add that it was an audience that had actually paid its money to hear me! If it would interest you to hear what others can say of me in this connection, you might inquire of Wm. B. Papin, one of the trustees of the St. Louis Art Museum, and O. E. Berninghaus, of the St. L. School of Fine Arts (at present in Taos, New Mexico, I believe), who could also tell you something of my artistic and technical qualifications…. So, although I have had no experience at all as a university lecturer, I believe it not unlikely that I could fulfill your requirements if given the chance.

You ask me for the names of two or three well-known artists who can speak knowingly of my ability as a painter, and especially as an instructor. Unfortunately I am not acquainted with any of the nationally-known painters on this side of the water. In the first place, I go about very little and, on the whole, prefer the society of a few intimates (not painters) to that of my confrères. I keep apart from them as much as I can, only because I dread the shop-talk and the studio-patter with which I became so full-fed during my long residence abroad. In the second place, I have been for a dozen years and until very recently, completely out of touch with people in this country, and with the painters in particular. Still, I do know Richard Miller pretty well (I believe he is in Paris again), and Ernest Lawton slightly. But they would be unable to give you any idea of my ability as an instructor. For such information I must refer you to Carl N. Werntz, director of the Academy of Fine Arts, Chicago (81 East Madison Street). And also — if you care to inquire of them — two of my fellow instructors at the Academy, both of them well-known Chicago artists, could speak of me both as a painter and instructor: Claude M. Buck, Palos Park, Chicago; and Bertram R. Elliott, 445 Garfield Avenue, Chicago, who was also a member of my class in color and composition during the past season. I do not know whether all the people to whom you are in the city just now; but doubtless letters would be forwarded to them from here.

Others to whom I could refer you are, Ferdinand Schevill, professor of history, U. of C.; Robert B. Harshé, director of the Art Institute of Chicago (who could say something of my qualifications as a painter), and Professor Robert Morss Lovett of the U. of C. (who, I believe, can be reached at present at 421 West 21st ST., New York).

An account of my experience as an instructor must be limited to this past year; for until then, my only work of this nature was with private pupils abroad. I can only say, that at the Academy I am considered a successful and competent instructor, and that I have been offered a reappointment for next term. My ideas of instruction — if you wish me to give them — are very simple and briefly this: —

My own painting is not in any degree "academic;" but it is my firm conviction that young people wishing to paint (unless they are God-sent geniuses), must have a pretty thorough training in the fundamentals before they may begin permitting themselves liberties. Therefore my instruction would be (and has been) based upon the time-honored theory: — Drawing first of all and above all things; drawing from the figure and from nature — a training of the memory through constant and accurate observation. And this, for beginners, would be also the foundation of my instruction in painting. Until now, however, my experience in painting instruction has been almost entirely confined to advanced students, who had already gone through a preliminary technical training, or to professionals. These came to me less for instruction than for help and criticism in the essentials of color and composition, and this was all that I ventured to offer them. Their work had to be criticised from their point of view, not from mine — at least that was my conscious endeavour. Two of my former pupils are today quite well-known painters in Germany: Klinker and Bromberger.

I have already told you, I think, that I am better known in Europe than in this country. I might be as well known here at home as abroad, if I had made any real attempt to gain recognition; but I have neither the gift nor the taste for using the methods that are considered necessary to catch public notice here. In Europe there was much less need of them. One single exhibition was all that was necessary; and since then I have exhibited practically all over the Continent — even in Russia (before the war) and in Sweden. Two works of mine are in public museums in Germany (Jena and — I believe — Stettin); and many of my pictures are in private collections here and abroad.

The Eddy collection in Chicago contains twenty-five canvases of mine; the Bixby collection in St. Louis, five. J. S. Watson of The Dial has one picture and several drawings in his collection. W. H. Mann of Lakewood (Cleveland) has about a dozen of my things. In the Macomber collection, Boston, I have two or three canvases. Arthur T. Aldis (a trustee of the Chicago Art Institute) has purchased two of my pictures.

I am enclosing a photograph of a portrait, which happens to be handy. It was painted early in 1911, when I was still practically a beginner, and was the first picture I ever exhibited, or ever submitted to a jury.

And now, my dear Mr. Butler, I must crave your indulgence for this interminable flow of talk about myself. But you asked for details;

and I have tried to give them — such as they are. I ask you to believe that it has been neither an easy nor a congenial task to hunt out as many nice things as possible to say about myself in the hope of making a favorable impression. But since it had to be done, let me express the hope that it will not be in vain, and that it has not altogether wearied you or exhausted your patience. And I do hope to hear from you. for though I could not wait upon you with the rehearsal of a distinguished career, yet I feel convinced that, given the opportunity, I could discharge

the duties of the position quite to your satisfaction. Please give me a chance at it. I really do want that job. I know something (by hearsay) of the charm of the little town of Lawrence. I have a sister who lived there for a year, and who has been longing ever since to go back again. Very cordially Yours,

Albert Bloch

IX. ALBERT BLOCH, DENVER LECTURE, 1934

The so-called "Denver Lecture" – "Kandinsky, Marc, Klee: Criticism and Reminiscences" – is one of three given by Albert Bloch in 1934 at the Denver Art Museum under the auspices of the Cooke Daniel Foundation. The "Kandinsky, Marc, Klee" lecture was held on 13 December 1934. In 1935/36 Bloch planned to publish the three lectures together with two earlier essays and an essay already published in 1922 under the title "Pictures and People: From a Painter's Point of View." Bloch wrote to Maria Marc, Wassily Kandinsky and Paul Klee in 1935/36 with regard to the publication of these lectures which was, unfortunately, never realized. An edited edition of these texts , as well as Bloch's arthistorical lectures, is in preparation by Professor Philipp Fehl, University of Illinois, Urbana/Vatican Library, Rome.

Again we would like to thank Mrs. Albert Bloch for her kindness and cooperation in permitting the publication of the last "Denver Lecture." This is a largely unknown document of quite considerable interest, dealing with the Blaue Reiter artists and Albert Bloch's artistic and personal relationship with them.

Die sogenannte ›Denver Lecture‹ – ›Kandinsky, Marc, Klee: Criticism and Reminiscences‹ – ist einer von drei Vorträgen, die Albert Bloch 1934 im Denver Art Museum, auf Einladung der Cooke Daniel Foundation, gehalten hat. Der Vortrag ›Kandinsky, Marc, Klee‹ fand am 13. Dezember 1934 statt. 1935/36 plante Bloch die Herausgabe dieser drei Vorträge – sowie den beiden, bereits 1922 veröffentlichten Aufsätzen ›Portraits and the Painter‹ und ›Whistler and the Pot of Paint‹ – unter dem Obertitel »Pictures and People. From a Painter's Point of View«. – Die Veröffentlichung dieser Schriftensammlung, für die Albert Bloch 1935/36 auch Maria Marc, Wassily Kandinsky und Paul Klee anschrieb, kam jedoch nicht zustande. Derzeit bereitet Prof. Philipp Fehl, University of Illinois, Urbana/ Vatikanische Bibliothek Rom, eine kommentierte Edition dieser Texte sowie der kunsthistorischen Vorlesungen Blochs vor.
Auch in diesem Fall danken wir dem freundlichen Entgegenkommen von Mrs. Albert Bloch, die uns den Abdruck der letzten ›Denver Lecture‹ gestattete. Sie ist ein unschätzbares, bislang weitgehend unbekanntes Dokument über die wichtigsten Künstler des ›Blauen Reiter‹ und Albert Blochs künstlerisches und persönliches Verhältnis zu ihnen:

KANDINSKY, MARC, KLEE
CRITICISM AND REMINISCENCE

Unfortunately I must preface this evening's discussion with a word of apology and an expression of diffidence and embarrassment. A diffidence and embarrassment arising from my fear that I do not know very much about my subject — certainly not enough to hold forth upon it as one speaking with authority; and the need for apology is born of my fear that in much of what I have to say I shall perhaps seem — if not to my hearers, at least to myself — rather insistently autobiographical. (Though really, if you dislike explanations as much as I do, you will feel rather, that I should first of all apologise for my apology!) We may take the matter of the autobiographical first, and my excuse for that must be, that since what I am to discuss is based primarily upon personal experience arising from direct and often intimate contact with the matters and the masters under consideration, I cannot very well avoid talking also about myself. This I do unwillingly and am usually able to dodge it with fair success — not because it is necessarily immodest, but because it is not my job. [...] And this brings me to the fear that I mentioned at the beginning — the fear that I know too little about this topic to speak upon it authoritatively. Now this, like everything else that is written or spoken, must be correctly interpreted: I believe, really, that I know as much about the subject as can be known; but when I pause seriously to review my knowledge, I am taken aback with the realisation of how little actually there is to say. Scientifically, sociologically, psychologically, even aesthetically, one might talk endlessly about it, and the critics and art historians, the experts and the aesthetes, in short all the solemnly speculating nincompoops who live as parasites upon the creative imagination, have talked endlessly about it in endless volumes, and no doubt they are still talking. [...] So when, in one of the telegrams that came to me

from the secretary of the Denver Art Museum, the hope was expressed that the general theme of this series, or at least the subject of one of the lectures, would be German Expressionism so-called, I could only wire back my regret that this would be impossible as a main theme; that, aside from my reluctance to mug up material for an assigned topic as it were, I do not regard myself as a modern or as an authority on modernism in painting; that there aint [sic] no such animal as German Expressionism; that the Snark was, in fact, a Boojum; that I should have to <u>fake</u> three lectures on the subject, which, in fairness to all concerned, I must refuse to do. [...] Meanwhile, however, a very interesting train of thought began to ensue upon my perception that this Snark was indeed a Boojum, and before the day was over and before I could receive the secretary's reply to my earlier telegram, I sent a second one, to say that one discussion could at least have German Expressionism for a point of departure. We left it at that; and now — how shall I begin?... If I could only be certain that all of you or most of you are at all familiar with the work of Franz <u>Marc</u>, Paul <u>Klee</u> and Wassili <u>Kandinsky</u>, the three chief figures of the movement in Munich, or that you know something of the background of the newer painting, not only in Germany, but particularly in France, my task would be simpler and I could feel a little less fearful that I may be completely wasting your time.

When I first went abroad at the end of 1908 Paul Cézanne had been dead only two years, and I had never heard of him. I knew nothing of the so-called New Movement‹ in painting, though I had seen, just a few months before, the first tentative small collection of the work of Henri-Matisse [sic], which had been held at the little gallery of Mr[.] Stieglitz in New York, where I was then living. The exhibition consisted almost entirely of drawings, I believe, or perhaps they were lithographs and etchings — I have forgotten, although I remember the work itself well enough. There was also one small painting — only one, I recall....

That was over twenty-six years ago; I was still full of the enthusiasm of youth, full of a completely misunderstanding enthusiasm, as I began to realise soon after. But the celebrated James Huneker, as I also realised a little later, was no better authority than I; and Huneker had not the excuse of youth and enthusiasm, for he was maturer than I by a good twenty years, and he had been for so long dangling in the greenrooms and behind the scenes of the various arts, had been for so long gracefully and a little jadedly chatting about them in the press, that the bloom had worn off his enthusiasm and his perceptions had become blunted. He and I both wrote and printed appreciative little essays on this work of Henri-Matisse, the only comments published upon that exhibition, so far as I know; and though I did not realise it then, Huneker was as far off the mark as I was. All I can say for and against myself is that I was aggressively enthusiastic and abysmally ignorant — like so many of the young writers and practitioners today. Huneker, the flâneur and aesthete, was sophisticated, informed and judicious. Be that as it may — here was my first contact with the newer painting, of which I had till then never heard, and quite honestly I confess, that I hadn't a notion what it was all about. But this at least I did know: that something had hit me with a terrific impact — so terrific indeed, that I literally didn't know what had hit me! A few months later I was in Europe — and not in Paris, curiously enough; for Paris it was toward which "my soul had yearned". [sic] I was in Germany, in Munich. I did not go to Paris until a year later, and since it is not of myself and my beginnings that I have to speak primarily, my reasons for going to Germany at that time (deeply thankful though I am now, that I did), rather than to France, with all my early love for the French Impressionists, is of no moment here. During that first year abroad (there were excursions to other capitols [sic], but I was saving Paris) I paid no attention to the newer painting — indeed I remained as ignorant of it as I had been before I came to Europe; Matisse had become only a pleasantly exciting memory, and it never occurred to me that this painter might not be a completely isolated and unique figure. And even if I had been curious about the new movement in painting, I could not at that time have come near gratifying such a curiosity in Germany; and particularly Munich, where I had settled, gave no surface indication that there had been a tremendous upheaval in the field of contemporary art. If any of you know anything at all of the typical painting of Germany at the beginning of the century — and the less you know about it, the less you are missing, although such figures as Max Liebermann, who is still living, Corinth and Slevogt will remain always interesting and important — ; those of you who know something of the representative German painting of thirty years ago, will be amused to be told that when I first went abroad, my chief enthusiasm side by side with my deep admiration for the great French Impressionists — and despite the glaring incompatibility — was that pretentious pseudo-classicist and vulgar mystagogue Franz von Stuck, although in fairness to my judgment, it must be said that direct contact with the original work of this highly gifted false god soon brought about a radical modification of my delight in it. And at the annual exhibition of the Munich Secession that spring (where a couple of years later, as I must defiantly confess, I myself was to be represented) — at that exhibition of the Munich Secession I came upon a roomful of Cézannes — and walked right through, unaware that I had been glancing, as I walked away, at anything out of the ordinary! Beside the work of the brilliant German Secessionists — and brilliant is the only word for them — Cézanne seemed to me drab and clumsy. I had until then never heard of him — and there he was, a giant confronting a pygmy. And the pygmy had no recognition for what he had found; felt no awe, but only a great indifference. I say it now to my shame. Only a few months later, however, I was to realise my sin with deep contrition, and I was able then also to suspect that what had so fascinated me at my first brief contact with Henri-Matisse was probably his surface brilliance, which since then I have come to distrust more and more, though I was soon to mature sufficiently to appreciate also something of the solid excellence beneath the brilliancy. During my first visit to Paris at the end of 1909 and the beginning of 1910, where I spent such time as I could spare from loafing in the Café du Dôme in the museums, familiarising myself as well as I could with the works of the great masters and the French Impressionists, the new movement, which was the predominant subject of café chatter, did not particularly interest me, nor did I make any effort to establish contact with any of its now famous exponents, as I might so easily have done. I was too absorbed in my explorations among the galleries and in my adventures with the Impressionists. Indeed, I have never been especially interested in the new movement in painting as such, as some of you may be amazed to hear, who happen to know that I am, and used to be, regarded, although mistakenly, as one of its exponents in this country. [...] But while I was away in Paris that first time, I missed an event of the greatest importance that had taken place in Munich, and which was to have a very marked effect upon the painting of many of the younger men throughout Germany as well as in other countries. This was the first exhibition of the Münchner neue Vereinigung, the New Society of Munich, whose leading spirit was Wassili Kandinsky, although he was not nominally the head of the organisation. When presently I saw an illustrated catalogue of this exhibition, I was immediately interested, and regretted that I had not been in town to see the show; for I recognised, even from the inadequate little black-and-white reproductions, that here were a few people — Germans, Russians, Frenchmen, Italians —, some of whom were striking out in a direction which seemed entirely sympathetic to the zigzag development which I was then undergoing myself, and that there was a certain kinship between some of this work and the groping experiments I was making independently and without previous knowledge of the existence of these others. Not that they were actually working together or at all in the spirit of a "school". Each was an independent painter, and they had simply been drawn together by the discovery that they had certain aims and sympathies in common, or at any rate, they thought they had. Among those now internationally known, who originally exhibited with the society are, beside Kandinsky himself, Picasso, Braque, Georges Rouault, Robert Delaunay, Pierre Girieud and Carl Hofer. Marc and Klee were at that time not yet of the number…. About a year later a visitor to my studio suggested that I invite Kandinsky and his associates to have a look at my work. This I was reluctant to do, for various reasons; but after some persuasion, I consented to see Kandinsky and ask him round to my place, if he would only come. As it turned out, Kandinsky was glad to come, and when he did come — well, the upshot was, that I was invited to cast my lot with him and his friends. However, this was not the immediate result. The immediate result, as I learned much later, was, that quite innocently and unwittingly, I was indirectly responsible for the breaking up of the New Society of Munich. There had long been dissension among the members, who very soon after the formation of the society divided sharply into two opposing factions of compromisers, or as we would call them: pussy-footers, and inexorables, or as we would call them: radicals. There is no point in calling over the names of members in the first group, for they would all be unknown to you, and it is indeed astonishing to realise how unknown almost every one of them has become in Europe since that day. Outwardly, when they came to my studio in a body, soon after Kandinsky's first visit, all was sweetness and light and harmony amongst them, and an outsider like myself could not suspect that there was anything else. The friction arose out of the fear and distrust felt by the compromisers, the backsliding respectables among the group, of the uncompromising independence and honesty shown by the radicals. The reactionaries feared that the radicals were going too far, and they had lost sympathy for their aims; while the other group were [sic] disgusted with the smugness and growing exclusiveness and snobbishness of the backsliders, and were by this time convinced that they were only a thinly disguised lot of not too capable academicians. And that was the situation when I came into the picture. It was simply the violent disagreement between the two factions concerning my worthiness to be admitted to membership that finally precipitated the already inevitable break. I had not put myself forward as a candidate for membership in the society, I did not particularly desire membership, and indeed, the thought of membership in any formally organised group of painters has always been unpleasant to me. But here the one faction was determined not to have me, while the other was quite as determined that I should be admitted — although I rather suspect that their determination was at least to some degree conditioned by the resistance of their opponents, and that I happened to be merely one of those convenient, though fundamentally unimportant bones of contention which are so often made the excuse for a decisive squabble and the ultimate showdown; although, to be just, I believe that the separation took place under all the dignified aspects of a gentlemen's disagreement. — Meanwhile, and some time before the final break, Franz Marc had been asked to join the society. During this first exhibition of the group, the newspapers and their more or less intelligent critics had been so scathingly abusive, that Marc, who at that time was still quite unknown, felt moved to write a letter of protest to the leading daily of Munich, one of the smuggest and most self-righteous sheets that ever defiled paper with printer's ink. I shall have a word to say of this letter of Marc's in a moment. Marc's intention was excellent, and his letter should have served as a fitting rebuke to the superciliousness and vicious self-complacency of the newspaper critics, and it might have done valuable service also in putting the public generally into a more receptive and tolerant frame of mind before such startlingly new painting as was shown in that first exhibition of the New Society. But the letter was not printed. [...] However, Marc was not easily discouraged; — he sent a copy of his letter to Kandinsky, whom, at that time, he had never met. Kandinsky and the other members of the society were so delighted with it, that they obtained Marc's permission to print the letter as a folder, which was inserted in the catalogues of the exhibition, for the show had still a fortnight or longer to run. And it was this incident that served to bring Marc into personal contact with Kandinsky and his group.

The ordinary Munich gallery visitor was ill-prepared to be suddenly confronted with such a radical overturn of all the commonly accepted standards of 19th century painting as was manifested in this first exhibition of the New Munich Society. Even though there were a good number of comparatively "harmless" pictures on the walls, the leaven of the work shown by so extreme a radical as Kandinsky alone, was sufficient to cause a ferment in the entire offering of the society, that made impossible even a dim recognition in the mind of the general public of some of the milder aspects of the show, which would inevitably have convinced some of the less prejudiced and clearer-headed among them, that nearly all of these painters displayed in their work some very definite points of contact with the painting of time-honored European tradition. And the critics, than whom there is no more venal gang in all German Journalism, being hand-in-glove with the long established groups that were allied with the official Royal Munich Academy and the Secession, found it to their personal interest to cry down out of hand any innovation in painting, which might threaten even remotely the supremacy or popularity of the established and universally sanctioned painting of the pedants and cheap-jacks. It is true, that German enthusiasts like Meier-Graefe were the first serious writers and connoisseurs of Europe to proclaim [and] broadcast the greatness of the founders of the newer painting: the greatness of Cézanne and van Gogh and of Gauguin, and that through the efforts of such Germans the interest of a large public was first aroused, not only in Germany, but throughout Europe and even in France, where a proper and general appreciation did not really begin, until their greatness had been pointed out to the world by <u>German</u> art-lovers; and it is equally true that more of the work of Cézanne, van Gogh and Gauguin was at that time to be found in Germany than anywhere else in Europe. But the German champions of the successors to the French Impressionists and Neo-Impressionists did not yet seem so interested in the activities of the successors to <u>these</u> French movements, of the so-called Post-Impressionist painters, as they were to become a little later on; and certainly it did not lie in the interest of the German picture-dealers, with their shops stocked full of the works of their own countrymen, [...]. Thus from the very outset the New Munich Society had to fight against an impossible condition; in the circumstances, and with the critics yelping them down, their chance for any sort of fruitful function in the community of painters and enthusiasts seemed to be doomed before ever they hung a picture.

And then Franz Marc's letter appeared as a kind of preface to the catalogue of the exhibition. How much actual good was accomplished by the printing of that letter, I cannot say; but it is certain that presently the public attitude became at least slightly less disrespectful — people no longer stood shouting, laughing and gesticulating before these pictures,

Wassily Kandinsky, Composition 2, 1911, destroyed in World War II, Städtische Galerie im Lenbachhaus, Photo Archive

Wassily Kandinsky, Komposition 2, 1911, im 2. Weltkrieg zerstört, Städtische Galerie im Lenbachhaus, München, Archivphoto

as though they had been so many mere monstrosities —, and it was noticeable even, that at the next exhibition the tone of the critics, though equally spiteful and malicious, was somewhat less vociferous. (After all — and we must not be led astray by the thoroughly false position into which the German people have been forced, by the criminally sinful Treaty of Versailles, into accepting blindly and supinely the dictates of a gang of psychopathic bandits — after all, the people of Germany are at bottom and as a whole fair-dealing, good-natured and tolerant; they are as lovable and well-disposed a folk as I have ever known — and my contact with them has been very close —, and they are hospitable to unfamiliar ideas to the point of gullibility; a characteristic of them, which, together with their really desperate straits, may help one to understand their pitiful enthusiasm for the present régime.) ... And so it was not long before a spirit of tolerance toward the newer painting began to prevail, and — despite the newspaper criticasters — a very lively interest in all the many varieties of its manifestations and even of its most absurd aberrations to be pretty generally shown. The nub of Marc's thesis — I can only state it baldly, for I can find no copy of his letter at the moment — the nub of the thesis was, that the public and critics, viewing the work of these new painters for the first time — and particularly the painted abstractions of Kandinsky — were shocked into condemnation of them, simply because they had never before been asked to contemplate abstract design as <u>pictures</u> and as <u>painting</u>. [...] <u>A picture is an image</u>. And an image — we need not trouble ourselves with etymology here — is a similitude, a similitude evoked in the imagination. [...] For a picture must infallibly represent something, however abstractly; and Kandinsky's pictures do represent something, though they represent it in an abstraction: they represent always an idea, a mood, an emotion — matters, we may agree, which cannot well or successfully be presented abstractly in pictures. [...] Now Kandinsky and all the other abstractionist painters place the unfamiliar beholder in a twofold quandary. Their compositions are not intended at all as decorative formal designs, but as pictures, and they look, to the uninitiated, neither like the one nor the other; though once we become aware of the idea that informs the painting, we must recognise, whether we admire the result or not, that these paintings are pictures, and not mere designs. If

point of the anecdote, let it be indicated, that to those who succumb so readily to the contemporary falsehood of art and culture — that is, to sentimentalists —, a work of human hands, a mere picture, will always seem of greater importance than a work from the hand of God.) … But what are the pictures of Franz Marc? What was he himself? Tall, slender, broad-shouldered, big-boned, big-muscled, a little ungainly-looking at first glance, for he walked with a certain stoop, bending down to speak or listen to a companion; yet he was quick in his movements and silent as the cats he loved, lumbering by turns like his dog, or graceful and sure of tread as one of his pet fawns; a man of clear feature; strong chin and nose, faintly smiling mouth and dark eyes gentle, by turns dreamy and sharp. That is his portrait, and his pictures are all in their kind images of this outer semblance. A stag and a doe lie, spread the length of the picture-plane, curled at their ease in a glade of the wood. The two great, broadly painted animal forms (not individualised animals) are the picture. There is little else — they occupy nearly all the space of the canvas. There is just enough suggestion of their environment, within them and about them, in the caressing interlinked rhythms, in the playful back-and-forth give-and-take of the color swelling to form, to make us aware of the forest depth — nothing more…. A great yellow cow, painted life-size in profile, kicks out her hind legs in ruttish abandon. The colors of spring play through her and about her…. Birds sit watchful in the treetops, birds fly through the thicket, dappled with summer sunlight, a beam of light darts through the silence into the dark of the forest solitude…. Cats play quietly in the corner of the room; there are only the cats — cat-forms, never an individual cat, never a portrait, always a symbol. For this painter sought to create his God in the image of His creatures, that so he might make himself worthy to have been created in God's image. And there is nothing to explain. We must not try to explain what is good, for fear of explaining it away from the heart of those who would learn to perceive. Let us leave explanations…. The romance of color! There must be no romance nowadays any more; it is cried down as sentimental, unless it be the romance of "business" or of politics or of gossip-mongering, of news-chasing. But Franz Marc was the great color-romancer, a greater than the Venetians, who were classical compromisers and who used color too often as a decoration, as an applied external thing. But Marc was no romanticist; his spirit, for all the fairy-land romance of his color, is classical, and toward the tranquillity of the classical, deviously, through mazes of doubt and struggle, he was forever striving. Already, before he was heard of, he had begun to recapture something of it; and then came the contact with Kandinsky — a stimulus that seemed for a moment like to overwhelm him. Yet it was during this period that he painted his greatest pictures. And what was perhaps his very greatest picture shared in his own tragedy: a year after his death it was destroyed by fire. Tierschicksale! Animal Destinies! They stand there, cowering, huddled, helpless, the center of a toppling world; heads reared aloft, stretched on craning necks into the threat and terror high over them. The seeking creature, lost in a world of wonder and strangeness and lurking danger, gropes back to the dark through his darkness. A sharp cry of color, a resonant roar, a tumult of tone; it subsides, there is a moan and a whisper, then stillness. Creation hurled down into the night of all beginnings — and this is the end…. But the picture was painted a year before the coming of the great débacle, and, when this was nearing its end, followed its painter through the fire. Animal destinies! Creature destiny! But it must not be thought that in Marc's mind, when he painted this picture, was anything like a romantico-philosophico-literary idea or notion. I have said and have demonstrated, that Marc was no sentimentalist, and certainly he was not a cheap-jack; and in this instance at any rate, I know definitely of what I speak; for, though I did not assist at the christening of the composition, I was consulted about the name. And this example will serve as well as any to give some notion of how a painter may sometimes work and think. It is only another anecdote, and again I was one of the parties to it. The other was Franz Marc. I was spending a few days with him at his home in a little mountain-valley near Munich, and this picture, in a way his masterpiece, had just been painted. Marc always invited the criticism of his friends, but how should I criticise this

picture? Suddenly he turned to me: What on earth shall I call this thing? — Good Lord, I said; don't ask me! That's something for you to decide. — I know; but I can't. — Well, but you must know what was in your mind when you painted it? — That's just it. I don't, exactly. I had been wanting to paint that picture for a long time. It was a kind of vague feeling, as much as anything else. I made a number of drawings and sketches and memoranda before I began, and it was constantly in my thought. But now that I've got it painted, I'm hanged if I know what to call it. — Well, I said, perhaps it doesn't matter very much. Why don't you take a leaf from Kandinsky's book, if you're up a stump for a title, and just slap a number on it? — He laughed. Klee, he told me, was out here a day or two before you came, and he suggests "Tierschicksale". What do you think? — But I thought not, and said so. — Afraid that might be a little pretentious-sounding; and it strikes me as rather too literary, though no doubt I'm wrong. — And no more was said; but as it turned out, that was the title he gave the picture, and afterwards, with the destiny of the picture itself in my mind, I was very glad that he had…. Toward the end — a few months before the coming of the cataclysm — Marc seemed to be feeling his way to something new. These last pictures were not shown until after his death, in a great memorial exhibition; but on my last visit to him, in the early summer of 1914, I saw all of them, some of them finished, some only begun. He was painting pure abstractions! Abstractions as only Franz Marc could have painted them. It was the same color, the same feeling, the same atmosphere — form and rhythm even were the same, but intensified, though one could recognise few of the forms objectively. These paintings presented a complete and perfected color-lyrism. Yet Marc himself was aware while he was at work on them, that this could be only a transitional development; a rather assured groping along a new path, which was leading him he knew not yet whither. But he was willing simply to be led. For already at this time, he was beginning to doubt that Kandinsky, to whose stimulus he owed so much, was himself upon the right track; and in such leisure as he found in the trenches and elsewhere at the front during the year and a half of his uncomplaining bondage, he thought himself through to a complete emancipation. This is manifest from many utterances in his published letters, letters written home from the slaughter-fields. To what these deep self-searchings might finally have led, had it been willed that Franz come back to us, no one need try to guess. But I refuse myself the sorry comfort of a belief that he had already given us all that had been given him to give; — for too much had been given him, and how thankful he always was to give of his abundance….

Perhaps Paul Klee is the strangest figure in all that group of painters, who were my friends and comrades in Munich. Whimsical, winsome, wayward, his little sheets of drawing and water-color, with an occasional small picture painted in oil, look at first sight like the daubs and scrawls of a wilful, destructive child — of a child never grown up, living alone, walled-off from the world in some undreamt garden of wonderland, or in some forgotten corner of hell. Symbol, all this — but symbol of what, no one can tell. Klee himself cannot. He has tried to give a hint now and then on a written page, but the reader is left the more confused. The play of a playboy of painting. And yet not play. This child — he is nearing sixty now — is a very careful and deliberate craftsman and an extraordinarily competent one. And I have seen early etchings of his that show what an excellent and powerful draftsman he is fundamentally. You may have seen some of his work here and there, some of you, reproduced in a book or periodical; or you may have come upon some bit of it in the original. Upon me the work of Paul Klee has from the beginning exerted a strange fascination, as great a fascination as the man himself, with his rare, impish humor. And for the life of me I could not say why I love much of his work, why some of it leaves me indifferent and why there is some that I detest. It is not in the least a matter of reasoned understanding. Rather, of knowing instinctively what is good for one's soul, what is definitely not good for it, or what, in between, can neither harm it nor delight it. People — that is, German art critics of the profounder sort, who should hardly be called people — well, people have tried to philosophise about Klee's work and they have made a sorry botch of the attempt. To be very honest about it — and thus display my ignorance or helplessness candidly — I haven't the least idea whether Klee's work as a whole should or even <u>can</u> be judged "seriously" as art. I know only that I cannot so judge it; but I have a few of Klee's pictures on my walls that I will not part with, while another lies hidden away in a portfolio somewhere, and I never look at it and never want to. I accepted it from him only because he so very solemnly assured me that it is one of the best things he had ever made. Well, perhaps it is; — what do I know about it after all; but, if it come[s] to that: what does he know about it himself? I have yet to meet the artist who is a trustworthy judge of his own work. And that Paul Klee is an artist, let there be no doubt, even though I confess myself incapable of judging his work. And Klee no more regards himself than I regard myself as a modern. Indeed, it is strange how unmodern many of these wild radicals of painting really are in their thinking and sympathies. Klee is an accomplished violinist — a really excellent one —, and he plays Haydn and Mozart, sometimes he will go as far as a little Beethoven; and he and his wife once played the Franck Sonata for me; but that is as near to contemporary music as he would come. Franz Marc loved music too; but to him music was Bach first of all, and anyone who knows his most characteristic work will easily understand why. Kandinsky used to play the piano rather well; but the only time I ever heard him at it, he was having a delightful time with some old Russian folk-tunes; he has no use for the "modern" Richard Strauss, and once, after a performance of Beethoven's mighty Missa Solemnis, which we both attended, he complained that such music was no longer written and that the confounded conductor had ruined the performance, because he obviously did not understand the score.

At bottom there is really nothing so very modern about any of these wild radicals. The convinced moderns are those who don't know what it is all about; and they don't count. Picasso, an artist of authentic gift, and regarded as the wildest of them all, is forever yearning back to the aloof tranquillity of the Greeks — I only wish he could make up his mind to one thing or the other; his constant hop, skip and jump from one point of view to the next and back again is irritating and distressing. No new painter has ever said a really new thing; when he has, it was not worth saying. Cézanne without Delacroix and the Venetians and the early Impressionists is unthinkable. Van Gogh at his best and most typical is impossible without the Japanese. The work of Franz Marc — which is typically German, and not in the least modern or cosmopolitan, is kin to the spirit of Cranach and Albrecht Altdorfer four hundred years ago. The best abstractions of Kandinsky derive pretty directly from the wild, free strain of his own Tatar [sic] ancestors. And Klee? Klee has only found his way home again. When the sentinel angel happened, for a moment, to be looking the other way, Paul Klee shinned over the wall, back into the forbidden garden. He has been playing there ever since he was reborn; and if sometimes his pranks make us uncomfortable, it may be that these are only projections of the bad dreams he dreams of the unimaginable that may await one who has sneaked back into Paradise.

X. ALBERT BLOCH - EDWARD MASER, 1955

Albert Bloch's letter to Edward A. Maser, formerly the Director of The University of Kansas Museum of Art (today the Spencer Museum of Art, University of Kansas, Lawrence) was first published in 1955 on the occasion of the exhibition "Albert Bloch: A Retrospective Exhibition of His Work from 1911 to 1955," at the Museum in Lawrence. Edward Maser had asked Bloch about his artistic credo and for a review of his painting. Bloch's letter provides considerable insight into his late works and lets us share his many memories of the Blaue Reiter forty years earlier.

Der Brief von Albert Bloch an Edward A.Maser, dem ehemaligen Director des University of Kansas Museum of Art (heute Spencer Museum of Art, University of Kansas, Lawrence) wurde anläßlich der Ausstellung ›Albert Bloch - a retrospective exhibition of his work from 1911 to 1955‹ im Museum in Lawrence 1955 erstmals veröffentlicht. Edward Maser hatte nach Albert Blochs ›künstlerischem Credo‹ und einem Rückblick auf sein Lebenswerk gefragt. Blochs Schreiben ist für die künstlerischen Überzeugungen seiner späteren Jahre höchst aufschlußreich, ebenso für die Erinnerungen an den ›Blauen Reiter‹ aus einem Abstand von über 40 Jahren.

June 20, 1955

Dear Maser—

I gather that you desire me to furnish you with material for the introduction to your catalogue of the "Retrospective" exhibition of my work which you have in mind. And that you are chiefly concerned to be given a resumé of my "career" and that I recite before the readers of the catalogue my craftsman's "credo." I need hardly tell you that it would be far easier (and ever so much more agreeable) to paint a picture to order at short notice — a task which I could never be persuaded to undertake and for which I am no more fitted than for what you ask of me.

My career, such as it is, I fear I cannot review for you. There may be those who have followed it — I haven't. I couldn't even tell you how and when it began. All I can tell you is that each year I seem to be beginning to learn a little about painting; as to the separate events of this apprenticeship which I am still serving and which I suppose I am fated to serve to the end, there don't seem to have been any. I don't seem to have become even a good journeyman, let alone a master. Apparently all I can remember about my journey from any one phase of my progress (if one may call it that) to another, makes it appear to me in retrospect as not so much a career as a more or less abrupt and jerky series of careenings from one dead end to the next, from the end of one blind alley to the next nearest stone wall, my head still bloody but unbowed, never knowing what hit me and caring even less. I had much the usual training, I suppose, — at the Washington University Art School in St. Louis (save the mark!) —; I did my stint of newspaper drudgery, magazine illustration and the like, sandwiched in amongst regular contributions of political and portrait caricatures to my dear old Bill Reedy's "Mirror" and occasional contributions to two or three satirical weeklies abroad — this last between fifty and forty years ago; I had the great benefit of a good bit of private criticism from painters whom I respected, in New York, Paris, Munich; and then, somehow, I came into contact, during the Munich days, with Marc and Kandinsky. I don't even remember the circumstances of our earliest meeting, but I do remember the first time they, with others, appeared in my studio, which, not being very large and stuffed to bursting with my pictures, most of them hopelessly bad and all of them long since destroyed, they managed to overfill outrageously. (Indeed — speaking of pictures destroyed —, I believe I may assert that in the course of this career of mine I have destroyed far more pictures than I was ever able to complete or save.) But before I go on with this unsatisfactory account, I had better say a very modest word about what you call my "artistic credo," because it may serve to explain what has always seemed to me Marc's and Kandinsky's peculiar failure to realise even in the days of my nonage that my conception of the painter's job and theirs were as the poles asunder. I may put this confession of faith quite briefly, I think; it comprises, reducing it as drastically as possible to its lowest common denominator, but two articles. Of these the first is, that all painting of our cultural era, i.e. from the days of the Byzantine mosaics down to our own, must be firmly rooted in tradition. Just as Giotto and his immediate forerunners would have been impossible without Byzantium, so would Cézanne and van Gogh have been impossible without the French impressionists and those in turn without Fontainebleau, and so on back to the beginning. And the second article is simply that the painter must have received adequate technical and mechanical training. Why it is and how it is that he virtually never receives it nowadays and has indeed not received it for the past several generations, not to say, actually, for the past several centuries, or ever since the workshop method of bringing a raw apprentice to the point where he can begin to be a profitable journeyman-assistant — this purely economical, sociological, historical aspect of the matter need not detain us; for remember, my dear Maser, I wish to be as brief as possible, and moreover I am quite sure you know all about such things anyway, or at least as much about them as I.

These two articles of faith, as you will of course have perceived, are pretty inextricably bound up together, being, so to speak "members of each other." So often, for example, you will find that the painter who has completely broken with tradition, couldn't help himself, because he had never received the necessary training which might have fitted him to help carry the venerable tradition forward (though more than we might imagine have, through independent hard work, overcome the lack). He is simply overpowered by an irresistible itch to paint, and he gives way to it, plunging headlong and hell-bent, without in the least knowing how to go about it. And of such as these is the evanescent republic of our "moderns." (I am not thinking now of such figures as Klee and Feininger, who certainly enjoyed a most thorough academic training and unquestionably did and do know how. Nor am I thinking —nomina sunt odiosa—of the bright particular galaxy of our head-liners, of the actual impostors, charlatans and mountebanks, whom the pundits of the cognoscenti and intelligenzia delight to exalt in their art weeklies and monthlies and their newspaper columns as "the greatest living painters," putting them on ice in separate niches amongst "the great creative spirits of the present century.") The poor art-students of today are so badly taught, the art-schools are so bad because the teachers there are unfitted to teach: they have never learnt anything themselves, except some fashion of the passing moment, whatever it may be, and, like barnyard fowl to pick up nimbly whatever may lie within easy reach of their beaks, most of which will stick in their gizzards anyway, caught up in their digestive mechanism without ever a chance of becoming properly assimilated. Is it any wonder, I ask you, that their "painting" (and never mind my mixed metaphors) has no roots in any living element? that the dernier cri, en vogue today will be forgotten tomorrow as though he had never lived (as indeed he never did live)? What is the philosophy of these Johnny-come-latelies? That because Cézanne and van Gogh had far greater genius than talent, it is unnecessary to learn anything! Now I ask you….

Well, so much for career and credo, and though I can tell you so little about either, you must at least realise that I take the latter very seriously indeed. And so I return to my good friend Franz Marc and his good friend Wassily Kandinsky, with whom I myself had only a most pleasant acquaintanceship. Marc, parenthetically, was one of the earlier "moderns" who really knew his stuff and who, in point of fact, was not really a modern at all in terms of present-day popular usage: he knew too much and he could do too much; in every stroke of his painting his profound scolarship is apparent. Even at the very end — just before he went off to the war from which he never returned —, when he essayed a few exercises in purely abstract painting, there is present throughout,

in these two or three beautiful experiments, and obvious to the practiced eye, the spirit of the craftsman who has learnt his trade from the beginning, who knew his job as only the masters of all the ages have known it: not one of these various non-objective forms but proves in all its simplicity and complexity that Marc never wished to break with tradition, that he could not have done it even had he wished to. He never could have written me Kandinsky's word of criticism of my pictures: "Sie zeichnen mir viel zu gut" (you draw much too well to suit me). But by then Kandinsky had broken completely with tradition, which he could never have done, had he truly absorbed any of it; if he had ever had any proper training; if he had ever really sat at the feet of the masters. Nor, on the other hand, could Kandinsky have written me as Marc did in reply to a puzzled inquiry and plea for help with a pictorial problem, ultimateley involving a question of drawing pure and simple: "Sie zeichnen genau so gut wie ich" (you draw exactly as well as I), for in passing I must say that it wouldn't have been true, since I always drew much better than Kandinsky, who had never really learnt how; nor, for that matter, is Marc's estimate correct, because his drawing was always superior to mine. Yet he did his best to help, went out of his way, taking time and trouble to demonstrate his point with drawings, even sending me a printed book of animal photographs and studies, from which I might take hints. It was certainly not his fault that he misunderstood the point of my questions; I had probably failed, with my very imperfect Geman of more than forty years ago, to state my trouble clearly. The point of Marc's and Kandinsky's misconception about me was simply that they believed in all good faith that I was a "modern," that it was my ambition to paint "modernist" pictures, whereas I desired to do no such thing. I was not a modern in any real sense of the word, neither in theory, performance, nor — and this is the truly important difference — in sympathy with many of the aims of the new movement, as it was called during the first years of the century. I was in actual fact — in aim and sympathy, even in such important externals as the mechanical and technical aspects of painting — a traditionalist to the core, however eager I was to avail myself of the stimulation the new men by their example in Paris and elsewhere were spreading abroad so generously. There is no question at all that the hints dropped by Matisse, for example, were fruitful to those who could profit by his inspiration without wishing to imitate him, nor dare I deny that there was much in the early Picasso (ca. 1908-12 and earlier, too) which I deeply admired then and still admire. But I was not a disciple of these stimulating painters, nor of any others (the incompetence of our art school faculty at home had cured me almost from the start, and once for all by their precept and practice, of any such futile longing if ever I had it). Vincent van Gogh I loved at first sight; Gauguin, too, I recognised without trouble for what he was, though with some serious reservation not so much concerning his painting itself, but of his personality as revealed through his painting, though at that time I knew nothing of his biography; but neither of these made me want to "go modern." At that time I was still too busy with the Impressionists, trying to learn what I could from the works of Manet, the earlier Renoir and of course Degas (who was really not an impressionist, i.e. a plein-airiste, at all), as I had been until recently occupied with their great forerunner Millet and, later on, with Daumier. In my earnest, bungling, uninstructed way, I was still only seeking, fumbling, groping toward whatever light might be vouchsafed me, trying honestly, though no doubt dunder-headedly, to find my own point of departure; for by that time had come to realise that painting had reached the end of the road which (with a few scattered but notable exceptions) it had been, in this country at least, following so smugly and unquestionably for a century and longer. And I felt that with the aid of those painters from whose pictures I could learn whatever I might, I must find my own road, come to my own starting-point. And it was while I was thus more or less helplessly bumbling about that Marc and Kandinsky came upon me and found in me what they regarded as a promising recruit.

It is to be remembered, whatever my critical reservations regarding the actual work of Kandinsky, that never had I listened to such inspired and inspiring talk upon the subjects which interested me most and that

I had never failed in those days to find his work itself most stimulating. He was bursting with ideas, and his work between 1909-1914 showed this in every canvas, every scrap of paper. He had thought long and earnestly, often fruitfully upon all aspects of the subject which so engaged my own thought. How could a receptive hearer sixteen years younger, fail to learn from a man like that, who was not trying to teach? As for Marc, my first experience of his work: a large one-man show at Die Moderne Gallerie in Munich early in 1911, before ever I had met the man himself, took me captive at first sight, even though I recognised immediately that Marc's external gift (though not his genius) was essentially decorative. Here at last I found painting which fed in full measure my need and my longing. Here was the <u>new voice</u>—something never yet heard —, the authentic new voice, yet speaking throughout in the revered, <u>traditional</u> mode. Less vocal, surely less tolerant than Kandinsky, who was his senior by fourteen years, there was yet a profundity in his rather reticent talk, in the man's silences and very bearing, in his often half-humorous obiter dicta, which the Russian, for all his more obvious charm, lacked entirely. What wonder, then, that an obscure newcomer like me, still in his twenties, who had until then shown only an occasional picture or two at the jury-shows of the Berlin and Munich Secessions, should feel delighted and flattered to be asked by two such men to join them in their planned enterprise of Der blaue Reiter, which in itself and for its own sake interested me very little, despite my awareness (or suspicion) that the group, or, rather the team of Marc and Kandinsky was to make Central European art history. Indeed I took very little actual part in their activities, preferring to remain withdrawn with my work, showing it when I could, and spending what leisure I allowed myself with a very few friends who claimed only a quite casual connection with painting and the other arts. Only of Franz Marc may I say that our acquaintance deepened to something like true friendship. I made no special secret of my rather cool indifference to modernism and the new movement in painting as such, and, I believe, by the time the war of 1914 dispersed the group, the others had begun, belatedly enough, to suspect my attitude. Not that it made any difference in our relations, indeed I feel that between 1914 and his untimely death in March 1916

Marc and I had drawn closer together than ever we had been. In truth, I had really very little contact with others of the group, some of whom I knew only slightly, while others I did not know at all and had never met — they did not all live in Munich, naturally, and during occasional sojourns in Berlin, Paris, Bonn or Cologne I felt no urgent impulse to look them up. With Klee, who joined the circle later, I exchanged pictures and visits, and found him an altogether delightful acquaintance. For a while also I saw a good deal of Campendonk, who would look me up when he was in town and whom I would visit in the country. Jawlensky and Werefkin I knew, but seldom saw, in Munich, though after the war I saw a great deal of them in Italian Switzerland. (It should be noted in passing, but well remembered, that neither Jawlensky nor Wereffkin ever showed their work with Der blaue Reiter, nor did poor Marsden Hartley or Lyonel Feininger, as the catalogue of a recent Blauer Reiter exhibition in New York erroneously asserts, with no shadow of excuse for the assertion. Whether Feininger was ever asked to join the group or to exhibit with them — as certainly he should have been —, I have no idea, though if he had been, I feel reasonably sure that he would have mentioned the circumstance during several years of most friendly intercourse. Jawlensky and Wereffkin, I know, were invited, but for compelling reasons were obliged to decline. Hartley was never asked.) So, then, though I remained throughout the existence of the circle one of the most inconspicuous of its members and after my return from Europe never made a point of mentioning, let alone advertising, my connection with Marc and Kandinsky, I was never left out of any of their shows and remain still grateful to both, not merely for their bringing me into notice and for the benefits to which this led, but even far more for the tremendous stimulus which association with them brought me.

This screed has grown to far greater length than it should have and than I had solemnly intended it to be, my dear Maser, and I hope if you have been able to read it through, you have not lost patience before you reached the end.

Sincerely,

Albert Bloch

SONNETS TO THE DEAD
SONETTE AN DIE TOTEN

FRANZ MARC

Before me on the wall above my table
your eye dreams quiet, changeless through the quiet
of the unchanging room in this unstable
night of a noisier world than was that riot
of hell let loose, in which your life went under
while we, expectant, ever hopeful, waited
on your return and the long longed-for wonder
of color-revelation, adumbrated
already, and, to the divining sense, so mightily
projected in those new last explorations
of palette-possibility. How brightly
your faith still burns amid hate-maddened nations!
    Unchanging dreams your clear eye through blind years
    that weave anew nightmare of blood and tears.

1937

M. DE V.; "THE BARONESS" [MARIANNE VON WEREFKIN]

Bei ihr ist der Kitsch schon
eine Kunst! - Paul Klee

We called her the old warhorse, which was mild
compared with what some others used to call her.
She made me think of Phorkyas when she smiled,
and that her mirrored face did not appall her
was proof of her strong nerves. As for her nerve,
imposing is the word for it - delightful,
how she imposed on all! And with what verve
she could backbite and wittily be spiteful!
She talked well, with a tongue that was a spear,
and he was wise who said no word to start her.
She was amusing, but one went in fear,
for scratch this Russian and you caught a Tartar.
    She painted. Badly, but by her own rules,
    Not badly like the dull and docile fools.

[1939 - 40]

PAUL KLEE

There was no word of comfort one could send
to those you left behind but this thought only:
The man is gone, the mate, companion, friend.
The spirit, whimsical yet lofty, lonely,
shall still remain, and not to us alone:
This to remember could bring comfort surely
in other, fairer days than these our own,
when men dared look on days to come securely.

But now that we must dread what morning brings,
even half hoping there be no tomorrow,
this word alone of envious comfort sings
through the dark dirge of helplessness and sorrow:
    Another gone, thus timely called away,
    who need not waken to the sunless day.

August 1940

Paul Klee at Possenhofen on Lake Starnberg, 1921, Städtische Galerie im Lenbachhaus, Photo Archive

Paul Klee, Possenhofen am Starnberger See, 1921, Städtische Galerie im Lenbachhaus, Archivphoto

Marianne von Werefkin and Alexej Jawlensky, Blagodan, 1895, Städtische Galerie im Lenbachhaus, Photo Archive

Marianne von Werefkin und Alexej Jawlensky, Blagodan, 1895, Städtische Galerie im Lenbachhaus, Archivphoto

CATALOGUE OF THE EXHIBITION
KATALOG DER AUSGESTELLTEN WERKE

*Kansas City Only/nur in Kansas City
**Munich Only/nur in München

Paintings/Gemälde

Cat. 1 (Pl. 1)
UNTITLED (TWO SEATED NUDES)
OHNE TITEL (ZWEI SITZENDE AKTE)
c. 1911
Oil on canvas/Öl auf Leinwand
21 x 26 7/8 in./53,3 x 68,3 cm
Mrs. Albert Bloch
EXHIBITIONS/AUSSTELLUNGEN
New York 1988, No.2

Cat. 2 (Pl. 2)
UNTITLED (CITYSCAPE)
OHNE TITEL (STADTLANDSCHAFT)
April 1911
Oil on canvas/Öl auf Leinwand
31 1/4 x 39 in./79,4 x 99,1 cm
Private collection
INSCRIPTIONS/BESCHRIFTUNGEN
"Albert Bloch" (c.r.)

Cat. 3 (Pl. 3)
CITYSCAPE WITH TOWER
HÄUSER MIT TURM
September 1911
Oil on canvas/Öl auf Leinwand
23 x 30 1/16 in./58,4 x 76,4 cm
Mrs. Albert Bloch
INSCRIPTIONS/BESCHRIFTUNGEN
"Albert Bloch" (l.r.)
EXHIBITIONS/AUSSTELLUNGEN
München 1913, No.14

Cat. 4 (Pl. 4)
HARLEQUINADE
HARLEKINADE
1911
Oil on canvas/Öl auf Leinwand
36 x 46 1/2 in./91,4 x 118,1 cm
The Museum of Modern Art, New York; given anonymously
INSCRIPTIONS/BESCHRIFTUNGEN
"Albert Bloch" (l.c.)
EXHIBITIONS/AUSSTELLUNGEN
München, Der Blaue Reiter, 1911/12, No.3; Berlin, Der Sturm, 1912, No.1; München 1913, No.22; Berlin 1988/89, No.2/2; Washington/Dayton/Chicago/Fort Worth, 1992/93, No.8

Cat. 5 (Pl. 5)
THE THREE PIERROTS NO. 2
DIE DREI PIERROTS NR. 2
1911
Oil on canvas/Öl auf Leinwand
30 1/8 x 22 3/4 in./77,2 x 57,8 cm
Mrs. Albert Bloch
INSCRIPTIONS/BESCHRIFTUNGEN
"AB" (u.c.)
EXHIBITIONS/AUSSTELLUNGEN
München, Der Blaue Reiter, 1911/12, No.7; Berlin, Der Sturm, 1912, No.5; Berlin, 1988/89, No.2/3

Cat. 6 (Pl. 6)
PORTRAIT OF A BOY
KNABENBILDNIS
1911
Oil on canvas/Öl auf Leinwand
35 1/4 x 28 in./89,5 x 71,1 cm
Kenneth James LaBudde
INSCRIPTIONS/BESCHRIFTUNGEN
"Albert Bloch 11" (u.r.)
EXHIBITIONS/AUSSTELLUNGEN
Berlin 1911, No.20; München 1913, No.3; Berlin, Der Sturm, Albert Bloch, 1913, No.3; Utica/Clinton 1974, No.3; Kansas City 1978, No.3

Cat. 7 (Pl. 7)
THE DANCER (RAGTIME)
DER TÄNZER (RAGTIME)
1911
Oil on canvas/Öl auf Leinwand
29 3/4 x 35 1/2 in./75,5 x 90,2 cm
Pamela and Allen B. Swerdlick
INSCRIPTIONS/BESCHRIFTUNGEN
"Albert Bloch 1911" (l.r.)
EXHIBITIONS/AUSSTELLUNGEN
München 1913, No.1; Berlin, Der Sturm, Albert Bloch, 1913, No.1

Cat. 8 (Pl. 9)
PROCESSION OF THE CROSS
KREUZTRAGUNG
1911
Oil on canvas/Öl auf Leinwand
23 5/8 x 30 3/8 in./60 x 77,2 cm
National Museum of American Art, Smithsonian Institution
INSCRIPTIONS/BESCHRIFTUNGEN
"Albert Bloch" (c.l.)
EXHIBITIONS/AUSSTELLUNGEN
München, Der Blaue Reiter, 1911/12, No.5; Berlin, Der Sturm, 1912, No.3; München 1913, No.15; Berlin, Der Sturm, Albert Bloch, 1913, No.12; Kansas City 1927, No.1; Chicago 1927, No.1; Tulsa 1961, No.2; New York 1963/64, No.1; München 1964/65, No.2; Ames, 1966; Wichita 1969/70, No.3; Utica/Clinton 1974, No.2; Kansas City 1978, No.1; Berlin 1988/89, No.2/5
REFERENCES/LITERATUR
George Shane, "Ames Showing of Bloch Art," *Des Moines Register*, 12 December 1966, p. 3; "The 25 Most Undervalued American Artists," *Art and Antiques*, October 1986, p. 73

Cat. 9 (Pl. 8)
HOUSES AT NIGHT
HÄUSER BEI NACHT
1911
Oil on canvas/Öl auf Leinwand
22 1/2 x 31 1/2 in./57,1 x 80 cm
Mr. and Mrs. James Hunter Allen
INSCRIPTIONS/BESCHRIFTUNGEN
"Bloch" (c.l.)
EXHIBITIONS/AUSSTELLUNGEN
München 1913, No.19; Berlin, Der Sturm, Albert Bloch, 1913, No.15

Cat. 10 (Pl. 12)
**RECLINING FIGURE
**LIEGENDE GESTALT
1911
Oil on canvas/Öl auf Leinwand
c. 17 x 26 in./45 x 67,5 cm
Sammlung Poppe, Hamburg
INSCRIPTIONS/BESCHRIFTUNGEN
"AB" (l.r.)
EXHIBITIONS/AUSSTELLUNGEN
München 1964/65, No.4

Cat. 11 (Pl. 10)
UNTITLED (PORTRAIT OF A MAN)
OHNE TITEL (PORTRÄT EINES MANNES)
1911
Oil on canvas/Öl auf Leinwand
25 7/8 x 19 3/4 in./65,7 x 50,2 cm
Mrs. Albert Bloch
INSCRIPTIONS/BESCHRIFTUNGEN
"Albert Bloch 1911" (u.r.)

Cat. 12 (Pl. 13)
PIPING PIERROT
FLÖTENDER PIERROT
1911
Oil on canvas/Öl auf Leinwand
39 3/16 x 30 5/8 in./99,5 x 77,8 cm
Private collection
INSCRIPTIONS/BESCHRIFTUNGEN
"Albert Bloch" (u.l.)
EXHIBITIONS/AUSSTELLUNGEN
Berlin, Der Sturm, 1913, No.2 (?); New York 1954/55, No.1; Lawrence 1955, No.2; Chicago 1956, No.2; Lawrence 1960/61, No.4

Cat. 13 (Pl. 14)
UNTITLED (FOUR PIERROTS)
OHNE TITEL (VIER PIERROTS)
1912
Oil on canvas/Öl auf Leinwand
25 1/2 x 19 1/4 in./64,8 x 48,9 cm
National Museum of American Art, Smithsonian Institution; gift of Arvin Gottlieb
INSCRIPTIONS/BESCHRIFTUNGEN
"AB" (l.r.)

Cat. 14 (Pl. 15)
DUEL
DUELL
1912
Oil on canvas/Öl auf Leinwand
39 1/2 x 50 3/8 in./100,3 x 127,9 cm
Dr. and Mrs. Nathan Greenbaum
INSCRIPTIONS/BESCHRIFTUNGEN
"AB" (c.r.)
EXHIBITIONS/AUSSTELLUNGEN
Köln 1912, No.377; München 1913, No.26; Berlin, Der Sturm, Albert Bloch, 1913, No.17; New York 1963, No.34; Annapolis 1966
REFERENCES/LITERATUR
Arthur Jerome Eddy, *Cubists and Post-Impressionism* (Chicago, 1914), p. 92

Cat. 15 (Pl. 16)
UNTITLED (INFERNAL FIGURES)
OHNE TITEL (HÖLLENSZENE)
1912
Oil on canvas/Öl auf Leinwand
30 3/8 x 35 1/2 in./77,2 x 90,2 cm
Alfred and Ingrid Lenz Harrison, Wayzata, Minnesota
INSCRIPTIONS/BESCHRIFTUNGEN
"AB" (l.l.)

Cat. 16 (Pl. 18)
LAMENTATION
KLAGELIED
1912-13
Oil on canvas/Öl auf Leinwand
38 1/2 x 40 5/16 in./97,8 x 102,4 cm
Private collection
INSCRIPTIONS/BESCHRIFTUNGEN
"AB" (middle)
EXHIBITIONS/AUSSTELLUNGEN
Berlin, Der Sturm, Albert Bloch, 1913, No.37; Chicago 1915, No.5; Chicago 1922, No.6

Cat. 17 (Pl. 17)
PRIZE FIGHT
BOXKAMPF
1912-13
Oil on canvas/Öl auf Leinwand
39 3/8 x 25 in./100,1 x 63,5 cm
Städtische Galerie im Lenbachhaus, München
INSCRIPTIONS/BESCHRIFTUNGEN
"AB" (l.l.)
EXHIBITIONS/AUSSTELLUNGEN
Berlin, Der Sturm, Albert Bloch, 1913, No.41; Dresden 1914, No.16; Chicago 1915, No.7; München 1964/65, No.5; München 1993/94, No.26
REFERENCES/LITERATUR
Hans Konrad Röthel, *Der Blaue Reiter*, Städtische Galerie im Lenbachhaus, München 1963, n.p., 1966[2], S. 10; Rosel Gollek, *Der Blaue Reiter im Lenbachhaus München: Katalog der Sammlung in der*

Städtischen Galerie im Lenbachhaus, München 1982, No.9

Cat. 18 SONG I
(Pl. 22) LIED I

November 1913 - April 1914

Oil on canvas/Öl auf Leinwand
41 1/2 x 38 1/4 in./105,4 x 97,2 cm
The Snite Museum of Art, University of Notre Dame; gift of Mr. Joseph Shapiro, 64.70

INSCRIPTIONS/BESCHRIFTUNGEN

"AB" (l.l.)

EXHIBITIONS/AUSSTELLUNGEN

Chicago 1915, No.19; Washington/Dayton/Chicago/Fort Worth, 1992/93, No.6

Cat. 19 THE GREEN DOMINO
(Pl. 20) DAS GRÜNE GEWAND

1913

Oil on canvas/Öl auf Leinwand
51 3/8 x 33 1/2 in./130,5 x 85 cm
Mr. and Mrs. Elliott Goldstein

INSCRIPTIONS/BESCHRIFTUNGEN

"AB" (c.l.)

EXHIBITIONS/AUSSTELLUNGEN

München 1913, No.36; Chicago 1915, No.20; Berlin, Der Sturm, 1916, No.23; New York 1972/73, No.4; Utica/Clinton 1974, No.4; New York 1977, No.1; München 1982, No.212

Cat. 20 SUMMER NIGHT
(Pl. 19) SOMMERNACHT

1913

Oil on canvas/Öl auf Leinwand
48 x 45 1/4 in./121,9 x 114,9 cm
Berry-Hill Galleries, New York

INSCRIPTIONS/BESCHRIFTUNGEN

"AB" (l.r.)

EXHIBITIONS/AUSSTELLUNGEN

Berlin, Der Sturm, Albert Bloch, 1913, No.40; Chicago 1915, No.14; Chicago 1922, No.2; New York 1972/73, No.7; Utica/Clinton 1974, No.6; New York 1977, No.2

REFERENCES/LITERATUR

Arthur Jerome Eddy, *Cubists and Post-Impressionism* (Chicago, 1914), p. 92; Eddy, 2nd edition, 1919, p. 92; David S. Rubin, "Der Blaue Reiter," *Arts Magazine*, 51 (June 1977), p. 18; *American Paintings VI*, (New York: Berry-Hill Galleries, 1990), pp. 150-51

Cat. 21 HARLEQUIN WITH THREE PIERROTS
(Pl. 21) HARLEKIN MIT DREI PIERROTS

1914

Oil on canvas/Öl auf Leinwand
40 x 53 3/8 in./ 101,6 x 135,6 cm
The Art Institute of Chicago; Arthur Jerome Eddy Memorial Collection, 1931.515

INSCRIPTIONS/BESCHRIFTUNGEN

"AB" (l.r.)

EXHIBITIONS/AUSSTELLUNGEN

Chicago 1915, No.24; Chicago 1922, No.7; Chicago 1931/32, No.1; Chicago 1933, No.766; Lawrence 1955, No.2; Chicago 1956, No.4; Tulsa 1961, No.4; Utica/Clinton 1974, No.7

REFERENCES/LITERATUR

John I. H. Baur, *Revolution and Tradition in Modern American Art* (Cambridge, 1951), p. 38; Peter Selz, *German Expressionist Painting* (Berkeley & Los Angeles, 1957), p. 208; Ernst Scheyer, Introduction, in Lawrence 1963, n.p.; Richard C. Green, "Albert Bloch. His Early Career: Munich and Der Blaue Reiter," *Pantheon*, 39 (Jan.-March 1981), p. 72

Cat. 22 STILL LIFE III
(Pl. 25) STILLEBEN III

April 1914

Oil on canvas/Öl auf Leinwand
20 x 25 5/8 in./50,8 x 65,1 cm
Des Moines Art Center Permanent Collections, Iowa; gift of Mary Mattern in memory of Karl Mattern, 1969.9

INSCRIPTIONS/BESCHRIFTUNGEN

"AB" (u.r.)

EXHIBITIONS/AUSSTELLUNGEN

Chicago 1915, No.1 (?); Berlin, Der Sturm, 1916, No.6 (?); New York 1921, No.2; Utica/Clinton 1974, No.8

Cat. 23 **ENTOMBMENT
(Pl. 23) **BEGRÄBNIS

1914

Oil on canvas/Öl auf Leinwand
27 3/4 x 39 3/4 in./70,5 x 101 cm
Städtische Galerie im Lenbachhaus, München

INSCRIPTIONS/BESCHRIFTUNGEN

"AB" (u.l.)

EXHIBITIONS/AUSSTELLUNGEN

Berlin, Der Sturm, 1916, No.5 (?); München 1964/65, No.6; München 1993/94, No.27

REFERENCES/LITERATUR

Hans Konrad Röthel, *Der Blaue Reiter*, Städtische Galerie im Lenbachhaus, München 1963, n.p.; 1966[2], S. 10; Rosel Gollek, *Der Blaue Reiter im Lenbachhaus München: Katalog der Sammlung in der Städtischen Galerie im Lenbachhaus*, München 1982, No.10

Cat. 24 NIGHT II
(Pl. 24) NACHT II

1914

Oil on canvas/Öl auf Leinwand
23 5/8 x 29 3/4 in./60 x 75,6 cm
David and Mary Winton Green

INSCRIPTIONS/BESCHRIFTUNGEN

"AB" (l.l.)

Cat. 25 PORTRAIT OF MR. A. M.
(Pl. 11) PORTRÄT DES HERRN A. M.

1914-15

Oil on canvas/Öl auf Leinwand
36 x 29 1/2 in./91,4 x 74,9 cm
The Regis Collection, Minneapolis, Minnesota

INSCRIPTIONS/BESCHRIFTUNGEN

"AB" (l.r.)

EXHIBITIONS/AUSSTELLUNGEN

New York 1988, No.1

Cat. 26 MOUNTAIN
(Pl. 28) GEBIRG

1916

Oil on cardboard/Öl auf Pappe
25 1/2 x 31 5/8 in./64,8 x 80,3 cm
Whitney Museum of American Art, New York; Blanche A. Haberman Bequest

INSCRIPTIONS/BESCHRIFTUNGEN

"AB" (c.r.)

EXHIBITIONS/AUSSTELLUNGEN

Berlin, Der Sturm, 1917, No.19; Frankfurt 1917, No.25; München 1918, No.11; München 1919, No.7; Utica/Clinton 1974, No.9

REFERENCES/LITERATUR

Richard C. Green, "Albert Bloch. His Early Career: Munich and Der Blaue Reiter." *Pantheon*, 39 (Jan.-March 1981), p. 72

Cat. 27 *FIGURES ON DARK GROUND
(Pl. 27) *GESTALTEN AUF DUNKLEM GRUND

1916

Oil on canvas/Öl auf Leinwand
50 x 36 1/2 in./127 x 92,7 cm
Mr. and Mrs. James L. Moffett

INSCRIPTIONS/BESCHRIFTUNGEN

"AB" (u.r.)

EXHIBITIONS/AUSSTELLUNGEN

Berlin, Der Sturm, 1916, No.16; Braunschweig, Der Sturm, 1916, No.2

Cat. 28 **NIGHT V
(Pl. 26) **NACHT V

1917

Oil on canvas/Öl auf Leinwand
27 1/2 x 39 3/4 in./70 x 101 cm
Dr. Horst Kollmann, Weitenau

EXHIBITIONS/AUSSTELLUNGEN

Berlin, Der Sturm, 1917, No.27; Frankfurt 1917, No.33

Cat. 29 WINTER
(Pl. 29) WINTER

1918

Oil on canvas/Öl auf Leinwand
50 1/4 x 36 1/4 in./127,6 x 92,1 cm
Spencer Museum of Art, University of Kansas, Lawrence

INSCRIPTIONS/BESCHRIFTUNGEN

"AB" (c.r.)

EXHIBITIONS/AUSSTELLUNGEN

München 1919, No.38; New York 1921, No.28 (?); Tulsa 1961, No.6; New York 1963/64, No.6; Kansas City 1978, No.6

REFERENCES/LITERATUR

Anna Bloch, "Albert Bloch's Silent Spirit," *Art and Antiques* (October 1987), p. 88

Cat. 30 INTERIOR
(Pl. 30) INTERIEUR

1920

Oil on canvas/Öl auf Leinwand
28 3/4 x 27 1/2 in./73 x 69,8 cm
Städtische Galerie im Lenbachhaus, München

INSCRIPTIONS/BESCHRIFTUNGEN

"AB" (l.l.)

EXHIBITIONS/AUSSTELLUNGEN

München 1964/65, No.11; München 1979, No.99; München 1993/94, No.157

REFERENCES/LITERATUR

Rosel Gollek, *Der Blaue Reiter im Lenbachhaus München: Katalog der Sammlung in der Städtischen Galerie im Lenbachhaus*, München 1982, No.11

Cat. 31 VERANDA
(Pl. 32) VERANDA

1920

Oil on artist's board/Öl auf Pappe
17 1/4 x 20 5/8 in./43,8 x 52,4 cm
Columbus Museum of Art, Ohio; gift of Ferdinand Howald, 31.108

INSCRIPTIONS/BESCHRIFTUNGEN

"AB" (l.l.)

EXHIBITIONS/AUSSTELLUNGEN

New York 1921, No.33; Lawrence 1955, No.7; Utica/Clinton 1974, No.11

Cat. 32 GROUP OF THREE
(Pl. 31) DREIERGRUPPE

1921

Oil on canvas/Öl auf Leinwand
39 3/8 x 29 1/2 in./100 x 75 cm
Michael Hasenclever Galerie, München

INSCRIPTIONS/BESCHRIFTUNGEN

"AB" (c.l.)

EXHIBITIONS/AUSSTELLUNGEN

New York 1921, No.40; Kansas City 1927, No.25; Chicago 1927, No.25; Annapolis 1966; Utica/Clinton 1974, No.12

Cat. 33 **SOUVENIR, ASCONA
(Pl. 33) **ERINNERUNG, ASCONA

March - April 1921

Oil on canvas/Öl auf Leinwand
35 3/4 x 43 1/2 in./90,8 x 110,5 cm
Sammlung Skulima, Berlin

Cat. 34 IMPROMPTU
IMPROMPTU
1926
Oil on canvas/Öl auf Leinwand
25 ½ x 19 ¾ in./64,8 x 50,2 cm
Private collection

INSCRIPTIONS/BESCHRIFTUNGEN
"B" (l.l.)

EXHIBITIONS/AUSSTELLUNGEN
Kansas City 1927, No.38;
Chicago 1927, No.38; Wichita
1969/70, No.7; Kansas City
1978, No.9

Fig. 3, see page 80/Abb. siehe Seite 80

Cat. 35 THE HOUSE NEXT DOOR
(Pl. 34) DAS HAUS NEBENAN
1934
Oil on canvas/Öl auf Leinwand
23 x 31 in./58,4 x 78,7 cm
Mr. and Mrs. Crawford L.
Taylor, Jr.

INSCRIPTIONS/BESCHRIFTUNGEN
"AB 1934" (u.l.)

EXHIBITIONS/AUSSTELLUNGEN
Birmingham 1987/88, No.3

Cat. 36 WINTER IN THE DEAD
(Pl. 36) WOOD
WINTER IM TOTEN WALD
1934 - 38
Oil on canvas/Öl auf Leinwand
30 ⅛ x 36 in./76,5 x 91,4 cm
Mrs. Albert Bloch

INSCRIPTIONS/BESCHRIFTUNGEN
"AB 1934" (l.c.)

EXHIBITIONS/AUSSTELLUNGEN
New York 1936, No.494; New
York 1963/64, No.9; München
1964/65, No.16; Kansas City
1966; Wichita 1969/70, No.10;
Utica/Clinton 1974, No.27;
Kansas City 1978, No.13

Cat. 37 GARDEN GLIMPSE
(Pl. 35) GARTENECKE
1936
Oil on canvas mounted on
masonite/Öl auf Leinwand,
auf Masonit aufgezogen
23 ⅛ x 35 ¼ in./58,7 x 89,5 cm
Mrs. Albert Bloch

INSCRIPTIONS/BESCHRIFTUNGEN
"AB" (l.r.)

Cat. 38 THE GARDEN OF ASSES (II)
(Pl. 37) DER ESELSGARTEN (II)
1938 - 39
Oil on canvas mounted on
masonite/Öl auf Leinwand,
auf Masonit aufgezogen
40 x 50 in./101,6 x 127 cm
Mr. and Mrs. Crawford L.
Taylor, Jr.

INSCRIPTIONS/BESCHRIFTUNGEN
"AB" (l.l.)

EXHIBITIONS/AUSSTELLUNGEN
Kansas City 1966; New York
1988, No.9

Cat. 39 OLD GRAVEYARD
(Pl. 40) ALTER FRIEDHOF
1940 - 41
Oil on canvas mounted on
masonite/Öl auf Leinwand,
auf Masonit aufgezogen
22 x 26 in./55,9 x 66 cm
Mrs. Albert Bloch

INSCRIPTIONS/BESCHRIFTUNGEN
"AB" (l.l.)

EXHIBITIONS/AUSSTELLUNGEN
Lawrence 1955, No.18; Chicago
1956, No.14; New York 1988,
No.12

REFERENCES/LITERATUR
Allen S. Weller, "Chicago,"
Arts, 30 (April 1956), p. 15

Cat. 40 GULLS
(Pl. 38) MÖWEN
1941
Oil on canvas mounted on
masonite/Öl auf Leinwand,
auf Masonit aufgezogen
36 x 32 in./91,4 x 81,3 cm
Private collection

INSCRIPTIONS/BESCHRIFTUNGEN
"AB 1941" (l.l.)

EXHIBITIONS/AUSSTELLUNGEN
Lawrence 1955, No.19; Chicago
1956, No.15; Tulsa 1961, No.16;
Wichita 1969/70, No.17; Utica/
Clinton 1974, No.28

Cat. 41 MARCH OF THE CLOWNS
(Pl. 39) DER MARSCH DER CLOWNS
1941
Oil on canvas mounted on
masonite/Öl auf Leinwand,
auf Masonit aufgezogen
36 x 40 in./91,4 x 101,6 cm
Mrs. Albert Bloch

INSCRIPTIONS/BESCHRIFTUNGEN
"AB 41" (l.r.)

EXHIBITIONS/AUSSTELLUNGEN
Wichita 1969/70, No.15; New
York 1988, No.11

Cat. 42 THE BLIND MAN
(Pl. 43) DER BLINDE MANN
1942
Oil on canvas mounted on
masonite/Öl auf Leinwand,
auf Masonit aufgezogen
40 x 36 in./101,6 x 91,4 cm
Dr. and Mrs. Nathan Greenbaum,
Kansas City, Missouri

INSCRIPTIONS/BESCHRIFTUNGEN
"AB 1942" (u.l.)

EXHIBITIONS/AUSSTELLUNGEN
Lawrence 1955, No.21; Tulsa
1961, No.17; New York 1963/64,
No.12; München 1964/65, No.20;
Wichita 1969/70, No.20; Alabama
1970/71; Utica/ Clinton 1974,
No.29

Cat. 43 *JORDAN
(Pl. 41) *JORDAN
1946
Oil on canvas/Öl auf Leinwand
25 x 30 in./63,5 x 76,2 cm
Mrs. Martin Scheerer

INSCRIPTIONS/BESCHRIFTUNGEN
"AB" (c.l.)

EXHIBITIONS/AUSSTELLUNGEN
Tulsa 1961, No.21

Cat. 44 PASSING TRAIN
(Pl. 42) VORBEIFAHRENDER ZUG
1947-48
Oil on canvas/Öl auf Leinwand
36 x 40 in./91,4 x 101,6 cm
Mrs. Albert Bloch

INSCRIPTIONS/BESCHRIFTUNGEN
"AB" (middle)

EXHIBITIONS/AUSSTELLUNGEN
Tulsa 1961, No.23; München
1964/65, No.23; Annapolis 1966;
Wichita 1969/70, No.30;
Utica/Clinton 1974, No.36

Cat. 45 FIGURES IN SILVER LIGHT
(Pl. 45) GESTALTEN IN SILBERNEM
LICHT
1950
Oil on canvas/Öl auf Leinwand
30 x 36 in./76,2 x 91,4 cm
Mrs. Albert Bloch

INSCRIPTIONS/BESCHRIFTUNGEN
"AB" (l.c.)

EXHIBITIONS/AUSSTELLUNGEN
Ames 1966; Wichita 1969/70,
No.36; Utica/Clinton 1974,
No.38

Cat. 46 THE GRIEVING WOMEN
(Pl. 44) KLAGENDE FRAUEN
1950/57
Oil on canvas/Öl auf Leinwand
30 x 36 in./76,2 x 91,4 cm
Mrs. Albert Bloch

INSCRIPTIONS/BESCHRIFTUNGEN
"AB 50/57" (l.l.)

EXHIBITIONS/AUSSTELLUNGEN
Lawrence 1955, No.34;
Chicago 1956, No.30; Tulsa
1961, No.25; Kansas City 1966;
Wichita 1969/70, No.34; Utica/
Clinton 1974, No.40

Cat. 47 CONFERENCE
(Pl. 46) KONFERENZ
1951
Oil on canvas/Öl auf Leinwand
28 x 36 in./71,1 x 91,4 cm
Mrs. Albert Bloch

INSCRIPTIONS/BESCHRIFTUNGEN
"AB" (c.r.)

EXHIBITIONS/AUSSTELLUNGEN
Wichita 1969/70, No.38;
Utica/Clinton 1974, No.43;
Kansas City 1978, No.26

Cat. 48 THE BLUE BOUGH
(Pl. 47) DER BLAUE AST
1952
Oil on canvas/Öl auf Leinwand
30 x 25 in./76,2 x 63,5 cm
Mrs. Albert Bloch

INSCRIPTIONS/BESCHRIFTUNGEN
"AB" (l.r.)

EXHIBITIONS/AUSSTELLUNGEN
Lawrence 1955, No.38; Chicago
1956, No.34; Tulsa 1961, No.27;
Decatur 1968; Wichita 1969/70,
No.40

Cat. 49 POSTHUMOUS PORTRAIT
(KARL KRAUS)
POSTHUMES PORTRÄT
(KARL KRAUS)
1955
Oil on canvas/Öl auf Leinwand
14 x 10 in./35,6 x 25,4 cm
Private collection

EXHIBITIONS/AUSSTELLUNGEN
New York 1963/64, No.16;
München 1964/65, No.27;
Kansas City 1966

*Fig. 26, see page 45/Abb. siehe
Seite 45*

Cat. 50 BLUE ECLIPSE
(Pl. 48) BLAUE DÄMMERUNG
1955
Oil on canvas/Öl auf Leinwand
16 x 30 in./40,6 x 76,2 cm
Mrs. Albert Bloch

INSCRIPTIONS/BESCHRIFTUNGEN
"AB" (l.c.)

Cat. 51 IMPROMPTU
(Pl. 49) IMPROMPTU
1959
Oil on masonite/Öl auf Masonit
34 ½ x 24 ⅛ in./87,6 x 61,9 cm
Mrs. Albert Bloch

INSCRIPTIONS/BESCHRIFTUNGEN
"AB 59" (l.r.)

EXHIBITIONS/AUSSTELLUNGEN
Annapolis 1966; Wichita
1969/70, No.52

Watercolors/Aquarelle

Cat. 52 **HARLEQUINADE
(Pl. 50) **HARLEKINADE
1911
Ink, graphite and watercolor/
Tuschfeder und Bleistift, aqua-
relliert
9 ⁵⁄₁₆ x 12 ⁵⁄₁₆ in./23,6 x 31 cm
Christian Strenger, Frankfurt

Cat. 53 (Pl. 51)

****For Clown-Picture IV**
****Zum Klownbild IV**

1914

Ink, watercolor/Tuschfeder, Aquarell
13 1/4 x 17 11/16 in./34,9 x 44,9 cm
Paul Klee-Stifung, Bern

Inscriptions/Beschriftungen

R: "Zum Klownbild IV. AB. 1.I.1914."

Exhibitions/Ausstellungen

Der Sturm. 36. Ausstellung, Graphische Werke, Berlin, 1916, No.15(?); Duisburg 1971, No.321; Villingen-Schwenningen 1975, No. 7, München 1982, No.445

Cat. 54 (Pl. 52)

Scherzo
Scherzo

1912/26

Ink, graphite, and watercolor/Tuschfeder und Bleistift, aquarelliert
7 1/4 x 11 5/16 in./19,7 x 28,7 cm
Mrs. Albert Bloch

Inscriptions/Beschriftungen

R: "AB 1912/1926" (l.l.)
"SCHERZO — $30.—" (l.r.)
V: ["Blatt" or "Blau"] VI" (u l.)
"Entwurf 'SCHERZO.'" (u.l.)
"AUGUST 1913" (u.r.)
"50.—" (c.)

Exhibitions/Ausstellungen

München, Der Blaue Reiter. Schwarz-Weiß, 1912, No.9 (?); Lawrence 1963, No.55; Cincinnati 1988; Lawrence 1992

Cat. 55 (Pl. 53)

Form and Color Study, No. 9: Railway Bridge
Form- u. Farbenübung, No. 9: Eisenbahnbrücke

1913

Watercolor/Aquarell
13 1/8 x 9 3/16 in./33,3 x 23,3 cm
Mrs. Albert Bloch

Inscriptions/Beschriftungen

R: "AB" (l.r.)
"9." (l.l.)
V: "Form= u. Farbenübung, No. 9." (u.c.)
"'Eisenbahnbrücke'" (u.)

Exhibitions/Ausstellungen

Berlin, Der Sturm, 1917, No.32; München 1919, No.71; Jena 1920, No.16; Lawrence 1963, No.45; Cincinnati 1988

Cat. 56 (Pl. 54)

Blue Waterfall
Blauer Wasserfall

1932

Watercolor and graphite/Aquarell und Bleistift
19 1/2 x 15 3/4 in./49,5 x 40 cm
Mrs. Albert Bloch

Exhibitions/Ausstellungen

Lawrence 1963, No.69; New York 1963/64, No.22; München 1964/65, No.46; Kansas City 1966; Annapolis 1966; Lawrence 1966; Wichita 1969/70, No.4; Decatur 1970; Utica/Clinton 1974, No.58; Kansas City 1978, No.34

Cat. 57 (Pl. 55)

Blue Ravine
Blaue Schlucht

1939

Watercolor and graphite/Aquarell und Bleistift
15 3/4 x 19 1/2 in./40 x 49,5 cm
Private collection

Inscriptions/Beschriftungen

R: "AB 1939" (l.l.)

Exhibitions/Ausstellungen

Lawrence 1963, No.79; Lawrence 1966; Decatur 1971; Utica/Clinton 1974, No.65; Kansas City 1978, No.39

Cat. 58 (Pl. 56)

Silver Night
Silberne Nacht

1943

Watercolor and graphite/Aquarell und Bleistift
16 x 20 3/4 in./40,6 x 52,7 cm
Mrs. Albert Bloch

Inscriptions/Beschriftungen

R: "AB 43" (l.l.)
V: "SILVER NIGHT 1943" (c.)

Exhibitions/Ausstellungen

Lawrence 1963, No.83; Ames 1966, No.7; Wichita 1969/70, No.8; Topeka 1969/70, No.16; Decatur 1971

Drawings/Zeichnungen

Cat. 59 (Pl. 57)

Untitled (Horse and Rider)
Ohne Titel (Pferd und Reiter)

c. 1910

Ink and graphite/Tuschfeder und Bleistift
12 3/4 x 8 1/4 in./32,4 x 21 cm
Private collection

Inscriptions/Beschriftungen

V: "(1910)" (l.)
"MS 3" (u.r.)

Cat. 60 (Pl. 58)

Rodin

n.d.

Ink and graphite/Tuschfeder und Bleistift
13 5/8 x 15 5/16 in./34,6 x 38,9 cm (sheet/Blatt); 11 3/4 x 14 in. 29,8 x 35,6 cm (image/Bild)
Mrs. Albert Bloch

Inscriptions/Beschriftungen

R: "Albert Bloch" (l.r.)
"Rodin" (l.c.)
" 35 " (l.r.)
V: "M44" (u.r.)

Exhibitions/Ausstellungen

Lawrence 1963, No.4

References/Literatur

Werner Mohr, "Albert Bloch as Caricaturist, Social Critic, and Authorized Translator of Karl Kraus in America". PhD. diss. University of Kansas, 1995, p. 89

Cat. 61 (Pl. 59)

J. S. Metcalfe of "Life"

n.d.

Ink and graphite/Tuschfeder und Bleistift
13 7/8 x 12 1/2 in./35,2 x 31,8 cm (sheet/Blatt); 9 5/8 x 8 1/16 in. 24,4 x 20,5 cm (image/Bild)
Mrs. Albert Bloch

Inscriptions/Beschriftungen

R: "Albert Bloch" (l.l.)
"J. S. METCALFE—OF 'LIFE'" (l.c.)
" 14 " (l.r.)

Exhibitions/Ausstellungen

Cincinnati 1988

Cat. 62 (Pl. 60)

Suicide
Selbstmörder

1911

Ink and graphite/Tuschfeder und Bleistift
13 x 8 7/16 in./33 x 21,4 cm
Mrs. Albert Bloch

Inscriptions/Beschriftungen

R: "1911" (l.r.)
V: ["Blatt" or "Blau"] "VIII" (u.l.)
"Selbstmörder" (u.l.)
"50.—" (c.)
"132 x 86" (c.)

Exhibitions/Ausstellungen

München, Der Blaue Reiter. Schwarz-Weiß, 1912, No.11(?); Cincinnati 1988

References/Literatur

Richard Green, "Albert Bloch. His Early Career: Munich and Der Blaue Reiter," *Pantheon*, 39 (Jan-March 1981), p. 74

Cat. 63 (Pl. 61)

****Figure Between Houses**
****Figur zwischen Häusern**

1911

Ink/Tuschfeder
12 3/4 x 8 1/2 in./33 x 21,6 cm
Marie-Louise Lankheit, Karlsruhe

Inscriptions/Beschriftungen

R: "1911" (l.l.)
"AB" (u.r.)

Exhibitions/Ausstellungen

München. Der Blaue Reiter, Schwarz-Weiß, 1912; München 1919, No.100; Lawrence 1963, No.18; New York 1963/64, No.25; München 1964/65, No.32; Annapolis 1966; Decatur 1968; Lawrence 1978; Bern 1986/87, No.170

References/Literatur

"Kultur in Kürze," *Amerikanischer Kulturbrief* (Bonn: United States Information Service), n.p.; Hans Kinkel, "Der Blaue Reiter aus Übersee: Albert Bloch Retrospektive in Stuttgart," *Stuttgarter Zeitung*, 14. Januar 1965, n.p.; CvH., "Neues von der Blauen Reiterei: Albert Bloch–amerikanischer Expressionist," *Frankfurt Neue Presse*, 18 March 1965, n.p.

Cat. 64 (Pl. 64)

Untitled (Hofbräu Nightmare)
Ohne Titel (Hofbräu-Alptraum)

c. 1911

Ink, graphite, and watercolor/Tuschfeder und Bleistift, aquarelliert
10 1/4 x 13 1/2 in./26 x 34,3 cm
Mrs. Albert Bloch

Exhibitions/Ausstellungen

Cincinnati 1988

Cat. 65 (Pl. 65)

Notes for 3 Cityscapes
Notizen zu 3 Stadtbildern

1911

Ink/Tuschfeder
9 1/8 x 24 in./23,2 x 61 cm (sheet/Blatt); ca. 6 3/4 x 6 3/4 in. 17,1 x 17,1 cm (image/Bild)
Private collection

Inscriptions/Beschriftungen

R: "[…] Notizen zu 3 Stadtbildern" (l.l.)

Exhibitions/Ausstellungen

München 1919, No.99 (?); Cincinnati 1988

Cat. 66 (Pl. 68)

Ink Study for *The Heights*
Studienzeichnung für ›Die Höhen‹

January 1914

Ink and graphite/Tuschfeder und Bleistift
13 1/2 x 10 1/8 in./34,3 x 25,7 cm
Private collection

Inscriptions/Beschriftungen

R: Various color and mood notations
V: "January 1914"

Cat. 67 (Pl. 62)

First Movement (Study for Song I)
Erste Bewegung (Studie für ›Lied I‹)

May 1912

Ink and graphite/Tuschfeder und Bleistift
13 5/8 x 12 3/4 in./34,6 x 32,4 cm
Mrs. Albert Bloch

Inscriptions/Beschriftungen

R: "1st movement" (l.r.)
V: "May, 1912" (u.r.)

Cat. 68

Working Drawing for a Picture
Studienzeichnung für ein Gemälde

1913

Ink and graphite/Tuschfeder und Bleistift
13 9/16 x 10 1/16 in./34,4 x 25,6 cm
Mrs. Albert Bloch

Inscriptions/Beschriftungen

R: various color notations
V: "1913" (l.r.)

EXHIBITIONS/AUSSTELLUNGEN

Utica/Clinton 1974, No.77; Cincinnati 1988; Lawrence 1992

Fig. 19, see page 67/Abb. siehe Seite 67

Cat. 69 (Pl. 67) **WORKING DRAWING FOR *Harlequin with Three Pierrots* STUDIENZEICHNUNG FÜR ›HARLEKIN MIT DREI PIERROTS‹**

1913

Ink and graphite/Tuschfeder und Bleistift
10 1/16 x 13 1/2 in./25,6 x 34,3 cm
Mrs. Albert Bloch

INSCRIPTIONS/BESCHRIFTUNGEN

R: Various color notations

EXHIBITIONS/AUSSTELLUNGEN

Lawrence 1963, No.22; Utica/Clinton 1974, No.76; Kansas City 1978, No.46; Washington/Dayton/Chicago/Fort Worth 1992/93

REFERENCES/LITERATUR

Anna Bloch, "Albert Bloch's Silent Spirit," *Art and Antiques* (October 1987), p. 90; Philipp Fehl, "Eine Begegnung mit Albert Bloch", *Kontinuität und Identität, Festschrift für Wilfried Skreiner*, Wien 1992, S. 229

Cat. 70 (Pl. 66) **STUDY FOR WRESTLING MATCH STUDIE FÜR RINGKAMPF**

1912 - 13

Ink-wash mounted on board/Tusche laviert auf Karton aufgezogen
13 3/4 x 12 in./34,9 x 30,5 cm
Städtische Galerie im Lenbachhaus, München

INSCRIPTIONS/BESCHRIFTUNGEN

"AB" (l.m.)

EXHIBITIONS/AUSSTELLUNGEN

Berlin. Der Sturm, 1913, No.51 (?); Der Sturm, Graphik, 1916, No.9 (?); München 1919, No.98 (?); Cincinnati 1988

REFERENCES/LITERATUR

Städtische Galerie im Lenbachhaus München, *Jahresbericht 1990-93*, pp. 15, 29

Cat. 71 (Pl. 63) ****UNTITLED **OHNE TITEL**

1913

Ink and graphite/Tuschfeder und Bleistift
13 1/2 x 20 in./34,2 x 50,9 cm
Franz-Marc-Museum, Kochel

INSCRIPTIONS/BESCHRIFTUNGEN

R: "A Bloch - s/l - Marc herzlichst zugeeignet. Sommer 1913"

EXHIBITIONS/AUSTELLUNGEN

München, Galerie Stangl, Vor 50 Jahren. Neue Künstlervereinigung und der Blaue Reiter, 1962, Nr. 11

Cat. 72 (Pl. 70) **UNTITLED (BUILDINGS WITH CLOCK TOWER) OHNE TITEL (GEBÄUDE MIT UHRENTURM)**

1917

Ink/Tuschfeder
11 7/8 x 9 3/4 in./30,2 x 24,8 cm
Mrs. Albert Bloch

INSCRIPTIONS/BESCHRIFTUNGEN

R: "AB" (l.r.)
V: "4" (u.l.)
"(1917)" (l.r.)

Cat. 73 (Pl. 69) **SELF-PORTRAIT SELBSTBILDNIS**

1918

Ink/Tuschfeder
8 5/8 x 8 1/16 in./21,9 x 20,5 cm
Private collection

INSCRIPTIONS/BESCHRIFTUNGEN

R: "AB/AETATIS SUAE/XXX/10 III 1918" (u.r.)
V: "drawn during an illness" (u.l.)
"M67" (u.r.)

EXHIBITIONS/AUSSTELLUNGEN

Utica/Clinton 1974, No.88; Kansas City 1978, No.51

REFERENCES/LITERATUR

Robert K. Sanford, "Bloch: American Blue Rider," *Kansas City Star*, 5 May 1963; "Albert Bloch 1882-1961," *Der Alleingang* (June 1984), n.p.

Cat. 74 (Pl. 71) **IN THE BEGINNING. FOR A CYCLE OF THE CREATION AM ANFANG. FÜR EINEN ZYKLUS DER SCHÖPFUNG**

1922

Ink/Tuschfeder
14 1/4 x 11 5/16 in./36,2 x 28,7 cm (sheet/Blatt); 11 3/8 x 8 13/16 in./28,9 x 22,4 cm (image/Bild)
Mrs. Albert Bloch

INSCRIPTIONS/BESCHRIFTUNGEN

R: "AB"/"1922" (l.r.)
"In the Beginning/For a Cycle of the Creation" (l.l.)

EXHIBITIONS/AUSSTELLUNGEN

Edgar Miller Gallery, Chicago, 1925 (?); Lawrence 1992

Cat. 75 (Pl. 72) **UNTITLED (LANDSCAPE) OHNE TITEL (LANDSCHAFT)**

1924

Ink/Tuschfeder
11 15/16 x 9 1/2 in./30,3 x 24,1 cm
Mrs. Albert Bloch

INSCRIPTIONS/BESCHRIFTUNGEN

R: "AB 1924" (l.r.)

Cat. 76 (Pl. 73) **NIGHT IN THE BLACK CITY NACHT IN DER SCHWARZEN STADT**

1931

Ink and graphite/Tuschfeder und Bleistift
14 3/16 x 10 1/16 in./36 x 25,6 cm (sheet/Blatt); 12 x 8 1/4 in.
30,5 x 21 cm (image/Bild)
Private collection

INSCRIPTIONS/BESCHRIFTUNGEN

R: "AB 1931" (l.r.)
"Night in the Black City" (l.l.)
"47" (l.l.)
V: "$175" (c.)

Cat. 77 (Pl. 74) **TEMPLETON VIGNETTES I, HOUSE ON THE TERRACE AT NIGHT TEMPLETON-VIGNETTEN I, HAUS MIT TERRASSE BEI NACHT**

1934

Ink and graphite/Tuschfeder und Bleistift
10 7/16 x 15 3/8 in./26,5 x 39,1 cm (sheet/Blatt); 8 1/2 x 9 in.
21,6 x 22,9 cm (image/Bild)
Mrs. Albert Bloch

INSCRIPTIONS/BESCHRIFTUNGEN

R: "AB 1934" (u.l.)
"Templeton Vignettes I, House on the Terrace at Night" (l.l.)

Cat. 78 (Pl. 75) **UNTITLED OHNE TITEL**

Summer 1936

Ink/Tuschfeder
4 15/16 x 7 7/8 in./12,5 x 20 cm
Mrs. Albert Bloch

INSCRIPTIONS/BESCHRIFTUNGEN

R: "Summer 1936" (l.r.)
V: " R " (u.l.)
" 6 , Untitled (landscape w farm buildings)" (c.) (written by Mrs. Albert Bloch)

EXHIBITIONS/AUSSTELLUNGEN

München 1964/65, No.44b

Cat. 79 (Pl. 76) **UNTITLED OHNE TITEL**

Summer 1940

Ink and graphite/Tuschfeder und Bleistift
4 1/2 x 7 3/4 in./11,4 x 19,7 cm (sheet/Blatt); 3 13/16 x 7 1/16 in.
7,1 x 17,9 cm (image/Bild)
Mrs. Albert Bloch

INSCRIPTIONS/BESCHRIFTUNGEN

R: "Summer 1940" (l.l.)
" 16 " (l.r.)
V: " R " (u.l.), "Untitled (Horses in a Landscape)" (c.) (written by Mrs. Albert Bloch)

EXHIBITIONS/AUSSTELLUNGEN

München 1964/65, No.44c

Cat. 80 (Pl. 77) **CONTINUATION OF A DRAWING BEGUN BY A. F. FORTFÜHRUNG EINER VON A. F. BEGONNENEN ZEICHNUNG**

1946

Ink and graphite/Tuschfeder und Bleistift
6 1/2 x 7 1/2 in./16,5 x 19,1 cm (irreg. sheet/unregelm. Blatt); 5 x 6 7/16 in./12,7 x 16,4 cm (image/Bild)
Mrs. Albert Bloch

INSCRIPTIONS/BESCHRIFTUNGEN

R: "1946" (l.l.)
"Continuation of a Drawing Begun by A. F." (l.r.)

Cat. 81 **AMERICAN STATESMAN AMERIKANISCHER STAATSMANN**

1951

Ink and graphite/Tuschfeder und Bleistift
8 15/16 x 5 15/16 in./22,7 x 15,1 cm (sheet/Blatt); 5 3/16 x 5 1/16 in.
13,2 x 12,9 cm (image/Bild)
Mrs. Albert Bloch

INSCRIPTIONS/BESCHRIFTUNGEN

R: "AB 1951" (l.r.)
"American Statesman" (l.l.)
V: "N73" (u.)

EXHIBITIONS/AUSSTELLUNGEN

Cincinnati 1988

Fig. 76, see page 83/Abb. siehe Seite 84

Prints/Radierungen

Cat. 82 (Pl. 78) **HOUSES AT NIGHT HÄUSER BEI NACHT**

1913

Drypoint/Radierung
14 11/16 x 19 5/8 in./37,3 x 49,8 cm (sheet/Blatt); 9 11/16 x 12 1/4 in.
24,6 x 31,1 cm (image/Bild)
Mrs. Albert Bloch

Cat. 83 (Pl. 79) **DUEL DUELL**

1913

Drypoint/Radierung
14 13/16 x 22 in./37,6 x 55,9 cm (sheet/Blatt); 8 1/16 x 10 3/8 in.
20,5 x 26,4 cm (image/Bild)
Mrs. Albert Bloch

INSCRIPTIONS/BESCHRIFTUNGEN

R: "AB 1913" (l.l.)
"10/20" (l.l.)
"Albert Bloch" (l.r.)

Cat. 84 (Pl. 80) **SELF-PORTRAIT, AETAT. 31 SELBSTBILDNIS AETAT. 31**

1913

Drypoint/Radierung
3 1/2 x 2 3/4 in./8,9 x 7 cm
Mrs. Albert Bloch

INSCRIPTIONS/BESCHRIFTUNGEN

R: "AETAT. 31" (u.l.)
"12/12" (l.l.)
"Albert Bloch" (l.r.)

(c.r.) center right = Mitte rechts
(c.l.) center left = Mitte links
(l.c.) lower center = unten Mitte
(u.c.) upper center = oben Mitte
(u.r.) upper right = oben rechts
(u.l.) upper left = oben links
(l.r.) lower right = unten links
(l.m.) lower margin = am unteren Rand
(c.) middle = in der Mitte
(u.) top = oben
R = recto
V = verso

LIST OF ABBREVIATED EXHIBITIONS
VERZEICHNIS DER ABGEKÜRZT ZITIERTEN AUSSTELLUNGEN

BERLIN 1911:
XXII. Ausstellung der Berliner Secession, Berlin, 1911

MÜNCHEN, DER BLAUE REITER, 1911/12:
Die erste Ausstellung der Redaktion Der Blaue Reiter, Galerie Thannhauser, München, 18. Dezember 1911 – 1. Januar 1912

MÜNCHEN, DER BLAUE REITER. SCHWARZ-WEIß, 1912:
Die Zweite Ausstellung der Redaktion Der Blaue Reiter. Schwarz-Weiß, Kunsthandlung Hans Goltz, München, 12. Februar – April 1912

BERLIN, DER STURM, 1912:
Der Blaue Reiter, Franz Flaum, Oskar Kokoschka, Expressionisten. Erste Ausstellung Der Sturm, Galerie Herwarth Walden, Berlin, 12. März – Mai 1912

KÖLN 1912:
Internationale Ausstellung des Sonderbundes Westdeutscher Kunstfreunde und Künstler zu Cöln, Köln, 25. Mai – 30. September 1912

MÜNCHEN 1913:
Albert Bloch – München. Der Neue Kunstsalon, Max Dietzel, München, Mai 1913

BERLIN, DER STURM, 1913:
Erster Deutscher Herbstsalon, Der Sturm, Galerie Herwarth Walden, Berlin, 20. September – 1. Dezember 1913

BERLIN, DER STURM, ALBERT BLOCH, 1913:
Albert Bloch. Der Sturm, 20. Ausstellung, Galerie Herwarth Walden, Berlin, Dezember 1913

BERLIN, DER STURM, DER BLAUE REITER, 1913:
Der Blaue Reiter, Der Sturm, 22. Ausstellung, Galerie Herwarth Walden, Berlin, 1913

DRESDEN, 1914:
Die neue Malerei. Expressionistische Ausstellung, Galerie Ernst Arnold, Dresden, Januar 1914

CHICAGO 1915:
Exhibition of Modern Paintings by Albert Bloch of Munich, The Art Institute of Chicago, July – August 1915 (Catalogue by Arthur Jerome Eddy) (St. Louis City Art Museum, September 1915)

BERLIN, DER STURM, ALBERT BLOCH/PAUL KLEE, 1916:
Albert Bloch – Paul Klee. Gemälde und Zeichnungen, Der Sturm, 39. Ausstellung, Galerie Herwarth Walden, März 1916

BRAUNSCHWEIG, DER STURM, 1916:
Expressionisten, Kubisten, Der Sturm, Erste Ausstellung, Herzogliches Museum, Braunschweig, 7. – 31. Mai 1916

BERLIN, DER STURM, GRAPHIK, 1916:
Graphische Werke, Der Sturm, 36. Ausstellung, Galerie Herwarth Walden, Berlin, 1916

BERLIN, DER STURM, 1916:
Expressionisten, Futuristen, Kubisten. Gemälde und Zeichnungen, Der Sturm, 43. Ausstellung, Galerie Herwarth Walden, Berlin, Juli 1916

BERLIN, DER STURM, 1917:
Albert-Bloch, Harald Kaufmann. Gemälde und Aquarelle, Zeichnungen, Der Sturm, 52. Ausstellung, Galerie Herwarth Walden, Berlin, Mai 1917

FRANKFURT 1917:
Albert-Bloch, Stanislaus Stückgold, Kunstsalon Ludwig Schames, Frankfurt, Juli 1917

MÜNCHEN 1918:
Albert Bloch, München. Eine Auswahl der Bilder aus den letzten fünf Jahren 1913 – 1918, Kunsthaus Das Reich, München, 15. März – 15. April 1918

MÜNCHEN 1919:
Albert-Bloch. Die Neue Kunst, Galerie Hans Goltz, 52. Ausstellung, München, Juni 1919

JENA 1920:
Albert-Bloch, Kunst-Verein zu Jena, 1. – 30. Mai 1920

NEW YORK 1921:
Exhibition of Paintings by Albert Bloch, Daniel Gallery, New York, 15 – 28 November 1921

CHICAGO 1922:
Exhibition of Paintings from the Collection of the Late Arthur Jerome Eddy, The Art Institute of Chicago, 19 September – 22 October 1922

KANSAS CITY 1927:
Exhibition of Paintings by Albert Bloch, Karl Mattern and Major Archibald Murray, The Kansas City Art Institute, 1 – 24 March 1927

CHICAGO 1927:
Exhibition of Paintings by Albert Bloch, The Arts Club of Chicago, 18 – 31 March 1927

CHICAGO 1931/32:
The Arthur Jerome Eddy Collection of Modern Paintings and Sculpture, The Art Institute of Chicago, 22 December 1931 – 17 January 1932

CHICAGO 1933:
Catalogue of a Century of Progress Exhibition of Paintings and Sculpture, Lent from American Collections, The Art Institute of Chicago, 1 June – 1 November 1933

NEW YORK 1936:
First National Exhibition of American Art, City of New York, International Building, Rockefeller Center, 18 May – 1 July 1936

NEW YORK 1954/55:
Der Blaue Reiter, Curt Valentin Gallery, New York, 7 December 1954 – 8 January 1955

LAWRENCE 1955:
Albert Bloch: A Retrospective Exhibition of His Work From 1911 to 1955, The University of Kansas Museum of Art, Lawrence, 15 September – 30 October 1955 (The Renaissance Society at the University of Chicago, 11 March – 7 April 1956, The Nelson-Atkins Museum of Art, Kansas City, Missouri, June – July 1957)

LAWRENCE 1960/61:
Paintings, Drawings and Prints of the 19th and 20th Centuries: The Collection of Dr. and Mrs. Otto Fleischmann. A Loan Exhibition, The University of Kansas Museum of Art, Lawrence, 4 December 1960 – 28 January 1961

TULSA 1961:
Albert Bloch: A Retrospective Exhibition of His Work from 1911 to 1956, Philbrook Art Center, Tulsa, Oklahoma, 7 – 31 March 1961, and further venues (Catalogue by Donald G. Humphrey)

NEW YORK 1963:
Der Blaue Reiter, Leonard Hutton Galleries, New York, 9 February – 30 March 1963, and further venues

LAWRENCE 1963:
Albert Bloch (1882 – 1961): An Exhibition of Watercolors, Drawings and Drypoints, The University of Kansas Museum of Art, Lawrence, 30 April – 4 June 1963

NEW YORK 1963/64:
Albert Bloch. Selected Paintings and Drawings (including works shown at Blaue Reiter exhibitions), Goethe House, New York, 3 December 1963 – 6 January 1964

MÜNCHEN 1964/65:
Albert Bloch: Ein amerikanischer Blauer Reiter, 1882 – 1961, Städtische Galerie im Lenbachhaus, München, November 1964 – August 1965 und weitere Stationen.

KANSAS CITY 1966:
Exhibition of Paintings and Drawings by Albert Bloch, Pembroke Country Day School, Kansas City, Missouri, April 1966 (no cat.)

ANNAPOLIS 1966:
Albert Bloch: Watercolors, Drawings, Oils, St. John's College, Annapolis, Maryland, October 1966 (no cat.)

LAWRENCE 1966:
Exhibition of Watercolors and Drawings by Albert Bloch, Public Libary, Lawrence, Kansas, October 1966 (no cat.)

AMES 1966:
Albert Bloch: Watercolors and Oils, Octagon Gallery, Ames, Iowa, December 1966 (no cat.)

DECATUR 1968:
Albert Bloch: Watercolors, Oils, Drawings, John C. Calhoun Junior College, Decatur, Alabama, March 1968 (no cat.)

TOPEKA 1969/70:
Exhibition of Drawings by Albert Bloch (1882 – 1961), The Mulvane Art Center, Washburn University, Topeka, Kansas, December 1969 – January 1970

WICHITA 1969/70:
Albert Bloch 1882 – 1961, Wichita Art Association, Kansas, 1969 – 70

DECATUR 1970:
Albert Bloch, John C. Calhoun Junior College, Decatur, Alabama, mid-April – mid-May 1970 (no cat.)

ALABAMA 1970/71:
The Image in Contemporary Art. A Series of Five Exhibits in the Representational Tradition: Eva Klein-Lamb, Paul W. Mannen, Albert Bloch, Richard Green, Arthur Bond, John C. Calhoun Junior College, Decatur, Alabama, November 1970 – April 1971

DECATUR 1971:
Albert Bloch, John C. Calhoun Junior College, Decatur, Alabama, February 1971 (no cat.)

DUISBURG 1971:
Paul Klee und seine Malerfreunde. Die Sammlung Felix Klee, Kunstmuseum Winterthur, 7. Februar – 18. April 1971; Wilhelm-Lehmbruck-Museum der Stadt Duisburg, 25. Mai – 22. August 1971

NEW YORK 1972/73:
German Expressionist Paintings, Drawings, Watercolors, Sculpture, Leonard Hutton Galleries, New York, November 1972 – February 1973

UTICA/CLINTON 1974:
Albert Bloch 1882 – 1961, An American Expressionist Paintings, Drawings, Prints. Paintings: Museum of Art, Munson-Williams-Proctor Institute, Utica, New York; Drawings and Prints: The Edward W. Root Art Center, Hamilton College, Clinton, New York, 3 February – 3 March 1974 (Foreword by James Penney)

VILLINGEN-SCHWENNINGEN 1975:
Der Blaue Reiter und sein Kreis (Der Blaue Reiter und die Neue Künstlervereinigung München): Gemälde, Aquarelle, Zeichnungen, Graphik, Villingen-Schwenningen, 26. April – 19. Mai 1975 (Vorwort von Klaus Lankheit)

NEW YORK 1977:
Der Blaue Reiter und sein Kreis, Leonard Hutton Galleries, New York, 18 March – May 1977

LAWRENCE 1978:
Albert Bloch Memorial Exhibition. Dedication of Art and Design Building, The University of Kansas, Lawrence, 2 – 22 April 1978

KANSAS CITY 1978:
Albert Bloch: Der Blaue Reiter Artist in the Midwest, Retrospective Exhibition, 1911 – 1958, Oils, Watercolors, Drawings, Friends of Art Sales and Rental Gallery, The Nelson-Atkins Museum of Art, Kansas City, Missouri, 8 October – 5 November 1978

MÜNCHEN 1979:
Die Zwanziger Jahre in München, Münchner Stadtmuseum, Mai – September 1979

MÜNCHEN 1982:
Kandinsky und München. Begegnungen und Wandlungen 1896 – 1914. Städtische Galerie im Lenbachhaus, München, 18. August – 17. Oktober 1982 (enlarged exhibition: Kandinsky and Munich 1896 – 1914, Solomon R. Guggenheim Museum, New York/San Francisco Museum of Modern Art, 22 January – 20 June 1982)

BERN 1986/87:
Der Blaue Reiter, Kunstmuseum Bern, 21. November 1986 – 15. Februar 1987

BIRMINGHAM 1987/88:
The Expressionist Landscape: North American Modernist Painting, 1920 – 1947, Birmingham Museum of Art and further venues, 11 September 1987- 21 August 1988

CINCINNATI 1988:
Albert Bloch 1882 – 1961: Drawings, Watercolors, Prints 1908 – 1958, Michael Lowe Gallery, Cincinnati, 1988 (Introduction by Anna Bloch)

NEW YORK 1988:
Albert Bloch (1882 – 1961): Paintings, Sid Deutsch Gallery, New York, 29 October – 23 November 1988 (Introduction by Richard C. Green, Foreword by Marla Prather)

BERLIN 1988/89:
Stationen der Moderne: Die bedeutenden Kunstausstellungen des 20. Jahrhunderts in Deutschland, Berlinische Galerie, Berlin, 25. September 1988 – 8. Januar 1989

LAWRENCE 1992:
Albert Bloch, Spencer Museum of Art, The University of Kansas, Lawrence, 22 March – 24 May 1992 (no cat.)

WASHINGTON/DAYTON/CHICAGO/ FORT WORTH 1992/93:
Theme and Improvisation: Kandinsky and the American Avant-Garde 1912 – 1950. The Phillips Collection, Washington D. C./Dayton Art Institute, Ohio/Terra Museum of American Art, Chicago/Amon Carter Museum, Fort Worth, Texas, September 1992 – August 1993 (Catalogue by Gail Levin and Marianne Lorenz)

MÜNCHEN 1993/94:
Süddeutsche Freiheit. Kunst der Revolution in München 1919. (Hrsg. von Helmut Friedel, bearb. von Justin Hoffmann), Städtische Galerie im Lenbachhaus, München, 10. November 1993 – 9. Januar 1994

ADDITIONAL SOLO AND GROUP EXHIBITIONS
WEITERE EINZEL- UND GRUPPENAUSSTELLUNGEN

XXIII. Ausstellung der Berliner Secession, Zeichnende Künste, Berlin, November – Dezember 1911

Zurückgestellte Bilder der Sonderbund Ausstellung Köln: Kandinsky, Marc, Jawlensky, Werefkin, Bloch, Münter, Der Sturm, 4. Ausstellung, Galerie Herwarth Walden, Berlin, Juni – Juli 1912

Nemzetközi Postimpresszionista Kiallitás, Budapest, Müvészház, April – Mai 1913

Graphische Werke, Der Sturm, 36. Ausstellung, Galerie Herwarth Walden, Berlin, 1916

Münchener Neue Sezession, II. Ausstellung, München, 1916

Albert-Bloch, Campendonk, Walter Dexel, Kunstverein Jena, Dezember 1916

Sturm-Ausstellung, Galerie Corray, Basel, 2. Februar – 2. März 1917; Galerie Dada, Zürich, 17. März – 30. April 1917

Sturm-Gesamtschau. Gemälde und Aquarelle, Zeichnungen, Der Sturm, 53. Ausstellung, Galerie Herwarth Walden, Berlin, Juni 1917

Albert Bloch, Emmy Klinker, Elisabet Niemann, Kurt Schwitters, Der Sturm, 64. Ausstellung, Berlin 1918

Neue Kunst, 54. Ausstellung, V. Gesamtausstellung, Galerie Hans Goltz, München, September – Oktober 1919

Albert-Bloch, Kunstverein zu Jena, 1. – 30. Mai 1920, St. Louis Artist's Guild, Missouri, 1920

Exposition internationale d'art moderne: Peinture, Sculpture, etc. Genève, 26. Dezember 1920 – 25. Januar 1921

Edgar Miller Gallery, Chicago, 1925

Midwestern Artist's Exhibition, Kansas City Art Institute, Missouri, 7 February – 1 March 1937

The Third Annual Exhibition of Paintings by Artists West of the Mississippi, The Colorado Springs Fine Art Center, 15 July – 31 August 1937

American Art Today. New York World's Fair, New York, National Art Society, 1939

Arts and Crafts of Kansas: An Exhibition Held in Lawrence, The Community Building, Lawrence, Kansas, 18 – 22 February 1948

Albert Bloch: Seven Paintings, The Willow, New York, June 1948

Der Blaue Reiter. München und die Kunst des 20. Jahrhunderts 1908 – 1914, Haus der Kunst, München, September – Oktober 1949 (Katalog bearb. von Ludwig Grote)

Der Blaue Reiter. 1908 – 1914. Wegbereiter und Zeitgenossen, Kunsthalle Basel, Januar – Februar 1950

Artists of the Blaue Reiter: Exhibition of Painting and Graphic Works, Busch-Reisinger Museum, Cambridge, Massachusetts, 21 January – 24 February 1955

Twentieth Century German Art, Fine Arts Festival, Kansas State College, Manhattan, Kansas, 2 – 12 May 1957

The Blue Rider Group: An Exhibition Organized with the Edinburgh Festival Society by the Arts Council of Great Britain, Tate Gallery, London, 30 September – 30 October 1960

Der Sturm. Herwarth Walden und die Europäische Avantgarde, Berlin 1912 – 1932, Veranstaltet von der Nationalgalerie in der Organerie des Schlosses Charlottenburg, Berlin, 24. September – 19. November 1961

Le Cavalier Bleu et son destin, Galerie Maeght, Paris, 1962

The Decade of the Armory Show: New Directions in American Art, 1910 – 1920, Whitney Museum of American Art, New York/City Art Museum of St. Louis/ Cleveland Museum of Art/Pennsylvania Academy of the Fine Arts, Philadelphia/The Art Institute of Chicago/Albright-Knox Art Gallery, Buffalo, February 1963 – February 1964

Albert Bloch (1882–1961): An Exhibition of Watercolors, Drawings and Drypoints, The University of Kansas Museum of Art, Lawrence, 30 April – 4 June 1963

Amercian Paintings in the Ferdinand Howald Collection, Columbus Gallery of Fine Arts, Ohio, 1968

Centennial Exhibition, St. Louis Artist's Guild, Missouri, September – October 1976

Pioneers: Early 20th Century Art from Midwestern Museums, Grand Rapids Art Museum, Michigan, 17 September – 1 November 1981

American Drawings and Watercolors from the Kansas City Region, The Nelson-Atkins Museum of Art, Kansas City, Missouri, July – August 1992

For a comprehensive bibliography see John Richardson, "Albert Bloch: An Annotated Bibliography" in *Albert Bloch: Artistic and Literary Perspectives*, edited by Frank Baron, Helmut Arntzen, and David Cateforis, also published by Prestel as a companion volume to this catalogue.

Eine ausführliche Bibliographie befindet sich bei John Richardson, ›Albert Bloch: An Annotated Bibliography‹, in *Albert Bloch. Künstlerische und literarische Perspektiven*, hrsg. von Frank Baron, Helmut Arntzen, und David Cateforis. Die Publikation erschien parallel zur Katalogausgabe.